T0291307

The Way the Money Goes

The project has been funded by the Nuffield Foundation, but the views expressed are those of the authors and not necessarily the Foundation. Visit www. nuffieldfoundation.org

The Way the Money Goes

The Fiscal Constitution and Public Spending in the UK

CHRISTOPHER HOOD
MAIA KING
IAIN McLEAN
AND
BARBARA MARIA PIOTROWSKA

OXFORD
UNIVERSITY PRESS

OXFORD
UNIVERSITY PRESS

Great Clarendon Street, Oxford, OX2 6DP,
United Kingdom

Oxford University Press is a department of the University of Oxford.
It furthers the University's objective of excellence in research, scholarship,
and education by publishing worldwide. Oxford is a registered trade mark of
Oxford University Press in the UK and in certain other countries

Published in the United States of America by Oxford University Press
198 Madison Avenue, New York, NY 10016, United States of America

British Library Cataloguing in Publication Data
Data available

Library of Congress Control Number: 2023942238

ISBN 978-0-19-886508-7
DOI: 10.1093/oso/9780198865087.001.0001

Printed and bound in the UK by
Clays Ltd, Elcograf S.p.A.

Preface and Acknowledgements

If public spending is so hard to control, as is so often claimed, why is it that spending blowouts exceeding the sums voted by parliament are rare in the UK? If public spending is so central to modern electoral politics, why has the UK parliament been peripheral in the process of planning and allocating expenditure? If 'austerity' is such a drastic policy shift as is commonly said, why did so much of the machinery for reviewing and controlling public spending that was developed in the boom years of rising public expenditure in the 2000s survive with little alteration into the lean years of the 2010s? If changes such as multi-year budgeting, accrual accounting, and performance metrics linked with budgetary settlements truly represent 'best practice' in the planning and control of public spending, why were they not adopted by leading international economies such as Germany? And why, despite the biggest constitutional changes in Scotland, Wales, and Northern Ireland for centuries, was there almost no change in the system for allocating public expenditure to those countries between the early 1990s and 2015?

This book, the result of more than five years' work by an interdisciplinary team combining a range of experience and disciplinary backgrounds, delves into such questions. Drawing on extensive interviews, archive material, statistics, and other published sources, we explore stability and change in the UK's 'fiscal constitution' for public spending over more than two decades from 1993 to 2015. Examples of the things we learnt from this study include:

- for some in the Treasury the planning and control of spending was if anything more challenging in times of spending growth than in times of restraint;
- there was a tension during much of the period between a 'contractual' approach to allocating spending (with specified Soviet-style performance targets) and a more tightrope-walking approach of continual balancing acts;
- efforts to limit what the Treasury considered to be 'gaming' by spending departments veered between a 'togetherness' approach aiming to limit the risk of unpleasant surprises and a cat-and-mouse approach based on changes in rules and classifications.

It has been a long journey and we have many debts to acknowledge. Our study was funded by the Nuffield Foundation and the Economic and Social Research Council, and we are especially grateful to Teresa Williams and Mark Franks of the Nuffield Foundation for their patience and support when the project ran over time as a result of long delays in security clearance in its first year and later, the more than two years of unexpected total disruption to everyone's life caused by the 2020–2021 Covid pandemic. We are grateful to past and present members of the Institute for Government (especially Julian McCrae, Catherine Haddon, and Gemma Tetlow) for their help in organizing events, giving advice and providing interview space. We owe a lot to the Institute for Fiscal Studies (especially to our co-investigator Paul Johnson and his colleagues Rowena Crawford and Ben Zaranko) for providing an authoritative survey of the statistical background to UK public spending over the period covered by this book. It was an essential starting point for our more qualitative analysis.

We are grateful to Sir Charles Bean for his sagacious and sympathetic advice as chair of our advisory group, and to the members of that group (Niamh Hardiman, Michael Kell, Richard Parry, James Richardson, as well as others mentioned elsewhere) for reading draft papers and making suggestions. We owe a huge debt to our Treasury liaison people (in order of appearance, Catherine Frances, David Penn, Niva Thiruchelvam, Kathryn Fairhurst-Jones, Claire Oxlade, Adam Crozier, Jenny Rowland, Michael Cotterell, Charles Lockwood and Thiri Sitharanjan), who were unfailingly helpful, sympathetic, resourceful, and indeed enthusiastic about our work. We are grateful to the Treasury's archive team and also to its IT staff who repeatedly rescued us when we lost access to the Treasury's changing digital archives. We are indebted to Oxford's Blavatnik School of Government for hosting the project and particularly to Ellie Haugh for handling the finances. As well as the advisory group mentioned earlier, we are deeply grateful to Jim Gallagher, David Heald, and Andy King whose expert knowledge we drew on repeatedly over the years, and also to contributors to a comparative workshop held in Oxford in 2019 (including Linda Bilmes, Lorenzo Condogno, Teresa Curristine, Richard Hughes, Maarten de Jong, Muiris MacCarthaigh, Donald Savoie, and Joachim Wehner, as well as others mentioned elsewhere) for helping us to see UK public spending control issues in international perspective.

Most of all we want to thank the 130 people from across the political and bureaucratic spectrum whom we interviewed for this book, who by convention we do not name (we interviewed them under a variant of 'Chatham House Rules'), but who generously gave up time, mostly in very busy lives, to contribute their ideas, reflections, and recollections about spending control. We would dedicate this book to them were it not that authors cannot dedicate their books to themselves, and we prefer to count them as co-authors.

Contents

III. FIVE ASPECTS OF PUBLIC SPENDING CONTROL

IV. UK PUBLIC SPENDING CONTROL IN PERSPECTIVE

List of Figures

List of Tables

List of Abbreviations

AC	Administration Costs
AME	Annually Managed Expenditure
AO	Accounting Officer
C and AG	Comptroller and Auditor General
DEFRA	Department for Environment, Food & Rural Affairs
DEL	Departmental expenditure limit
DH	Department of Health
CBG	Consolidated Budgeting Guidance
CDEL	Capital Departmental Expenditure Limit
COINS	Combined Online Information System
CST	Chief Secretary to the Treasury
DWP	Department of Work and Pensions
DTI	Department of Trade and Industry
EDX	Economic and Domestic Policy (Expenditure) Committee
ERG	Efficiency and Reform Group
ERM	Exchange Rate Mechanism (of the European Community)
EYF	End-Year Flexibility
FCO	Foreign and Commonwealth Office
FD	Finance Director
FER	Fundamental Expenditure Review
FLF	Front Line First
GEP	General Expenditure Policy Group of HM Treasury
HFE	Horizonal Fiscal Equalisation
HMT	Her Majesty's Treasury
IfG	Institute for Government
IFS	Institute for Fiscal Studies
LASFE	Local Authorities Self-Financed Expenditure
MOD	Ministry of Defence
NAO	National Audit Office
NCT	New Control Total
NHS	National Health Service
OBR	Office for Budget Responsibility
ODA	Overseas Development Agency
OGC	Office of Government Commerce
OSCAR	Online System for Central Accounting and Recording
PAC	Public Accounts Committee
PESA	Public Expenditure Statistical Analyses
PEX	Public Expenditure Committee

PFI	Private Finance Initiative
PSA	Public Service Agreement
PSBR	Public Sector Borrowing Requirement
PSND	Public Sector Net Debt
RAB	Resource Accounting and Budgeting
RD	Relational Distance
RDEL	Resource Departmental expenditure limit
SpAds	Special Advisers
TME	Total Managed Expenditure
VFG	Vertical Fiscal Gap

PART I

PUBLIC SPENDING CONTROL AND THE UK'S FISCAL CONSTITUTION

1

Introduction

...Britain's parliamentary supply process today would perhaps be the one aspect of twenty-first century government that a medieval monarch could relate to...The root problem... springs from the historical constitutional convention of the right of the Crown to 'Financial Initiative' (Davey 2000: 12 and 14).

I persuaded John Major [the then prime minister] to emphasise to the members of EDX [Cabinet public expenditure committee] that they were only to consider expenditure and nothing else (Lamont 1999: 303).

...any...unauthorised expenditure shall, unless sanctioned by the Treasury...be regarded as not being properly chargeable to a Parliamentary grant (Exchequer and Audit Departments Act 1921, sec.1 (3) (Examination of Appropriation Accounts)).

The Treasury had to keep shifting the goalposts [because] after a while everyone worked out a way to game the system (ex-Treasury interviewee).

Vignette: Why the Small Print Matters—the 2005 Health Near-Cash Overspend and the Politics of Public Spending Control

After a landslide Labour election victory in 1997, the most sacred cow in public spending for Tony Blair's new government in the UK was the National Health Service (NHS, the UK's free-at-point-of-delivery public healthcare system). In 2000, when all other central government departments were given three-year budgetary settlements, the Department of Health (DH, responsible for funding the NHS in England[1]) had a special five-year deal involving annual spending increases of 7 per

---

[1] DH's health expenditure mainly applied to England only, since subnational governments were responsible for healthcare spending elsewhere in the UK. But changes in English spending shaped the amount available to spend in the rest of the UK through the funding formula described in Chapter 7.

The Way the Money Goes. Christopher Hood, Maia King, Iain McLean, and Barbara Piotrowska,
Oxford University Press. © Christopher Hood, Maia King, Iain McLean, and Barbara Piotrowska (2023).
DOI: 10.1093/oso/9780198865087.003.0001

cent or so in real terms. But despite such largesse, DH's so-called 'near-cash' budget was overspent by a hefty £2.6bn by mid-2005. That overspend threatened New Labour's 'golden rule' for prudent fiscal management requiring that current public spending should be paid for out of tax revenue over the course of an economic cycle.

The measures taken to correct that DH overspend (which included compulsory redundancies in the NHS, closed hospital wards and delayed operations) caused political damage to the government over its handling of a flagship public service that was highly salient to voters and for which Labour traditionally was more trusted than the Conservatives. Beleaguered by political opponents in the House of Commons Health Select Committee, the Secretary of State (minister) for Health, Patricia Hewitt, was obliged to declare in 2006 that she took 'personal responsibility' for returning the NHS to financial balance (BBC 2006). Hewitt was reshuffled out of the Labour Cabinet the following year.

In mid-2005 (shortly after Labour had been re-elected with a much-reduced parliamentary majority), the Management Board of the Treasury (HMT) received a report about how the overspend had happened.

Formally, the report explained, NHS Trusts (the bodies delivering public health care in England) were legally obliged to break even. Trusts in deficit were expected to repay any overspend the following year. But these formalities did not actually stop Trusts from running deficits. Over a third of them were doing just that by 2005/2006, thereby breaching DH's overall spending limit by about £½bn in that year. At the centre, DH took advantage of a new accrual accounting and budgeting system that had been introduced in 2002 (and which we explore in Chapter 10), switching more than £1bn in 2005/2006 between accounting categories to give itself spendable money to fill the funding gap.

What that switch involved was moving money from a budgetary category (so-called 'non-cash') which did not impact on New Labour's 'golden rule' into one that did ('near-cash'). And DH was able to make such a move because its 2002 budgetary settlement with the Treasury included generous allocations of non-cash (to cover items like depreciation, capital charges and provisions for clinical negligence claims). Those allocations had been lavish precisely because non-cash did not count towards the golden rule and for that reason it was evidently treated as 'free money'. (Interviewees told us that most ministers at that time still thought wholly in terms of cash despite the shift to accrual accounting in the early 2000s.)

So how was it that HMT apparently failed to spot that DH overspend until some £2.6bn had been transferred from non-cash to near-cash over two financial years? Part of the reason was that DH spending—probably not accidentally—was structured in such a way as to make Treasury monitoring particularly difficult. DH distributed some 80 per cent of its budget to the 300 Primary Care Trusts

(PCTs) that provided NHS services in England.[2] DH's practice of passing the bulk of its money straight through to the provider organizations lined up with strong political emphasis on funding the NHS 'front line' adequately. But one interviewee told us that handing out the money in that way was also a defensive strategy by DH, designed to deter NHS Trusts from running up deficits and then going to the central department for bailouts.[3]

Further, DH's own central capacity to monitor Trusts' finances was limited, which in turn meant the Treasury could not glean reliable and up-to-date spending data from DH. DH's monitoring rested on Trusts' end-year financial forecasts, not on actual cash outlays or monthly expenditure compared to profile. But those Trust forecasts were unreliable because DH's practice was to confiscate any forecasted surpluses[4] and reallocate them to Trusts in deficit—meaning Trusts had no incentive to forecast accurately. Against that background, HMT's health team apparently did not pick up any early warnings about the scale of the looming overspend.

More broadly, the report said, DH and NHS financial management at this time reflected a view that budget balance was less important than improved service delivery (particularly in cutting waiting times for emergency and other treatment). It said: '...in practice, NHS budget constraints are relatively "soft", since the NHS perceived (correctly) that financial management was not a priority for DH in an era when ministers, from the PM down, were focused on reducing waiting times...the...performance management system was strongly focused on service improvement rather than financial balance'. As well as extra costs from new policy initiatives launched by each successive Secretary of State for Health (there were three between 2002 and 2005), the central political focus on cutting wait times loaded extra costs onto the system. Such additional costs included more expensive weekend working and plummeting productivity resulting from hiring inexperienced doctors and nurses on expensive new pay contracts[5].

Further, in the early 2000s personal relations between DH and HMT were described by one ex-Treasury interviewee as 'very bad' at both official and ministerial level, despite the unprecedented funding increases going to DH at that time. Relations evidently improved later when DH hit financial trouble, but in the early 2000s, ministerial letters between the two departments were said to have been 'a

---

[2] The other 20 per cent of DH's budget was held at the centre and distributed to trusts for purposes such as training, IT, and capital projects.

[3] DH's approach resembled HMT's own tactic at that time of keeping the Reserve (unallocated spending for unforeseen emergencies) small to discourage claims from spending ministers.

[4] Even though a weighty twenty-eight-page 'settlement letter' from HMT in 2000 setting out conditions for DH's budget allocation had stipulated that Primary Care Trusts should be allowed to keep half of any underspends, to provide incentives for efficiency savings.

[5] Rosy assumptions about health care productivity growth failed to materialize, while new pay deals negotiated by DH without Treasury involvement led to income surges of some 42 per cent for general practitioners over those three years, over 36 per cent for consultants and 20 per cent for nurses and other health professionals.

formulaic exchange of hostilities' and there were evidently times when some DH ministers expressly told their officials not to share information with the Treasury.

But friction between ministers seems to have been only part of the reason for HMT's lateness in spotting and moving to correct the developing overspend. According to the report, the Treasury did not anticipate the threats to the 'golden rule' from DH's 2002 budget settlement, which left the department awash with capital and non-cash spending and thereby posed a risk of big switches between budgetary heads. Nor did the Treasury impose separate spending limits for cash and non-cash spending until 2005, such that DH thought it was fully entitled to switch funds between the two categories within the rules of the then new accrual accounting system.

Further, the HMT spending team's institutional memory was limited by high staff turnover and much of its attention seems to have been focused on policy development rather than financial oversight. Work on spending reviews and the policy issues they raised was apparently seen as more glamorous than spending control in a narrower sense, so the job of monitoring and challenging how money was spent after the high-octane spending review deals had been done was seen as of lower priority. Nor did HMT 'read across' from earlier threats to its golden rule by other departments switching from non-cash to near-cash (notably the Ministry of Defence, in an episode we discuss in Chapter 10). Indeed, several interviewees said Treasury spending teams in the mid-2000s had little grasp of the then new accrual-based Resource Accounting and Budgeting system and the associated risks. One declared, 'No-one on the spending side understood it [resource accounting] ...not one [spending] Director knew what "near-cash" was'. Another acknowledged that HMT's health spending team had been 'asleep at the wheel' on this issue.

The upshot was that in 2005 the Treasury formally blocked switches between near-cash and non-cash spending by departments and DH agreed to pay back its near-cash overspend by 2007–2008, to avoid a hit on the 'golden rule' over the economic cycle. The first move negated the core idea animating the recently introduced resource budgeting regime—that better use could be made of public money if departmental managers were free to shift resources across different categories of spending. The second caused real political pain to Labour over the consequent NHS cuts.

The UK's Fiscal Constitution and How It Worked

What do the vignette, and the quotations before it, have in common? Touching variously on long-standing parliamentary rules, power-plays in Cabinet, high politics, bureaucratic folkways, and accounting technicalities, they all relate to the constitutional and institutional arrangements for managing public spending in the

UK—which we hereafter call the 'fiscal constitution' for short. This book describes and evaluates how that constitution operated and developed over two eventful decades from the early 1990s to the mid-2010s. The DH overspend described in the vignette is just one tiny part of that story, but as we shall see, it brings out some recurring themes, notably the way the world of ministers and party politics intertwined with the workings of bureaucracy and how the big picture linked to the small print, especially over matters of classification.

During that quarter century or so, the economic backdrop varied from historically exceptional boom conditions to two major busts, one involving a severe global financial crisis of (normally) once-in-a-century proportions—and a curtain-raiser for the huge fiscal upheaval brought by the coronavirus pandemic and other crises a decade or so later. The politics varied too. At UK level, the period included rule by right-of-centre and left-of-centre parties, forming successively:

- a single-party government that lost its slim majority in Parliament to end up as a minority government in its final days;
- a single party government with a landslide majority so large that there were only seats for about half of its MPs on the government benches in the House of Commons;
- and the first formal coalition at central government level since 1945.

Figures 1.1 and 1.2 summarize what happened to public spending against that economic and political backdrop over the decades of our study, and Figure 1.3

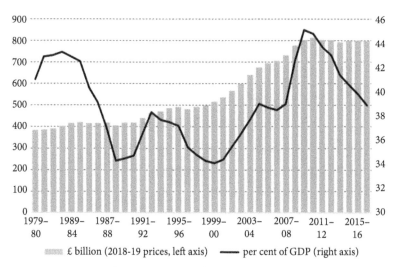

Figure 1.1 UK 'Total Managed Expenditure' 1979–1980 to 2015–2016
Source: Office for Budget Responsibility

compares the UK's spending profile with a handful of other developed democracies over a longer period. During our period, as Figure 1.1 shows, overall, UK public spending rose by over 70 per cent in real terms. The spending-to-GDP ratio began at 38 per cent in 1992–1993 and ended at 41 per cent in 2014–2015—hardly a dramatic difference. But the in-between period includes both the second highest (45 per cent) and the lowest (34 per cent) ratios of spending to GDP since World War II and the 1930s respectively. A big spending surge in the 2000s was exceeded in the post-World War II era only in the mid-1970s and (after our period) by the spike in spending in and after the Covid pandemic.

We would therefore miss some of the major twists and turns in the story if we just compared the beginning and end of our period and indeed that period comprises most if not quite all the logically possible combinations of public spending relative to GDP. There were times of economic recovery (in the 1990s and early 2010s) when spending growth was held back after episodes when the Treasury had lost control; a time (in the early and mid-2000s) when public spending growth was allowed to outrun GDP growth; and another time (in the aftermath of the 2008 global financial crisis) when public spending rose dramatically while GDP shrank. Each of these policy stances—and the political circumstances they reflected—posed different challenges for the fiscal constitution.

Figure 1.2 shows how the distribution of public spending changed across policy domains during the period. As can be seen, spending on defence, the fourth

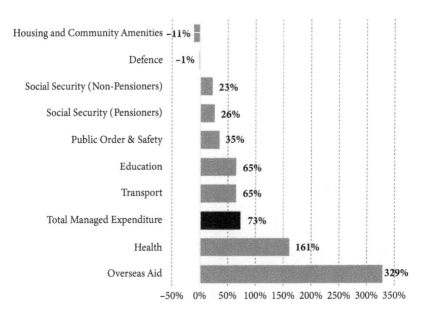

Figure 1.2 Real-terms UK spending changes 1992–1993 to 2015–2016

Source: Institute for Fiscal Studies

largest item of public expenditure, had a more or less 'flat real' profile over the period, against a background of big changes in the security environment. The sudden fall of the former Soviet Union in the early 1990s put an end to defence plans based on preparations for war in central Europe against the Soviet bloc (only for that scenario to return with war in Ukraine going on as we completed this book). The Provisional IRA cease-fire in Northern Ireland in 1994 and the subsequent peace settlement under new constitutional arrangements led to a demilitarization in Northern Ireland too. But a big post-Cold War 'peace dividend' of substantial cuts in military spending, though widely expected, failed to materialize. Instead, there were new unanticipated—and expensive—post-9/11 'Global War on Terror' military operations in Iraq and Afghanistan.[6]

In contrast to that defence spending profile, health spending grew by over 150 per cent. In the early 1990s the amount spent on health care had been similar to that spent on education, but it had become by far the biggest single spending item in the UK budget by the end of our period after repeated major spending uplifts following a succession of NHS financial crises. Another notable contrast is that between spending on overseas aid and on the operations of the Home Office. Those two items were approximately the same at the outset of our period, but—partly as a result of functions being taken away from the Home Office—the aid spending ended up some three times that of the Home Office.

So how did such striking divergences in different areas of spending come about? Allocation and planning of public spending is sometimes said to be subject to strong pressures for inertia and automaticity, with budgetary 'baselines' fiercely defended and demand for 'fair shares' leading to pressure for similar incremental spending increases across different policy domains. Indeed, in the 1970s Hugh Heclo and Aaron Wildavsky (1974: 351–352) described a 'fair shares' tendency as 'always-present' in the UK public expenditure community. They thought such pressures were built into the system by its practice of multi-year cross-government spending surveys (adopted in the early 1960s), which enabled (too) ready comparison of spending growth across different parts of government. But clearly over successive planning periods some decidedly non-incremental outcomes in spending allocations occurred, so there is far more to the story than inertia and 'fair shares'.

Anticipating a theme to which we return later in the book (Chapter 11), Figure 1.3 depicts the public spending picture comparatively, showing what happened to the UK's reported public spending relative to GDP as compared with a set of other developed countries over more than a century. It shows three things. First, in earlier times the UK was an extreme outlier in the extent to which

---

[6] Operations which counted as 'campaign expenditure' and were therefore funded from special reserves decided on by the Cabinet without normal Treasury control.

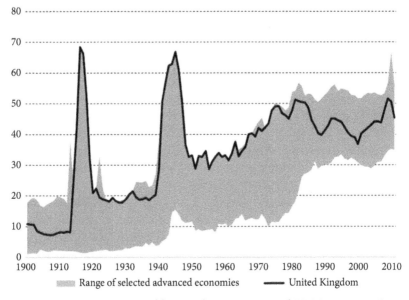

Figure 1.3 Long-term UK public spending as per cent of GDP in comparative perspective

Source: IMF (2022)

its recorded public spending rose and later fell in and after the two twentieth-century world wars. Second, up to the 1980s it had one of the highest recorded proportions of public spending relative to GDP, before privatization of much of what had been a large state-owned industry sector meant that the newly privatized firms' financing no longer counted as public spending. Since then and during the period covered by this book the UK occupied a more 'middle-of-the-pack' position. Third, as we will explore further in Chapter 11, it was by no means alone in the 'up and down' pattern of its public spending relative to GDP over time.

Our aim in this book is to go beyond those overall spending numbers into some of the less readily quantifiable realms of bureaucracy and politics. We explore how the UK's fiscal constitution operated in shaping public expenditure, what some of the key players said about how it worked in practice, and what lay behind those ups and downs of spending, debt and deficit. As we shall see, some of those spending shifts were anticipated or planned, while others were not. Some lined up with declared political commitments in party election manifestos and some seemed to owe more to shocks, happenstance and personalities. Some of the key changes in the fiscal constitution over that period have been much commented on. But others have received less attention and there are still only a few overall qualitative assessments of how the process of planning and controlling public spending worked over the period as a whole—a gap at which this book is aimed.

Four Faces of the Fiscal Constitution

So what does the term 'fiscal constitution' mean in this book? As already mentioned, we use the phrase to denote the constitutional and institutional arrangements for planning and controlling public spending and the associated levels of tax and debt.[7] The epigraphs to this chapter point to at least four features of such arrangements, and our vignette contains examples of all of them. As the first and second epigraphs indicate, there are some more obviously 'political' parts relating to the world of political parties, parliamentary committees and debates, cabinet and cabinet committees, prime ministers, ministers, and their political advisers and acolytes. Such actors figured prominently in our vignette, with close ministerial and Prime Ministerial attention focused on the politically central issue of waiting times for NHS treatment.

One of the eleven former CSTs (Chief Secretary to the Treasury, the minister responsible for planning and controlling public expenditure) that we interviewed for this book stressed the different perspectives of the political and the more technocratic players, commenting that 'All the key decisions are [made] in a very political context' and that 'techie-type issues' in public spending did not have 'much practical impact on what we were doing'. (We think the story in the vignette points to a more nuanced conclusion, since it clearly shows how those apparently 'techie-type issues' of accounting categorisation could have a strong and sometimes unexpected impact on ministers.) Another CST during our period, William Waldegrave (2015: 171), quotes advice he received from a party colleague: 'All the decisions where there is a rational balance of argument will have been taken by civil servants or your junior ministers...the ones that reach you will be evenly balanced...'.

Our third and fourth epigraphs point to those more 'techno-bureaucratic' parts that involve the inner workings of departments and agencies, and the activities of the officials who populate them (such as the way the DH chose to handle the distribution of funds to healthcare Trusts in the vignette). Further, as the first and third epigraphs indicate, some parts of the fiscal constitution are more formal, enacted and written-down, while the second and fourth epigraphs refer to parts that are more implicit, partially or wholly unwritten, customary or taken for granted, perhaps even honoured in the breach (as in the

---

[7] The phrase is partly borrowed from other scholars, notably Martin Daunton (1999; 2002).

Table 1.1 Public spending and the fiscal constitution: four elements

| Arenas | Rules and Conventions | |
	Formal	Informal
'Political'	**(1) Example:** The 'Crown Initiative' rule (stated in Standing Order 48 of the House of Commons) prohibiting MPs other than ministers from proposing increases in public spending to the House of Commons (Epigraph 1)	**(2) Example:** The agreement between the then Chancellor and Prime Minister in 1992 that members of the Cabinet PEX committee considering spending bids should not propose tax changes in the committee (Epigraph 2)
'Bureaucratic' or 'Technocratic'	**(3) Example:** The Exchequer and Audit Departments Act provision that audited spending not specifically sanctioned (by delegation or authorization) by the Treasury is not properly chargeable to a Parliamentary grant (Epigraph 3)	**(4) Example:** the common Treasury practice of official staff in spending teams moving on to different positions (by promotion, transfer etc.) after the conclusion of Spending Reviews (Epigraph 4)

break-even rule for NHS Trusts in the vignette). So a rounded account of the working of the fiscal constitution needs to include all four of those elements (Table 1.1).

'Political' elements: formal and informal

What ministers and their political appointees could do in planning and controlling public spending was shaped by formally enacted rules of several types. Some of those rules consisted of Standing Orders of the House of Commons, of which perhaps the leading example is the 'Crown Initiative' rule (S.O. 48) noted in cell (1) of Table 1.1 and referred to by Ed Davey in the first epigraph to this chapter. That historic rule restricts to ministers the right to propose extra public spending in Parliament. Some of our interviewees defended it as a way of limiting 'pork barrel' spending (that is, public expenditure on localized projects to help incumbent MPs secure re-election) but others deplored it as an excessive restriction of backbench initiative. Another example (set out in S.O. 55) was a rule enabling the Treasury to present the Main Estimates to Parliament several months after the start of the financial year, an unusual and often criticized feature of the UK public spending system in international perspective. Other rules were expressed as statute law, such as balanced-budget obligations of various types and statutes obliging Chancellors to publish specific documents as part of the Budget papers. As we will see in later chapters, some of those formal rules changed little or not at all over our period. Others were more changeable, such as the four successive statutory requirements on governments to limit public debt and deficit over our period.[8]

Sometimes more elusive were less formally enacted conventions or understandings about how the various political players should interact over public spending issues. The example given in our second epigraph and noted in Table 1.1 is a political agreement between Prime Minister John Major and Chancellor Norman Lamont at the start of our period as to how the Cabinet should decide public spending allocations. Lamont's proposal, discussed further in Chapter 3, was a rule that ministers on a newly created Cabinet committee set up to decide departmental budgetary allocations (within an overall spending 'envelope' to be decided by the Cabinet at an earlier meeting) could not propose tax rises to provide room for extra expenditure.[9]

Bureaucratic or technocratic elements: formal and informal

The rules and understandings applying to the more bureaucratic or technocratic players in the public spending world also had both formal and informal elements. As we shall see in Chapter 10, the Treasury issued voluminous documents setting out formal guidelines and prescriptions for reporting and accounting over the fiscal cycle as well as less prescriptive advice. Many of the legal foundations of those prescriptions date back to measures enacted in the nineteenth century by William Gladstone (Chancellor of the Exchequer from 1853 to 1855 and 1859 to 1865, later going on to serve four terms as Prime Minister). One is the Exchequer and Audit Departments Act 1921, noted in cell (3) of Table 1.1 and our third epigraph. That statute, a modification of an 1866 Act of the same title, requires Treasury authorization of all central government spending, whether by specific approval or by agreed delegation, even if the expenditure concerned is for purposes already provided for in statutes.[10] That rule gives the Treasury the option—powerful in principle, hard

---

[8] Namely the 1998 Code for Fiscal Stability, the 2008 'Temporary Operating Rule' adopted by triggering an escape clause in the 1998 Code, the 2010 Fiscal Responsibility Act and the 2011 Budget Responsibility and National Audit Act. Strictly, those codes required government to publish documents reporting performance against prescribed limits for debt and deficit (or trigger an escape clause, as happened in 2008), rather than actually meeting such limits (Hughes, Leslie, Pacitti and Smith 2019: 16–17).

[9] An earlier example is the convention noted by Heclo and Wildavsky (1974: 153) that disappointed departmental spending ministers could not appeal expenditure decisions by the CST over matters such as claims on the Reserve by going up to the Chancellor, only to the Cabinet as a group.

[10] For Scotland, Wales, and Northern Ireland, however, that regime under the 1921 Act ended in 1999, when each of these territories acquired its own parliament and tax powers.

to deploy as a matter of practical politics—to put recalcitrant departments 'in the clinic' at any time by subjecting them to heavy-duty approval processes.

Other formal elements of the Gladstonian fiscal constitution include the statutory powers of the Treasury to designate a senior official from each spending department as 'Accounting Officer' (AO), to be personally answerable for the department's spending to the parliamentary Public Accounts Committee (PAC), a powerful backbench committee working together with the Comptroller and Auditor General (the public auditor). Officials designated as AOs were not permitted to delegate their responsibility to answer to Parliament to a deputy, and during the twentieth century the Treasury came to name Permanent Secretaries (official heads of departments) as AOs, thereby raising the political stakes for such players in their dealings with ministers over spending issues (discussed later in Chapter 6).[11]

In contrast to those formal powers and duties in the Gladstonian fiscal constitution, numerous accounts of the bureaucratic working of the expenditure control system portray the interactions between Treasury controllers and spending departments as shaped more by informal understandings and personal relationships (good or bad) among the people involved rather than by hard-and-fast rules. One example of such conventions from our period was the common practice of turning over the Treasury's controlling staff in the aftermath of spending reviews (a feature of our vignette and noted in cell (4) of Table 1.1), meaning that the Treasury officials who had negotiated multi-year spending settlements and laboriously drafted the associated 'Settlement Letters' were not those who oversaw the subsequent implementation process. Such 'churn' was far from new,[12] but it meant that institutional forgetting of such settlements was almost built into the system. Other unwritten customs or conventions included the expectation that meetings between the Treasury and spending department officials and ministers should ordinarily be held in the Treasury's building rather than in departments and that before 1999 Treasury spending teams were expected to avoid getting involved in 'too much detail on non-English social policy business'.[13]

Some of those customary practices were more durable than others and some may have been part of longer cycles. Heclo and Wildavsky (1974: 78–79) claimed there had been a century-long cycle of alternating hostility and efforts at collaboration between Treasury and key spending departments, and if so there was at least

---

[11] A further example, based on a 1932 agreement ('concordat') with the House of Commons Public Accounts Committee rather than in statute law or parliamentary Standing Orders, is the Treasury's power to approve proposals for 'new' spending by departments before the anticipated legislation for which the spending is intended to prepare has been enacted.

[12] One of Heclo and Wildavsky's (1974: 66) interviewees in the 1970s commented that 'The Treasury makes everyone's job especially difficult by their tendency of switching their own expenditure. controllers around'.

[13] Described by Deakin and Parry (2000: 157–159) as an unwritten 'default position' of Treasury spending teams in the 1990s.

one fresh iteration of that cycle over our period. Some informal understandings were overturned over that time as well. A case in point is an unwritten convention, upset by a landmark court ruling in 1994 (discussed in Chapter 6), that AOs' formal objections to ministerial spending proposals on grounds of 'regularity' were routinely notified to the National Audit Office and the Public Accounts Committee, but objections based on grounds of 'economy' were not.

Of course, those categories of formal/informal and political/bureaucratic overlap. Indeed, as we will see in later chapters, many of the interesting developments in the fiscal constitution took place precisely in that middle ground between politics and bureaucracy[14] or came somewhere between formal rules and informal understandings. But the point of drawing attention to such distinctions is that official speeches, published policy documents, and enacted rules, can only take us so far in portraying how the fiscal constitution worked and changed over our period. Accordingly, our account draws not just on published material but also on unpublished documents from the Treasury archives, plus in-depth interviews with both official and political players involved in spending control. The Treasury archives relating to the period, to which we had some access on a privileged basis, mutated over our period from a traditional paper-based system to some three generations of digital records based on the changing office software used in the Treasury. Our interviewees—130 altogether—included all the Chancellors of the Exchequer over our period, most of the Chief Secretaries to the Treasury (the minister responsible for public spending), all the Permanent Secretaries (official heads) and a large group of former or serving officials at different levels in the Treasury and spending departments, as well as some key observers. By agreement, we quote such sources anonymously.

Analytic Perspectives on Control of Public Spending

The large practitioner and academic literature on the planning and control of public spending spans history, economics, political science and accountancy, among other disciplines. Some of that literature consists of how-to-do-it prescriptions, while some is more descriptive or analytic, and approaches range in style from abstract modelling of budgetary behaviour to 'thick' practico-descriptive accounts of specific developments over time.

We do not attempt any exhaustive review of that enormous literature here. But Table 1.2 picks out a few of the major studies that align with the distinctions we drew earlier between officially enacted rules and less formal conventions or understandings, and between a focus on the activities of the political actors as those of

---

[14] For instance, in the role played by Special Advisers—political appointees with no formal power to direct regular civil servants—in running spending reviews.

Table 1.2 Some different analytic perspectives on control of public spending

Arenas	Rules and Conventions	
	Formal	Informal
'Political'	**(1) Example:** prescriptive writing on the design of political arrangements for taxing and spending	**(2) Example:** descriptive/analytic writing on public opinion and other political shapers of public spending
	Cross-cutting literature	
'Bureaucratic' or Technocratic	**(3) Example:** mainly prescriptive literature on international 'best practice' processes in budgeting	**(4) Example:** descriptive/analytic literature on bureaucratic behaviour in public spending

bureaucrats or technocrats in public spending control. Our own study aims to cut across the four cells in Table 1.2.

In cell (1) of Table 1.2 (political-formal), just one of the classic contributions is Vincent Ostrom's (1971) exposition of the compound-republic ideas of the eighteenth-century founding fathers of the United States. Another is Aaron Wildavsky's (1976) argument for constitutional limits to public spending (as reflected in those balanced-budget rules in US state constitutions adopted in the aftermath of the 1830s crash when half the states in the Union defaulted on their debts, or the EU Stability and Growth Pact in the 1992 Maastricht Treaty on European Union that paved the way for the Euro). A third is Geoffrey Brennan and James Buchanan's (1980 and 1985) ideas about the importance of formal rules to fiscal policy-making, reflecting a long-standing preference for 'rules-based order' by liberal economists. Also influential is Torsten Persson and Guido Tabellini's (2005) work on the fiscal consequences of different constitutional arrangements.

In cell (2) of Table 1.2 (political-informal), Alan Peacock and Jack Wiseman's (1961) pioneering study of long-term expenditure growth in the UK modified Adam Smith's idea that war is the main driver of public spending growth, by depicting long-term UK public spending growth up to the early 1960s as a mixture of peaks and rising plateaux, bounded by the electoral limits of taxable capacity in peacetime politics ('It is harder to get the saddle on the horse than to keep it there', as they put it). In the same decade Aaron Wildavsky (1964) classically described budgeting behaviour in the United States as an incremental or disjointed process driven by log-rolling in the legislature and with bureaucracies and their legislative allies and lobby groups fighting to protect their budgetary 'base' (a view subsequently modified in Wildavsky 1988 and Wildavsky and Caiden 1997) We could add a vast literature on the electoral determinants of spending choices by governments, including the 'electoral cycle' (or 'political business cycle') theory that tax and spending behaviour is shaped by expected election dates (Lewin 1991).

Equally, there is a large prescriptive and often practitioner-led literature on good or 'best practice' in public financial management that is mainly directed at official bureaucratic and executive-government behaviour, broadly fitting into cell (3) of Table 1.2. It includes a growing set of standards, ratings and evaluative frameworks from bodies like IMF, OECD, PEFA and the international Public Sector Accounting Standards Board (Heald and Hodges 2015). We explore how the UK figured in some of those ratings in Chapter 11. There is also a domestic UK literature with similar emphasis, mainly in the form of frequent proposals from think-tanks of ways to improve the rationality of the formal processes of planning and controlling public spending (Institute for Government 2018). Such literature typically stresses the desirability of greater transparency, clearer rules, wider parliamentary and public participation in decision-making and a more evidence-based approach to spending allocations.

Finally, in cell (4) (informal-technocratic or bureaucratic) there is a smaller and mainly academic literature looking at the way bureaucratic behaviour plays into the planning and control of spending. Such literature includes William Niskanen's (1971) classic theory of bureaucracies seeking to capitalize on policy monopolies and information asymmetry to maximize their budgets, and Patrick Dunleavy's (1991) related analysis of senior bureaucrats as 'bureau-shapers' with more concern for their core budgets than their programme budgets. It also includes literature about the bureaucratic process of budgeting that draws heavily on interviews with practitioners, such as Nicholas Deakin and Richard Parry's (2000: 12) 'administrative anthropology' account of the UK Treasury's role in social policy; Donald Savoie's (1999) account of the politics of the Treasury and other central agencies in the Canadian federal government; and Hugh Heclo and Aaron Wildavsky's classic (1974) account of how public money was managed in the UK fifty years ago, to which we have already referred. They depicted the process as a largely closed-door affair within Whitehall, dominated by a small group of powerful personalities who knew each other (perhaps too) well. A final example is 'Miles' Law', (Miles 1978), the assertion that in bureaucracies 'where you stand depends on where you sit'. Rufus Miles, a Truman-era civil servant in the United States Bureau of the Budget (BoB), framed this eponymous 'law' after observing a colleague who moved from BoB to one of the spending agencies for which he had previously been responsible, and quickly became as critical of the BoB as he had been of the spending agency in his previous life.

We aim to draw on all four perspectives shown in Table 1.2 and certainly do not claim to be the first or only scholars working at that intersection. But our approach differs at least in detail from some of the earlier studies in the field. Unlike studies of an older historical period (notably Martin Daunton's (2001) account of how the UK in Victorian times evolved a coherent 'fiscal constitution' comprising a set of related practices and attitudes in the legislature and the bureaucracy which worked together to limit the growth of public spending), we were able to combine documentary sources with in-depth interviews with politicians, officials and a few key observers. Unlike most contemporary-history studies of the UK, we were able to access Treasury papers not yet released to the National Archives (subject to long-drawn-out security clearance and restrictions on citation) which gave us a chance to see some internal documentary material on how the spending control system worked. Further, the Institute for Fiscal Studies, the UK's main non-governmental institution for analysis of fiscal statistics, provided us with a comprehensive quantitative analysis of the main public spending numbers over our period against which we could set our more qualitative analysis (Crawford, Johnson and Zaranko 2018).

Three Questions

We use the sources mentioned above to chart public spending developments in the UK fiscal constitution over our period, looking both at different eras and at different functional types of spending. In particular, we explore three cross-cutting questions.

One: how much change really took place in the spending control system over that quarter-century, and how fundamental or lasting was it? The answer to that question depends of course on who counts what as 'fundamental', what time-period is to be considered and how much weight is to go on what aspects of the system (formal or informal, political or bureaucratic). That is tricky, because some changes that appear linear in a shorter time frame may look more like cycles in a longer one. A case in point is the several shifts over our period between insistence on strict annuality in spending control (with wasteful end-year expenditure surges or long delays in paying suppliers as the inevitable concomitant) and the alternative 'end-year flexibility' (EYF) approach of allowing unspent funds to be carried from one year to another (with resultant hoarding into reserves). There were two more or less complete swings between EYF and annuality over our period. Similarly, practices that were familiar enough to earlier generations may seem novel when new names are coined for them (such as switching of extra responsibilities as unfunded mandates into notionally protected budgets, known as 'tuck unders' for part of our period). Several of our long-serving interviewees thought most of the fundamentals of the spending control game did not alter out of recognition over the period, as ministers and crises came and went, but there were some exceptions, as we will see.

Two: what was the direction of change in the arrangements for planning and control of spending over the period? Did it become more evidence-based, professional, and technocratic as knowledge diffused and new accounting standards aimed to underpin and promote more rational handling of public spending and assets? Did it become more political as battles over spending went deeper and wider in each successive crisis, inexorably raising the stakes in the power-play among rival contenders for funding? As we will see in later chapters, several developments over the period were intended to take some of the key public spending control processes out of 'politics' (notably in statistical classification and fiscal reporting and forecasting). Efforts were made to inject more rationality into project and investment appraisal through new evaluation formulae, explicit adjustments for optimism bias and multi-stage 'gateway' reviews. Further, policy generalists were replaced by qualified financial professionals in departmental Finance Director roles, with the declared intention of securing better spending outcomes. How did such changes affect the balance between political clout and technocracy in the public spending system?

Three: what developments occurred between the cracks or in the overlaps of the formal/informal, politics/bureaucracy categories depicted in Table 1.1? Was it a story of ever-more explicit and predictable rules and categories, increasing transparency and a narrowing gap between official statements and what happened in practice in the handling of public spending? Or were developments less tidy and dramatic, continuing to produce bendable rules, fuzzy-edged institutions and flexible or contestable categories? 'Public spending by other means' in one way or another (by shifting of categories and dexterity in classification) is a thread that runs through several of the chapters that follow. Fifty years ago, 'quangos' (quasi-non-government organizations) or 'fringe bodies' were much discussed as an organizational type that spanned the public and private sector and presented challenges to conventional accountability systems (see for example Pifer 1967; Barker 1982). As later chapters will show, new creations of quasi-non-government expenditure posed similar challenges in our period.

The Plan of the Book

Our account of how the UK's fiscal constitution developed from the early 1990s to the mid-2010s combines four elements, and the rest of the book divides into three parts and eleven chapters. The next chapter gives an overview of the period as a whole. Instead of focusing on change, it identifies some of the fixed points, picking out seven elements of the fiscal constitution (many of them dating back to the Gladstonian reforms already mentioned), that persisted or recurred over the period.

That overview is followed in Part II by chapters about the management of public spending under the three governments in power in Westminster over the period, namely, John Major's Conservative government after its unexpected re-election in 1992; the New Labour era from 1997 to 2010 under two prime ministers and economic conditions that went from boom to slump; and the Conservative-Liberal Democrat coalition government of 2010–2015, which took office pledged to reduce debt and deficit through austerity measures combining stringent spending restraint and tax increases.

Part III comprises five chapters devoted to different aspects of public spending control. These chapters focus on:

- capital, investment, project or infrastructural spending, often seen as a particularly challenging form of public spending to control properly;
- sub-national spending by devolved governments and local authorities;
- control of running or administration costs and associated measures intended to deliver better and/or lower-cost public services;
- arrangements for the forecasts which formed the background to spending allocations under the various fiscal rules in operation over the period;
- the changing framework of metrics for tracking and accounting for public spending.

Each of the eight chapters in Parts II and III includes an approximate timeline and a vignette giving an account of a telling episode or issue relating to the theme of the chapter.

The final two chapters are more wide-ranging. One looks at the UK's fiscal constitution from a comparative perspective, looking at some of the ways in which its performance in controlling public spending could be rated relative to the performance of other developed democracies over the period. The concluding chapter returns to the questions that we posed earlier: how much stability and change there was in the fiscal constitution over the period; how business was done in planning and controlling spending: whether it involved predictable application of transparent rules; and what went on in the grey zones between politics and technocracy and between public and private spending. We add a short epilogue commenting on the public spending implications of three dramatic developments occurring since the period covered by our study, and how those developments relate to our analysis. We conclude by sketching out four possible directions (not mutually exclusive) in which the UK's fiscal constitution might develop in the future.

2

Dogs That Didn't Bark

Seven Continuing Features of the Fiscal Constitution

> ...the essence of [UK] financial administration has been to force taxation...and expenditure to compete with one another, by making the same minister responsible for both...
>
> (Heclo and Wildavsky 1974: 385).

Introduction

This chapter picks out seven persistent or recurring features of the UK's fiscal constitution that emerged from our interviews and the literature we read. They are:

- A limitedly codified parliamentary process for allocating expenditure.
- A 'strong/weak' profile of committee oversight in parliament, with heavy emphasis on *ex post* control of public spending but little on *ex ante* control.
- A system comprising a large gap between amounts spent and revenue raised by lower levels of elected government, with long-lasting formula-funding arrangements for allocations to subnational governments.
- A spending review process formally comprising synchronized and competitive reviews of spending across the whole public sector.
- A system formally comprising a top-down, fixed-envelope approach to allocating 'controllable' spending to departments.
- A system centred on pre-parliamentary review of departmental spending bids by the department responsible for levying taxes.
- An executive government system with review and control of spending at the centre largely organized on the 'porthole principle'. with official review teams 'marking' or mirroring spending departments, together with an overall central coordinating unit.

Most of these traits figured in Heclo and Wildavsky's (1974) classic account of the UK's fiscal constitution fifty years ago. Their study, focused mainly on the workings of the Whitehall bureaucracy, had much less to say about the world of Parliament, ministers, and the Cabinet and did not go at all into the division of fiscal powers

The Way the Money Goes. Christopher Hood, Maia King, Iain McLean, and Barbara Piotrowska,
Oxford University Press. © Christopher Hood, Maia King, Iain McLean, and Barbara Piotrowska (2023).
DOI: 10.1093/oso/9780198865087.003.0002

between central and sub-national governments that we see as a central feature of the UK's fiscal constitution. We do not claim this list to be exhaustive or innovative. Nor do we claim that these features remained wholly unaltered. Several were eroded or diluted over our period. But given that commentators on systems of governance tend to focus on reform and innovation, it is important not to lose sight of the continuities and recurrent elements in the public spending system, to put the many changes of nomenclature and shifting of bureaucratic deck chairs into context.

A Limitedly Codified Parliamentary Process for Allocating Expenditure

Heclo and Wildavsky (1974: 37) comment, 'One way to begin coming to grips with [UK public spending control]...might be to list the Treasury's formal powers. However...definitions of these powers are scarcely to be found in documents, much less statutes'. They quoted a 1960s report from a parliamentary committee: 'What is called Treasury control is better described as a complex of administrative practice...empiric rather than theoretical'.[1] More than three decades later, Colin Thain (2010: 35) wrote that: 'Unlike most of its comparators internationally, the Treasury gains its authority for managing and controlling public expenditure, setting tax rates, managing borrowing and setting the overall fiscal framework from convention, quasi-legal rules and precedent. Little of its authority is statute-based'. And in 2016, an IMF review team commented on the UK's 'convention-based budget process' [which is] 'largely uncodified, allows the budget to be presented just before the start of the financial year, forces Parliament to approve the budget well into the fiscal year to which it refers, and has seen the Autumn Statement become, in effect, a mini-budget which sometimes dwarf[s] the Budget itself in fiscal significance' (IMF 2016: 9). Indeed, no budget at all was presented in the calendar year 2019—a year of deep political crisis over Brexit which included a third general election in four years. (The Budget for FY2019-20 was presented in October 2018, and that for the following year FY2020-21 not until March 2020.)

Labelling the system as 'convention-based' and 'largely uncodified' does not mean that public spending control was a wholly rule-free, Wild-West zone. It only takes a glance at some of the official rule books in operation during our period[2] (as we show later) to see that it was anything but. Several features of the control framework, such as the reporting arrangements at fiscal events, the form in which

---

[1] House of Commons Select Committee on Estimates, HC 347 1967–1968: xxxvi.
[2] Including *The Government Accounting Manual* (up to 2008–2009), *Consolidated Budget Guidance, Managing Public Money* and *The Estimates Manual.*

accounts were to be kept by government departments and even (for some of the time) overall budget-balance rules, were enacted in legislation over the period.

What was missing, though, was a single comprehensive legal code for the various rules and the sources of authority for them. Some of the key parliamentary rules governing the annual Supply process were set out in the Standing Orders of the House of Commons[3] (notably the crucial 'Crown Initiative' rule, already mentioned, that prevents MPs other than ministers from proposing increases or even switches in public expenditure in the House of Commons). Others were a mixture of convention and statute, such as the rule that supply estimates could only be presented to Parliament with the Treasury's approval and the associated Treasury claim to act as Parliament's agent in controlling the spending of other departments.[4] The latter claim rested on various non-statutory authorities, notably an 1884 report from the House of Commons Public Accounts Committee (stating that the Treasury is responsible to Parliament for the regularity and propriety of government expenditure) and a 1932 'Concordat' between the PAC and the Treasury (naming the Treasury as the body responsible for specifying the rules under which expenditure can be authorized before a Bill becomes law).[5] And for those provisions relating to public spending control which were set out in statute, there was no clear equivalent to French organic law or German Basic Law.

A 'Strong/Weak' Profile of Committee Oversight in Parliament, Putting Heavy Emphasis on *Ex Post* Review but not *Ex Ante* Control

Among the numerous major changes in the handling of public spending by the Westminster parliament over our period were the following, all featuring in later chapters:

- the creation of new devolved parliaments and governments in three of the component countries of the UK, that developed their own arrangements for controlling and allocating spending at subnational level;
- the drastic simplification of parliamentary supply estimates from 1996–1997 by the removal of detailed line-item presentation of spending (something

---

[3] Described as 'arcane and impenetrable' by Davey (2000: 14).
[4] A claim extended for part of our period (1998 to 2010) by requiring departments to sign up to 'Public Service Agreements'—statements about policy and service-delivery objectives—formally agreed with the Treasury.
[5] The so-called 'pre-emption' or 'new services' rules agreed between the Public Accounts Committee and the Treasury under which departments had to have 'vires' (legal power) to undertake new spending ahead of legislation—an issue described to us as a 'highly stressful' part of the work of the Treasury Officer of Accounts, with more than one argument about the issue typically running at any one time. See House of Lords Constitution Committee (2013), Chapter 2: §18–22.

adopted during the two twentieth-century world wars and a change which followed years, indeed decades, of discussion). Shortly after that (2001) parliamentary estimates were changed from the traditional cash basis to an accruals approach—another move that had long been mooted, going back at least to the 1940s;

- the creation of an Office for Budget Responsibility in 2010 to give parliaments a more independent source of forecasts and analysis of spending plans;
- the reporting changes that after half a century finally (in 2011) aligned the Estimates numbers presented to Parliament with the numbers used by the Treasury for expenditure planning and negotiations with departments.

But one thing that did not change was the marked disparity between the amount of attention and scrutiny given by the Westminster parliament to spending after the event, as compared to the scant attention paid to challenging spending bids at the initial grant-of-supply stage. That *ex post* review operated through forensic hearings by a heavy-duty cross-party parliamentary committee, the Public Accounts Committee (PAC), working with the public auditor (the National Audit Office (NAO) headed by the Comptroller and Auditor-General) and calling departmental Accounting Officers to account for overspends and other breaches of Treasury spending rules. Over our period, PAC's *ex post* reviews went well beyond its Victorian-era preoccupation with 'regularity' in public spending[6] and focused heavily on value for money issues as well. We will see in later chapters that in some areas at least such scrutiny drew blood.

The long-term asymmetry in parliamentary attention paid to *ex ante* as against *ex post* examination of spending is strikingly reflected in the resources provided for such scrutiny. With 800 or so staff, NAO was over fifty times the size of the House of Commons' Scrutiny Unit (created in 2002 as part of the Committee office), which with fourteen or so staff had to service public bill committees and advise select committees on draft legislation along with its responsibilities to provide advice and analysis on estimates and other financial matters. It is also notable that the very opposite type of asymmetry applied to parliamentary oversight of taxation, where *ex post* scrutiny was typically perfunctory while the annual Finance Bill containing tax proposals was usually debated in depth. The opposite bias arguably also applied to the operations of the Treasury, which typically gave far less official and ministerial attention to post-mortems and lessons-learned exercises than to future-oriented plans and projects, leading to frequent complaints about weaknesses in institutional memory (Ussher and Walford 2011).

---

[6] Commenting on the PAC in Victorian times, Basil Chubb (1952: 40) says, 'The Committee tended…like Gladstone, like the Treasury and like MPs generally, to stress regularity rather than true economy—the maximum result at the minimum cost. It concentrated on the crime of unauthorised spending rather than the crime of unwise spending'.

A set of parliamentary select committees was established in the 1970s to shadow the major departments. These select committees often touched on spending issues and some of them reviewed estimates within their domains, but not all did so. And despite repeated calls for creation of a parliamentary Budget committee (as in the German Bundestag and many other parliaments) for approval of prospective spending bids to match the *ex post* heft of the PAC, no such committee was established over our period. Despite the pieties surrounding Westminster's historic 'power of the purse', the granting of supply remained a perfunctory affair, since parliamentary votes to change estimates were taken as an issue of 'confidence', meaning they would risk precipitating the fall of a government unless reversed. The consequence was that no estimates vote was changed or modified by backbenchers over our period. Days assigned for debates on the Estimates were typically used for dog fights between government and opposition parties over the contentious policy issues or events of the day, and rarely if ever used for in-depth scrutiny of spending plans. The same broadly went for the parliamentary debates on spending reviews, covering annual expenditure 'survey' White Papers at the start of our period and the multi-year spending reviews that replaced those 'surveys' from 1998.

That parliamentary bias towards *ex post* control conforms to a classic argument by Matthew McCubbins and Thomas Schwarz (1984) on US Congressional committees' oversight of executive government. They distinguish so-called 'fire-alarm' and 'police patrol' approaches to scrutinizing the executive (that is, following up on scandals, complaints or other signs of trouble as against trying to survey activities routinely and prospectively across the board). They argue that laying more emphasis on 'fire-alarms' is a rational strategy for legislators, because it avoids time spent on fruitless searches for possible failures or errors. Under the 'fire alarms' approach, much of the effort in monitoring the bureaucracy comes from complaints and protests by citizens, interest groups or whistle-blowers. This elegant analysis is consistent with the behaviour of the Westminster parliament over spending, but it does not readily explain why some other legislatures gave more attention to *ex ante* scrutiny of expenditure.

A Large 'Vertical Fiscal Gap' with Established Formula-Funding Arrangements for Allocations to Subnational Governments

A further longstanding feature of the UK's public spending system over our period relates to intergovernmental fiscal relations, a key element in any fiscal constitution (other than those of micro-states or city-states).[7] It took the form of a notable

---

[7] There is a substantial literature on 'fiscal federalism', both in general (Tiebout 1956; Musgrave 1956; Oates 1999) and specifically on the UK (McLean 2005a and b; 2018a and b; McLean et al 2008).

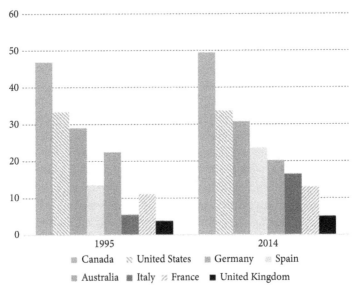

Figure 2.1 Subnational tax revenue as per cent of overall tax revenue
Source: OECD (2022b)

'vertical fiscal gap' (VFG), which we discuss more fully in Chapter 7. VFG denotes the difference between the taxing power of the central government and that of subnational government(s). Such a gap has long applied to the financing of elected local authorities in the UK relative to that of central government. At the end of our period approximately a third of local government expenditure in England was funded through central grants from revenue collected by central government, and only 14 per cent of taxes were collected at local or regional level (Institute for Government nd.). Figures 2.1 and 2.2, derived from OECD's *Fiscal Decentralisation Database*, give an indication of the UK's VFG relative to its other member states.[8]

Figure 2.1 shows that The UK had a lower share (around 5 per cent) of tax collected by subnational governments than any other comparator OECD state and therefore potentially a larger VFG. Indeed, until the Scotland Act 2012, whose effects had not been felt by OECD's last sample year of 2014, the only subnational tax was Council Tax. The other local property tax (Business Rates) was collected by local authorities but in each of the four countries (England, Northern Ireland, Scotland, and Wales), the rate was set, and the proceeds pooled, that is, redistributed to all authorities on the basis of their population. Since rich authorities had robust business rate receipts and fewer demands for local spending than poor authorities, the pooling formula led to Horizontal Fiscal Equalisation (HFE)

---

[8] OECD's expenditure data are available for all years, the tax data only for the data points shown in the figures.

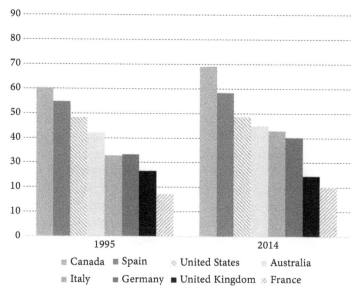

Figure 2.2 Subnational government expenditure as per cent of general government expenditure

Source: OECD (2022a)

at least within each of the four component countries of the UK, but at the cost of weakened local autonomy. Figure 2.2 shows that the UK was also towards the bottom of the OECD league in the proportion of general government expenditure disbursed by subnational government: only France was lower. Indeed in England (85 per cent of the UK population), a large proportion of local public expenditure was disbursed by the UK government, including almost all social protection, health, and school education.

That VFG, a longstanding feature of the UK's fiscal constitution, inevitably limited local responsibility for local expenditure. The 2010–2015 Coalition government reduced 'ring-fencing' of the various central grants issued to local authorities, allowing switching of funds across different policy domains at a time of severe spending restraint, but the general imbalance between local expenditure and local taxes inevitably invited local authorities to pass the blame for cuts or limitations in local services onto central government. Local authorities' self-financed expenditure of various types (LASFE), which included not only the proceeds from local property taxes but also from other sources of revenue such as parking fines,[9] could also be problematic for fiscal management from the centre because such

---

[9] For example the 'Compare the Market' price-comparison website in a survey of 204 UK local authorities in 2019–2020 named the London Borough of Newnham as the 'parking fine capital of the UK', issuing some 239,000 fines over that period yielding £10.6m (Hull and Gausden 2021).

self-funded expenditure counted towards aggregate public spending for the purpose of fiscal rules and targets. That is why a decade or so before the start of our period the Treasury was locked in battle with some local authorities pursuing sale-and-leaseback arrangements designed to increase the spendable funds available to them—only to champion similar expedients at central government level a decade later.

At the time of writing OECD[10] classified the UK as a unitary state (unlike Spain which it counted as 'quasi-federal', or the eight of its thirty-six member states classed as 'federal'). But the UK's subnational government arrangements, as we show later in Chapter 7, were complex, changing, disputed and politically hot over the period. Changes included: devolution of spending control to new (or renewed) elected governments and parliaments in Scotland and Wales; transformed arrangements for government in Northern Ireland on a consociational power-sharing model; the creation of new directly elected metropolitan mayors and police and crime commissioners in England; and a closely fought referendum on Scottish independence towards the end of our period in which Scotland's fiscal prospects figured large in political contention But those VFG levels shown in Figures 2.1 and 2.2 did not alter greatly over a quarter of a century. And despite devolution, the fact that devolved spending, like that of local authorities, counted towards overall fiscal targets for the UK meant the Treasury could not stay out of issues such as switching between capital and current expenditure by devolved governments without endangering legally enacted budget-balance fiscal rules for the UK as a whole.

A Spending Review Process Formally Comprising Synchronized and Competitive Reviews of Spending across the Whole Public Sector

A generation before our period, the legendary 1961 Plowden committee on Public Expenditure[11] prescribed a rational-planning process to correct what was seen as a loss of control over public spending under Conservative governments during the previous decade. Heavily guided by a few top Treasury officials, the committee proposed a system that was to be (a) comprehensive, in that it should apply to expenditure across the whole public sector, broadly defined; (b) synchronized, with all plans and proposals considered together at the same time in a 'gathered field' competition; and (c) prospective, with allocations to be made in the light of economic forecasts extending over several years.

---

[10] OECD (2019b) Fiscal Balance and Debt by Level of Government, Methodology and Definitions.
[11] See for instance Plowden 1961; Mackenzie 1963; Heald 1983: 174–176; Likierman 1988: 39; Lowe 1997; Hood and Himaz 2017: 102–110.

The comprehensiveness aimed at by the Plowden scheme meant that 'public expenditure' in the surveys was widely defined. It included both the borrowing costs of state-owned enterprises (even those supposedly managed on business principles at arm's-length from government) and the spending of elected local authorities from taxes, borrowing and other income. That broad definition of public spending meant that the question of how far (or what aspects of) LASFE should be controlled by central government was a recurring issue.

Critics found limitations of the Plowden approach in theory and practice[12] and some of its key original features had disappeared well before the start of our period. Some critics (such as Bosanquet 1988) saw the approach as better geared to the management of public utilities or wartime physical production planning—Plowden's own background[13]—than to other types of spending, especially of cyclically variable expenditure. Under political stresses, the original Soviet-style five-year planning horizon was cut to four years in 1981 and then to three. And, as Plowden's 'volume terms' approach to expenditure planning became politically inconvenient, it was first undercut by a parallel cash limit approach to expenditure planning introduced by the 1970s Labour government (Wright 1977), after which volume-terms planning was scrapped altogether by the Thatcher government in 1983 (Thain and Wright 1995: 461). Ever since then, the Treasury tenaciously maintained a cash-limit approach to expenditure planning, even during times of stable or falling prices when a volume-terms approach might have been easier for the Treasury to handle.[14]

Over our period, the Plowden principle of 'comprehensiveness' was eroded by reducing the amount of public expenditure deemed to be 'controllable' in the planning process, with the adoption of a 'New Control Total' in 1992 and a further reduction under New Labour's regime six years later, dividing public spending into Departmental Expenditure Limits (DEL) and Annually Management Expenditure (AME), before the 2010 Spending Review put AME back into contention with DEL. The Plowden 'synchronicity' principle was also notably breached by some out-of-sequence or exceptional deals that we describe later.

Even so, some version of all three Plowden principles survived as recognizable features of the UK's spending-control landscape throughout our period. Medium-term economic forecasting continued to be integral to the expenditure planning system and indeed the development of longer-term fiscal sustainability forecasting from the late 1990s extended the Plowden 'forward look'. A related continuity

---

[12] A leading critic, Wynne Godley, said, 'We have not got a proper planning system and we have not got a proper control system' (House of Commons Expenditure Committee 1975: 223; see also Else and Marshall 1981).

[13] Plowden's own career included economic and production planning during World War II, in the Ministry of Economic Warfare and the Ministry of Aircraft Production.

[14] Because it would have avoided the politically challenging task of trying to claw back expenditure set in cash, as happened on occasion in the 1990s and after the 2008 financial crash.

was the production of comprehensive cross-government spending plans to be debated in parliament but kept separate from the annual parliamentary process of approving supply to departments (so much so that the two processes did not even use the same numbers until 2011). That planning process was also augmented by attempts to link performance targets to spending allocations over part of our period (mooted but not applied to executive agencies under the 1990s Major government and applied to government departments under New Labour after replacing its predecessor's plans for reporting spending against objectives in accrual accounts). And while, as already noted, there were special-deal breaches in the Plowden 'synchronicity' principle during our period (and some much more spectacular ones after 2015), that principle never quite disappeared and indeed re-emerged in a high-stakes cross-government evaluation of major capital projects early in the life of the 2010–2015 Coalition government.

A System Formally Comprising a Top-Down, Fixed-Envelope Approach to Spending Allocations to Departments

The top-down approach to budgeting holds that the total sum ('envelope', in the jargon) available for public spending should be fixed separately and—in principle—in advance of any decisions as to how that total sum is to be allocated among departments and policy domains. Several of our ex-Treasury interviewees laid heavy stress the political importance of this 'agree on the total, then fight over the share-out' approach to spending allocations.

Some aspects of top-down budgeting were more persistent over our period than others, as later chapters will show. The specific 'veil of ignorance' arrangements adopted at the outset of our period in 1992 were remodelled by New Labour six years later (enshrining fiscal rules constraining the size of the envelope in statute). The Conservative-Liberal Democrat coalition that replaced New Labour brought in another player to calculate budget affordability constraints (the Office for Budget Responsibility), and also changed the content of the envelope such that cyclically variable and entitlement-led spending had to be traded off against other types of spending in the bargaining process. Even the basic 'top down' principle itself was precarious: for instance, in New Labour's final long-drawn-out (twenty-eight-month) spending review in 2007, several departmental settlements, including one for the Treasury itself, were agreed before the overall envelope had been announced (House of Commons Treasury Committee 2007: 48, §80).

Reflecting on this issue, several ex-Treasury officials said that in practice budget negotiations had continued to be a mixture of bottom up and top-down processes. Indeed, some thought such negotiations could never be strictly top down, because economic forecasts kept changing in a way that made neat sequencing impossible or because the political feasibility of any given total sum could only be established by exchanges between the Treasury and departments on concrete department-specific proposals rather than abstract global figures. An ex-minister pointed to the extreme unrealism of the technocratic assumption that spending ministers would ever stick to an overall spending total when the political going got rough, for example when departmental officials applied the trusty bureaucratic tactic of leaking scare stories to the media to get their ministers' attention.

And yet the top-down principle never quite disappeared over our period, and the pre-1992 free-for-all 'bidding culture' preceding decisions over total government spending never fully returned. All three governments more or less maintained the procedural formality of starting the allocation process with an envelope agreed by the Cabinet, such that the subsequent political bargaining over division of spending among departments amounted to a zero-sum game.

Pre-Parliamentary Review of Departmental Spending Bids by the Department Responsible for Levying Taxes

In the twentieth-century world wars, Treasury control of departmental spending was suspended and replaced by a 'vote of credit' system in which departments largely controlled their own spending. Against that background, the report of the Haldane Committee, a cross-party committee of experts set up towards the end of World War I to review machinery-of-government issues for the post-war period declared: '...the conviction appears to have grown that it is essential to a sound system of finance that the Minister responsible for raising the revenue should also have a predominant voice in deciding on the amount and...character of the expenditure' (Ministry of Reconstruction, 1918, 18).[15] The principle that, namely that the bureaucratic architecture of spending control should focus political decision-making on the trade-offs between taxing and spending, broadly applied throughout our period (together with an overall but not invariable bias towards general fund financing rather than 'hypothecation' or earmarking of taxes to fund specific items). The Chancellor and the Treasury largely continued to combine the responsibility for levying taxes and overseeing the tax bureaucracy with that of planning and controlling public spending. The Haldane principle was somewhat modified in the early 1960s after the Plowden report with the creation of the office of Chief Secretary to the Treasury, as a second minister of Cabinet rank within the Treasury alongside the Chancellor, to be specifically concerned with public spending. But the political clout of Chief Secretaries over public spending

---

[15] Edward Bridges (1957: 261) surmises that Sir George Murray was the member of the Committee most likely to have been the source of this statement of orthodoxy. Murray (1849-1936) was a former Permanent Secretary of the Treasury who in 1909, two years before his retirement, had taken the decidedly unorthodox course of urging members of the House of Lords to reject his own Chancellor's budget (McLean 2009).

policy varied in practice over our period and so did the extent of Prime Ministerial and Cabinet Office involvement in shadowing or sharing Treasury powers.

While the combination of tax-raising and expenditure-planning responsibilities in one department meant that ministerial attention unavoidably had to be focused on trade-offs between taxing and spending, the same did not necessarily apply down the line, and numerous critics argued that the two functions tended to co-exist in different parts of the official Treasury rather than coming together, at least at the start of our period. In fact, before the introduction of a so-called 'Unified Budget' in 1993, the annual budget documents presented to Parliament did not even combine information on tax plans with corresponding plans for expenditure.

All three governments in office during our period bent and stretched the Haldane approach in one way or another. Under the Major government from 1992, expenditure scrutiny was in effect shared between Treasury and other ministers, since spending bids were formally made to EDX, the Cabinet's expenditure committee (described by William Waldegrave (2015: 268) as 'where power really resided in John Major's government') rather than to the Treasury alone. Under New Labour, the Haldane principle was diluted in a different way, in that the Treasury itself became a *de facto* spending department, running a huge tax credits empire dispensing benefits for working families and the disabled, without review of that quasi-spending by any other department.[16] Under the 2010–2015 Coalition government (Chapter 5), review of procurement, major projects and a large block of administration costs, such as IT and consultancy, was in practice shared between the Treasury and an 'Efficiency and Reform Group' directed by a powerful Cabinet Office Minister to provide extra scrutiny, albeit formally within the overall system of Treasury control. Prime Ministerial involvement in tax policy always cut across the Haldane principle as well.

Even so, that principle was another feature of the fiscal constitution that broadly continued over our period. The next chapter describes a vividly remembered 1992 incident in which the Chancellor strongly resisted attempts by fellow-ministers on the Cabinet expenditure committee to debate specific tax-spending trade-offs and one of the former senior officials we interviewed said firmly, 'The one thing the Treasury is never going to agree to is…a collective process [of decision-making] on the tax side'. And although the 1993 'unification' of the budget process, as mentioned earlier, does not seem to have had an instant effect on the way tax-expenditure trade-offs were handled within the Treasury, it may later have empowered the small group of SpAds and high officials in the Treasury and No. 10 who handled fiscal events in the early New Labour period. Ed Balls (2016: 226), one of the leading players at that time, recalls that in handling fiscal events: 'Ed Miliband and I would sit with [the key Treasury officials] and go through two sets

---

[16] Since the tax department that ran the credits scheme (Inland Revenue, later merged with Customs and Excise in 2004) was within the Chancellor's group of departments.

of spreadsheets: one—the Scorecard—setting out every potential Budget measure; and the other—the Fiscal Tables, originally called the Fry Tables after my private secretary who devised them—setting out every aspect of the forecast and telling us whether we were on track to meet our fiscal rules'.

The 'Porthole Principle' for Organizing Spending Control at the Centre

A seventh relatively stable element of the public spending control system over the period is the Treasury's basic administrative structure for handling public spending. Portrayed in a simplified and schematic form in Figure 2.3, that structure combined a set of departmentally focused oversight units approving movements of money across input-focused ring-fences as well as monitoring and review, together with a powerful inward-facing central planning and coordinating unit and other cross-cutting policy teams.

Counting on a consistent basis is problematic because of changes and ambiguities in reporting, but the total numbers of Treasury officials in dedicated spending

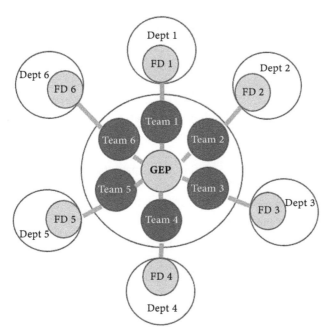

Figure 2.3 The porthole principle: GEP, Treasury spending teams, departmental Finance Directors (FD), and spending departments

roles ('spending controllers' in the terminology used by Thain and Wright (1995)[17] do not seem to have changed out of recognition over our period.[18] They amounted to some two hundred or so, if we exclude those exercising routine civil service pay and grading approvals in the early 1990s. But their grade profile altered markedly over the period, as a result of drastic de-layering at the top, a marked reduction in 'support' roles reflecting the move to digital-age working, for example with the disappearance of messengers and typists, and a substantial growth in middle-graded staff which increased the Treasury's graduate-level analytic capability over the period (a change remarked on by several interviewees).

Writing in 1994, a senior Treasury civil servant approvingly characterized the structure depicted in Figure 2.3 as analogous to traditional military organization, with a general staff and line regiments, and saw its longevity as proof of its efficacy (others were more critical[19]). Even the title of the 'general staff' unit, known as GEP (General Expenditure Policy), remained unchanged over the whole period, a rarity in UK bureaucratic life during a time of frequent shake-ups, makeovers and revamps in other parts of the bureaucratic forest.

As the centre of the spider's web, working closely with Treasury ministers and their SpAds, GEP had three main responsibilities. One was to develop plans for the totality of public spending that were affordable and reflected the policies and priorities of the government of the day. GEP did so by managing public spending reviews (annually under the Major government, every other year in the early New Labour period, and at three-year intervals in the late New Labour and Coalition period), as well as Budgets and other fiscal events. GEP set the rules, organized the process and 'kept the score' by operating the secret and sensitive database of bids and allocations. Its second main responsibility was to plan, monitor, control, and report overall spending, involving parliamentary Estimates, cash limits, and monthly spending returns, plus the Chief Secretary's powers to approve claims on the Reserve (described to us by one ex-CST as involving 'hand-to-hand combat' with spending ministers). Its third major task was to define and refine the conceptual and classificatory framework for public spending, an all-important element that runs through many of the chapters that follow.

Along with the GEP as 'general staff', the 'line regiments' consisted of a varying number (ten or more) spending 'divisions'—later renamed teams, in line with usage elsewhere in the civil service. The teams were organized on the traditional porthole principle' (Shapiro 1978: 1), a term that denoted a 'marking' system

---

[17] Thain and Wright (1995: 97–98) used the term to denote officials above the rank of Senior Executive Officer (equivalent to Range D today) in dedicated 'spending' roles or under public spending commands, as distinct from those providing advice or specialized services.

[18] For indicative sources see HM Treasury 1994; Treasury Select Committee 1999; https://data.gov.uk/organogram/hm-treasury/2015-03-31

[19] Two years earlier another senior Treasury official had described the department's structure as 'a mess...if one is looking for...clear chains of command...'. He added, 'If it is a mess that works well, we should not worry. But it is not...clear that it is'.

consisting of teams each shadowing a department or set of departments, along with some cross-cutting teams. The 1962 reorganization of the Treasury following the Plowden report aimed to replace the porthole principle with a 'functional' structure reflecting different aspects of economic management. But the principle survived, despite criticisms that it led to fragmentation within the Treasury in the handling of the many cross-cutting policy issues such as housing or procurement and that it contributed to repeated breakdowns of Treasury control over spending. For instance, before the start of our period, a former Treasury official, David Shapiro (1984), saw the Heath Conservative government's creation of the Central Policy Review Staff within the Cabinet Office in 1971 as 'a devastating criticism of the public-sector side of the Treasury'. He noted that the nineteen heads of the Treasury's spending divisions in 1978 approximated to the size of the Cabinet itself, with much the same preponderance of 'spending' interests, and asked rhetorically, 'Viewed in this light, should the [Treasury public sector group] have been expected to do a satisfactory job in controlling public expenditure?' (Shapiro (1978: 4).

The job of those spending teams was to immerse themselves in the policy issues relating to the departments they oversaw, and to operate as interlocutors, intelligence-gatherers, reviewers, and authorizers where spending required Treasury approval.[20] One interviewee described the work of the officials working in those teams as 'intellectual gymnastics', notably by mounting challenges to find possible 'slack' in spending programmes which could be removed without provoking strong political defensive action from the relevant spending minister. Others highlighted the importance of the Treasury teams in averting major political damage to incumbent governments that could arise if services collapsed as a result of too much cost cutting by excessive raids on apparently soft targets. Another saw the essence of the teams' work as 'interpolating' in the different and often conflicting pressures and groups within spending departments, notably in efforts to strengthen finance directors and their staff in departments against their policy colleagues or their delivery organizations (as in the health overspending episode described in the vignette in the previous chapter).

In principle, the combination of the departmentally specific knowledge of its porthole units with GEP's overall birds-eye-view of government gave the Treasury the advantages both of a cross-government view of the spending scene and also of specific intelligence or in-depth policy expertise in the domain of each department. And since GEP officials did not deal routinely with individual departments, and indeed rarely left the Treasury building (we came across

---

[20] As noted in the previous chapter, under the 1921 Exchequer and Audit Act no expenditure can be incurred without Treasury approval in advance, unless the Treasury chooses to delegate its powers. As well as spending above delegation limits, departments need Treasury approval for 'novel or contentious' spending, for carrying over unspent funds from one financial year to another, for accessing departmental reserves or the central reserve, and for virements across 'ring-fenced' categories such as capital and current or administration and programme costs.

several jokes on that theme), the combination of GEP and the porthole teams was also believed by some to combine the advantages of social closeness between spending teams and departments with those of social distance, for example in 'good cop/bad cop' ploys). Perhaps that is why the porthole principle proved resilient in the face of criticisms by David Shapiro and others even though the Treasury's organization and operation was subject to frequent reviews of different kinds over our period. Those reviews ranged from Treasury-instigated reviews and 'inside' lessons-learned post-mortems after events such as spending reviews, through reports to Parliament from the National Audit Office, to externally commissioned reviews by public-interest think-tanks or international bodies such as the IMF. Without claiming to be comprehensive, Table 2.1 lists a dozen or so illustrative examples of such reviews over the period, varying widely in their provenance, depth and how laudatory or otherwise they were. But none of those reviews argued for the wholesale abandonment of the 'porthole principle'.

Some of the Treasury reviews listed in Table 2.1, notably the landmark 1994 Fundamental Expenditure Review (discussed further in the next chapter) correctly predicted that the department would need more cross-cutting team working in the future. As in previous decades, the porthole principle was sometimes diluted or overlaid by cross-cutting functional policy units for pan-government initiatives (such as efficiency reviews, the promotion of private finance, cross-departmental ventures). The question of how closely the porthole teams should work together with GEP and other oversight teams, for instance in sharing intelligence, also recurred in various ways over the period, but arguments for maintaining some degree of social distance continued too. One interviewee recalled the apparently uncontroversial idea (emerging from an internal report on improving spending control) that spending teams and GEP should 'join up more' being summarily dismissed as heresy within the Treasury in the mid-2000s. The 1994 Fundamental Expenditure Review of the Treasury had aimed to go in precisely the opposite direction, fostering more 'creative tension' between the spending groups and GEP by putting them into separate directorates.

Likewise, some reviews were concerned with how the Treasury should staff its spending control units, in the sense of what grades, analytic skills, experience, and professional knowledge were needed for effective control, how often their officials should move from one position to another and how they should do their work. And on several occasions over our period, questions arose of whether Treasury officials with particular professional skills—micro-economists, statisticians, accountants, and management or delivery experts—should be concentrated into specialist functional groups or be 'bedded out' (in Treasury gardening terminology) into the porthole teams, with varying outcomes. Such issues could be consequential: as we showed in the vignette to the previous chapter and discuss further in Chapter 10, poor communication between the 'policy wonks' in the porthole units and the

Table 2.1 Some selected reviews of the Treasury 1992–2016

Year	Review	Comment
1992	2 pre-FER reviews of HMT 'to give management the unvarnished truth' of how HMT viewed itself and how its main customers saw it. Portrayed an inward-looking organization with poor people skills	Internal; unpublished
1994	Fundamental Expenditure Reviews of HMT (running and programme costs). Stressed a 'strategic' approach to control and put spending teams and GEP into separate directorates	Internal but with outside chair; unpublished but later released through FOI (Chapter 4)
1999	IMF Experimental Report on Transparency Practices: United Kingdom	External; published (Chapter 11)
2002	Thompson Review of Treasury External Relations	Internal; unpublished
2003	Hay Review of 'flexible management' in HMT	Internal; unpublished
2006	Government Economic Service Peer Review Report on HM Treasury	Cross government; unpublished
2007	Capability Review of HM Treasury (HM Treasury 2007b)	External; published
2008	Internal Audit Report on Business Continuity Management in the Treasury	Internal; unpublished
2010	Strategic Review of the Treasury	Internal; unpublished
2012	(White) Review of HM Treasury's Management Response to the Financial Crisis (HM Treasury 2012a) Followed calls from PAC and NAO for a post-mortem following the 2008 financial crisis	Internal; published
2012	NAO Report on Managing Budgeting in Government	External; published
2013	Review of Financial Management in Government (White-Douglas review)	Internal; published (Chapter 5)
2013	Government Office for Science: Science and Analysis Assurance Review of HM Treasury	External; published
2016	National Audit Office Report on the 2015 Spending Review	External; published
2016	IMF Fiscal Transparency Review of the UK	External; published (Chapter 11)

accountants in other parts of the Treasury seems to have limited some spending teams' capacity to keep track of departments' expenditure during the adoption of a major new accounting system in the 2000s.

But while several of our interviewees expressed unease about the division between GEP and spending teams—with the accompanying risk that spending teams could be dismissed as 'the voice of departments' by the GEP and Treasury ministers, along the lines of Shapiro's (1984) view—none floated the idea of scrapping the porthole principle altogether. Nor did any of the reports listed in Table 2.1. Broadly, the porthole principle survived unscathed since Plowden.

Conclusion

In an era of ever-changing bureaucratic acronyms, policy initiatives, reform plans, and digital technology, readers might expect a discussion of those elements that were unchanged or recurring over our period to be the shortest chapter in this book. It is undeniable that all seven features of the UK's fiscal constitution that we have discussed here changed in detail over our period, and where the line is to be drawn between continuity and change is always debatable, as Heclo and Wildavsky (1974: 340) also found. But even so, a Rip Van Winkle who revisited the UK's public spending system at the end of our period after slumbering for two decades could be expected to recognize these seven features as familiar parts of the political and bureaucratic landscape of spending control. Some of these features proved to be more problematic in international best-practice assessments than others, as we will see in Chapter 11. And whether the same continuities might be found two decades hence is a question to which we turn in the final chapter.

PART II

UK PUBLIC SPENDING CONTROL UNDER THREE GOVERNMENTS 1992–2015

3

Fear, Shock, and Spending Control under the Major Government, 1992–1997

Vignette: How to Limit Information Asymmetry in Spending Reviews: 'Front Line First', 1993–1994

2528. [Sir Nicholas Bonsor, MP, chair of the Committee] So would it be fair to say that, had you not found the savings that you have, the front line would have been cut?

(Malcolm Rifkind [Minister of Defence]) No question about it

(House of Commons Defence Select Committee (1994): 2).

Defence presents special challenges for public spending control, and indeed for civilian control of the military more generally, because of its scale, technical complexity, high security and political clout. One ex-Treasury interviewee described the Ministry of Defence (MOD) as 'huge', 'impenetrable', with 'lots of layers', communicating in acronym-studded language incomprehensible to outsiders, and carefully editing all information leaving the department. MOD is also unique among major Whitehall spending departments in having its main 'producer group' (the armed forces) located inside the ministry at high executive level.

One ex-MOD official breezily described the department's strategy in the early 1990s as: '...ask for twice what you want and expect to get half; "play the Prime Minister card" [that is, mobilize the Prime Minister to resist Treasury pressure for cuts in defence spending]; and encourage "chuntering" by the military top brass, who in turn talked to the PM'. Another said that in its dealings with the Treasury, MOD had been adept at padding the baseline (that is, exaggerating the costs of delivering existing policy). Given that much defence spending involves complicated procurement projects liable to delays (featuring in many critical NAO reports), MOD ran the risk of running underspends that could be pocketed by the Treasury. To limit its exposure to Treasury 'raids' on capital underspends (and satisfy the conflicting claims of the different armed services) MOD tended to run an overcrowded procurement programme, juggling with more projects than could easily be funded at any one time if they all went according to plan.

One interviewee said MOD was not hit as hard as it had expected by budget cuts immediately after the collapse of the Soviet Union. But after the pound's

The Way the Money Goes. Christopher Hood, Maia King, Iain McLean, and Barbara Piotrowska,
Oxford University Press. © Christopher Hood, Maia King, Iain McLean, and Barbara Piotrowska (2023).
DOI: 10.1093/oso/9780198865087.003.0003

sudden ejection from the European Exchange Rate Mechanism (ERM) in 1992 and an unexpected £50bn deficit and fiscal squeeze that followed it (discussed in Chapter 9), the 1993 spending round went badly for MOD. The Treasury took a tough line in the bilateral bargaining, after which the Cabinet's public spending committee (EDX) sided with the Treasury and agreed on a 5 per cent cut in MOD spending over the years 1994–1995 to 1996–1997. That decision put at risk the political credibility of the then Secretary of State for Defence (Malcolm Rifkind) with the armed service chiefs and the defence community, and indeed ran the political risk that some or all of those service chiefs might resign.

The main difficulty for Rifkind and MOD concerned the final year (1996–1997) of the three years covered by that 1993 spending round. Of the first two years, the 1993 agreement implied a reduction from previous plans of £260m in 1994–1995, half of which was expected to come from lower than forecast inflation, and of £520m in 1995–1996, almost all of which was expected to come from the sale of most of MOD's huge 'married quarters' estate to a housing trust (Dodd 1994).[1] The challenging year was 1996–1997, when the 1993 settlement implied a cut in MOD spending of a daunting £750m below previously agreed plans (Defence Select Committee 1994b, Evidence, p. 1).

Rifkind's political riposte was to announce a review of non-front-line defence spending, the Defence Costs Study, or 'Front Line First' (FLF) and ask it to find a dramatic £1bn-worth of savings in MOD's then £23bn budget—but without any reduction in the 'fighting strength' of the armed forces. The outcome of the review was announced in July 1994 after some thirty-three studies of 'non-front-line' spending items. The decisions included: plans to cut 18,700 defence jobs by closing and co-locating numerous offices, bases, depots, and training areas (including Rosyth naval base in Scotland, with a loss of some 700 jobs); a major reduction of the UK's then large military presence in Germany; rationalization of what were seen as non-frontline functions such as medical care, fire services, and research; civilianization of support posts; and a big cut in MOD's headquarters staff in Whitehall. After FLF UK defence spending was set to fall from some 3.7 per cent of GDP in 1993–1994 to 2.9 per cent in 1996–1997—a long way down from the 5.1 per cent of GDP devoted to such spending in 1985–1986 (Asteris 1994: 42).

In one sense, FLF followed a pattern commonly observable in 'waste finding' reviews and was perhaps less radical than it seemed at first sight (Dodd 1994: 27–28). Many of the cuts picked up on developments already in train, such as moves towards a tri-service approach that had begun with the creation of a unified defence ministry thirty years before, the transfer of forces from Germany to the UK, and further reductions in what had once been a dedicated hospital system

---

[1] The initial plans for that sale fell through, but four-fifths of MOD's married quarters estate was sold to the Annington Group in 1996 for £1.6bn in a controversial sale and leaseback arrangement (NAO 1997).

for military personnel and their families. FLF was short on specifics about how some of the claimed cost savings would be achieved (House of Commons Defence Select Committee 1994: 9), and what counted as 'acceptable risk', for example when stores or bases were consolidated into single locations potentially subject to catastrophic loss, was inevitably contested. The same went for the long-standing and imponderable issue of where exactly the line was to be drawn between military 'teeth' and 'tail', for instance over the issue of military music. Should the £6m a year it then cost to train fifteen to twenty military bandsmen at the Royal Marine Music School in Deal be seen as expensive 'tail' or was martial music a vital part of the 'teeth' in what it did to promote fighting spirit?

But at least three things made FLF unusual from a 'fiscal constitution' angle. First, the tricky poisoned-chalice job of heading the review was not given to a business or similar expert with links to politics (a common pattern in such efficiency exercises). Instead, the task was handed to a newly appointed non-Cabinet Defence minister at a crucial point in his political career (Jonathan Aitken, Minister of State for Defence Procurement). It was unusual for MOD non-Cabinet ministers to be involved in budgeting and public spending issues, but Aitken was a far from typical minister: he had spent eighteen years on the back benches, had worked in business and journalism and knew how to read a balance sheet. In his memoirs, Aitken (2000: 159) recounts how much time and energy he put into FLF, engaging with MOD at the 'colonel' level and not just those of 'general' rank. His reward was promotion to the Cabinet (as Chief Secretary to the Treasury (CST), responsible for public expenditure control across government) just a week after FLF was published. Evidently FLF greatly helped his political career at that point.[2]

Second, within the bureaucracy, the Treasury's involvement in FLF differed from its normal approach to departmental spending proposals, since Treasury Defence spending team officials were actively involved in every one of the thirty-three FLF studies. Such involvement contrasted with the Treasury's earlier operating style of leaving MOD to frame proposals and limiting its own role to sceptical questioning in meetings held in the Treasury building. That approach reflected a deliberate break with the past by a new official head of the Defence spending team, and it raised some eyebrows among those who thought the Treasury would run the risk of being blamed for whatever went wrong later. But some of our ex-Treasury interviewees thought the new approach (along with secondments from MOD to Treasury) had improved previously strained MOD-Treasury relations at that time and reduced information-asymmetry between Treasury and MOD.

Third, FLF crossed another line away from the traditional Treasury approach to 'savings' exercises. Aitken did a deal with the Chief Secretary to the effect that

---

[2] In the event, Aitken's political career ended a year later when he resigned as CST to pursue a libel action against the *Guardian* which he lost and was later convicted of perjury and sent to prison (Aitken 2000: 153–176).

MOD could pocket half of the proceeds of cuts above the £1bn savings target, both to encourage MOD officials to look for 'back-office' savings and give MOD ministers a chance to sweeten the pill by announcing increased funding for front-line defence capability. This 'keep the change' approach contrasted with the traditional Gladstonian principle that any savings should be recovered by the Treasury, and bids for any new spending considered on their merits on a clean-slate basis.[3]

The result was an 'efficiency' initiative that strongly incentivized MOD Ministers and officials to look for savings and (most unusually for such exercises) broadly achieved the spending reductions it originally aimed for. FLF cuts inevitably led to loud complaints by those facing job losses and base closures, and in particular the cutbacks in defence medical services were criticized as weakening front line capability (House of Commons Defence Select Committee 1998) but the FLF approach enabled MOD ministers and the top military brass to package such bad-news announcements together with higher planned 'front line' spending. Examples of the latter were plans to take ships and aircraft out of reserve and put them back into active service, to fund a new Joint Rapid Deployment Force, and buy new Tomahawk ground attack missiles.[4]

FLF thus represents an unusual combination of circumstances that produced a serious spending review, substantially reducing and reallocating expenditure in a department often said to be hard for any outsider to penetrate. The 'protecting the front line' theme was seized on by the Chancellor as a political credit-claiming opportunity a few months later in the 1994 Budget and extended to the civil service generally in the following year's Budget speech[5] (a theme we pursue in Chapter 8). So FLF is part of a wider story of efforts to cut back-office and 'administration' spending by John Major's Conservative government after 1992. The timeline at the end of this chapter lists some of the key changes to the planning and control of public spending during the five years of that government, while the rest of the chapter shows how the same circumstances that lay behind FLF (the political shock and fear associated with a sudden move from the illusion of budget surplus to a large structural deficit) also played into some other notable developments over that period.

---

[3] In the nineteenth century Gladstone as Chancellor refused to guarantee that the proceeds of the sales of insanitary barracks by the then War Office could be used to fund new barracks. The result was that 'every grant for barracks meant a fight with the Treasury ... improvements in barracks were postponed and soldiers were still housed in barracks ... where there was a high death-rate from typhoid fever' (Woodward 1962: 180, fn 1).

[4] Rifkind claimed: '... we have both protected the fighting strength and ... identified the savings ... we have ... been able to fund ... significant enhancements ... that is a very satisfactory outcome' (House of Commons Defence Select Committee 1994, Proceedings, §2542).

[5] 'In practically every Department ... we have found significant savings while protecting the front line of public service delivery' (HC Debs 28 Nov 1995 c.1060).

The Shock Effect and the 1992 Move (Back) to Top-Down Budgeting

The previous chapter identified aspirations to top-down budgeting as a long-term feature of the UK fiscal constitution over our period, and several of our veteran interviewees saw a shift (or return) to a more 'top-down' approach to negotiation over spending settlements in the early 1990s as a development with long-term significance (even though some of the specifics of those changes proved to be short lived). The new system, which had not been trailed in a White Paper or in the Conservatives' 1992 election manifesto, was introduced after the 1992 election. And it took effect against the high drama of the pound's ignominious ejection from the then European Exchange Rate mechanism (ERM) in September 1992, and the political damage that episode did to the incumbent Conservatives.

That 1992 reform package was much discussed (see for instance Heald 1995; Thain and Wright 1995, Chapters 12 and 13; Chapman 1997, Chapter 3; Lamont

Table 3.1 The 1992 shift to a more top-down approach to budget negotiations

	Before	After	Comment
What spending was subject to control	Negotiations between Treasury and departments focused on a 'Planning Total' excluding debt interest and a few other items	Treasury-departments negotiations focused on a smaller 'New Control Total' that excluded cyclically variable social security expenditure	Developed into DEL-AME under New Labour; did not come explicitly into the parliamentary approval framework until 2009
How negotiations over budgetary allocations began	Negotiations began with 'bidding letters' from departments in May, followed by bilateral meetings between Treasury and departments	Negotiations began with Cabinet fixing total NCT spending in July, followed by a (theoretically) zero-sum allocation of NCT among departments	The affordable NCT envelope kept changing in practice as forecast numbers altered
Who did the negotiating	Bilateral meetings between Treasury and departments, with the threat (not invoked for 5 successive years) to take disputes to a 'Star Chamber' cabinet committee chaired by a non-Treasury minister	A cabinet committee (EDX) chaired by the Chancellor received bids and allocated budgets after bilateral Treasury-department negotiations	Conflict arose over whether members of EDX could propose and discuss tax-spending trade-offs

1999: 300–303) and Table 3.1 summarizes its main elements. One was a change in the 'controlled' spending that negotiations between the Treasury and spending departments focused on, involving a 'New Control Total' (NCT) for spending the Treasury deemed to be non-cyclical and which could therefore be restrained in both boom and slump.[6]

Second and closely related was an attempt to move away from 'bottom up' budget negotiations that had begun in practice with open-ended bids from departments in May before the Cabinet agreed on a total for public spending. Several veteran interviewees talked about the 'theatricals' of this process, with departmental bidding letters parading what were termed 'bleeding stumps' and painting lurid pictures of political disaster if their bids were rejected, while the stock Treasury riposte had been a so-called 'talk of doom' emphasizing the political risks of spending blowouts necessitating election-losing tax hikes. A common expectation at that time, it appears, was that departments would eventually get about two thirds of the increases they demanded, setting off a predictable dynamic of bid inflation. By contrast, under the 1992 changes, budget negotiations formally began in July with the Cabinet fixing on an overall total for NCT. The designers of the new system intended NCT to be a credible budget affordability constraint, such that allocation among departments would turn into a zero-sum game for shares of a fixed total sum and thus limit the 'tragedy of the commons' risk associated with the bottom-up bidding approach (Lamont 1999: 301).

Third was a certain shift from the earlier model of budget negotiations between spending departments and the CST, which included a deadlock-resolving mechanism (not actually invoked since 1987) in the form of a special Cabinet Committee chaired by a non-Treasury minister. But from 1992 to 1998 departmental bids went to a Cabinet Committee (EDX: Economic and Domestic Policy (Expenditure) Committee). EDX was chaired by the Chancellor and included the Chief Secretary, but also contained other ministers with whom the Treasury had to share some of its carefully guarded information over bids and allocations (Lamont 1999: 302).

The 1992 package affected both 'political' and 'bureaucratic' aspects of the fiscal constitution and none of its components was wholly new. Committees of non-spending ministers were not a novelty and nor was the idea of making departments compete for a fixed sum (indeed, decades earlier that approach was described by one of Heclo and Wildavsky's (1974: 95) interviewees as 'the Treasury's ever-present dream'). The changes amounted to a package deal in that the introduction of EDX for negotiating spending allocations was a political *quid pro quo* for the top-down and zero-sum approach to budgeting that NCT was designed to facilitate (Thain and Wright 1995: 304).

---

[6] NCT as a component of central government expenditure was about 7.5 per cent smaller than the previous 'planning total' (Heald 1995: 216).

Norman Lamont, the Chancellor (and former CST) who introduced the new system, said he did so for two reasons (Lamont 1999: 301–302). One was to hold public spending growth below the long-term rate of GDP growth—a rule of thumb that (re)emerged after the 1992 general election and was known to some in the Treasury as the 'Robinson rule'.[7] The other was to bolster the Treasury's position in Cabinet under a Prime Minister (John Major) who Lamont saw as less inclined to support Treasury ministers in Cabinet over public spending restraint than his predecessor Margaret Thatcher.

Some of our official ex-Treasury interviewees gave us a different perspective. For them the top-down system was as much a way for the Treasury to bind the Chancellor as for the Chancellor to bind the Prime Minister. The need to do so had been demonstrated by the Conservatives' spending splurges of the late 1980s and early 1990s, in which (those interviewees said) the Treasury had not so much lost control of public spending as lost control of the Chancellor. Another perspective was offered by a 1992 Treasury memo setting out the thinking behind the NCT:

> We invented it [the New Control Total] because we don't want a target that is likely to be missed because of irresistible bids in the economic upturn … when Social Security starts to grow more slowly (as it will in the upturn). That leaves room for other programmes to grow faster if Social Security is in the planning total. But if it is outside, the benefit comes straight through into the PSBR [that is, reducing deficit]. The NCT is a crucial part of our strategy for getting the maximum reduction in [the deficit] in the upturn ….

David Heald (1995: 231–232) commented that the new approach was 'a reassertion of how the PES (expenditure survey) system was always supposed to operate', and suggested that firm control of public spending owed more to vigorous political leadership and clarity of ideological purpose than formally enacted rules. Developments over later decades seem to bear out Heald's view. It is hard to distinguish the effect of the new top-down NCT/EDX system on spending growth, from the political fear and shock induced in the Major government by the 1992 ERM fiasco and the subsequent massive deficit. But it does seem that those 1992 changes (announced shortly before the ERM debacle) were underpinned by that political climate and that something similar happened in later reassertions of the top-down approach by the Treasury.

Published statistics are of limited help here, because (as a result of definitional changes), NCT spending was reported for only seven years before the 1992 NCT/top-down control system began and six years afterwards. Figure 3.1, compiled by the Institute of Fiscal Studies, shows what happened to spending growth

---

[7] After Bill Robinson, former Director of the IfS, then Special Adviser to Chancellor Lamont, who outlined the rule in May 1992 (see Robinson 1993a and 1993b).

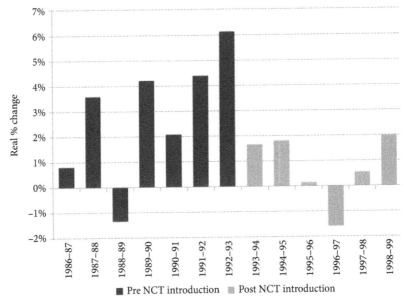

Figure 3.1 Real growth in New Control Total spending, 1986–1987 to 1998–1999
Source: Crawford, Johnson and Zaranko (2018): p. 18

over those thirteen years, and the pattern is consistent with the idea that top-down budgeting was associated with lower growth in non-cyclical expenditure, at least in the short term. But from a longer-term perspective, looking at growth of Total Managed Expenditure (TME) over four decades or so, the slope of TME growth is not markedly different as between the decades before and after the 1992 changes. Indeed, from that longer-term perspective, the most dramatic reduction in TME spending growth (and its fall relative to GDP) did not come after the 1992 ERM fiasco but after the financial crash of 2008, which also breathed new life into top-down budgeting.

In the short term, though, a change in the bargaining climate was noted in the Treasury's post-mortem documents (after-the-fact 'lessons learned' evaluations) over budgetary negotiations with departments. The post-mortem on the pre-NCT (and pre-election) spending survey in 1991 said attempts to exhort ministers to limit their opening bids had failed, even though the CST had urged the Prime Minister to stress the political need for restraint. By contrast, the corresponding post-mortem on the 1993 negotiations said that while some spending ministers had approached their bilateral meetings with the CST 'in the old style as propagandistic, chest-beating devices', the bargaining atmosphere had 'changed radically', with much greater collective restraint than the previous year, caused—at least in part—by the political 'threat of further tax increases'.

Reflecting on that 1992 move (or move back) to top-down budgeting nearly three decades later, interviewees offered a range of views. Some saw the shift to top-down budgeting, facilitated by the invention of NCT, as the most important single development in spending control over the whole period covered by this book, because after 1992 Chief Secretaries no longer had to 'negotiate blind' with their ministerial colleagues, but instead had a constraint agreed by the Cabinet that helped to shape the subsequent bargaining. But other interviewees argued that public expenditure planning was always and inevitably a mixture of top-down and bottom-up processes in practice. Part of the reason was that fiscal forecasts could change rapidly and dramatically (as we will see in Chapter 9), meaning the size of the available spending envelope was always contestable. Some thought negotiations with ministers over specific budgets were a vital element in forming the Cabinet's collective view about what the global total should be. One said, 'In practice you have to go through the negotiations to let Ministers know what they are signing up for ... to get the political consensus you have to start talking about individual budgets'. And several echoed the point made in the 1993 spending-round post-mortem quoted earlier, that any moderation of departmental spending bids after 1992 came more from ministers' political fears of needing to raise taxes than from formal rule changes.

The Unified Budget of 1993: 'Better Decision-Making Through More Carefully Considered Trade-Offs'?

Chapter 2 identified relatively strong *ex post* scrutiny of spending by parliamentary committees together with weak *ex ante* scrutiny as a continuing feature of the UK fiscal constitution, whereas exactly the opposite mix—stronger *ex ante* parliamentary engagement but weaker scrutiny *ex post*—applied to taxation. Indeed, until 1993 the Westminster Parliament in effect considered public spending and taxation separately. Tax proposals were made in Budgets, normally presented in the spring close to the beginning of the financial year and leading up to a Finance Act authorizing the government to levy taxes for that year. On the expenditure side, Parliament was presented every autumn with government multi-year spending plans (a system that went back to Plowden (1961) and indeed had antecedents in the 1930s) and later went through the annual process of granting 'supply'—that is, approving provision from the Consolidated Fund to fund the work of each government department. That process began with a 'Vote on Account' before the start of the financial year, then moved to approval of Supply Estimates and culminated in an Appropriation Act in the summer, plus supplementary estimates presented three times (later twice) a year.[8]

---

[8] For a useful summary of the traditional timetable, see Likierman 1988: 146, Table 7.2.

That system had plenty of critics. David Heald (1983: 165 and 169–170) described parliamentary control of public spending as 'a hollow myth', said the Estimates system was 'irrelevant to the needs of a modern legislature' and that the system bred 'compartmentalized minds: enthusiastic spenders can urge higher expenditure without simultaneously considering how it would be financed; and enthusiastic tax cutters can advocate sweeping reductions without specifying comparable expenditure changes ... none of the difficult choices are ever explicitly posed'.

As we shall see, some of those issues were still being fought over decades later, and even in 1993 the idea of unifying the budget was far from new. Back in 1980 an independent committee chaired by a former top Treasury mandarin and Head of the Civil Service (William Armstrong) recommended that a provisional budget covering both taxation and expenditure should be presented in December, ahead of final spending decisions in the spring budget (Armstrong 1980; Thain and Wright 1995:52). What happened instead, in the face of Treasury objections about administrative burden and timetabling difficulties, was a more modest scheme in the form of an annual 'Autumn Statement' from 1982 containing spending plans, tax revenue projections and economic forecasts, but in practice detailed expenditure decisions continued to be made first, with specific tax changes following on in the spring budget.

Shortly before the 1992 general election, the Major government issued an apparently unprompted White Paper (HM Treasury 1992) declaring its intention to have a unified autumn budget, to include detailed proposals on both tax and spending in a single, once-a-year fiscal event. The White Paper claimed the change would produce: better decision-making, through more carefully considered trade-offs between tax and spending; clearer presentation; more informed parliamentary debate; and earlier announcement of tax proposals before new taxes took effect. The plan was endorsed in the 1992 Conservative manifesto.

The first such Budget was in 1993, but the one-main-fiscal-event-a-year part of the change proved short lived. In 1997 the incoming New Labour government went back to two such events, in the form of a Pre-Budget Report in November—a renamed version of the earlier Autumn Statement—followed by a Budget in the spring). But while a single fiscal event per year is a sufficient condition for bringing tax-spending trade-offs to a single decision point, it is arguably not a necessary one. And at least officially the top-down feature of the 1992 reforms that involved setting the spending envelope in advance of departmental bids survived even when New Labour and its successors reverted to multiple fiscal events per year.

Indeed, several interviewees distinguished the issue of how many parliamentary fiscal events there should be per year from that of how tax and spending decisions should relate to one another. Several thought the choice between one or more fiscal events a year made little difference to the public spending control and were just a matter of political style. One said, 'The more technocratic the Chancellor the less they want to do budgets; the more political ... the more they want to do budgets'. Another said the choice reflected how far Chancellors 'had their ego under control'. A third pointed to the political credit-claiming opportunities for Chancellors: '... it's a great opportunity for Chancellors twice a year to be at the centre of events and ... organize government around them' (for instance by commissioning reviews or orchestrating policy announcements from departments).

By contrast, there were long-standing arguments for a one-fiscal-event-a-year approach, often said to be international best practice. Several interviewees thought multiple fiscal events encouraged short-termism and led to higher spending. One said, 'Every time you come to the Despatch Box, you have to bring gifts' and another believed that a perceived political need to announce extra largesse at every fiscal event had led to spending being increased too fast in the early 2000s. A third thought telling examples of serious underlaps between tax and spending decisions could still be readily found over a quarter of a century later. One ex-Treasury official described the idea of a unified budget as an 'IFS (Institute for Fiscal Studies) policy' (implying it had more enthusiasts outside than inside the Treasury). Another said it reflected 'a recurring Treasury view ... one of the cyclical things in Treasury theology'.

The 1992 announcement of the move to a unified budget came before the ERM episode and before the Treasury had grasped the size of the likely future deficit. But the timing of the move was confirmed by Norman Lamont in the aftermath of the ERM episode, and his successor Kenneth Clarke opted to go ahead with the plan the following year, at a time when the government was unpopular with its own backbenchers after a big VAT hike in the spring budget. It therefore seems likely that the change was politically underpinned by the impact of unpopular tax rises and a deficit comparable in size to that of 1976 which preceded the downfall of the Callaghan Labour government in 1979.

When it comes to more micro-level trade-offs and interactions between tax and spending policies, interviews and documents both indicated that the introduction of the Unified Budget in 1993 did not immediately bring the tax and spending sides of the Treasury closely together. One senior ex-Treasury interviewee said that, while GEP and the tax side of the department were briefly put under the same command in the Treasury after 1994 and thus 'sort of' reflected the move to a Unified Budget, the change made no difference to spending departments' dealings with their Treasury teams. Another said the Treasury was 'close to being two departments' (over tax and spending) at that time.

Part of the reason for that separation at official level seems to have been simply 'bandwidth' or 'headspace' limits on the capacity of top Treasury officials to concentrate on the detail of both of those issues at once at that time. Indeed, some months before the first Unified Budget, a frank official submission to the Chancellor stressed that its effects would be limited: 'Running the two big annual exercises at the same time will place a huge burden both on you personally and on the Treasury ... A raft of new problems has been created, and a lot of expectations raised, when in practice little of substance is likely to change. Expenditure will continue to be determined in one box, tax in another ... Among the most disappointed will be those who had hoped for a genuine unification of tax and spending, with decisions taken together and alternatives traded against one another, rather than a process still driven by the expenditure side of the account ...'. The following year, the 1994 Fundamental Expenditure Review of the Treasury, to be discussed shortly, said much the same:

> [The budget] ... was not fundamentally a *unified* budget ... the 'tax' and 'public expenditure' sides of the Treasury carried on pretty much as if nothing had changed; and the final Red Book and Budget Report was largely just the conflation of the old FSBR [*Financial Statement and Budget Report*] and Autumn Statement documents ... (HM Treasury 1994a: 89).

Further, the integration of spending and tax deliberations at the political level seems to have been limited by Treasury determination to protect its 'closed circle' on tax. One interviewee said the political thinking behind the Unified Budget had been that if Chancellors could make credible threats of electorally painful tax increases when pressed by their Cabinet colleagues to spend more, it would help to limit such demands. But at the same time the Treasury aimed to avoid collective Cabinet discussion of tax policy. Norman Lamont says in his memoirs that he was determined to prevent his EDX colleagues from going into tax-expenditure trade-offs, and to uphold what he saw as a key convention that tax proposals concerned the Chancellor and Prime Minister alone. He describes an angry scene in 1992 when he stormed out of an EDX meeting he was chairing because the committee had raised the issue of reducing tax reliefs to allow more spending (Lamont 1999: 304–305).

Table 3.2 summarizes what interviews and official documents indicated about three aspects of the 1993 move to unified budgeting. Several interviewees described it as 'a good idea in principle', or words to the same damning effect.[9] But while parts of the Unified Budget scheme proved short lived, all budgets after 1993 included extensive documentation of both tax and spending (in the 'Red Book', FSBR). Tax-expenditure issues also figured large in the application of New Labour's fiscal rules (as we will see in Chapter 4), with extensive discussions of such issues by the small group of SpAds and officials who ran spending reviews under New Labour. At the same time, new forms of 'spending' grew up at the boundaries of tax and expenditure, serving both to underline the need for unified budgeting and the challenges of achieving it in practice.

---

[9] One thought there was a case for going in the opposite direction, separating the Treasury's 'Office of Management and Budget' functions from its tax-raising responsibilities.

Table 3.2 Three aspects of unified budgeting during and after the Major government

Theme	What Happened	Comment
Single (major) fiscal event per year	Adopted in three successive years (1994, 1995 and 1996), thereafter replaced by two or more events per year	A short life only and its impact on spending pressures is hard to distinguish from that of the political climate
More debate over trade-offs between spending and tax revenue at micro level	Little sign of more trade-off deliberation in Cabinet or at official department-Treasury level immediately after UB	Micro-level tax-spending deliberation later became a feature of Spending Reviews under New Labour
Alignment of spending and tax documents and combined announcement of tax and ending plans	Further alignment of what had begun with adoption of Autumn Statements a decade before	A permanent change to bring tax and spending documents together in the Budget 'Red Book'

The 1994 Treasury Makeover: In Search of 'Controlled Culture Change'

A third notable development in spending control which took place in the aftermath of the ERM debacle and the unexpected return to a spending squeeze on a scale not seen since the early 1980s was the 1994 Fundamental Expenditure Review of the Treasury's running costs (henceforth FER). FER was one—arguably the most high-profile—of a set of zero-based in-depth reviews of spending departments launched by CST Michael Portillo in 1993 (HM Treasury 1994a). Unlike the 1994 MOD review described in our vignette (led by a junior minister), the Treasury FER was headed by a senior business figure (Sir Colin Southgate of Thorn EMI) and orchestrated by a young Treasury high-flier, Jeremy Heywood,[10] working closely with the Permanent Secretary, Sir Terry Burns.[11] Like the other two developments in this chapter, FER took place at a time of fear and uncertainty about the Treasury's capability and future.[12]

---

[10] With Richard Thomas and Suzanne Cook. For Heywood FER was an early chapter in a stellar civil service career up to his untimely death in 2018 (Heywood 2020).

[11] FER also involved a heterogeneous steering group of ten top Treasury officials (whose opinions were said to vary from the idea that there was little wrong with the *status quo* to the view that the Treasury should run like a merchant bank, paying huge bonuses to its highest fliers).

[12] Spending squeezes always lead to pressures for the Treasury to 'lead by example' (though it can be argued that cutting Treasury staffing in such conditions runs the risk of making spending cuts more ill-considered or self-defeating than they would otherwise be) and rumours of 20 per cent staff cuts apparently circulated in the Treasury in mid-1994.

Drawing on three other reviews,[13] FER went deep into the Treasury's structure and operation, making recommendations that ranged from scrapping the typing pool to reorganizing the top-level command structure. It led to big cuts in Treasury staffing,[14] and also broke new ground in its proposals aimed at changing the department's culture, particularly in spending control, at which its most contentious proposals were directed.

FER aimed at what it called 'controlled culture change' in spending control, involving people, structure and processes. As for people, it backed a mix of staffing cuts, particularly at the top through de-layering, together with the integration[15] of a formerly separate corps of economic specialists into spending teams. It did not frontally attack the 'porthole principle' of Treasury organization discussed in the previous chapter (though it said more cross-team working was likely to be needed), but it led to a striking new Treasury organogram putting most of the spending teams in an 'expenditure and policy review' directorate divided from the central GEP team in the public finances directorate.

The declared aim was to separate GEP's single-minded concentration on hitting overall spending targets from the balancing act expected from the Treasury's spending teams, exposing them to pressures to support policy choices to improve overall economic performance and not just to deliver spending cuts. It also emphasized the need for an approach to spending control that was 'strategic'. That key word was not defined at the outset, though the FER document mentioned the need to take 'a five or ten year view [rather] than what happens from one April to the next' (p. 20)[16] and to focus on 'outputs not inputs' (p. 33). But the definitive meaning was given (at p. 90) as '*more* reliance on maintaining bottom line control over departments' expenditure and *less* reliance on detailed controls over sub-components of departmental running costs' (p. 90: emphasis in the original). The general message, redolent of criticisms made in earlier eras,[17] was

the needs of short-term public expenditure control tend to over-rule the requirements for long-term economic performance,

---

[13] Those reviews covered the Treasury's central Personnel, Finance and Support group, office efficiency and—most controversially—de-layering. FER also involved surveys of staff and 'customers', reports from senior officials and many meetings, including one of the entire department, gathered in a large conference centre.

[14] The view that the Treasury might be overstaffed at ministerial level, with five ministers and the associated support staff, was raised but unsurprisingly not pursued.

[15] Termed 'bedding out' in Treasury jargon, meaning co-location with spending teams and inclusion within the team command structure.

[16] One former Director of Public Spending said 'upstream' Treasury intervention in policy formulation was the only way to keep public spending in check because, 'By the time you get to control the money (in approving Supplementary Estimates, for instance), it's too late'.

[17] For example, the Programme Analysis and Review (PAR) system, introduced under the Heath government in the 1970s, was intended to focus on what departmental goals were, how spending related to those goals and whether those goals were actually being reached (Heclo and Wildavsky 1974: 351).

And

> ... there is ... significant ... second-guessing of ... detailed spending and management decisions; and a reluctance ... to 'let go' of detailed casework. (HM Treasury 1994a: 105-106).

One member of FER's steering group decoded the term 'strategic' for us as meaning that spending teams should not get into political fights with departments that they could not win. But that still left questions open about how to 'lose well' in such conditions (for example by extracting agreements for future reviews when the political climate might have altered), the issue of when the Treasury should stop taking an interest in policy discussions, and what to do when the pressure for second-guessing came from the Treasury's ministers rather than officious civil servants—subtleties that unsurprisingly FER did not mention.

Advocacy of a 'strategic' approach in government in general and the Treasury in particular was much in vogue in the early 1990s. Sir Angus Fraser, the Prime Minister's Adviser on efficiency, used the term to mean avoidance of excessive Treasury second guessing in a key 1991 report[18] and in 1992 a senior consultant discussed that theme with top Treasury staff. In 1993 the Chancellor himself (who had been a minister of several large spending departments and who indeed chose to devote time when on holiday that year to write a paper on how the Treasury should treat departments), asked the FER team to consider the loaded question, 'Should the Treasury expenditure divisions seek to micro-manage other departments' spending or exert bottom-line control?' He also questioned whether the department needed so many top-level staff.

Some of the accounts of the work done by Treasury spending teams that emerged during FER indicate the pressures they were under, both from departments and from their Treasury colleagues, and the consequent obstacles to a big-picture strategic approach. For example, a member of the agriculture and fisheries team reported that the team was aiming to be more 'strategic' by raising delegation limits, moving from assessing individual cases to agreeing departmental decision procedures over proposed flood defence schemes and getting 'out of the pay policy loop' for arm's-length agencies. His team was also disengaging from other areas of work, resisting pressure from other parts of the Treasury for 'scouring the backwaters for privatization candidates'. It was pulling out of 'figurework' it had hitherto done in checking the then Ministry of Agriculture, Fisheries and Food's returns for official statistics and Parliamentary Estimates,

---

[18] 'The public expenditure side of the Treasury should focus increasingly on key measures of outcome as it moves to a more strategic style of control of the public sector. The detailed management of resources to achieve those outcomes should be left to agencies and information gathering should be limited accordingly' Fraser (1991) §2.15.

meaning there would inevitably be more flaws in those returns in the future.[19] But detailed checking responsibilities did not end there. Treasury spending teams had to check departments' form-filling for annual reports of contingent liabilities to Parliament and were also expected to police Treasury Officer of Accounts rules on fees and charges. Those rules involved legal obligations, so the checking could not be abandoned altogether. But, the writer of the aforementioned report remarked, '... arguments about what constitutes a "chargeable service" and whether there is cross-subsidization often look to me like the sort of thing that brought medieval theologians into disrepute'.

One interviewee who had been in a different spending team (social security) at that time also commented that the Treasury's approach to spending control in the early 1990s was 'fraught with "wood-for-trees" risks'. There had been a sense of running to stand still, dealing with symptoms rather than causes, facing a constant heavy load of ad hoc business and 'unpleasant surprises'. The spending team 'didn't have the headspace' to deal effectively with underlying issues, could not 'step back and exit' and were preoccupied with 'the daily disaster' ('the unending stream of bad news from the department'). FER aimed to limit the amount of specific casework done by the Treasury, notably by taking it out of the business of approving specific pay and pension arrangements, which involved transferring almost 10 per cent of the Treasury's backroom staff to the then Office of Public Services and Science.

A few years after FER, Richard Chapman (1997: viii), described the restructuring that followed as 'the most fundamental and radical change in the Treasury's approach to its work during the twentieth century'.[20] Chapman, a careful historian not given to hyperbole, seems to have been referring in particular to the post-FER Treasury organogram which separated formal responsibility for giving advice on how big the overall public spending envelope should be from the responsibility for negotiating the individual departments' spending settlements. A quarter of a century on from Chapman's judgement, Table 3.3 summarizes what can be concluded about FER's long-term significance from interviews and official documents.

Several interviewees with experience going back to the 1990s did indeed think FER had been the most searching review of the Treasury's public spending control activity over our period, but their verdicts on its efficacy were mixed. Some saw it as 'a solution in search of a problem'. Some thought it led to a dangerous loss of in-depth policy expertise. Most remembered it as a time of painful staff cuts. Only

---

[19] So it seems to have proved. One of us led a review of regional expenditure statistics in 2002–2004 and discovered that DEFRA simply apportioned all its expenditure to the English regions by population share, such that London was recorded as receiving the second highest amount of farm support payments in the country (Cameron, McLean, and Wlezien 2004: 126).

[20] Other commentators at that time (such as Parry, Hood, and James 1997 and Deakin and Parry 2000) were more sceptical.

Table 3.3 What happened to three FER changes in spending control

FER Theme	What Happened	Comment
GEP and (most) spending teams placed in separate directorates, to expose teams to 'cross pressures'	The post-FER organogram lasted only four years but variants recurred in later reorganizations	Indicates both short term impact and recurrence
Reduction of specific approvals and detailed case work for a more 'strategic' bottom-line and result-oriented approach	Some approvals were removed (such as pensions and pay) and delegation limits rose but administration cost controls remained (Chapter 8) and some detailed approvals returned after 2010 (Chapter 5)	Indicates some circularity but detailed pay approvals did not return over the period
Reshaping Treasury spending control into a flatter hierarchy, younger and more economics-focused	Stringent post-1994 cull of senior staff, not reversed later	Indicates a permanent change

one spontaneously named that post-FER organogram as a notable development while several were more doubtful about it ('moving the deck chairs').

We also heard from several interviewees that FER did not change the fundamentals of Treasury spending teams' relationship with departments and that the Treasury's ability to be 'strategic' depended much less on official or managerial culture than on the political context, particularly the stage of the electoral cycle and the size of a government's parliamentary majority. As for FER's 'strategic' doctrine that spending controllers should focus on the big picture and switch from 'managing irrelevant transaction approvals' to concentrate on the 'upstream' stage of policy which then determined spending patterns, we see a different picture. We were told that delegation limits rose and some specific approvals were removed after FER, to the point that one interviewee remarked that the Treasury had in fact done little 'controlling' of public spending in the traditional sense in the early days of New Labour. But as we will see in later chapters, ring fences and specific approvals did not disappear altogether in the New Labour years. And low delegation limits and detailed specific approvals came back in the early 2010s, drawing exactly the same sort of criticisms about self-defeating short-termism and narrow focus that FER had made of spending control a decade and a half earlier.

The one post-FER change that all our interviewees of the relevant vintage noted was the reshaping of the Treasury spending teams. The 'de-layering' of those teams through cuts in higher-level staff resulting from the review was never reversed and led to a notable 'younging' of the spending control community. We were told that before FER, Grade 3 officials normally signed off any papers going to ministers, thereby second-guessing the work of those below them, while post-FER, it was Grade 5s who largely assumed that role. One interviewee recalled that FER 'cleared out a whole generation of officials', transforming the Treasury's internal labour market. Another said FER 'established the idea that the Treasury should be extremely lean and young, with a very limited number of experienced people, and largely staffed by graduate economists'. Several saw downsides in the younger and leaner Treasury that emerged from FER. One thought it 'led to a world of fast-streamers moving about too rapidly to get on top of their briefs' (a theme that recurred in numerous critical reports) and several thought post-FER staff cuts had meant the spending teams risked losing intimate knowledge of their departments. But all saw the change as permanent. Such verdicts lend some support to Chapman's 1997 judgement of FER as having made a decisive break with the past.

Conclusion

This account of three developments in public spending control under John Major's Conservative government, summarized in Tables 3.1 to 3.3, shows that a combination of political shock, serious reputational damage and the prospect of having to impose steep tax increases, can lead to the adoption of tough fiscal rules and top-down budgeting. The story also shows how such an environment can be conducive to a once-a-year approach to budgeting (when there is little scope for more frequent giveaways) and to searching reviews of the Treasury's own operations. That is not a new observation and chimes with the conclusion of a Conservative Chancellor (R. A. Butler) struggling to deliver on tax-cutting election promises in the 1950s that 'we shall not get any sense till Whitehall is frightened'.[21]

But fear, shock, and reputational damage does not seem to be the whole story of spending control changes under the Major government. Those 'don't-waste-a-good-crisis' factors cannot plausibly account for other changes set out in the timeline to this chapter which we explore further in later chapters. Such changes included the early development of performance metrics as a form of output control alongside input spending controls; the creation of a new category of public spending derived from a National Lottery; the first decisive steps in the move from cash to resource accounting and budgeting; and the start of the Private Finance Initiative in central government and other near-substitutes for public spending. Such innovations were rebranded and taken much further under the subsequent New Labour government, to which we turn in the next chapter.

---

[21] T233/926. Note from R. A. Butler to Sir E. Bridges 16 November 1952.

Timeline

Some pre-1992 developments

1980: Armstrong Committee recommended a provisional Autumn Budget bringing together tax and spending proposals ahead of the spring budget.

1981: 'Star Chamber' cabinet committee set up to adjudicate unresolved disputes between spending ministers and the Treasury.

1983: End-year-flexibility (EYF) introduced for cash-limited capital spending.

1986: Running costs control introduced, replacing an older common services regime.

1988: EYF for running costs introduced.

1988: Start of 'Next Steps' initiative to spin service delivery functions out of ministerial departments to be managed at under arm's-length under 'framework agreements' including performance indicators.

1991: Introduction of Citizen's Charter, with accompanying performance measures, and 'Competing for Quality' Initiative.

1992

March: Budgetary reform White Paper announced plans for a unified budget in 1993, bringing together tax and spending proposals (proposed also in the Conservative election manifesto).

April: General election produced a surprise Conservative victory with a narrow (twenty-one seat) majority; Norman Lamont remained Chancellor, but Michael Portillo replaced David Mellor as CST.

Spring and Summer: New Control Total replaced the New Planning Total for budgetary settlements; EDX Cabinet committee replaced the previous 'Star Chamber' committee; Cabinet agreed the total spending envelope for the following fiscal year in July, ahead of Treasury-department bilateral meetings in a revamped 'top down' budget decision procedure; 'Robinson rule' adopted for spending (to keep NCT growth below the long-term rate of growth in GDP, set at a maximum of 1.5 per cent a year).

September: 'Black Wednesday' shock ejection of sterling (and the Italian lira) from the European Exchange Rate Mechanism, followed by a sustained slump in the Conservative party's poll ratings for economic competence.

October: Chancellor's Mansion House speech announced: establishment of 'wise men' independent forecasters to supplement official Treasury forecasts; separate reporting of capital spending in Budget documents from 1993; the introduction of an inflation target (1 to 4 per cent) to replace the ERM monetary policy framework; and an examination of ways to foster private financing of capital projects.

November: Autumn Statement (the last before the unified budget) stated an intention to keep the growth in public spending below that of GDP over time and announced three elements of what became the Private Finance Initiative (more use of leasing, active encouragement of joint public-private ventures and relaxation of earlier requirements for comparison with public sector provision).

1993

February: Chief Secretary Michael Portillo announced a programme of Fundamental Expenditure Reviews (FERs) to cover running and programme costs.

April: Council Tax introduced for Great Britain (replacing the controversial Community Charge 'poll tax' as the main source of locally raised revenue).

May: Kenneth Clarke replaced Norman Lamont as Chancellor.

September: Professor Andrew Likierman succeeded Sir Alan Hardcastle as Chief Accountancy Adviser to the Treasury and Head of the Government Accountancy Service; Chancellor wrote to the Prime Minister recommending a move to accrual or resource accounting and budgeting across central government.

November: First Unified Budget announced an intention to return PSBR to balance by the end of the decade, to equalize state retirement pension ages for women and men at sixty-five from 2010 and to introduce electronic user charges for motorways when the technology allowed it; and announced the (Front Line First) Defence Costs study.

1994

May: Franchise awarded for running a National Lottery, with the first draw in November and profits allocated on an 'additionality' principle by twelve distributors to 'good causes' including sport, arts, and heritage.

July: Green Paper on RAB ('Better Accounting for the Taxpayers' Money') published; Defence Costs Study ('Front Line First') published and MOD dropped out of running cost controls for an MOD-specific regime (with a wider 'operating costs' regime covering all defence costs except for major equipment procurement and related research); Civil Service White Paper ('Continuity and Change') published, followed by three-year efficiency plans with output and performance indicators to figure in annual departmental reports; Jonathan Aitken became Chief Secretary.

October: Fundamental Expenditure Review of the Treasury's running costs completed; IRA conditional ceasefire in Northern Ireland.

November: Pergau Dam judgment by the English High Court (Chapter 6); second unified budget.

December: Government defeated (by eight votes) by a backbench revolt on its proposal to increase VAT on domestic fuel and power (in breach of the Conservatives' 1992 general election pledge not to increase VAT).

1995

June: Following the introduction of the National Lottery, the Summer Economic Forecast introduced 'GGE(X)' as a new metric for government spending targets (to reduce spending to below 40 per cent of GDP), excluding lottery financed spending as well as privatization proceeds and interest/dividend receipts from GGE, while retaining the smaller NCT as the item by which those targets were to be achieved.

July: William Waldegrave became CST.

White Paper on Resource Accounting and Budgeting announced plans to implement RAB across central government by 2001–2002 and included plans for capital charging, reporting of performance against objectives for each item of spending and the establishment of an independent advisory group for accounting standards in government (Financial Reporting Advisory Board).

Summer: Final FERs completed (for the Foreign and Commonwealth Office and Overseas Development Administration).

November: Budget report announced extension of EYF for running costs.

1996

March: Simplified form of Estimates introduced (following agreement between the government and the Parliamentary Public Accounts Committee and Treasury and Civil Service Select Committee the previous year), with the declared intention of making it easier to relate the figures given in the Estimates with the information on outputs objectives and performance contained in departments' reports.

October: Jobseekers Allowance replaced Unemployment Benefit and Income Support for unemployed people.

November: Budget 1996 included funding to deal with BSE fallout (worldwide ban on UK beef exports prompted by government announcement in March of a link between consumption of BSE-infected beef and variant CJD) and 'spend to save' measures of extra spending intended to raise revenue or decrease future spending (more funding to counter social security fraud and combat tax evasion).

1997

January: Labour Shadow Chancellor, Gordon Brown, committed Labour to retain the Conservatives' forward spending plans announced in the 1996 Budget for its first two years in office

May: General election won by Labour with a landslide 179-seat majority.

4

Public Spending by Other Means?

New Labour, New Labels, 1997–2010

Vignette: When the Treasury Spends Money on Itself: Transforming GOGGS

In the early 2000s the Treasury's physical setting changed 'almost out of recognition' according to one senior minister. After decades of neglect, the building that had housed most of the Treasury since World War II was completely remodelled in two stages, with the Treasury's half reopening in 2002 and the other half (for the tax department, HMRC) in 2005.

Before that transformation, the Grade II listed heritage building—'Government Offices in Great George Street', a.k.a. 'GOGGS', a large, grandiose edifice completed in 1917[1]—was in such need of repair that it was valued at nil in 2000.[2] The basement was flooded, the electrical wiring was a fire risk urgently needing replacement and the bomb-blast curtains were covered in mould. Norman Lamont (Chancellor of the Exchequer 1990–1993) is reported to have said that the building resembled 'a Russian psychiatric hospital' (HM Treasury n.d.) and several interviewees commented on how the old GOGGS shaped working life in the Treasury. A former member of one of the spending teams recalled using the state of the building as a bargaining ploy, with officials from spending departments called to justify their bids for extra funding in late-afternoon Friday meetings in a building so dilapidated that it projected an image of the utmost parsimony. Even Treasury ministers had a threadbare carpet in their second-floor corridor and one described a meeting with the Chancellor huddled over an old-fashioned electric fire, which he saw as emblematic of the state of the building at that time. Echoing the very frustrations about fragmented administration that had led to the construction of GOGGS a century before, a senior Treasury official described the building as 'a millstone round our necks' in 1994, mainly because the layout

---

[1] The original GOGGS took decades (and several Acts of Parliament) to complete. It was funded through a lump sum from the Consolidated Fund with a form of end-year-flexibility (HC Debs 17 March 1898 Vol 55 c.107–125, Ways and Means Committee, Public Buildings Expenses).
[2] Even the land on which the building stood was valued at only £30m at that time.

The Way the Money Goes. Christopher Hood, Maia King, Iain McLean, and Barbara Piotrowska,
Oxford University Press. © Christopher Hood, Maia King, Iain McLean, and Barbara Piotrowska (2023).
DOI: 10.1093/oso/9780198865087.003.0004

of corridors and rooms inhibited free communication[3] and facilities for large meetings were so poor.

By the mid-2000s GOGGS had been remodelled into a largely open-plan workspace combined with meeting rooms and informal break-out areas. Before the reconstruction each spending control team had its own room, but in the new GOGGS all but three of the teams[4] were grouped together in a single open-plan space. Whether the change fundamentally altered the quality and nature of the Treasury's work by increasing information flow is not clear. But the remodelling made informal ad hoc team meetings and social gatherings easier, enabled all the Treasury's staff to work in the same building for the first time for over fifty years and projected a new, more modern image of the department.

So how was this costly once-in-a-century transformation possible? The Treasury is normally under political pressure to set an example to spending departments by practising 'conspicuous abstention' when it comes to spending on itself (see for instance Hood and Himaz 2017: 96 and 103).[5] Such political pressure was at least part of the background for decades of neglect of GOGGS, along with other self-denying features of Treasury life such as the pay 'discount' for economists working in the Treasury as against other parts of government.

The answer seems to be twofold.

First, timing. The binding agreement to fund the GOGGS transformation was signed off by the then Chief Secretary (Alan Milburn) in 1999, within a rare political window of opportunity when there was unusually low pressure to cut government administration costs. Arguably the most politically opportune time to spend more on the Treasury's headquarters and administration costs opened towards the end of Labour Chancellor Gordon Brown's 1997 hair-shirt pre-election commitment to stick to his Conservative predecessor's plans for tight spending restraint for the first two years of the new government. That political window closed again around the time of Labour's third spending review in 2002 when Treasury ministers and their SpAds in the renovated GOGGS began to worry about the political risks of continuing growth in government administration costs, particularly for 'back office' activity (an issue we explore further in Chapter 8).[6]

Politically agreed in 1999 and completed (for the Treasury's part of the building) in 2002, the timing of the project fits exactly into that window. Recognition of the dire state of GOGGS and the need for complete renovation went back at least to the

---

[3] The top officials who formed the Treasury Management Board were said to have been 'remote and invisible' because they were grouped around the central 'drum' on the second floor rather than with their Directorates.

[4] Three exceptions were Work and Pensions, Overseas Aid, and Defence, Security and Intelligence.

[5] See for example HC Debs 5 February 2002 vol 379 c836–41W, written answers (Mr Bacon), Treasury Building PFI Deal.

[6] Or, had the Conservatives won the 2001 election, their manifesto pledge to cut central government administration costs by £1.8bn by 2003–2004 would probably have required a moratorium on new PFI deals as part of a freeze on departments' administration cost budgets.

early 1990s,[7] and after 1993 a serious process of planning began which led to the selection of a developer in the Major government's final year. But the deal was not finalized before the 1997 general election and after that election it was promptly postponed by the incoming Labour government on the grounds that spending should not go ahead on a big Treasury project when all other departments were facing zero-based comprehensive spending reviews.

Second, method. Rather than funding the new GOGGS through the conventional capital expenditure route (with the reconstruction costs of about £141m[8] at 2000 prices funded out of public spending as construction happened and the subsequent costs of running and maintaining the new offices allocated and managed ad hoc) the project was funded under the Private Finance Initiative (PFI). As mentioned in the previous chapter, PFI was a way of financing public facilities by long-term leasing-type arrangements that bundled together financing with construction and operation of buildings and facilities. In fact, the GOGGS project itself added a new twist to PFI, because it included a competition for financing the building's remodelling and a separate competition for reconstruction, operation and maintenance of the new building. Though the National Audit Office never reported on the GOGGS project as a whole, it concluded in a glowing 2001 report that the financing competition had cut the first year PFI payment by some 7 per cent from the PFI provider's initial bid.[9]

The GOGGS project therefore epitomized the 'PFI mood' of the early New Labour years for financing new infrastructure. Indeed, the bulk of the extra funding that New Labour's second (2000) spending review allocated to central government administration costs between 2000–2001 and 2003–2004 was earmarked for PFI payments. PFI financing meant that the costs of reconstructing and operating the new GOGGS were rolled up together into annual charges for a thirty-five-year servicing and maintenance agreement, paid to the consortium which developed and managed the project.[10] The implication of paying for it that way was that the government's cash outlay in the early years of that thirty-five-year span was much lower than it would have been if the project had been financed in the traditional capital expenditure style. The deal obliged the Treasury to pay the PFI developer some £14m at 1999 prices every year up to 2037.

---

[7] Indeed, there is said to have been a proposal to demolish the building altogether in the mid-1960s (HM Treasury n.d.).

[8] The figure given by the Treasury in 2003 as the cost to the PFI provider in reconstructing and redeveloping GOGGS (See Letter and Memorandum Submitted by HM Treasury, House of Commons Treasury Committee 2003).

[9] Because it involved a lower-cost way to finance the capital expenditure (an index-linked insured bond) than the fixed-rate insured bond originally offered by the PFI provider (NAO 2001b, Part 1: 17 §1.50).

[10] The PFI contract for GOGGS went to Exchequer Partnership (EP) a consortium consisting of Bovis Lend Lease Holdings Ltd, Chesterton International PLC, and Stanhope PLC. The contract provided that the site and building would be returned to the government estate in 2037 in the same condition as it had been after renovation.

Funding the new GOGGS through PFI was politically convenient because under the accounting conventions of that time, all PFI projects were excluded from Public Sector Net Debt (PSND).[11] That made it easier to fit the GOGGS project into fiscal rules limiting government debt (which we describe later and which New Labour stressed as a sign of its financial prudence). Beyond that, the detailed accounting treatment of PFI projects depended on whether NAO and the department's accountants agreed that the bulk of financial risk (of delay, default, cost overruns etc.) had been transferred from government to the PFI provider. If so, all that appeared in the department's resource budget was the annual PFI 'unitary charge',[12] whereas if the project was on balance sheet, the budget also had to include provisions for depreciation and a cost of capital charge, as applied to conventionally financed capital expenditure at that time. When the new GOGGS came into use in mid-2002, the project was classified as off balance sheet and that treatment was reflected in the Treasury's 2001–2002 accounts and in its Parliamentary Estimates for 2002–2003. But a later review, conducted by a leading accountancy firm and agreed by NAO, inconveniently concluded instead that most of the risks lay with the Treasury. The project came back onto the balance sheet and the Treasury had to face the political embarrassment of making a supplementary estimate claim for £141m in 2003 and putting those extra costs into its accounts (House of Commons Treasury Committee 2003).

Once the 1999–2002 political window for extra spending on administration closed, pressure on such spending steadily increased, as we will see in Chapter 8. And as time went on the negative effects of PFI financing became more apparent (that is, cash outlays lower than they would have been under traditional financing in the early years of the new GOGGS's life were balanced by correspondingly higher cash outlays later on).[13] Further, the fixed contractual terms of the PFI approach made it harder for the Treasury to adapt to a colder climate in the traditional way by means such as postponing maintenance expenditure. (Indeed, stopping deferred maintenance was one of the main arguments for PPI). Instead, as several of our interviewees pointed out, it had to limit its administration costs by reducing the amount of GOGGS it occupied and sharing ever more of the building with other departments to help pay for the £14m per year at 1999 prices that GOGGS cost to occupy. Such an expedient meant adapting to increasingly cramped conditions. For instance, as time went on the building's hot water points could not boil water quickly enough for the ever-lengthening queues trying to make their mid-morning cup of tea, and private kettles were also banned because the power supply was not designed to cope with the extra wattage.

---

[11] From 2006, on-balance sheet PFI projects counted towards PSND.

[12] The combined charge for debt repayment, financing costs, maintenance, and any other services provided.

[13] See for instance Hawkes (2010).

The GOGGS story therefore links both to the boom in PFI financing and the tightening input controls over back office administration costs that marked the long reign of New Labour under Tony Blair and Gordon Brown from 1997 to 2010. The next section of this chapter sets the GOGGS story into context by summarizing the overall New Labour approach to handling public spending during that period. We then return to the broader PFI story of which GOGGS was a small part and to two other major policy shifts that created giant new realms of public spending outside traditional categories.

A New Public Spending Framework and a New Style of Fiscal Management

Immediately after Labour's landslide electoral victory in 1997, the Treasury's responsibilities were reduced by the dramatic creation of an independent Monetary Policy Committee (MPC) to set Bank of England interest rates. There were also new arrangements for the management of the public finances. These included a new division of spending into DEL (departmental expenditure limits, replacing the New Control Total described in the previous chapter) and AME (Annually Managed Expenditure, a new term for spending that was deemed to be forecastable but not readily controllable by departments via expenditure limits, for instance because it depended on numbers of eligible claimants). The reporting of capital spending initiated by the previous government was taken further by separating budgets for capital from current spending in both DEL and AME. Budgets forecasted AME and set an envelope for DEL expenditure, to be allocated in spending reviews, conducted every two or three years and replacing the previous Survey. Those allocations were accompanied by agreed policy objectives with quantified performance targets (Public Service Agreements (PSAs)). Further, responsibilities for 'territorial' spending were devolved to new elected parliaments and assemblies in Scotland and Wales, in addition to new consociational arrangements for the governance of Northern Ireland introduced in 1998 following peace talks.

Along with these formal changes, according to several observers (Thain 2010: 58; Allen 2014), the style of Treasury decision-making over spending operated in a distinctive and different 'top down' way in this period, with many departmental allocations determined not so much by the traditional meetings between the CST and departmental ministers, but rather by bilateral negotiations between a high-level Treasury team (largely comprising key SpAds) and Tony Blair's Prime Ministerial team.

Further, a new fiscal framework, announced in the 1997 Budget and later written into statute (though without penalties for non-achievement or independent statistical validation), committed the government to two fiscal rules. One was a 'golden rule' of budget balance for current spending over the course of any given economic cycle. The other was a 'sustainable investment rule' that required the level of public sector net debt relative to GDP to be kept at a 'stable and prudent level' (interpreted as no more than 40 per cent of GDP) over each economic cycle. The government claimed to have met that rule over an economic cycle that it eventually deemed to have run from 1997 to 2006. But according to the Institute for Fiscal Studies (Chote, Emmerson, and Tetlow 2009, Ch 5: 81) those rules 'had already lost credibility as a meaningful constraint on policy' before the global financial crisis of 2008 led the government to suspend them and replace them with a 'temporary operating rule' imposing little constraint on tax and spending decisions.

We discuss several of New Labour's changes to the public spending system in more depth in Part III of this book, for instance in devolution funding and administration costs. But here we concentrate on three developments that took place at the margin of what counted as public spending, because those initiatives (some of which began under the previous government) can be partly understood as a way of living with those trademark New Labour fiscal rules. One is the boom in PFI projects, of which GOGGS was only a tiny part. A second is the development of tax credits into one of the biggest-ticket categories of public spending (though a sizeable amount of it did not at first count as 'public spending' in the National Accounts) which in effect turned the Treasury into a spending department in its own right. A third is a switch in the funding of an ever-expanding number of students in higher education away from government grants to students and provider institutions. The sector's growth was funded through tuition fees paid through loans financed by an arm's-length government company, which (until the accounting rules were eventually changed) reduced the size of the government's reported deficit by counting these loans, including debt never expected to be repaid, as government lending rather than government spending. How did these new empires grow up at the edge of what counted as 'public spending' and what were their consequences?

The quintupling of the Private Finance Initiative, 1997–2010

Central government is usually able to borrow at lower rates of interest than local authorities or private firms, given lower risk of default. That value-for-money assumption provided the justification in the UK for traditional arrangements that restricted borrowing by individual public sector bodies and provided for funding the bulk of public capital or similar projects by money borrowed through sale of government stock on the capital market by the Treasury or its agencies.

There had been departures from that approach in both central and local government before 1997. In particular, as mentioned in Chapter 2, in the 1980s several local authorities (most Labour-controlled, such as the city councils of Liverpool and Manchester and the London Borough of Lambeth), responded to central

government caps on their power to increase local taxes by new forms of borrowing from the private sector. Those new arrangements included sale and leaseback
arrangements for real estate and facilities such as streetlights and parking meters
(Likierman 1988: 135–136; Heald 1997; Allen and Tommasi 2001: 238). The
Treasury's response in 1982 was to restrict private financing by local or central
government by introducing stringent new rules (the 'Ryrie rules'[14]) covering such
activity (Heald and MacLeod 2002: §502).

But those rules were scrapped by John Major (then Chief Secretary to the Treasury) in 1989 to allow private financing of transport projects and as we saw in the
previous chapter, Chancellor Norman Lamont in 1992 announced a new scheme
for private financing of government projects that involved 'a sensible transfer of
risk to the private sector' and provided greater value for money. That scheme
became the Private Finance Initiative (PFI), a development presented as a way to
reduce the cost overruns, delays and subsequent cuts in preventive maintenance
that commonly arise in public projects managed in the traditional style. Archival
records show that when the PFI scheme was first mooted in 1992, several senior
Treasury officials thought there was a risk that funding capital projects that way
would be poor value for money and increase rather than reduce public spending
over time.[15] One of our interviewees thought PFIs initially had the attraction of
'bypassing the institutional inertia of Whitehall and helping to fill the gap left by
the heavy emphasis on cuts in capital spending in 1993–1994'. And as mentioned
in the GOGGS story, PFI financing also offered the prospect of taking debt off the
government's balance sheet under the accounting conventions of that time.

Figure 4.1 shows that PFI funding was modest in scale at first, with PFI projects
totalling about £6bn agreed between 1992 and 1997. They were mainly transport
projects with a revenue stream attached, and by far the largest was the Channel
Tunnel Rail link (HS1), to be discussed in Chapter 6.[16] Commenting on this era,
several interviewees said Treasury scepticism over the feasibility of shifting the
financial risks of project failure onto the private sector limited the number of deals
signed in the early days of PFI.

Before the 1997 election, some Labour frontbenchers (including the then
Shadow CST, Harriet Harman) attacked PFI as backdoor privatization that would
increase the cost of public services.[17] But a 1994 paper by three other heavyweight

---

[14] The Ryrie rules, named after a Treasury mandarin, permitted private financing of public projects
only if (a) there were no government guarantees or equivalents; (b) projects were likely to achieve
higher efficiency and profit commensurate with the extra cost of private finance (c) private finance
replaced rather than supplemented public finance (see Heald and MacLeod 2002; Musson 2009: 5–6;
Parker 2009: 3).

[15] They thought a leasing approach cut the cost in the first few years of the life of an asset—because
the payments were spread over its whole lifetime—but that since government could borrow more
cheaply than private firms, private finance would lead to higher public spending in the long run.

[16] Others included the Skye bridge, the Dartford crossing and the Heathrow express rail service.

[17] In 1993 Harman argued, '[PFI] is not about partnership. It is about the Government abandoning
their responsibility to modernise our economy and our infrastructure...' HC Debs 7 December 1993
(Budget Resolutions and Economic Situation) Vol 234, c.229.

Labour frontbenchers—Gordon Brown, Robin Cook, and John Prescott (Brown et al. 1994)—advocated more private sector involvement in public services, 'putting a left-wing gloss on PFI', as one of our interviewees saw it. Labour's 1997 election manifesto declared that Labour-controlled local authorities had led the way with public-private partnerships and promised to 'overcome the problems that have plagued the PFI at national level'.

Figures 4.1 and 4.2 show that from 1997 to 2010, the size of the PFI sector quintupled (as PFI spread from its original concentration on transport to public service projects without a clear revenue stream, such as schools or hospitals). Interviewees described the PFI policy boom using phrases like 'letting rip' and 'the only game in town', and thought at least three factors enabled New Labour to put PFI quickly into 'warp drive'.

First, the new government inherited a stock of candidate PFIs from its predecessor—of which the GOGGS remodelling was one. Second, some Labour ministers put a lot of effort during the government's first two years into modifying PFI contractual terms, moving further away from the Ryrie rules to make PFIs more tempting to private providers.[18] Indeed, the very first piece of New

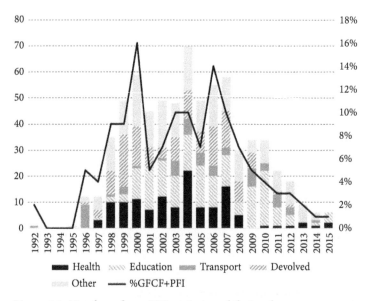

Figure 4.1 Number of new PFI projects and their value as a proportion of all government investment[a]

Source: PFI: HM Treasury (2018); Investment: the sum of GFCF (ONS identifier JW2U) and PFI data.
[a]Investment is here calculated as the sum of GFCF (ONS identifier JW2U) and PFI data.

---

[18] In 2003, a Treasury review concluded that PFI was unsuitable for small projects and bespoke IT projects and should therefore be concentrated on larger non-IT projects. One interviewee thought PFIs worked best in managing projects for standardized facilities like prisons.

Labour legislation was the National Health Service (Private Finance) Bill 1997,[19] a measure inherited from the previous government and intended to reassure banks that NHS trusts had the legal power to enter into agreements financed by third parties (an issue which had caused major NHS PFI hospital projects to stall; see Wright 1997; Pollock 1998: 1). Third, while GEP and the Treasury spending teams were said to have been less enthusiastic (continuing to doubt whether this financial instrument really transferred investment risk to the private sector on a scale that matched the profits involved and fearing that its attraction to governments for balance sheet reasons would trump value for money considerations), policy responsibility for PFIs lay with the Treasury's Private Finance Policy team, which vigorously championed the approach.

As we saw in the GOGGS vignette, the essence of PFI financing was to package charges for capital repayment for the provision of a facility together with other related services (such as maintenance or cleaning) into an annual index-linked 'unitary payment' running over two or three decades (NAO 2018). Figure 4.2

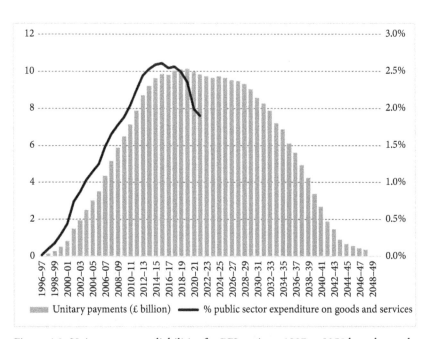

Figure 4.2 Unitary payment liabilities for PFI projects 1997 to 2050 by value and as a proportion of all public sector current expenditure on goods and services

Source: PFI unitary payments: HM Treasury (2018); expenditure on goods and services (ONS identifier FV4W), commonly used as the closest National Accounts proxy for RDEL/public services.

[19] Introduced in the House of Lords on 15 May 1997, the day after the State Opening of Parliament, unopposed by the Conservatives and described by Baroness Cumberledge, Conservative Health spokesperson, as straight from 'the must-do pile of our administration' (HL Deb 3 June 1997 c578; see also Wright 1997).

shows the aggregate unitary payment liabilities incurred by PFI projects over half a century or so, as of 2018.

Figure 4.1 shows that the PFI boom peaked in the mid-2000s, with the rate of growth falling back noticeably after 2008. Figure 4.2 shows that the continuing and index-linked cost of unitary payments for PFI projects bit deeply into central and local government budgets as the fiscal climate cooled from the mid-2000s. Those PFI contracts were hard for public authorities either to fulfil or buy out and stretched ahead long after the governments and politicians who agreed them had left the scene.

One gloss on those numbers came from an interviewee from the Treasury local government team in the 2000s, who said that in the early New Labour years the sums involved for PFI payments had been 'trivial', but that as time went on PFI credits had been 'handed out like sweeties' to local authorities, becoming an ever-increasing proportion of the money available to local government (and local authority budgets were 'top sliced' with unitary PFI payments as the first call on the authorities' funds). As for school (re)building, we were told that by 2010 both the Treasury spending team and education department officials were seriously alarmed by the build-up of PFI liabilities. By then unitary PFI payments were eating up half of some local authorities' school budgets. In such conditions, paying for buildings came at the expense of hiring teachers, despite evidence that the critical factor for educational efficacy was the quality of the teachers, not the buildings.

As for the politicians, one former Labour minister unapologetically stressed the value of PFIs in delivering projects on time and within budget. That interviewee thought negative NAO evaluations of PFIs on value for money grounds were largely based on projects early in the life of the PFI programme and did not take proper account of the fact that the government had to bring a new market into being for PFIs. He thought prices for those early PFIs inevitably reflected a risk premium that could be expected to fall as that market matured. By contrast, other former Labour ministers, expressed some 'buyer's remorse' over PFIs, while expressing a belief that PFIs had led to real improvements in public infrastructure that could not have been achieved with conventionally financed capital spending. One pointed to the problematic outcomes that could result from traditional financing as well, giving the example of new schools built in the 1960s with flat roofs that subsequently leaked because of cost-cutting over maintenance—a problem PFI was designed to avoid. Another noted that parties that succeeded Labour in government (the post-2007 SNP government in Scotland and the 2010–2015 Coalition in Westminster) had chosen to rename rather than scrap PFIs.

Still, far from becoming an accepted and taken-for-granted part of the fiscal constitution over time, PFIs faced a different climate in the last few years of the New Labour period. After Gordon Brown became Prime Minister in 2007, he was succeeded as Chancellor by Alistair Darling, who had been a 'PFI sceptic' in opposition. The 2008 global financial crash drastically weakened market appetite for risk-taking on PFI projects and led to several government bailouts of troubled PFI contractors, contrary to the doctrine that PFI transferred financial risk to the private sector.[20] Growing pressure to bring PFI liabilities onto the balance sheet of recorded public debt meant PFI became a less certain way of keeping official debt levels down. As budgets tightened, NAO became increasingly critical of the value for money offered by PFI. At the same time hostile journalists and academics continued to criticize the costs and rigidity of PFI contracts, the large profits made by some PFI companies, the incentives PFI created (or reinforced) for preferring projects of an unnecessarily large scale, and the opaque accounting that under-recorded the real level of government debt (see for example, Pollock 1998; Foot 2004; Shaoul 2005).

Altogether, PFI was always 'small in the vast scheme of things, in terms of the money involved'. PFI unitary payments never exceeded 20 per cent of overall capital spending. But while PFI spending was a negative for New Labour's 'golden rule' (since it turned capital into current spending), it really mattered for observance of the sustainable investment rule with the debt limit of 40 per cent of GDP. And as the forecasts for debt got closer to 40 per cent, 'classification risk' came to be managed ever more carefully in an effort to ensure that PFI projects remained off balance sheet.[21] Hence the amount of ministerial and SpAd time and effort put into championing PFI projects and facing the associated political flak.

Who marks the Treasury's homework? The tax credits saga

In Chapter 2, we noted the 'Haldane principle' (that spending proposals by government departments should be scrutinized by the department responsible for levying taxes) as one of the relatively enduring features of the UK's fiscal constitution over our period. But how does 'spending' through the tax system fit into that precept?

In the 1970s 'tax expenditures' (tax reliefs etc., which substitute for public spending through revenue foregone) began to get more attention among UK academics and commentators (Willis and Hardwick 1978; Heald 1983: 20–22). At the same time, the idea of tax credits (using the tax bureaucracy to pay out benefits in the form of negative or reversible income taxes) also rose to prominence, with claims

[20] In particular, the Metronet consortium which had been awarded a thirty-year contract by Transport for London to upgrade London Underground infrastructure, collapsed into administration in 2007, resulting in a £1.7bn Treasury bailout early in 2008 (NAO 2009; House of Commons Public Accounts Committee 2010). The following year the Chief Secretary announced a £2bn 'investment bank' to bail out PFI operators hit by the recession (Webb 2009).
[21] The Office for Budget Responsibility (OBR 2017: §7.67) suggested that similar considerations shaped the design of Network Rail, the quango that took over the duties over the privatized Railtrack after the latter collapsed in 2002, in financing rail investment off balance sheet and thereby more expensively than through gilts.

that such an approach could help to incentivize work by limiting the 'poverty traps' built into means-tested welfare benefits. In 1975 the US federal government introduced 'Earned Income Tax Credit', a tax credit for lower-income families, while in the UK, ambitious proposals for doing something similar (harking back to ideas floated in World War II) were developed under the Heath Conservative government in the early 1970s (Lenkowsky 1986; Sloman 2016). After that government fell, its tax credit plans were rejected by its Labour successor, but the main state support for lower-income families was re-badged as 'Family Credit' in 1988, with payments dependent on family income net of income tax and National Insurance contributions (Dilnot and McCrae 1999). Subsequently, the idea of turning child benefit payments into tax credits paid out by the tax bureaucracy came up from time to time, for instance under John Major's Chancellorship and fleetingly under that of Kenneth Clarke in 1993.

The issues at stake included: how to move from benefit payments to tax credits without creating politically important losers; tricky gender-politics issues (should family credits or benefits go to mothers or fathers, and should the unit for tax and benefits be the individual or the household?); and the challenges of gearing up the tax bureaucracy to gather information about family circumstances and in-year changes in household income that was not routinely used in tax collection. The idea of moving to a hybrid of tax credits and welfare payments for child benefits was floated in the early 1990s but witheringly dismissed by a senior Treasury official:

> ...To switch to an allowance for taxpayers and a benefit for non-taxpayers would just give you one benefit for the price of two. You would be spending more money, and employing more bureaucrats, to deliver the same benefit in a less efficient way. You would be doing it only to get round the public expenditure limits, and that would be pretty clear to everyone.

In the 1997 general election, Labour's manifesto promised to 're-examine' the relationship between taxation and welfare benefits to reduce poverty and welfare dependency. And in the following year Chancellor Gordon Brown announced that two welfare benefits (Family Credit and Disability Working Allowance) would become tax credits (Working Families Tax Credit (WFTC) and Disabled Person's Tax Credit), more generous than the benefits they were replacing and operated by the tax bureaucracy rather than the Benefits Agency (Brown 1998).

As Figure 4.3 shows, that announcement was the start of something big. Between 1996 and 2002 annual average real-terms spending on tax credits grew by 8.7 per cent, as against 5.1 per cent for health, 4 per cent for education, and 5.1 per cent for law, order, and protective services. By 2010, when New Labour left office, tax credit payments amounted to 1.9 per cent of GDP, roughly the size of the Defence budget, the equivalent of 4 or 5p on the standard rate of income tax, and it amounted

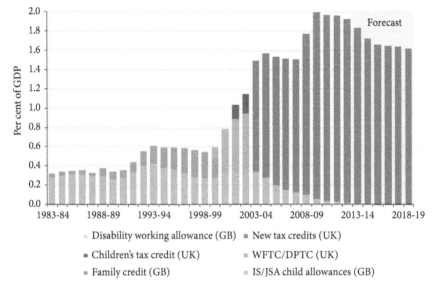

Figure 4.3 is depicted above with the following legend:

- Disability working allowance (GB)   ■ New tax credits (UK)
- ■ Children's tax credit (UK)   ■ WFTC/DPTC (UK)
- ■ Family credit (GB)   IS/JSA child allowances (GB)

Figure 4.3 Tax credits and other benefits as per cent of GDP 1983–1984 to 2018–2019

Source: OBR (2014) p. 125

to the second-largest item in the social security budget after the state pension (Rawnsley 2000; Sloman 2015).

This rapidly growing spending domain was 'hybrid' in at least three ways. First, unlike the previous welfare payments system run by the Benefits Agency under the Department of Social Security (later the Department of Work and Pensions (DWP)), it did not involve the normal Treasury-spending department interaction over spending plans. DWP seems to have played little part in developing tax credits, and the tax bureaucracy came under the Chancellor's control as one of the Treasury group of departments.[22] Colin Thain (2010: 58) commented, 'For the first time the Treasury as a finance ministry was seen to be partial to certain...programmes because the Chancellor was...sponsoring spending initiatives'.

Second, the public spending element of tax credits counted as annually managed expenditure (AME), a class of spending subject neither to control totals nor to the periodic spending reviews which largely concentrated on DEL spending during the Labour years. AME expenditure also provided fewer opportunities for approval or intervention by the Prime Minister and the No 10 apparatus (Tony Blair (2010: 587) says in his memoirs that he was 'not...a fan of tax credits'.)

[22] The Paymaster General (then Dawn Primarolo), a Treasury junior minister, answered parliamentary questions on tax credits and piloted the legislation through the House of Commons.

Third, not all the tax credits money formally counted as 'public expenditure' at first. After 2014 a new set of European National Accounting rules (ESA10) counted all tax credits as additional public spending, but before that, tax credit money was split between 'negative tax' for those who were liable for tax and 'public expenditure' for those who were not. About 90 per cent of the total sum fell into the second category, but that still left several billion pounds classified as 'negative tax'. Those classification issues did not impinge on the fiscal 'golden rule' of the Brown Treasury (of budget balance over the economic cycle, except for 'investment' spending), for which it did not matter whether the money counted as extra spending or negative tax. But the classification conventions did have the politically convenient effect of lowering the measured tax burden and the growth in public spending.

The two new tax credits were launched in 1999 and three years later a further change was announced, comprising a new child tax credit and a working tax credit to extend tax credits to those without children. The new tax credits were intended to be more responsive to changes in income and circumstances than WFTC,[23] but the new working tax credit was introduced with no piloting and little evidence of its efficacy in reducing poverty or increasing work incentives.

An IFS report at the time said prophetically, 'Success or failure...depends as much on the practicalities of administration and delivery as on...the precise amounts of money involved' (Brewer 2003: 14). The practicalities certainly proved challenging. In 2003 Sir Nicholas Montagu, then head of the income tax department, admitted the rollout of the new credits had gone 'spectacularly wrong' (House of Commons Public Accounts Committee 2003, Q87). At least three kinds of 'practicalities' beset the system, raising serious questions about the quality of the Treasury's formally elaborate 'gateway' project-approval process to limit optimism bias and provide reality checks when political 'pet projects' were at stake (discussed further in Chapter 6).

No fault with the governance of the project appears to have been found through that approval process, then operated by the Office of Government Commerce (a body set up in the Treasury in 2000, with a brief to promote 'best practice' in project appraisal). Yet Sir Nicholas Montagu later suggested the absence of a third party (to challenge the tax department and the outsourced IT provider, Electronic Data Services (EDS)) contributed significantly to the delivery failures (House of Commons Public Accounts Committee 2003: Q84). Snags in the IT led to severe delays in payments, causing distress to many of those whom tax credits were meant to help. In the first year, out of about two million applicants, some 300,000 found their credits delayed. The result was bad publicity and pressure in Parliament,

---

[23] Claimants for WFTC had to produce verifiable information about their circumstances and then the tax credit was fixed for six months. The system thus did not adapt to changes of circumstances happening within any six-month period, leading to hardship and political embarrassment.

including committee inquiries and investigations by the Parliamentary Ombuds-man. Costly legal action had to be taken against EDS, which eventually lost its contract to provide IT services for tax credits.

Second, the greater responsiveness to changing family income and circum-stances that was built into the new tax credit system created a different problem in the form of frequent overpayments to claimants that had to be clawed back later, leading to hardship for claimants and more political damage. Overpayments in 2003–2004 ran to almost £2bn and although that figure fell to £1.23bn by 2009–2010, a fifth of all claimants were still being overpaid, affecting more than a million individuals and families (King and Crewe 2013: 147).

Third, the system proved costly to run through the tax bureaucracy. The reported cost of delivering tax credits through the tax department (HMRC) in 2003–2004 and 2004–2005 was over 3 per cent of the sums paid out—higher than the cost of levying most taxes, but also higher than the costs of running WFTC and nearly three times what it cost to administer Child Benefit (a flat-rate payment per child at that time). And amid a storm of negative publicity about overpayments (during which the Prime Minister chose to apologize publicly for the hardship involved), the 2005 Pre-Budget Report raised the amount by which income could increase from one year to another without changing entitlement to tax credits (from £2,500 to £25,000 in 2006–2007), making the system even more costly.

Critics of this departure from the 'Haldane' principle of expenditure scrutiny include Andrew Rawnsley (2010: 69) who says '...there was no-one to invigilate [Gordon Brown's] spending, which was notorious for its waste and incompetence in the administration of tax credits'. Anthony King and Ivor Crewe (2013) also include tax credits in their chronicle of major UK government 'blunders' over three decades. They see it as the result of a 'cultural disconnect' between the worldview of the well-meaning policymakers who pushed the scheme through and the expe-rience of many of those at the bottom of the income scale, who struggled to fill out complex forms detailing their previous year's earnings, to estimate future earn-ings and notify the tax bureaucracy every time their circumstances altered. The rocky road of the subsequent government's Universal Credit system shows that such problems were not unique to New Labour's tax credits scheme. But the tax credits story remains a notable case of a large public spending empire develop-ing without 'the vigilant supervision of some authority not directly involved in the expenditure itself...' (Ministry of Reconstruction 1918:17–18).

Funding undergraduate teaching in higher education by loans and fees

A third major realm of spending at the edge of what counted as debt and public expenditure that grew markedly under New Labour was £30bn or so of loans to HE students issued by a government-owned company, the Student Loans Company

(SLC)[24] and intended to be repaid from students' subsequent earnings via the tax bureaucracy. The terms of the loans changed over the period, but broadly they were repayable when the borrower's income exceeded a stipulated level. They were issued to help pay for student living costs ('maintenance') and later tuition fees as well. Scotland was different, as we will see shortly.

That system replaced earlier arrangements by which the teaching and maintenance costs of HE students had been mostly funded by government financing of universities and polytechnics (through intermediary arm's-length funding bodies) both for capital spending and for teaching and research, and of maintenance grants (non-repayable and partially[25] means-tested) to cover the living costs of home undergraduates. These arrangements reflected a view that an HE-trained workforce led to faster economic growth and productivity and should therefore be financed from general taxation. We focus here on funding of teaching rather than research, and of undergraduates rather than graduates.

Like the PFI story, the shift from the old to the new student finance system began under the Conservatives, who set up the SLC in 1989 to provide loans to students to supplement shrinking maintenance grants. In its final year the Major government also commissioned a heavyweight inquiry[26] into HE funding, which by at least tacit agreement between Labour and the Conservatives was timed to report immediately after the 1997 election. The Dearing review concluded that the only way to correct underfunding of HE was to enable teaching institutions to charge up-front tuition fees and put more emphasis on repayable loans issued to students.

The incoming Labour government broadly accepted these recommendations. Aiming to raise the HE participation rate and increase support to poorer students, it promptly withdrew the previous maintenance grant system (while Dearing had argued for a mixture of grants and loans) and replaced mortgage-style[27] loans introduced by the Conservatives in 1990 with income-contingent loans (that is, loans repayable, via the tax bureaucracy, when the borrower's income reached a minimum level). It enabled HE institutions to charge upfront tuition fees of up to £1000 per year (means-tested and paid by about half of all students). And it sold much of the earlier loan stock at a heavy discount in 1998 and 1999. As already noted, the first two of those moves substantially cut DEL spending from what it would otherwise have been at a time of HE expansion, while the third reduced debt levels, albeit by heavily discounting the value of the student loan book.

---

[24] The £30bn figure refers to the total value of loans issued by 2009/2010: student debt amounted to £160bn by 2020/2021 (Bolton 2022). At the time of writing, SLC was jointly owned by the UK government and the devolved governments of Scotland, Wales and Northern Ireland.

[25] 75 per cent of the maintenance grant was paid to all students, 25 per cent means-tested against parental income.

[26] Chaired by a senior civil servant (Sir Ron Dearing). It produced nine volumes, over 1,500 pages and ninety-three recommendations.

[27] Graduates normally paid off loans over five years in sixty equal monthly instalments.

The case for funding expanded HE undergraduate training by loans and upfront tuition fees was hotly contested. It got a bad press from the start and the enacting legislation provoked New Labour's first major Parliamentary backbench revolt.[28] It also split the Labour/Liberal Democrat coalition that governed Scotland after devolution in 1999, because of an electoral pledge to scrap tuition fees by the Liberal Democrats. Against that background the Scottish government set up its own inquiry into funding HE teaching, conducted by a leading tax lawyer, Sir Andrew Cubie, who recommended a modest retrospective graduate tax (of up to £3000, carefully branded as an 'endowment' to support poorer students) rather than upfront tuition fees.[29] So the Scottish government retained loans, introduced the 'endowment' tax from 2000, but scrapped tuition fees for home students studying in Scotland (and also EU students, who had to be treated the same as home students under EU rules).

Thus barely two years after the new loans and fees system had been adopted, there was no longer a single UK-wide HE funding model. The alternative 'user pay' approach of a retrospective graduate tax was not adopted by the Westminster government in the 2000s, even though after the 2001 UK general election the idea of replacing the unpopular loans-and-fees approach with a retrospective income tax on graduates had some powerful advocates inside New Labour in intra-party battles over HE funding (Wintour 2002; O'Leary 2009: 476). Those advocates thought students should contribute to tuition costs (because the average university graduate earned more than the average taxpayer) but that a graduate tax would be fairer. 'Loan aversion', especially among students from lower socioeconomic groups, was widely claimed to have limited the greater participation in HE that New Labour wanted, and a retrospective graduate tax would in principle avoid that problem.

But the alternative arrangements adopted in Scotland presented a major political obstacle to any such scheme, exacerbating the basic conundrum of who would be liable for tax and what the tax base would be. Under the devolution legislation the Westminster government had 'reserve powers' to impose a graduate tax on a UK-wide basis, but a proposal strongly backing a UK graduate tax after the 2001 election conceded that it was not politically feasible to 'drive a coach and horses through Cubie' in that way. The alternative, of levying a graduate tax in some parts of the UK but not others, presented complications such as how to track student movement across countries within the UK, how to treat EU students, what to do

---

[28] Although in 1998 the government won a comfortable majority on the relevant amendment in a late-night sitting, thirty-one Labour MPs voted against it and fifteen abstained.

[29] One commentator at the time (MacLeod 2000) saw the Cubie tax as a possible forerunner of other moves to get round restrictions on the Scottish government's tax raising powers in the devolution settlement, but in fact the tax was scrapped eight years later when the SNP formed its first government in Scotland.

about part-time students, and whether to earmark the tax like the Cubie 'contribution' in Scotland. But in any case, the tax department (Inland Revenue) was in such difficulties over the tax credits system by then (described earlier) that it probably did not have the bureaucratic bandwidth to grapple with yet another complicated personal tax scheme at the same time.

The other serious political obstacle to the introduction of a UK graduate tax in the early 2000s was the huge short-term increase in HE spending it would have necessitated. Even if graduate tax receipts had eventually covered the costs of withdrawing upfront tuition fees (and the extra spending on reinstated means-tested student maintenance grants that some graduate-tax advocates were calling for, to correct 'loan aversion'), it would have taken some two decades to get to that point. In the short term it would have necessitated extra DEL spending on HE, estimated by the Treasury at over £2.5bn per year in early 2000s prices.[30]

So despite the evident disadvantages of the fees-and-loans system, greater emphasis was placed on that system as the fiscal position tightened, with maximum tuition fees for new students tripled from £1000 to £3000 per year from 2006–2007. Figure 4.4, charting the growth of loan-financed university education against what happened to direct public spending on HE institutions, indicates the size of the sums involved. Higher education loans and fees had become 'spending substitutes' to the tune of more than £2.5bn a year by the end of New Labour's first term and over £5bn a year by the time Labour left office (House of Commons Library 2021). Several of our interviewees saw this funding substitution as one of the biggest public spending shifts over the period covered by this book.

The new funding model raised longer-term issues too. One, already mentioned, was the matter of how much student debt would actually be repaid. The other concerned the Labour government's sales of its predecessor's 1990 mortgage-style loan book at heavy discounts in 1998 and 1999.[31] Such discounting raised questions about the desirability of sacrificing longer-term value for money in exchange for ready cash in the short term. Unprompted, one of our seasoned ex-Treasury interviewees picked out those loan book sales as a key example of what he saw as a prevalent Treasury tendency to engage in 'clever ruses to get things off balance sheet' in managing debt and deficit. Another from a different background said the Treasury had countered the education department's value-for-money objection to selling off the loan book at a heavy discount with a 'theological' claim that the sales

---

[30] Arguably, a classic case of policy shaped by 'fiscal illusion': in principle issuing gilts to fund student loans to be repaid slowly and only in part is economically equivalent to issuing gilts to fund public spending to be recouped slowly and only in part via a graduate tax (indeed, probably fiscally more costly if high-earning graduates 'overpaid' for their studies under a graduate tax, cross-subsidizing lower earners). But the accounting treatment of the two was very different at that time.

[31] The government also announced plans to sell student loans debt in 2007/2008, but that sale was postponed until after the 2010 election because of market conditions after the 2008 stock crash.

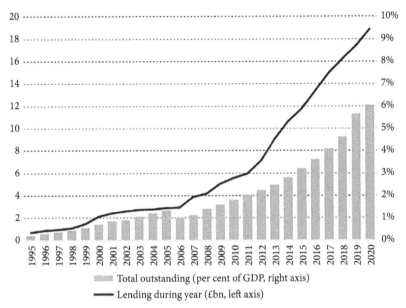

Figure 4.4 Student loans in-year lending and total outstanding 1995–2020

Source: Analysis based on House of Commons Library (2021)

were a matter of 'policy'. He added gloomily, 'All this guff about value for money is just that—all they...care about is the numbers'.

Indeed, as with PFI and tax credits, public-sector accounting conventions at least partly explain why the loans-and-fees approach to funding HE expansion grew so dramatically under New Labour, while the graduate tax idea (McQuillan 2016) failed to replace it, despite the advantages claimed for the latter as a way of avoiding 'loan aversion' by potential students from less affluent backgrounds. Lending (in contrast to the grants the lending replaced) did not count as 'spending' for the purpose of calculating accrued Public Sector Net Borrowing (i.e. the budget deficit) in National Accounts conventions during most of the New Labour period.[32] As such, the (substantial) non-recoverable part of SLC's loans did not count as public spending until write-offs took place at the end of each loan's term. By contrast, all the borrowing to fund the loans SLC paid out to students counted towards the cash-based Public Sector Net Debt under National Accounts conventions. What that means is that the reported deficit numbers substantially understated the true fiscal cost of higher education, while the figures for debt overstated its ultimate cost while accurately reflecting the timing of the

---

[32] According to McGettigan (2015) loan outlay was classed as expenditure in the 1990s and repayments as receipts, as with taxation and spending, but the conventions were changed in the early 2000s, following the recommendation of the 1997 Dearing review. The accounting conventions were changed by ONS in 2018 to count part of SLC's lending as spending.

associated cash flows.[33] Here, in short, is another case of small print having big consequences, in this case concerning how much of the student loans operation counted as 'spending' and 'debt'.

At the end of its tenure, like its Conservative predecessor, New Labour commissioned a further major review of HE student funding (this time chaired by a senior business figure, Lord Browne). As with the 1996–1997 review, Browne's review was timed to report after the 2010 general election, enabling both Labour and the Conservatives to avoid the subject during the election campaign: 'The big numbers...were kicked down the road'.[34] But in contrast to the PFI and tax credit booms, which both reached their peak under New Labour, the fees and loans approach to financing higher education expansion in England and Wales was taken even further by the subsequent Coalition government.

Conclusion

The PFI, tax credit, and student finance stories all reflect impressive effort and ambition to expand public provision while staying within demanding fiscal rules limiting debt and deficit—at least until reclassification caught up with practice. This pattern was not unique to New Labour. PFIs and the first moves to student loans began under the Major government, which also created the National Lottery Fund as a special field of public spending running to several billion pounds a year outside the Treasury's formal control. And the succeeding Coalition government put yet more emphasis on loans and fees to fund HE (tripling student fees and selling off more student debt), at heavy cost to the Liberal Democrats' electoral support. These changes in government produced differences in emphasis rather than outright policy reversals.

As we have seen, two of these 'spending substitutes' led to major political trouble for New Labour in the form of opposition from inside the party, while the niceties about what counted as what kind of spending may have been lost on many voters. Perhaps the most striking case of public (mis)perception of that kind occurred when New Labour ran into political trouble over its controversial Millennium Dome project to mark the year 2000 (also inherited from the Conservatives but

---

[33] Departmental resource accounts arguably provided a better measure of the loans' fiscal costs, because the Treasury's funding to SLC to cover the difference between the face value of existing loans and their 'net present value' (the discounted value of future repayment) was recorded in the form of 'impairments', known as the 'RAB charge'. But these 'impairments' were 'non-cash' items in the resource accounts, and the lower impaired value of student loans in the resource accounts versus the cash outlays recorded in the figures for Public Sector Net debt is the reason why the sale of chunks of the student loan book at heavy discounts could reduce recorded debt.

[34] A senior politician thought it was 'a very sensible device...[both main political parties] knew it was...a vehicle for raising fees after the election'.

enthusiastically relaunched as a flagship project). In several opinion polls after the project's re-launch in 1998 a large majority of respondents considered the Dome to be a waste of money that ought to be going to schools or hospitals,[35] when in fact (precisely to avoid such political charges) the Dome had been carefully funded from the National Lottery Fund. (Under the 'additionality' principle applying to such expenditure, the proceeds of that Fund could not be used to replace regular public spending.) As in that case, the PFI, tax credit and student loan stories suggest that 'public spending by other means' is not always politically cost-free.

Timeline

1997

May: Announcement of operational independence for Bank of England; NHS (Private Finance) Bill introduced to facilitate PFI funding.

July: Post-election Budget announced the 'golden rule' and 'sustainable investment rule' and a commitment to stick to two years of the control totals in the Conservatives' 1996 Survey. Dearing Report recommended a shift to tuition fees and loans for HE undergraduate teaching.

1998

March: Budget enacted fiscal rules in a statutory Code for Fiscal Stability (HM Treasury 1998); plans announced for tax credits and a Comprehensive Spending Review (CSR).

June: Economic and Fiscal Strategy Report set out DEL/AME control framework and the CSR spending envelope.

July: CSR set out: spending plans and efficiency targets for 1999–2002; Public Service Agreements (PSAs) alongside spending settlements; more asset sales and PFIs. Legislation introduced £1,000 a year HE tuition fees from 1998/1999 and loans replacing maintenance grants for most students. Stephen Byers became CST.

December: Alan Milburn became CST.

---

[35] A 1998 Gallup poll found 72 per cent of respondents opposed the use of Lottery funds to finance the Dome and thought those funds should go to schools and hospitals. A 1999 poll found 40 per cent thought the Dome was mainly funded by regular taxes, while 90 per cent thought it was funded partly from taxes (BBC 1999), quoted in Jennings (2004).

1999

March: Budget announced tax cuts.

October: Working families' tax credit replaced family credit for low-income working families with children. Andrew Smith became CST.

November: Pre-Budget Report (PBR): basic state pension uprated by only 75p a week, backfired politically (leading eventually to the 'triple lock' in 2010).

December: Millennium Dome opened.

2000

January: In a TV interview Tony Blair announced a rise in health spending, to the EU average as a percentage of GDP by 2006.

March: Budget set the envelope for SR2000 (2½% real spending growth with 5.6 per cent a year for the NHS). A stock crash ended the dotcom boom.

July: SR2000 set out 2001–2004 spending plans and updated PSAs.

September: Fuel tax protests around the UK.

November: PBR announced that £22.5bn from 3G spectrum licence auction would go to reducing PSND.

2001

February: A major episode of Foot and Mouth (serious cattle disease) began.

March: Pre-election Budget forecast allowed fiscal easing of almost £5bn.

June: Labour re-elected with 167-seat majority.

September: The 9/11 attacks in the US set off a chain of events leading to the creation of the Special Reserve (for funding military campaigns) the following year.

November: PBR and Interim report of the Wanless Review of NHS funding published.

2002

April: Budget set the SR2002 spending envelope (real growth of 7.5 per cent for NHS England and 2½% for non-health current spending, with PSNI to rise to 2 per cent of GDP), partly financed by increased National Insurance contributions.

May: Paul Boateng became CST.

July: SR2002 set out 2003–2006 spending plans.

August/September: GOGGS reopened (by Alan Greenspan), under a thirty-five-year PFI contract.

2003

March: Iraq War began. Budget introduced a new Child Trust Fund.
April: Working Tax Credit and Child Tax Credit replaced WFTC and Disabled Person's tax credit.

2004

March: Budget set the SR2004 envelope (real spending growth to slow to 2.7 per cent a year).
July: SR04 announced 2006–2008 spending plans. HE Act tripled maximum HE tuition fee from 2006–2007. Gershon efficiency review published.

2005

May: Labour re-elected with a reduced majority (66 seats). Des Browne became CST.
July: Treasury claimed the cycle then in progress started in 1997 not 1999 (making it easier to meet the golden rule).
December: PBR announced plans for: CSR2007 (with no SR in 2006) and changes to tax credits to limit overpayments.

2006

March: A modest tax-raising Budget met the Golden Rule.
May: Stephen Timms became CST.

2007

March: Budget removed the 10p starting rate of income tax; golden rule still met.
April: Independent National Statistics Authority established.
May: Minority SNP government took office in Scotland.
June: Gordon Brown became PM, with Alistair Darling as Chancellor and Andy Burnham as CST.
July: Metronet (the main PFI contractor on London Underground) collapsed.
September: Run on Northern Rock bank.
October: Combined PBR and CSR07 set out spending envelope and plans for 2008–2011.

2008

January: Yvette Cooper became CST.

March: Budget: the final fiscal event to predict that the 1997 fiscal rules would be met.

September/October: Several US financial institutions collapsed or were bailed out; UK government bailed out RBS, Lloyds TSB, and HBOS.

November: PBR acknowledged a structural fiscal deficit. The 1997 fiscal rules were replaced by a 'temporary operating rule' to reduce the deficit after the crisis, but with a VAT cut and accelerated capital spending in the short term.

2009

March: Quantitative easing began.

April: Budget announced further fiscal stimulus to be followed by fiscal consolidation. Cost-cutting operational Efficiency Programme published.

May: Standard and Poor's outlook on UK sovereign debt went from stable to negative.

June: Liam Byrne became CST (Labour's 10th).

November: PBR announced plan to halve the deficit over four years, with real current spending growth cut to 0.8 per cent and PSNI by two thirds to 1¼% of GDP; creation of Infrastructure UK within the Treasury to advise on long-term infrastructure needs and support major projects.

2010

February: Fiscal Responsibility Act.

March: Pre-election Budget stuck to PBR plans for fiscal consolidation.

May: UK general election: no party won an overall majority.

5

Austerity, Coalition, and Public Spending Control under the Cameron-Clegg Government, 2010–2015

Had there been a lot of money, the Coalition would have been...harder
(ex-Treasury official).

Vignette: Opening up the Private World of Public Money? The 2010 'Spending Challenge'

One of the seven persisting features of the UK's fiscal constitution featured in Chapter 2, was the executive and specifically Treasury dominance of *ex ante* scrutiny of spending proposals. In contrast to federal budgeting in the United States, with extensive wheeling and dealing in legislative committees lobbied by interest groups, Hugh Heclo and Aaron Wildavsky (1974) portrayed the UK's equivalent as a 'private world' where key money matters were settled by elite bureaucrats behind closed doors in Whitehall. But the Conservative–Liberal Democrat coalition government formed after the 2010 general election expressed ambitions to change that world into a less exclusive, less Whitehall-dominated affair. Its Programme for Government published a fortnight after that election, announced a full spending review to be completed in the autumn, 'following a fully consultative process involving all tiers of government and the private sector' (HM Government 2010: 16).

Indeed, in the honeymoon atmosphere of its early weeks, the new government committed itself to a process that would be 'more open, transparent and collaborative than any previous [spending] Review', giving 'the whole country...the opportunity to be engaged and involved in the decisions that will have to be taken'. Against the background of the Coalition's commitment to spending cuts and deficit reduction, the aim of the public engagement was to identify the best suggestions for doing more with less ('Whitehall does not have the monopoly on ideas'), build consensus for spending reductions and 'lay the foundations for action', allowing people to prepare mentally and practically for a new spending landscape.

The Way the Money Goes. Christopher Hood, Maia King, Iain McLean, and Barbara Piotrowska,
Oxford University Press. © Christopher Hood, Maia King, Iain McLean, and Barbara Piotrowska (2023).
DOI: 10.1093/oso/9780198865087.003.0005

In pursuit of these unexceptionable sentiments the Coalition opted for a three-pronged 'engagement' strategy for its post-election Spending Review.

One prong consisted of an 'independent challenge group' (ICG) of thirty-nine people to bring fresh ideas, experience, and perspectives to the review. Those 'Challengers' were mostly upper-level civil servants (several ex-Treasury) from across government. ICG was tagged as 'a leadership group within Whitehall to champion and challenge ideas...' but outside the normal bilateral interactions over budget allocations between the Treasury and spending departments. It had the lofty but somewhat cloudy remit 'to think innovatively about the options for reducing public expenditure and balancing priorities to minimise the impact on public services'. One interviewee translated this mandarin language to mean ICG was intended 'to get top people on the Treasury's side' and 'lock Whitehall...into the process' of the Spending Review. Another saw it as an official-level variant of the 'Star Chamber' approach to Cabinet decisions over departmental budget allocations (discussed in Chapter 3), reflecting a presumption that senior civil servants would be more disposed to challenge spending when dealing with departments other than their own.[1] To signal their top-level status, the Challengers were chaired by the Treasury's Permanent Secretary and divided into eleven report-writing teams, seven focusing on the main spending departments and four on cross-cutting themes embraced by the government, such as 'localism'. They also met as a group to talk about the review with Treasury ministers, once with the Chancellor and twice with the CST.

The Treasury post-mortem on the 2010 Spending Review guardedly described ICG as having 'moved Treasury and Department thinking on a number of issues'. But it also noted difficulties, including an implied tendency by Treasury officials to be polite rather than candid with the ICG sub-groups about their ideas ('a stronger push on sending early and frank feedback...would have helped') and the bureaucratic security roadblocks that obstructed access to classified Treasury documents. None of the interviewees we asked about the ICG thought it had had much impact on the Spending Review, commenting variously that the group 'didn't come up with things', had 'no clout' because it was outside the formal bargaining process and therefore had no leverage, or that it was simply too hard for outsiders, however eminent, to grapple with the relevant issues in the necessary detail when it was invariably the small print that mattered. Less diplomatically, one of the Challengers laughingly dismissed ICG as 'an absolute and utter waste of time'. ICG's impact on the outcome of the Spending Review seems to have fallen well short of other 'outside looks' designed to cut public spending in times of fiscal crisis, such as the 1921–1922 Geddes Committee or the 1931 May Committee in the

---

[1] This presumption echoed ideas about the effect of social distance on enforcement behaviour in Black's (1976) classic 'relational distance' theory that we discuss further in Chapter 10.

UK,[2] or some of the several audit commissions appointed to suggest spending cuts to incoming (mostly right of centre) state and Commonwealth governments in Australia (Weight 2014: 4).

A second strand of engagement over the spending review seems to have been partly modelled on the SAVE ('Securing Americans Value and Efficiency') award initiative begun by the Obama administration in the United States the previous year.[3] It comprised a website portal for all public sector employees to offer ideas on how to achieve 'more with less'. This form of engagement was arguably more successful than ICG in producing specific money-saving ideas and both the Prime Minister and Chancellor used its suggestions as a credit-claiming opportunity in public statements. Over 60,000 submissions were made (over 7,500 in the first day alone), proposing possible measures with savings that were estimated by the Treasury at up to £0.5bn in total from ideas such as greater cross-government collaboration to exert greater buying power over suppliers. But in the context of a process designed to cut public spending plans by £80bn or so overall, the significance of this engagement operation was contested and the novelty of some of the proposals was questioned too. For instance, the House of Commons Treasury Committee, in its report on the Spending Review, said, 'We are sceptical about how new some of the claimed savings from the Spending Challenge are in reality...the Office of Government Commerce's Collaborative Procurement Programme has been running since 2007' (House of Commons Treasury Committee 2010: 17–18). The Institute for Government was also unimpressed, commenting that the Spending Challenge 'produced some announcements, but of a relatively micro nature...the top ideas highlighted by the Treasury saved a few million pounds each' (McCrae 2011: 37).

The third, most ambitious line of engagement was a website aimed at the public at large. It was not intended to be just a one-way forum for floating money-saving ideas (the way the Public Sector Employee website worked, as essentially a mailbox). Rather, in the age of interactive reality-TV and social media, it was intended as a facility for enabling ideas to be proposed, commented and voted on, such that proposals with most support would rise to the top. That wisdom-of-crowds initiative went online only a week after a 'Your Freedom' website initiated in a YouTube video by the Deputy Prime Minister Nick Clegg, inviting the public to put forward unnecessary legislation or regulations for repeal and declaring 'We're hoping for virtual mailbags full of suggestions' (Duffet 2010; Heaven 2010). The Spending Challenge website clearly reflected a similar enthusiasm for digital-age

---

[2] See McDonald 1989; Hood and Himaz 2017, chapters 3 and 4.

[3] SAVE was an online consultative system introduced in 2009 to fulfil President Obama's call for 'a process through which every government worker can submit their ideas for how their agency can save money and perform better', by enabling all Federal employees to propose savings during the annual Budget process. It was expanded the following year to enable those employees both to make proposals and vote on ideas submitted by others.

crowdsourcing of ideas for better or lower-cost government (rather than the more *realpolitik* approach of only asking questions to which the answer was already settled).

The basic idea of inviting public suggestions for economies in public spending was not new, either in the UK or elsewhere. For instance, there was extensive public consultation in Canada over its 1994–1997 'Program Review' deficit reduction scheme (McCrae 2011; Savoie 2014: 213). And in the UK, long before the digital age, the Treasury had put advertisements in newspapers at the start of World War II in 1939 asking people to report waste in war work, an invitation which produced a huge correspondence.[4] What was different in 2010 was the digital interactive facility of the initiative—the commenting and voting element—but that was the feature which proved to be its undoing.

Hastily designed to fit the Spending Review's highly time-pressured schedule, the website went live to the public on 9 July. Chancellor George Osborne launched it with a fanfare, writing in *The Sun*—the UK's highest-circulation tabloid newspaper with over three million daily readers at that time—asking for views. 'You pay the taxes that fund our public services...Your ideas will help us decide how to save money... So, Sun readers, please get thinking. Your Government needs you!' Osborne rashly said that the website (jointly managed by the Cabinet Office and the Treasury's productivity team) would stay open until the end of August (Hartley 2010). But its interactive facility lasted barely a week before the managers had to close the site (on 15 July) and then, the next day, disable the voting and commenting element. That shutdown was caused by a stream of malicious attacks and 'inappropriate' submissions that overwhelmed the slender resources the Treasury had chosen to put into moderating the site, leading to negative media coverage (Apps 2010). The cyber-attacks included links to pornographic websites posted within comments, and the 'inappropriate' ideas submitted and voted upon included submissions that were flippant (for example proposals for jokey windfall taxes), irrelevant (for example a recipe for beef and vegetable casserole, described by one visitor as 'the most sensible thing I have read on this site') or racist (such as anti-migrant rants (Jeffery 2010)). So after just a week of full interaction, the website was switched to the same one-way mode as the Public Sector Employee website, with the public allowed to submit ideas but not to see or rate other suggestions. The site was then closed to new proposals after another two weeks, but to deliver on the Chancellor's bold pledge in *The Sun* to keep it going through August, the public was allowed to rate a (laboriously moderated) set of ideas for the rest of the consultation period but not to put in any new ones.

After the Review, the Chief Secretary defended this 'crowdslicing' approach in parliament, denying it was a gimmick: 'It is important with decisions of this scale that you seek to engage with people' (House of Commons Treasury Committee

---

[4] See National Archives Treasury file T161/1453.

2010: 18). But the digital interactive reality-TV approach to handling proposals from the general public was not repeated in later spending reviews in the UK up to the time of writing. Only public sector workers (in non-interactive mode) were asked for their views in the 2015 Spending Review, although public suggestions (again in non-interactive mode) continued to be invited (or at least received) from individuals and groups for 'Budget Representations' at Budget times.

This episode brings out some of the challenges facing attempts to change the fiscal constitution by opening the 'private world' of public spending allocation to wider public engagement—and perhaps of crowdsourcing policy decisions more generally (see, for example, Rodgers (2016)). It was one of several efforts to modify the handling of public spending by a government which was itself constitutionally unusual (as the first formal coalition government at Westminster since 1945) and which claimed to deal with fiscal matters differently from its predecessors.

As in the previous two chapters, the timeline at the end of this chapter summarizes some of the major developments in public spending under the Coalition government, but we now discuss three key episodes relating to the fiscal constitution in some more detail. They are:

- The Coalition's adaptation of the DEL/AME planning process that it inherited from its Labour predecessor, to effect a major fiscal consolidation. In its post-election Spending Review, it cut some £80bn out of public spending plans, sharply putting on the brakes to produce a decade of 'austerity' that had deep political reverberations.
- The fate of an effort (reflecting election pledges by both Coalition parties in support of strengthening parliament's power) to modify parliamentary procedures to enable stronger *ex ante* scrutiny of spending proposals.
- The operation of what was billed as a joint 'corporate centre' approach to control of key elements of administration, procurement and project spending between the Treasury and an 'Efficiency and Reform Group' headed by a powerful minister in the Cabinet Office.

Reviewing Spending in a Cold Climate: Cutting £80bn out of RDEL Spending Plans in the 2010 Spending Review

After the 2010 general election resulted in the first formal coalition at Westminster for 65 years, a central feature of the agreement between the Conservatives and the Liberal Democrats was a commitment to accelerate the previous government's plans to reduce a budget deficit running at some 11 per cent of GDP in 2009–2010. That agreement aimed to eliminate most of the structural deficit by 2015, while protecting some favoured domains of spending. The Coalition also aimed to start reducing the deficit sooner than Labour planned to do by immediately cutting £6bn out of spending (on 'non-front-line services', of course) in-year in 2010–2011.

Ten days after the new government took office it duly announced spending cuts of £6.25bn, mostly from resource DEL, within the then current financial year (2010–2011). A 'mini-spending review' took only a week to allocate departments' contributions to those in-year cuts. About half of the £6bn came from subnational spending (local and devolved government) and, following a familiar pattern in earlier spending squeezes, more than half the savings came from tighter restraints on hiring and 'discretionary spending' (on consultancy, temporary staff, advertising, travel and the like). At a time when ministers were still new to their departments, these in-year cuts were not negotiated individually between the CST and each spending minister (as had happened with the £5bn emergency in-year spending cuts after New Labour's 2007 Spending Review). Instead, the new Cabinet simply agreed a flat percentage cut across all departments, thus avoiding the need for the usual lengthy wrangling between Treasury and departments over the accuracy of the Treasury's centrally held data and over how much spending had already been cut.

Three weeks after that announcement, the government set up a new Cabinet PEX (public expenditure) committee chaired by the Chancellor. Such a committee was a familiar part of the furniture for allocating public spending, as we have seen in earlier chapters, but it was proclaimed in this case to reflect the more collective approach to planning spending to which the Coalition aspired, as well as serving as an arbitrator when departments and Treasury deadlocked in negotiations.[5] At the same time, also following a familiar pattern of post-election fiscal events, the government published plans for a high-stakes multi-year Spending Review over the summer, stressing that the Review would prioritize spending in some areas over others, not just make uniform percentage cuts across the board.

A fortnight after that announcement, a post-election 'emergency' budget set out the overall spending reductions the Coalition was aiming for. The ambition was to reduce spending plans by some £83bn between 2011–2012 and 2014–2015 (without making further cuts to capital spending plans on top of those already announced by the previous government) and to bring down total UK public spending to 41 per cent of GDP from the 48 per cent it hit in 2009/2010. As well as setting the total envelope for the Spending Review, the budget announced some early spending decisions, notably a two-year public sector pay freeze to save over £3bn a year by 2014–2015 and £11bn of cuts in AME spending from changes to benefits uprating, tax credits and housing benefit. (In the event the planned reductions in AME welfare spending went deeper than that, running to some £18bn.)

---

[5] The original members were the Chancellor (chair), Chief Secretary, Foreign Secretary and two Cabinet Office ministers (Oliver Letwin and Francis Maude). Other spending ministers were able to join the committee after their departments had agreed a spending settlement with the Treasury.

The post-election budget also announced that the government was 'reviewing...commitments' under New Labour's 'end year flexibility' scheme (EYF, for carrying over unspent funds into later financial years). The background was that in its efforts to contain spending after its 2007 Spending Review the previous government had done some £7bn of ad hoc 'deals' with departments involving promises of access to EYF drawdown in 2010–2011 as a reward for spending less in earlier years (the biggest of those deals was a promised £2bn to the Department of Children, Schools and Families). But the Treasury's May 2010 estimate of likely underspending indicated that no more than £1.8bn in total of EYF drawdown could actually be funded from the Reserve available for the Spring Supplementary Estimates. The October 2010 Spending Review proceeded to cancel EYF entitlements and the following year's (2011) Budget introduced a much less generous end-year-flexibility scheme, 'Budget Exchange', which required departments to surrender unspent funds before the end of the financial year in order to get Treasury permission to spend the corresponding amount in the following year.[6]

That 2010 spending review differed from New Labour's five spending reviews in several ways. First, as already indicated, it was overwhelmingly concerned with cutting rather than increasing planned spending, for current expenditure at least (it did not go beyond the previous Labour government's plans for cuts in capital spending and in fact allocated more for capital spending than Labour had planned). Second, it was politically managed in a different way. According to one interviewee the review was actively led by the Chancellor throughout, in contrast to a pattern in earlier Reviews when Chancellors had only engaged closely in person in the endgame or over a few pet projects. Further, the Review had to be politically tailored for coalition rather than single-party government, with plans to be cleared with two political parties rather than one, and against the background of a Coalition Agreement, which according to one interviewee meant 'less scope for last-minute theatricals'. For the same reason, the Review set out plans for four years of public spending—the expected political lifetime of the coalition—rather than the three-year plans of the New Labour-era reviews. And in contrast to EDX, where the Treasury was permanently outnumbered, the Treasury had two ministers out of four of the all-important 'Quad'—an initially informal group comprising the Prime Minister, Deputy Prime Minister, Chancellor and Chief Secretary, which became a central decision point, embedding coalition government and elevating the Chief Secretary to the centre.

Third, in contrast to 'bolt from the blue' episodes like the ERM fiasco that was the backdrop to Chapter 3, the official Treasury was primed and ready to

---

[6] Different rules applied to the devolved governments, which did not have to surrender unspent funds before the financial year-end, but carry-overs were formally capped and subject to Treasury agreement.

go with spending cuts in 2010, well aware that a major fiscal squeeze would follow that election whatever the party composition of the government.[7] In contrast to the deep political divides over 'austerity' in the subsequent decade, all three main UK political parties campaigned in the 2010 election on manifestos that committed them to fiscal consolidation. What they differed over was when spending cuts should start, what the mix of tax rises and spending cuts should be, and how long it should take to return to some approximate budget balance.

Fourth, as we will see in the next chapter, capital spending on major projects was subject to a comparative zero-based review across government for the first time, so that, formally at least, there were no departmental baselines from which negotiations began over such spending.[8]

Fifth, the 2010 Spending Review differed from its five New Labour predecessors in the way DEL and AME spending was allocated. Before 2010, Budgets had forecast AME spending (about a third of total public spending at that time) and set an envelope for DEL, to be allocated via Spending Reviews. By contrast, in 2010 the June Budget set an envelope for Total Managed Expenditure and thereby allowed AME and DEL to be traded off against each other in the subsequent Spending Review. So the issue of how much to cut spending on welfare (by cuts in benefit rates or entitlements) as against spending on other items was central to the endgame politics of the 2010 Review. The post-election June Budget announced big cuts in both AME and Resource DEL, but with the promise that any further AME cuts found in the Spending Review would be used to reduce the extent of cuts in RDEL (HM Treasury 2010: 17 §1.40).

Indeed, the general political background to AME spending altered with the development of the 'benefits cap', announced by George Osborne in the 2010 Conservative party conference (limiting the total amount that any individual household could claim in welfare benefits) and the subsequent 'welfare cap' announced four years later and taking effect in 2015. The welfare cap limited the total amount that could be spent on a range of welfare benefits and tax credits (excluding Housing Benefit, Jobseeker's Allowance and the state pension), under legislation that modified the Charter of Budget Responsibility by obliging the Office of Budget Responsibility (OBR) to monitor and report and by providing for ministers to account to Parliament for breaches of the cap. One interviewee described the cap as 'an attempt to manage what was really Annually Unmanaged

[7] Though Gordon Brown's government chose not to conduct a Spending Review in 2009 and Brown as Prime Minister frowned on talk of spending cuts, his Chancellor Alistair Darling set out plans for fiscal consolidation in his 2009 Pre-Budget Report (including some £20bn of 'efficiency savings' and a 'public value' programme) and his 2010 pre-election budget contained plans to halve the deficit in four years, while protecting spending on health care, international aid, and schools.

[8] Further, although the June 2010 Budget stated that the overall capital spending envelope had been fixed up to 2014–2015, the Spending Review increased that envelope by £2bn a year.

Expenditure until then' and as 'kind of halfway house' between the New Control Total of 1992 (Chapter 3) and the boundaries of DEL under New Labour (Chapter 4).

Sixth, there was a new institutional player in the process, albeit only existing in a 'shadow' form at that time, in the form of the newly created independent Office for Budget Responsibility (as already mentioned), responsible for economic and fiscal forecasting and for acting as a watchdog on the government's fiscal performance.[9]

Seventh and finally, the 2010 Review differed from its New Labour predecessors in that there were no Public Service Agreements accompanying the spending allocations (even in the attenuated form of the 30 or so PSAs in the 2007 spending review). The abolition of PSAs had been one of the Conservatives' manifesto commitments since 2005 (policy aims and metrics were to be included separately in departmental reports).

One interviewee described the Treasury's general political strategy for allocating resource (RDEL) spending to departments in this Spending Review as 'allocating pro rata for the unprotected departments and then doing fine-tuning adjustments in the final stages, plus coming up with a few eye-catching announcements to bind the process together politically'. Less than a fortnight after the post-election budget set the envelope for the Spending Review, the Cabinet agreed 'scenarios' for all departments. Those scenarios were intended to lower expectations, with most departments asked to aim for real terms cuts of between 25 and 40 per cent in planned RDEL spending. But in line with the Coalition agreement to protect some spending domains, there were exceptions, notably for education (schools), defence, international development and health (which was originally asked to assume 'flat real' resource spending). Departments were also asked to produce unit cost data and plans for 'efficiency' savings equivalent to at least 15 per cent of their administration costs.

In a pattern reminiscent of earlier cutback exercises (Hood and Himaz 2017: 92, 102, 106), departmental responses to these drastic demands yielded only patchy data and offers of reductions in spending plans amounting to about half of the government's target (£31bn by 2014–2015 as against an overall target of £66bn). Following those responses, the (Liberal Democrat) Chief Secretary to the Treasury, Danny Alexander, began bilateral negotiations with ministers in July. The bargaining went on until the week before the Spending Review document was published in October, with the most contentious negotiations predictably coming at the end of the process.

That RDEL bargaining went in three main phases. Early September saw quick wins on soft targets, in an 'early settlement' phase. It was followed by a month

---

[9] We discuss OBR further in Chapter 9: it was not established by statute until 2011, but several interviewees thought the shadow OBR had had a disciplining influence on the 2010 spending review, especially given that many ministers had little experience of government at that time.

of 'ground clearing', whittling down areas of disagreement and doing deals with smaller departments. Early in October, during and after the Conservative Party Conference, the process moved into the endgame, focusing on big or difficult departments.

The early settlement phase, intended to signal momentum, included deals with Cabinet Office and Treasury (obliged as always to set an example in such cut-back exercises). It also included the Foreign and Commonwealth Office, the Department of Communities and Local Government and the Department of Environment, Food and Rural Affairs—all 'non-protected' departments led by Conservative Ministers amenable to settling for major spending cuts.

The later ground-clearing phase in September saw deals struck with small and medium sized departments and some government-wide policies developed—such as efficiency plans, the 'de-ring-fencing' of central funding for local government that was a key feature of the Review, and less generous public sector pensions. To deter holdouts, the Cabinet agreed that allocations to departments with an RDEL baseline of less than £6bn (a number chosen for tactical reasons to exclude the Ministry of Justice) would go to the PEX committee for arbitration if they were not settled bilaterally by early October. That phase produced RDEL settlements averaging −25 per cent for small departments and deals with several others, including the Department of Energy and Climate Change (−15 per cent), the tax department HMRC (−16 per cent) and the Home Office (−30 per cent, excluding police).

By the time the endgame began after the Conservative party conference, seven big spending domains still had to be settled, most of which had been held back so they would compete with one another for the remains of the DEL envelope: local government, BIS, welfare, education, defence, police and justice. At this endgame stage the 'quad', not PEX, was the central player in the deal-making. Indeed, according to the Treasury's post-mortem on the review, PEX was never used as a 'star chamber' to break deadlocks between Treasury and departments. But that post-mortem claimed PEX had 'served as an effective deterrent to gaming' during the RDEL bargaining and had encouraged a few spending-hawk ministers to set-tle early so they could join the committee. It also seems to have played a bigger role in the capital spending allocations, in that it endorsed the capital allocations which were then imposed on departments by the Chief Secretary acting on behalf of PEX.

The final settlement comprised greater reductions in AME spending on welfare than had originally been floated, to make room for concessions on RDEL funding for police, justice, defence. and education. A deal with the BBC was agreed at the last minute (affecting three departments' budgets) and there was also a late change to the welfare cuts package on the weekend before publication of the Review. Even so, the RDEL deals were all concluded several days before that publication date—in sharp contrast to the endgames in previous spending reviews, or pre-Budget reports, when the deal-making often went on until the final print deadline for the document.[10]

As Table 5.1 shows, the eventual outcome of the Review was an overall reduction of some 8.3 per cent in resource spending,[11] but with a remarkably wide variation in settlements across departments ranging from a 37 per cent increase in spending by the Department for International Development to a 51 per cent reduction in core spending in communities and local government. Far from the inertia-driven

Table 5.1 RDEL allocations (excluding depreciation) by department, SR 2010

Department or Spending Domain	£ billion		Per Cent
	Baseline 2010–2011	Plans 2014/2015	Planned Cumulative Real Growth 2011/2012 to 2014/2015
CLG Communities	2.2	1.2	−51
HM Treasury	0.2	0.1	−33
Environment Food and Rural Affairs	2.3	1.8	−29
CLG Local Government	28.5	22.9	−27
Business, Innovation and Skills	16.7	13.7	−25
Culture, Media and Sport	1.4	1.1	−24
Foreign and Commonwealth Office	1.4	1.2	−24
Home Office	9.3	7.8	−23
Justice	8.3	7.0	−23
Transport	5.1	4.4	−21
Energy and Climate Change	1.2	1.0	−18
HM Revenue and Customs	3.5	3.2	−15
Defence	24.3	24.7	−7.5
Wales	13.3	13.5	−7.5
Scotland	24.8	25.4	−6.8
Education	50.8	53.9	−3.4
NHS (Health)	98.7	109.8	−1.3
Work and Pensions	6.8	7.6	2.3
Northern Ireland	9.3	9.5	6.9
Cabinet Office	0.3	0.4	28
International Development	6.3	9.4	37
Total	326.6	328.9	−8.3

Source: HM Treasury 2010

[10] We heard stories about officials working far into the small hours on some of those earlier reviews, in a style described by one interviewee as 'massively dysfunctional'.
[11] Near-cash RDEL, to be precise.

pattern of uniform incremental growth from fiercely defended baselines famously portrayed in Aaron Wildavsky's (1964: 15) *Politics of the Budgetary Process*,[12] those variations reflected strategic political decisions to protect or increase some spending (notably health, state pensions, overseas development, childcare and social care) at the expense of deep cuts elsewhere. The latter included a tripling of higher education tuition fees (turbocharging the shift in HE funding discussed in the previous chapter and breaching Liberal Democrat election promises), plans for increased employee contributions and scaled-back benefits in public sector pensions, and highly contentious welfare savings that included withdrawal of child benefit payments to better-off taxpayers.

The 2010 Spending Review shows that an instrument developed by a centre-left single-party majority government broadly for planning an orderly increase in public spending in return for demonstrable public service improvements (New Labour's spending review system) could be used in different circumstances for slamming on the brakes. As we have noted earlier, the Treasury was 'locked and loaded' after a year or more of time to prepare for the review, all three major UK political parties had fought the 2010 election on manifestos that embraced fiscal consolidation, and the post-election Coalition agreement committed both parties in the government to reducing debt and deficit. Indeed, several interviewees thought the 2010 Spending Review, with its deep cutbacks, had only been possible because the political glue holding the Coalition together was its mission to 'save' the public finances—the issue highlighted in the epigraph to this chapter.

Efforts to Increase Parliamentary Scrutiny of Budget Estimates

The second selected episode from the Coalition era concerns parliamentary scrutiny rather than executive-government review of public spending plans. In this case, the Treasury aimed to contain or limit change. The issue at stake served if anything to divide ministers in the Coalition government rather than to hold them together, and (not coincidentally) the episode produced a non-event.

The Liberal Democrats' 2010 election manifesto promised (p. 88) to 'strengthen the House of Commons to increase accountability. We will increase Parliamentary scrutiny of the budget...' The Conservatives' manifesto did not specifically mention budget scrutiny but it highlighted (p. 18) the creation of an independent Office for Budget Responsibility that would keep the Treasury honest by better informing the UK public and parliaments over the background to public spending decisions

---

[12] Two decades later Wildavsky (1988) argued that incrementalism had been abandoned in the US budgetary process.

(discussed in Chapter 9), and declared more generally that the party's aim was to redistribute power from government to Parliament (p. 74).

Enhancing Parliamentary scrutiny of budget proposals was a far from new idea in 2010. Indeed, a plan to do just that had been proposed ten years earlier by Ed Davey (then Liberal Democrat Economic Spokesman). In a forty-eight-page pamphlet containing ten proposals for reform (quoted in Chapter 1), Davey (2000) said the UK had the weakest parliamentary scrutiny of draft budgets in all the OECD countries because it had no Budget committee and departmental select committees did not routinely analyse estimates. Davey saw Sweden and New Zealand as models for the Westminster Parliament to follow and called for an independent 'Office of the Taxpayer' modelled on the National Audit Office, to provide adequate analytic support to MPs in challenging spending plans.[13]

Although the recruitment and acculturation of MPs in all parties does not usually favour individuals who wish seriously to hold the executive to account over an extended period, Davey was not alone in advocating such changes. Some Conservative MPs, notably Andrew Tyrie (who became chair of the Treasury Select Committee in 2010) held similar views and some of our official interviewees thought the traditional pattern was indefensible. But while the Coalition agreement committed the Cameron-Clegg government to taking action on other constitutional matters and to several changes to parliamentary procedure, it did not commit the government to specific new parliamentary procedures for scrutinizing budgets.

However, the Treasury developed its 'Clear Line of Sight' (CLOS) project, a major accounting exercise to align the numbers used in Treasury expenditure planning with those used in Supply Estimates. Although apparently a technicality, CLOS was a necessary step for any real enhancement of parliamentary scrutiny, and the first CLOS-based Estimates were presented in 2011. In September 2010 the Chancellor invited two influential backbench MPs (Sir Edward Leigh from the Conservatives and John Pugh from the Liberal Democrats) to provide 'independent challenge, advice and support' to the development of financial management across central government, including parliamentary engagement.

That arrangement only lasted a few months. Leigh and Pugh both resigned from their advisory roles early in 2011 on taking up other appointments and on their departure wrote a report for the Chancellor strongly advocating the formation of a well-staffed Budget Committee in Parliament for *ex ante* scrutiny of Estimates and major project proposals.[14] The following year, the composition of the Cabinet changed when Ed Davey, author of the 2000 pamphlet described earlier, succeeded his fellow Liberal Democrat Chris Huhne as Secretary of State for Energy and

---

[13] Perhaps a partial echo of Beatrice and Sidney Webb's more general idea of dividing the civil service in half, with roughly one half working for parliament and the other half working for government (Webb and Webb 1920).

[14] Edward Leigh MP and Dr. John Pugh MP 'Options to Improve Parliamentary Scrutiny of Government Expenditure: A Report to the Chancellor' 2011 (unpublished).

Climate Change when the latter resigned, thus bringing to the Cabinet a long-standing advocate of increased parliamentary scrutiny of spending proposals.

However, as the Coalition's third year approached, three of the four pieces of constitutional reform to which it had committed itself were politically dead,[15] and the fourth, namely the pledge to introduce in that year a House Business Committee to control the House of Commons agenda (House of Commons Reform Committee 2009) also came to nothing. (The Leader of the House, Andrew Lansley, announced that no such committee would be formed because of lack of consensus over its function and composition (Kelly 2015: 3)). Various proposals for strengthening parliamentary scrutiny of departmental budgets—including Davey's 2000 pamphlet and the 2011 report by Leigh and Pugh proposing a budget committee—were floated again in 2013 both in the Cabinet and by a group of ministers from both parties meeting with the Leader of the House. But no substantial changes were made.

Why did such proposals get nowhere, despite successive arguments for greater parliamentary scrutiny of budget proposals? There were certainly tricky issues affecting the role of existing players in the system, such as NAO, with its traditional focus on *ex post* analysis for the Public Accounts Committee, and indeed the PAC itself (whose role in approving pre-emption or 'new services', covered by its 1932 Concordat with the Treasury, as mentioned in Chapter 2, would be likely to disappear with the creation of a Budget Committee). And the Treasury seems to have been fearful of losing control over public spending if it lost control over financial debates. It continued to block proposals that might limit its room for political manoeuvre, even after discussions among Cabinet ministers in 2013 dropped consideration of more far-reaching options such as new parliamentary committees with NAO-type servicing.

Another scheme that failed to progress at that time was an apparently modest proposal to spread the House of Commons' then three 'Estimates Days'[16] more evenly throughout the year and thereby make it possible to hold these debates on a wider range of issues and documents. On the face of it a minor tweak of the existing arrangements for debating estimates, the proposal envisaged scheduling one Estimates Day in the autumn, possibly on the 'Autumn Statement' (given that the Coalition's Autumn Statements were major fiscal events, on a par with the Spring Budgets). But even that very limited modification to parliamentary procedure came with the political risk that Chancellors might lose their unilateral power to set the date of the Autumn Statement at the point they judged most politically opportune and that an Autumn Estimates Day vote would count as a 'vote

---

[15] A referendum on changing the electoral system for the Westminster parliament produced a 'no' vote, Conservative backbenchers blocked reform of the House of Lords and in retaliation the Liberal Democrats voted against equalizing the size of parliamentary constituencies.

[16] Normally one day in March for Parliament to consider Supplementary Estimates and two in the summer for Main Estimates.

of confidence' on the Autumn Statement (that is, a vote which if lost would trigger a dissolution of Parliament and a general election). Such political qualms over power and control seem to be the most likely explanation of why the Coalition's appetite for constitutional reform proved to be limited when it came to parliamentary scrutiny of spending proposals and the proposals for enhancement of that scrutiny stalled. As a result, the budget allocations arising out of the Coalition government's second spending review in 2013 received no more *ex ante* scrutiny by House of Commons select committees than had applied to its first spending review three years earlier. Indeed, no House of Commons budget committee or equivalent had been established at the time of writing, though such a move still had serious advocates.[17]

Sharing Spending Controls between Treasury and Cabinet Office 2010–2014: Replaying the 1990s 'Strategic Control' Debate?

As already noted, all three main UK political parties committed themselves in their 2010 general election campaigns to some measure of fiscal consolidation to reduce post-2008 deficit and debt levels. And during the election campaign, heavy stress was laid on the amounts that could be saved simply from better management and avoidance of egregious waste, rather than by running inferior services or cutting benefits. Table 5.2 gives a flavour of what the three parties' election manifestos said about cutting what they saw as wasteful spending.

In pursuit of those promised efficiency savings, the Coalition set up an 'Efficiency and Reform Group' (ERG) in the Cabinet Office in 2010. ERG was headed politically by the Minister for the Cabinet Office, Francis Maude, an influential and experienced Conservative frontbencher who was committed to changing the way government financial management worked. ERG was announced as a partnership between the Cabinet Office and the Treasury and branded as a 'corporate centre' of government. That branding reflected a view held by Maude and others that UK government should be reshaped to be run more like a large corporation rather than a federation of departments, with a powerful central finance function located at the centre of government to keep spending departments on a tight financial rein and collective buying power being wielded vigorously to strike hard bargains with suppliers. In line with that vision, ERG absorbed the Office of Government Commerce (itself assembled from earlier organizations in 2000 to lead on public sector procurement policy, as noted in the previous chapter[18]). As well as reducing costs

---

[17] For example, in 2019 the House of Commons Procedure Committee (2019: 27 §92) again recommended the establishment of a Budget Committee.

[18] The 'Office of Government Commerce' brand disappeared in 2011, but most of OGC's functions continued under ERG.

7

Table 5.2 2010 election claims on efficiency or waste reduction in public spending

Conservatives (p. 9)	Labour (p. 4)	Liberal Democrats
'We will...cut a net £6bn of wasteful departmental spending in...2010/2011, with further savings in future years...former government advisers [say] ...that savings of £12bn across all departmental spending are possible in-year without affecting the quality of frontline services'	'...£15bn efficiency savings in 2010/2011 '...£11bn of further operational efficiencies and other ...savings to streamline government...by 2012/2013' Other savings mentioned: Public pay and pensions: £4.4bn Lower priority spending: £5bn Welfare reform: £1.5bn Asset sales: £20bn by 2020	'Not only must waste be eliminated, but we must also be bold about finding big areas of spending that can be cut completely...we have already identified over £15bn of savings in government spending per year' (pp. 13–15) Proposed savings included: cuts in quangos across government, cuts in the use of consultants in the public sector and scrapping of civil service bonuses (pp. 102–103).

Source: Conservative Party (2010), Labour Party (2010) and Liberal Democrat Party (2010).

by exerting centralized buying power, ERG aimed to make public services 'digital by default', eliminating old-style paperwork, and to be the central repository of knowledge about how to make the public sector cut costs and work better.

ERG's work was expected to result in large savings over the lifetime of the Coalition by providing central advice and consultancy (disseminating central expertise or 'Crown insights' to improve project management capability and risk management) and by exercising strict control over designated areas of spending. Indeed, in much the same vein as numerous earlier efficiency reviews, ERG stressed how much could be saved from government operating costs by such interventions and heavily publicized its target to cut such costs by some £20bn by 2014–2015 (perhaps coincidentally, a sum exactly the same as the 'efficiency savings' announced by Labour Chancellor Alastair Darling in the 2009 Pre-Budget report mentioned earlier).[19]

Apart from cutting costs, ERG aimed to improve the quality and delivery of government capital or investment projects, a type of spending that we explore further in the next chapter. After the 2010 election it reviewed some thirty-one major government projects and identified several familiar and recurring weaknesses in the way they had been managed (delays, cost overruns, quality problems). Developing the 'gateway' review process initiated by the Office of Government Commerce

[19] For an examination of ERG's claimed savings, see NAO (2014c), which found strong methods and evidence for nine out of fourteen ERG 'savings lines', but weaker evidence about what a counterfactual 'business as usual' approach would have meant for five of them.

a decade or so earlier, ERG set up a new Major Projects Authority to provide a centre of expertise to oversee such spending across Whitehall, '...by working with departments to ensure the fitness and quality of major projects throughout their life'.

In one way ERG belonged in a long line of high-level 'efficiency' or 'better management' units at the centre of government, including Margaret Thatcher's Efficiency Unit, whose name ERG echoed, Tony Blair's Prime Minister's Delivery Unit or the Gershon Efficiency review initiated by Gordon Brown. But it differed from those earlier cases in that it routinely exercized ten 'category' spending controls on behalf of the Treasury, including approval of proposed spending on items like consultancy and IT that had increased markedly as a proportion of administration costs in the period from 1987–1988 to 2003–2004 (Hood and Dixon 2015: 81). That development modified the 'Haldane principle' of Treasury review of expenditure proposals in so far as the advent of ERG meant some controls over UK spending were shared or delegated rather than exercized exclusively by the Treasury.[20] Further, in most cases, departments' delegation limits were set very low, in what one interviewee saw as a symbolically charged 'reign of terror' approach, because it meant departments had to apply to ERG for approval of proposals involving small sums (counted in thousands rather than millions of pounds) within those ten categories. As a result, ERG had a lot of work to do. By 2013 its efficiency empire stretched across four different cities—Liverpool, London, Newport, and Norwich—and mustered a total of some 990 full-time-equivalent staff, roughly the same size as the Treasury itself.)[21]

As had applied to many of the earlier central units in the efficiency world, this shared-power regime led to tensions and conflicts between the Treasury and ERG. Part of the problem—the well-known turf-battle or coordination issue where more than one department occupies the same policy space (see for instance Wilson 1989; Peters 1998)—was that in numerous cases both ERG and the relevant Treasury spending team were involved in assessing the same departmental proposals, from different perspectives. Even where that did not apply, Treasury spending teams' views about how specific proposals should be evaluated sometimes clashed with what their ERG counterparts thought, for example over nuclear decommissioning or climate change modelling software.

Disagreements between the Treasury and ERG seem to have been triggered or exacerbated in several cases by the failure of one organization to inform or involve the other at an early stage of the decision-making process—another classic bureaucratic coordination issue. But as well as the turf-battle element in the

[20] A line that had already been crossed over control of devolved spending.
[21] But only about thirty-five of those FTEs were routinely approving 'business cases' from departments within the ten category controls (receiving more than 100 cases a month on average, of which roughly half were approved as submitted).

tension between the two organizations (commented on by some of our inter-viewees), there seems to have been a difference in overall vision or philosophy about how spending control should operate—a difference that harked back to the debates of the 1990s over 'strategic' as against routine control that we discussed in Chapter 3. As already noted, ERG reflected the idea that the finance function in government should be tightly centralized, following the 'loose-tight' pattern of numerous private corporations. But that vision of tightly centralized control over finance rubbed up against a contrasting Treasury vision of delegated self-control in departments on the basis of earned autonomy and of UK central government as a 'federation of departments' (in the words of a former head of the civil service quoted in Chapman and Dunsire 1971: 319). A 2013 Treasury briefing document argued for a more risk- or capability-based approach to spending approvals on the grounds that 'the most efficient and effective approach to realising objectives on efficiency, improved capability and digital and procurement strategies is to incentivize departments to take ownership of this agenda'. Such tensions between blanket central oversight and a more selective approach to spending control were at least in part a reprise of the 'strategic control' debate surrounding the Trea-sury's Fundamental Expenditure Review some two decades before, although little reference seems to have been made to those earlier debates.

A 2013 Treasury document discussing spending controls and earned auton-omy described ERG's exercise of controls using a plethora of negative words and phrases, including 'shambolic', 'inconsistency', 'incoherence', 'counterproductive', 'obstructive', 'poor judgement', and 'narrow'. The Treasury argued that the way ERG exercized its controls tended to slow or stop expenditure with little regard and no accountability for the consequent delays or disruptions in major reforms, such as Universal Credit (the Coalition's flagship welfare benefits scheme, intended to replace the former tax credit and means-tested benefit systems). The Treasury spending teams also thought the split between ERG's controlling function and its advisory function was unclear, such that in some cases ERG as controller was sign-ing off on its own advisory work; and that ERG's focus on draconian controls over ten narrow categories of spending, representing a fairly small proportion of overall expenditure, had the effect of taking up a disproportionate amount of the time of senior officials within departments on relatively low value, low risk expenditure.

One instance of ERG failing to exercize its spending control powers 'strategi-cally', in the opinion of one of its Treasury critics, was a long delay in approving £14m or so of consultancy costs, which held up for months a proposal supported by the Treasury for outsourcing a major department's estates management calcu-lated to save about £360m a year. Another was ERG's insistence on the national museums conducting their procurement by rigidly following the standard central government contracting procedure, when the Treasury supported a more flexible approach on the grounds that the museums' status as charities enabled them in some cases to buy supplies more cheaply than government departments (because as charities those museums could ask suppliers to offer them special deals, as part of those firms' 'corporate social responsibility' programmes). Nor do these examples seem to have been isolated cases. One report of a discussion among heads of Treasury spending teams in 2013 revealed that 9 out of 12 of them agreed to the proposition that 'ERG takes a narrow view of expenditure, fail to adopt a strategic approach'.

This reprise of that long-running risk-based versus search-every-suitcase debate over spending control was of course different from its 1990s predecessor in that it concerned division of responsibilities between Treasury and another department, rather than practices within the Treasury. But as with the debate of two decades before, views about it varied. Some of our interviewees shared the view of the ERG's low-autonomy approach as 'penny-wise, pound foolish', in line with the criticisms noted earlier. One of them who had high-level experience both in government and the private sector thought the ERG regime had had only a short-term effect because spending departments quickly learned to game the system, for example by arguing for exceptions for political pet projects and creating corporate bodies to get round rules limiting civil service pay costs. But that interviewee, while describing ERG's approach as 'medieval', said it had been a necessary 'short, sharp shock' to departments at a time of major fiscal challenge.

Such tensions between the Treasury and ERG over financial controls, and NAO concerns over the operation of ERG's working, seem to have been at least part of the background to the institution of a high-level Review of Financial Management in Government in 2013—significantly, at a time when the political clout of ERG was passing its peak, according to several interviewees. The Review was driven politically by the (Liberal Democrat) Chief Secretary to the Treasury and conducted at official level by the top Treasury mandarin responsible for overseeing public spending (Sharon White) together with the Head of the Government Finance Profession who was also Finance Director of one of the biggest spending departments (Richard Douglas of the Department of Health).

This review differed from its FER predecessor of two decades before, in that it was notionally a cross-government affair rather than exclusively Treasury-owned, and its investigative method consisted largely of elite interviews rather than the extensive documentary material gathered for the FER, which (as we noted in Chapter 3) had drawn on multiple reviews covering different aspects of Treasury working. Its report was pitched as a set of recommendations to strengthen the finance function in government through 'empowered leadership' under a professionally qualified Director-General of Finance located in the Treasury and a new framework for financial management that included a system of earned autonomy (essentially a tweak or repackaging of the Treasury's traditional ability to vary delegation limits for spending) in which departments could take greater responsibility for spending decisions on the basis of their track record. ERG itself (in a classic instance of efficiency revolutions devouring their own children) was dissolved the following year as part of a 'Public Bodies Transformation Programme' but most of its component parts survived.

Conclusion

The three issues explored in this chapter show that as well as the deep cutbacks it made in public spending, the 2010–2015 Coalition government grappled with varying success with at least three basic issues in the fiscal constitution, namely public engagement, parliamentary scrutiny and the operation of spending control within executive government.

Each of those three episodes reveals something about how political conditions shape the working of public spending control. The 2013 episode over proposals for enhanced parliamentary scrutiny of supply estimates shows that even apparently small changes in parliamentary procedure could be seen as presenting significant political risks to executive government management of the budgetary process and the Treasury's power. The ERG story, including the tension between the 'corporate centre' vision of spending control and the variable-geometry Treasury version, shows that the conundrum of how to achieve 'strategic' control of public spending had by no means been settled for good in the 1994 Fundamental Review of the Treasury that we discussed in Chapter 3. And the 2010 Spending Review saga showed that expenditure classed as AME (outside the DEL control total and in principle forecastable rather than controllable in any given year) did not always have to be left out of contention with other expenditure items when the stakes were high enough. What was to be counted as controllable was a political judgement of what items of spending were to be fixed or settled sequentially, and what could be traded off against what. Nevertheless, the DEL/AME framework itself did not disappear and the 2010 Spending Review is one of several tests of the framework's resilience in the face of major changes in context, including financial crisis, and austerity (and, after our period, Brexit and the Covid pandemic).

Timeline

2010

February: George Osborne's Mais lecture foreshadowed the OBR, an emergency post-election Budget and an Autumn Spending Review if the Conservatives won government.

March: Labour's pre-election Budget detailed £11bn of spending reductions already announced under the 'Smarter Government' scheme, and an extra £5bn of savings, plus tax changes including frozen inheritance tax thresholds and changes to Stamp Duty (transaction tax) for house-buyers.

May/June: After the General Election a Conservative-Liberal Democrat Coalition was formed, with a Conservative Chancellor (George Osborne) and

Liberal Democrat Chief Secretary (David Laws for seventeen days, thereafter Danny Alexander). OBR was set up de facto and produced forecasts for the post-election Budget. That Budget announced £6bn in-year spending cuts and plans for further reductions up to 2014–2015. It set a spending envelope for Total Managed Expenditure in the subsequent Spending Review, meaning that AME could be traded off against DEL. The Efficiency and Reform Group was set up in the Cabinet Office.

October: Universal Credit announced at the Conservative party conference to (eventually) replace tax credits. Publication of Defence and Security Review, the public service pensions commission interim report, and the Spending Review covering spending up to 2014–2015. That review included an average 19 per cent cut in planned spending except for health and overseas aid (but also a £2.3bn increase in the capital spending envelope compared to that announced in the June Budget). The review cancelled the earlier End Year Flexibility system and announced a Benefit Cap policy to limit how much state benefit any individual household could claim per year, to take effect in 2013.

November/December: Strategic Review of the Treasury, in the wake of a spending settlement that implied cost savings of one third and staff falling to around 1000 by 2015.

2011

March: Final Report of Independent Public Service Pensions Commission (Hutton Review). Fiscally neutral Budget continued fiscal consolidation and included plans for a further one percentage point cut in Corporation Tax, to 23 per cent in 2014.

June: Report by Lord Levene on the Structure and Management of the Ministry of Defence.

November: Autumn Statement announced plan to raise state pension age to sixty-seven in the late 2020s and added £6.3 bn to infrastructure spending. Revised OBR forecasts led to an extra year of fiscal austerity being planned.

2012

March: Welfare Reform Act enacted the Universal Credit system. Review of Treasury response to the financial crisis in 2007–2009. 'Omnishambles' Budget (followed by climb-downs over proposed VAT increases on hot food and static caravans) continued fiscal consolidation including an announcement of means testing of Child Benefit while cutting top income tax rates.

April: Sovereign Grant replaced former Civil List and grants-in-aid for funding the monarch; HM Treasury Capability Action Plan published (HM Treasury 2012b).

July/August: Treasury Select Committee published (negative) report on PFI. Olympic Games held in London, costing about £10bn, most coming from central government and National Lottery funds.

October: NAO report on managing budgeting in government.

December: Autumn Statement announced another year of austerity in fiscal plans following forecast revisions. PF2 ('a new approach to public-private partnerships') launched as a successor to PFI.

2013

February: UK debt downgraded by Moody's.

March: Budget fixed the envelope for the 2015–2016 (one year) Spending Round and announced protection for health, schools and ODA in that Round.

April: UK debt downgraded by Fitch; Personal Independence Payments began to replace Disability Living Allowance for working-age people, with an expected reduction of DLA caseloads and expenditure by 2016–2017 (in fact it resulted in increased costs despite a higher rejection rate).

May: Andrew Lansley, Leader of the House, stated that the Coalition's pledge to introduce a House Business Committee in its third year would not be met because of lack of consensus.

June: Spending Round for one year only (2015–2016), making over £11bn of claimed savings. Announcement of a cap on welfare spending and a rolling programme of efficiency reviews, beginning with BIS, HMRC and DWP, with 5 per cent RDEL reductions as the default savings target.

September: OSCAR replaced COINS as the Treasury's spending control IT system. NAO report on 'The performance of HM Treasury 2012–2013'.

December: Autumn Statement cut most departmental budgets for 2014–2015 and 2015–2016 by 1.1 per cent. White/Douglas Review of Financial Management in Government.

2014

March: Budget set out the welfare cap (a complement to the benefits cap, with performance against the cap assessed by OBR) and announced tax cuts funded by spending cuts. OBR forecast £7bn underspending in 2013–2014 with further underspending until the end of the Parliament.

September: Scottish Independence referendum (Chapter 7).

October: Efficiency and Reform Group dissolved.

November: Against a £27bn improvement in the public finances forecast by OBR, the Autumn Statement set out plans to cut the forecast deficit by three quarters from its peak by 2016–2017, eliminate it by 2019–2020 and then deliver a £10.1bn surplus. OBR observed that the then current spending plans would shrink the state to its lowest share of GDP since 1938.

2015

March: The Chancellor's pre-election Budget, agreed between the Coalition parties, continued fiscal consolidation while cutting income tax and altering public spending plans such that spending no longer fell to a post-World War II low. But the CST (Danny Alexander) also presented an alternative Liberal Democrat ('yellow') budget to Parliament with a slower path of fiscal consolidation and a shift away from spending cuts to tax increases.

May: General Election produced a narrow overall majority for the Conservatives.

PART III
FIVE ASPECTS OF PUBLIC SPENDING CONTROL

6

Hunting an Elephant with a Pea-Shooter

Power Politics and Cost-Benefit Analysis in Investment and Infrastructure Spending

Vignette: Who Decides What Is Value for Money? Building the Pergau Dam

Pergau Dam (Steson Janaelektrik Sultan Ismael Petra) is Malaysia's third biggest hydroelectric power station (though at 600MW it is quite small by world standards). Opened in 2003 after a decade of construction, it is run by peninsular Malaysia's privatized electric utility company, Tenaga Nasional (TNB). Its construction, by a consortium of British and Malaysian companies that included Balfour Beatty, General Electric, and Cementation International,[1] was initially funded by some £234m of UK overseas aid from the Overseas Development Administration[2], then part of the Foreign and Commonwealth Office. That spending was authorized in 1991 by the then Foreign Secretary, Douglas Hurd, following a political deal struck three years earlier between then UK Prime Minister Margaret Thatcher and Malaysia's long-term Prime Minister Dr. Mahathir Mohamad. That deal, recorded in an unpublished protocol (Hurd 2003: 548), linked approximately £500m worth of UK arms sales to Malaysia with UK aid funding in the form of a prestigious hydroelectric project.

The Pergau project made the news in the UK in 1993 after a NAO report revealed for the first time that the Overseas Development Administration's official head (Sir Tim Lankester)—in his role as Accounting Officer (AO) for the department—had asked in 1991 for a formal 'Direction' from the Foreign Secretary to authorize spending on the Pergau project. Lankester took that step because he and other Overseas Development Administration civil servants thought the dam was 'a very bad buy', failing one of the four tests in the official rules for evaluating public expenditure projects at that time, namely economy.[3] Lankester based his view on a technical appraisal of the Pergau Dam proposal by TNB

---

[1] Lankester (2013: 29) notes that Cementation's parent company, Trafalgar House, was a substantial donor to the Conservative Party.

[2] Then commonly known as 'ODA', but that acronym had come to be used to denote overseas development aid' (the UK's overseas aid budget) at the time of writing, so we give the organization's name in full here to avoid confusion.

[3] The other three criteria then were 'effectiveness' or 'prudence', 'propriety' (lawfulness) and 'regularity' (meaning money was spent as specified in the relevant Parliamentary Vote).

The Way the Money Goes. Christopher Hood, Maia King, Iain McLean, and Barbara Piotrowska,
Oxford University Press. © Christopher Hood, Maia King, Iain McLean, and Barbara Piotrowska (2023).
DOI: 10.1093/oso/9780198865087.003.0006

in Malaysia, which concluded that the project was uneconomic because other options for increasing Malaysia's power supply by the same amount would be far cheaper (almost £100m)—a conclusion endorsed by both World Bank and Overseas Development Administration officials.

Already mentioned earlier in this book (Chapters 1 and 2), Accounting Officers, normally the permanent heads of government departments or agencies, are a feature of the UK's fiscal constitution that goes back to the 1866 Exchequer and Audit Act (s.22). Under that Act, the Treasury assigns the duty of submitting each department's accounts to Parliament not to ministers but to a named permanent official (Harris, 2013: 9).[4] AOs are directly and individually accountable to Parliament for the observance of Treasury public spending limits and rules in their departments and cannot delegate that accountability—a feature said by several of our interviewees to build a strong bias to underspending into the fiscal constitution because Permanent Secretaries are highly averse to the prospect of a grilling from the House of Commons Public Accounts Committee (PAC) if their spending goes over budget. When AOs ask for a formal 'Direction' (or 'Instruction') from a Minister over an item of proposed spending, it amounts to a refusal to be accountable for such decisions if Ministers insist on going ahead. Such requests are high-level bureaucratic weapons, not used lightly or often (as we show later in this chapter) and signify serious divergences of view between officials and Ministers.

Describing the political context of the Pergau project, Lankester (2013: 101) says the Overseas Development Administration, '...was under immense pressure from other parties within Whitehall and from the British contractors—to speed up, slow down, cut corners, compromise. That [the department] did all of these things went completely against the professional ethos of the organisation, and can only...be understood in terms of the political environment... With so many others in powerful places working on a different agenda...it was extremely difficult for [the department] to apply its usual standards'.

The 1993 NAO revelation about the Direction request on the Pergau project attracted media and parliamentary attention, much of it focused on the link between aid and arms sales. The PAC duly launched an investigation resulting in a report highly critical of the Overseas Development Administration, followed by the Foreign Affairs Committee, which also probed the arms linkage. The drama moved into the judicial sphere the following year, with a case brought in the English High Court by a small UK development NGO, the World Development Movement (WDM). WDM claimed the Overseas Development Administration's spending on the project was a breach of the 1980 Overseas Development and Cooperation Act which in Section 1 (1) enabled ministers to provide aid to any other country 'for economic development or the welfare of its people'. WDM

---

[4] The title 'Accounting Officer' is said to date from a Treasury minute of 1872 (First Report of the Public Accounts Committee 1873 (HC 110), Appendix: 78).

argued that a project that did not constitute 'sound development' (in that it had been shown to be much more costly than available alternatives) could not meet such a condition. In a surprise ruling in November 1994 (*Regina v Secretary of State for Foreign and Commonwealth Affairs, ex parte World Development Movement Ltd*),[5] the English High Court agreed with WDM, consequently ruling the Overseas Development Administration's spending on the project to be unlawful under the 1980 Act.[6]

The judgment, which remains 'good law' because it was not appealed (though some lawyers criticized it[7]), led the Comptroller and Auditor General to 'qualify' the Overseas Development Administration's 1993/1994 accounts, on the grounds that the money spent on the project was not a proper charge on the relevant parliamentary vote. To allow the project to continue, the Treasury routed the spending via another government department, the Export Credits Guarantee Department, whose spending was not covered by the 1980 Act on which the High Court had ruled. So the moral victory went to cost-benefit analysis (and related methods of expert evaluation of investment project proposals)—but the dam was built anyway.

This episode raised three related 'fiscal constitution' issues about who decides what and how in project or infrastructure spending. One concerns the relative position of politicians and ministers as against bureaucrats or technocrats when their judgements differ. Pergau was a case in which technocrats' views diverged from those of elected politicians. In Malaysia the dam project was favoured by Prime Minister Mahathir Mohamad but not by TNB officials, and in the UK it was backed (perhaps equivocally) by the Prime Minister and Foreign Secretary but not by Overseas Development Administration officials. The High Court's 1994 decision in effect sided with the technocrats against the politicians.

A second issue concerns the weight to put on subjective political judgement as against what was taken to be more 'objective' economic or technical evaluation. The subjective doctrine applying to this case was the view held by Overseas Development Administration officials at that time that if ministers said they *believed* some item of spending would assist a country's development, then any such expenditure was lawful under the 1980 Act (Lankester 2013: 87). Similar assumptions about the status of ministers' subjective views on matters of economy seem to have applied to the way Direction requests to ministers from AOs on grounds

---

[5] [1994] EWHC 1 (Admin), [1995] WLR 386, [1995] 1 All ER 611, [1995] COD 211 http://www.bailii.org/ew/cases/EWHC/Admin/1994/1.html

[6] Lord Justice Rose's judgment said, 'If Parliament had intended to confer a power to disburse money for unsound developmental purposes, it could have been expected to say so expressly . . . Where the contemplated development is...so economically unsound that there is no economic argument in favour of the case, it is not, in my judgement, possible to draw any distinction between questions of propriety and regularity on the one hand and questions of economy and efficiency of public expenditure on the other'.

[7] Lankester (2013: 112–113) notes that Lord Irving of Lairg (Labour Lord Chancellor 1999–2002) wrote in 1996 that the Pergau ruling went too far in 'curbing a valuable and legitimate facet of administrative autonomy'. Lord Sumption (2011) also criticized the ruling as judicial over-reach.

of economy were treated by the parliamentary system at that time. The Pergau affair led the PAC to recommend a change from previous practice in which AO requests for Directions on grounds of economy were not automatically notified to the Comptroller and Auditor General (the Pergau Direction just lay in the files until NAO decided to investigate and found it), while requests for Directions on grounds of propriety or regularity were routinely notified to NAO. Although the Pergau project went on to completion under a different funding route, the PAC report and the High Court's judgment made a notable dent in the 'subjective' view that what ultimately counted in matters of economy was the political judgement of ministers.

In fact, as Lankester's account shows, UK government ministers were far from united on their views on the issue, so it was not a simple case of ministers versus technocrats. A 1991 meeting of five ministers over whether to go ahead with the project resulted in deadlock and strong protests from the Chief Secretary to the Treasury on the grounds that he had not been given a chance to review the proposal in advance (the Treasury was said by one interviewee to be normally sceptical about linking aid to other deals). The then Foreign Secretary, Douglas Hurd, acknowledged the values in conflict when he wrote to the Prime Minister, 'Although it goes against the grain to support an uneconomic project, we face a test of Britain's good faith and Mrs. Thatcher's in particular...we must honour Mrs. Thatcher's word...we have no choice but to proceed' (Hurd 2003: 548).

The weight attached to Mrs. Thatcher's word links to a third issue raised by the Pergau case, that is, the balance between formal rules and less formal customs and understandings. Overseas Development Administration assumptions about the weight to be given to the views of ministers relative to professional economic assessments are described by Lankester (2013: 87, referring to a conversation with the Department's Chief Finance Officer), as long-standing 'custom and practice', generally assumed to be legally correct, thought to be widely shared in the legal profession and never previously challenged in court. The court's rejection of that understanding made the rules about how 'economy' was to be treated in public spending decisions more explicit and formal, and assigned no weight to the political agreement between the Malaysian government and UK ministers. Indeed (Judge) Stephen Sedley (2011: 351) saw the judgment as 'a sharp illustration' of a trend towards greater judicial activism in the 1970s and 1980s to 'fill lacunae of legitimacy in the functioning of democratic politics' both in the UK and across the common law world.[8]

The Pergau story highlights the central theme of this chapter, which explores how rational analytic appraisal (of the kind represented by TNB's cost-benefit evaluation of the Pergau project) fared in different political circumstances during our period when applied to those 'lumpy' or discrete kinds of public spending

---

[8] Harden, White and Hollingsworth (1996) also discuss the changes that followed the case.

projects that are variously designated as 'capital', 'investment' or 'infrastructure'. Was the Pergau episode a sign or even a cause of a clear shift to greater emphasis on rational economic assessment of those kinds of spending? Or did such assessment have more purchase in some political contexts than others?

After a brief look at what exactly can be counted as 'capital' (or not) in public spending, this chapter explores the handling of capital, infrastructure, or project expenditure from three angles. First, following the Pergau case, we look at what happened to requests by Permanent Secretaries for formal Directions from their ministers over spending on such items during our period. Then we explore how the official guidelines for appraisal and evaluation of project proposals developed over that time, especially in relation to so-called 'optimism bias'. Finally, we review evidence from other sources about how the rules and principles were applied and what effect they had. Clearly much official effort went into developing economic appraisal and more systematic analysis of management and delivery issues in capital and similar spending, with the development of elaborate systems of 'traffic lights', multi-staged evaluations and peer reviews. But high-profile, politically favoured 'pet projects' do not appear to have triggered many requests for Directions even when outsiders suggested major question marks about them.

'Capital', 'Infrastructure', or 'Investment' Spending: Easy to Venerate, Trickier to Define?

Capital expenditure has long presented challenges to traditional forms of spending control because of its typical 'lumpiness', multi-year timescale, and vulnerability to cutbacks in times of fiscal stringency through delay or cancellation.[9] The GOGGS building (Chapter 4) exemplifies such spending, not only in its 2000s makeover but also in its original construction. it took thirty-two years (1866–1898) and four Acts of Parliament to buy the land and another nineteen years to construct the building. And as we also saw in Chapter 4, when PFI was developed in its original form, it allowed at least part of such spending to be funded off-balance sheet.

As with PFI, New Labour's stress on capital expenditure had antecedents in the previous government. A month after the ERM debacle in 1992 Chancellor Norman Lamont announced that he had 'decided that the Government accounts should be drawn up in a way which makes a proper distinction between current and capital transactions. I believe this will help to underpin the Government's commitment to infrastructure investment in the longer run'.[10]

Six years later, Chancellor Gordon Brown took the capital/current distinction further by introducing separate budgets for current and capital spending, and

---

[9] See for instance Chubb 1952: 74; Heclo and Wildavsky 1974: 105.
[10] Chancellor's Mansion House speech, 24 October 1992: §23–5.

(as described in Chapter 4) adopting a variant of the German 'golden rule' by excluding 'investment' spending from a commitment to balance the budget over the course of the economic cycle. Introducing New Labour's first comprehensive spending review, he said: 'We are raising capital investment for...three years...to tackle the backlog of under-investment... [while] current spending will grow by no more than 2¼ per cent'.[11]

In 2013, Chancellor George Osborne also emphasized the importance he attached to capital and infrastructure spending in his Budget speech: 'We've switched billions of pounds from current to capital spending since the [2010] spending review. But on existing plans, capital spending is still due to fall back in 2015–16. I don't think that's sensible. So by using...extra savings from government departments, we will boost our infrastructure plans by £3 billion a year from 2015–16. That's £15 billion of extra capital spending over the next decade...public investment will now be higher on average as a percentage of our national income...than it was in the whole period of the last Government'.[12]

Thus Chancellors from different parties over our period repeatedly represented 'capital' as an important and valuable type of spending that deserved protection.[13] Further, the words 'capital', 'investment', and 'infrastructure' were often used interchangeably and approvingly, although, as Figure 6.1 shows, the term 'investment' appeared more often than 'capital' or 'infrastructure' in budget speeches over our period, particularly during Gordon Brown's Chancellorship (when 'investment' often seems to have been a synonym for public spending in general).

Further, as always happens when one type of public spending is given more weight than another, what exactly is to count as the 'capital', 'infrastructure', or 'investment' part of public spending can be debatable. Several such issues emerged as the official Treasury worked on how to deliver on Lamont's 1992 announcement of separate reporting of ('good') capital and ('bad') current spending.

One related to spending on defence *materiel*. Did battleships or tanks count as 'capital' items, even 'investments' in that they were big-ticket lumpy purchases intended to produce some notional return in extra security or world peace? Or were the implications of treating armaments like that just too contestable? The UK's national accounts conventions until almost the end of our period (2014)[14] counted spending on so-called 'dual use' military assets—for instance, airfields or

---

[11] HC Debs 14 July 1998 Vol 316, c189.

[12] HC Debs 20 March 2013 Vol 560, c.937.

[13] But for those who supported 1980s Thatcherite policies of privatizing former SOEs (such that their privatised successors raised funds on the private capital market) a fall in public sector capital spending relative to GDP might be expected and desired. Indeed, commenting on a fall in public sector capital spending since the mid-1970s, a 1993 Treasury document said, 'The difficulty is to know whether this indicates success or failure'.

[14] In 2014 spending on single use military assets was reclassified as 'capital' in UK national accounts following a change in the European System of Accounts (ESA) (Office of National Statistics 2014).

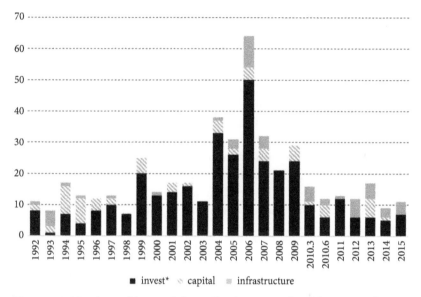

Figure 6.1 Mentions of the words 'capital', infrastructure', and 'investment', in Chancellors' Budget Speeches

hospitals that could in principle be used for civilian purposes—as capital expenditure. 'Single use' assets—items like rocket launchers, held not to be usable for any non-military purpose—counted in this mental universe as current spending. At the same time, under the resource accounting and budgeting framework applied in UK central government from 2001 (to be discussed in Chapter 10) all spending on military assets counted as 'capital', regardless of their treatment in national accounts. So between 2001 and 2014 spending on 'single use' military assets scored as 'current' for national accounts but 'capital' in the resource accounts presented to Parliament. Part of the reason for the Treasury sticking to that messy and confusing approach to accounting for military spending seems to have been defensive in a political or bureaucratic sense, to avoid accusations of fiddling the figures or giving other departments any opening for bids to reclassify parts of their spending. An internal 1993 document said, 'Anything else the government chose would arouse suspicion'.

A second issue, noted by Norman Lamont elsewhere in his 1992 speech and raised by several interviewees, was that of how to treat 'human capital' spending, notably in the form of education or professional training. Such spending was also not counted as 'capital' in the national accounts, which focused on physical objects (buildings, machinery, plant, dams...), not people. But if the distinction that advocates of separate treatment of capital spending were trying to make was between spending that provides only current benefits, as against that which yields a return in the form of an income stream or continuing additional benefits into the future, the exclusion of human capital was obviously problematic. Indeed, educational spending was commonly referred to as 'investment', especially but not only in the New Labour era, even though most of it did not officially count as 'capital'. One interviewee went so far as to declare that excluding human capital, together with the absence of a clear revenue stream for many projects dubbed as capital, made the capital/current distinction 'bogus'. Several others insisted that a closely related distinction ought to be drawn between preventive and remedial expenditure. They saw such a distinction as vital for effective public spending control, given that cuts in preventive spending so often meant higher remedial spending later, but said that preventive/remedial distinction was obscured, and the underlying problem arguably exacerbated, by the DEL-AME framework.

Other tricky issues bound up with delivering on Lamont's 1992 Mansion House pledge included:

- How to treat research and development (which, like military single-use spending, counted as 'current' expenditure in national accounts until it too was reclassified as 'capital' under new EU accounting rules in 2014).
- Whether and how depreciation should be netted off against capital spending. Before 1995–1996 the Treasury did not publish aggregate numbers for public sector investment net of depreciation (the available numbers were seen as too 'ropey') and when it began to do so, depreciation turned out to amount to about half of Public Sector Gross Investment.[15]
- How to report the capital spending element of the Reserve (the unallocated part of the budget, to be used for unexpected spending needs), which at that time was not committed to either 'capital' or 'current' expenditure.
- What aggregation of government or public sector to use in reporting (central government only, 'general government', or the whole public sector). In 1993 the Treasury opted to stay with the 'public sector' basis of reporting public spending, a modified form of the broad 'Plowden' approach era of the early 1960s,[16] as discussed in Chapter 2. But capital spending showed a much steeper decline relative to GDP when calculated on that basis than it would have done had figures been reported for central government alone.
- How to deal with the inevitable borderline cases, such as the long-standing issue of how to treat 'temporary fix' pothole repairs (road maintenance not expected to have a life beyond a year did not count as capital spending, creating perverse incentives to neglect short-term remedial spending).[17]

---

[15] But that was by no means always the case, since depreciation was a fairly stable share of the capital stock whereas PSGI varied substantially.

[16] Although public expenditure was redefined in 1977 to exclude capital spending by SOEs that was wholly funded from user charges (Heald 1997: 576).

[17] One interviewee even said that GEP in the early 2000s toyed with the idea of adding to the distinction between 'resource' and 'capital' spending a further arcane sub-categorization of 'resource' into 'investment resource' and 'consumption resource' spending.

Such conundrums did not wholly disappear over our period. But as some of the examples given above show and is also noted in the timeline, there was a marked shift over the period to standardize accounting conventions over such matters, notably with the adoption of international accounting conventions in the form of the European standards ESA95 and ESA2010. Connected to that standardization was the removal of discretion over statistical definitions, frameworks, and classifications from Treasury officials into the hands of autonomous bodies staffed by experts, notably the Office of National Statistics and the Office for Budget responsibility. We return to those developments in Chapter 10.

Asking for Directions: Was Pergau Dam Followed by a Flood?

As we noted in the vignette, the power of Permanent Secretaries acting as 'Accounting Officers' (AOs) to ask their Ministers for formal written 'Directions' overriding their (AOs') objections to spending proposals, goes back to the UK's Victorian fiscal constitution. In principle the Public Accounts Committee could recommend that AOs be held personally liable and 'surcharged' for any irregular or unauthorized expenditure (Marre 1957: 172–173). But an 1883 Treasury circular that envisaged such surcharges said AOs would be discharged of any personal liability if, when instructed to make a payment they considered improper or irregular, they stated their objections in writing, the political head of the department overruled them with a written Direction to make the payment, and that Direction was reported to the Treasury.[18]

At first those appointed as AOs had mainly been Chief Finance Officers of departments, whose views could be and were overridden by higher-grade officials. That defect of the 1866 system was eventually corrected in the twentieth century when it became standard practice for departmental permanent secretaries to be designated as AOs. And AOs' individual accountability over spending came to be extended from propriety or regularity (that is, avoidance of embezzlement or fraud or using funds for purposes other than those voted by Parliament) to financial management and control more broadly, including efficiency and economy, the key issue in the vignette. Before 1994, only requests for Directions concerning 'propriety' and 'regularity' had to be reported to the Treasury and the Comptroller and Auditor General (C and AG). But AOs were certainly making requests for Directions on value for money grounds before the Pergau Dam episode. Indeed, in 1994, according to internal documents, the Treasury knew of eight such Directions in the recent past, some but not all of which were also known to the C and AG.

Some nine months before the 1994 Pergau judgement, a move to report all value for money Direction requests to the Treasury and C and AG was triggered by

---

[18] Treasury Circular 21670/82, October 1883.

a set of parliamentary questions from Ted Rowlands MP (Lab, Merthyr Tydfil) asking ministers for lists of Directions.[19] Rowlands' questions led a meeting of Permanent Secretaries to discuss whether an answer could be limited either to Directions based on propriety and regularity (routinely sent to Treasury and the C and AG) or alternatively to whatever value-for-money Directions the C and AG had happened to turn up in investigations, as in the Pergau case. The meeting concluded that neither of those positions would be defensible and the Treasury needed to have a complete list of value-for-money Directions, information that thereby became accessible through parliamentary questions and later through Freedom of Information Act procedures, until eventually (from 2011), a full list of Directions appeared on the UK government website. Even then, what was recorded referred only to instances when AOs were formally overruled by Ministerial Directions. 'Near misses' when AOs submitted reservations and Ministers thereafter altered spending proposals were not recorded (NAO 2016: 25). The same applies to informal threats or warnings about the possibility of Direction requests unless Ministers changed course, which seem to have been more common.[20]

Those changes in reporting procedures mean there is no official list of Directions made on both value for money and propriety/regulatory grounds before 1994, from which we could definitively assess whether the Pergau Dam case proved to be a turning-point in the incidence of Directions. In one narrow sense it apparently did not: no further Directions were requested within the domain of overseas aid during our period (though there were several Directions relating to export credits deals involving developing countries and some interviewees said the Pergau case had lingered in official memory). But the picture looks a little different when we turn from overseas aid specifically to such numbers as are available for Directions in all public spending domains, as shown in Table 6.1. Three features stand out.

One is that over our period more Directions do seem to have been requested than in the previous decade or so. But they rose from a low base, never amounting to more than a handful per year. Assuming that by 1999 the Treasury had garnered a full list of Directions since 1981, the incidence of reported Directions in the decade or so prior to our study was eleven (just over one per year on average), compared with some fifty-three over the 1993–2015 period (over twice the 1981–1992 yearly incidence on average). It is of course debatable whether that higher incidence of official Directions should be interpreted as meaning Permanent Secretaries were exerting firmer control over public spending, or the very

[19] HC Deb Vol 238 1993–94 (written answers 24 Feb 1994, 25 Feb 1994, 28 Feb 1994, 1 March 1994, 8 March 1994, 10 March 1994, 22 March 1994).
[20] Harris (2013: 15) reports one interviewee saying the Treasury dealt with 'a couple of inquiries' about possible Directions every week and another from a spending department said to have seriously considered a Direction request every three months.

Table 6.1 Incidence of Ministerial Directions over time, 1981–2015

'Before' (1981–1992)	'After' (1993–2015)		
11	53, of which		
	Major Government 1993–1997	Blair/Brown Government 1997–2010	Cameron/Clegg Coalition Government 2010–2015
Overall	6	37	10
Per Year in Office	1.2	2.8	2

Source: HC Official Report Vol. 326 1999, written answers, Prime Minister 'Notes of Dissent', 23 February 1999; HMT reports of Direction requests 1990–2005; Institute for Government (2015)

opposite (with their requests for Directions to be understood as futile 'protest votes' indicating less control and influence on their part).

Second, there was a notable jump in formal Direction requests during the New Labour period. New Labour had the highest incidence of such Directions per year in office over our period. But the Coalition was not far behind, especially in its final year when Direction requests spiked, and there were further spikes under the May and Johnson governments after our period.

Third, capital and infrastructure spending proposals featured prominently in those Direction requests during our period. Table 6.2 gives a few examples of such cases between 1993 and 2015, taken from a list of some forty-six Directions over that time, compiled by the Institute for Government (2021). Those cases include several procurement decisions over military hardware, such as the purchase of eight Chinook military helicopters in the aftermath of the 'Front Line First' review (Chapter 3) in 1995, which led to a damning NAO report thirteen years later when none of the aircraft were yet in operation (Hencke 2008; NAO 2008). The list also includes development or regeneration projects in politically sensitive areas, one complex IT project covering benefits payments through the Post Office, and a few prestige projects such as the controversial Millennium Dome to mark the year 2000 and the HS1 high speed rail project, to which we return later in this chapter.

Still, arguably the more striking feature of this list is what is *not* there—'the ones that got away'. By that we mean major capital, project, or infrastructure items that were not challenged by requests for Directions even though they attracted serious criticism on feasibility or value for money grounds from the NAO or Public Accounts Committee, media, or forensic academic studies and might therefore be expected to be candidates for AO challenges. Specifically, of the twenty major UK government 'blunders' over three decades identified in a classic study by Anthony King and Ivor Crewe (2013), only two of the eleven non-IT cases were challenged by requests for Directions and only one out of the nine IT cases. Many of the

Table 6.2 Nine selected requests for Ministerial Directions on value for money grounds concerning 'project' or 'capital' spending, 1993–2015

Year/Government	Department	Description	Nature of Spending
1995/Conservative	Ministry of Defence	Medium Support Helicopters	Military procurement
1997/Labour	Department of Environment, Transport and the Regions	Millennium Exhibition	Prestige millennium project
1997/Labour	Department of the Environment, Transport and the Regions	Channel Tunnel Rail Link (HS1)	High Speed Rail mega-project
1998/Labour	Department of Social Security	Benefits Agency/Post Office Counters Ltd—automation project	Ambitious IT project involving two departments
2001/Labour	Ministry of Defence	Roll-on/Roll-off Ferries	Military procurement
2002/Labour	Department of the Environment, Transport and the Regions	A43 Silverstone by-pass	Major road project in the vicinity of Silverstone race track
2003/Labour	Ministry of Defence	Acquisition of BAE Hawk trainer aircraft	Military procurement
2009/Labour	Department for Business, Enterprise and Regulatory Reform	Leeds Arena project	Big regional entertainment venue development
2010/Labour	Department for Business, Innovation and Skills	North-West Development Agency's Funding for Blackpool Leisure Assets	Investment to support leisure assets in a major regional tourism centre

Source: Data Extracted from Institute for Government (2015)

projects that did produce Direction requests were only medium in scale. A 2016 NAO report (analysing sixty-two Directions between 1990 and 2015, 77 per cent of which were requested by AOs on value for money grounds) showed that about half of those Directions involved sums of less than £20m, while the average value of a project in the Government Major Projects Portfolio at that time was £2.6bn (NAO 2016: 24).[21]

That report also gave examples of major capital spending projects—all involving ambitious IT ventures that went seriously wrong, all dating from the New Labour period—in which PAC, NAO or other oversight bodies raised serious concerns about value for money and issued loud warnings, but AOs did not ask for Directions. Those examples included: a 'Single Farm Payment' scheme to merge several EU farming subsidies into a single payment based on size of farms; a major project (FiRe Control) to replace local fire and rescue control centres with regional control centres, and the National Programme for IT in the (English) National Health Service (NAO 2016, Figure 10: 28–29), which cost about £10bn before it was finally scrapped in 2011. NAO's 2016 report also named the procurement of two aircraft carriers as a big-ticket defence project in the 2000s for which AOs should have sought Directions (NAO 2016: 25).

Overall, such documents indicate three things about how the Direction system operated in relation to capital or similar spending over our period. First, such requests became more transparent due to the changes in logging and reporting Direction requests sparked by parliamentary questions in 1994 and arguably buttressed by the Pergau Dam judgement in the same year.

Second (anticipating the theme of the next chapter), the equivalents of the Direction system for the devolved governments also seem to have been little invoked over our period, albeit perhaps for different reasons. There were a few instances in Northern Ireland during times when its Assembly was in operation and its Public Accounts Committee functioning,[22] five in Scotland since devolution in 1999 (but no reported 'written authority' cases between 2007 and the end of our period in 2015) (Scottish Government 2021)[23] and none in Wales, except for one request coming after our period in 2019. A fairly low incidence of AO Direction requests was evidently not peculiar to the world of Whitehall and Westminster.

Third, while the incidence of such value-for-money challenges increased at UK level to some extent during our period, particularly during the New Labour era,

---

[21] There were two exceptions, both concerning Treasury decisions during and after the 2008 financial crisis, namely £3.4bn of financial guarantees to UK depositors in the failed Icelandic bank Landsbanki and £37.2bn on the Asset Protection Scheme, protecting banks from losses on their assets.

[22] See for example Northern Ireland Public Accounts Committee (2015), End of Session Report. 2014-2015.

[23] In 2022 Audit Scotland reported that it could find no record of a ministerial direction to issue a ferry-building contract to a Clyde shipyard that later failed, despite civil service warnings. The contract had gone two and a half times over budget and the two ships in question had yet to be delivered four years after they were due to be completed. See Audit Scotland (2022).

Direction requests that focused on 'pet projects' at the highest political level were rare at that time.[24] That observation supports NAO's (2016) conclusion that AOs' incentives to prioritize value for money during our period were weak compared with those associated with the day-to-day job of satisfying ministers. But NAO did not discuss how to change those incentives and left aside questions such as whether some move towards imposition of personal surcharges on AOs (as the Treasury had apparently envisaged for regularity and propriety in the 1880s) would improve the system or break it by leading AOs to ask for Directions on everything.

Doing It by the (Green) Book: Appraisal and Evaluation of Business Cases

As mentioned in the vignette, the main official Treasury guide for appraising and evaluating public spending project and investment proposals is the so-called 'Green Book'.

Efforts to develop rational-evaluation procedures for project and capital spending proposals have a long history in the UK, stretching back at least as far as the early post-World War II period when there was a big nationalized industry sector (and arguably long before that, with SOEs such as ordnance factories and the Post Office). After World War II, borrowing for investment by the large SOE sector had to be rationed because it counted as part of overall public sector debt. To assess SOE investment proposals within that rationing process, the Treasury developed time-discounting analysis and cost-benefit analysis to set cost-recovery and rate-of-return requirements (Spackman 2004 and 2013; Groom and Hepburn 2017). That experience led to the distillation of some general official principles for investment appraisal and evaluation, set out in a 'Green Book', which first appeared as a slim unpublished volume written by the Treasury's micro-economists in 1973, but came to outlive the era of 1940s-style nationalized industries. It also outgrew the original focus on capital spending proposals, came to be applied to policy and regulation more generally and became mandatory in providing a framework for the submission of 'business cases'—that is, proposals for spending projects for approval by the Treasury or other bodies.[25]

---

[24] But in the era of Brexit turmoil and the Covid pandemic shortly after our period, there was a big spike in Direction requests, only some of which took the 'supportive' form of declaring support for the measure proposed but asking for a Direction for form's sake in the absence of a clear way of showing that the scheme was value for money.

[25] The Treasury's 'Green Book principles' were binding on the UK and Welsh Assembly governments over our period, but not on the Scottish and Northern Ireland governments, which had their own documents, albeit closely following the UK Green Book.

As shown in the timeline for this chapter, there had already been four 'Green Books' before 1993 and over the period of our study that Book went from its fifth to its seventh edition, entered the digital age and acquired sixteen notes of 'supplementary guidance'. An eighth, ninth and tenth Book appeared a few years after the end of our period in 2018, 2020, and 2022 respectively. Table 6.3 offers a summary and comparison of four editions in or around our period.

The dominant preoccupation of the early Green Books was how to quantify and discount future returns from public investment proposals. The 1991 edition devoted a whole chapter and two rather professorial appendices to the subject, and discounting, which does indeed raise deep philosophical issues, figured prominently in later editions as well. But, as Table 6.3 shows, the Green Book guidance was later broadened to include several other matters.

One was the question of how to appraise proposals for public or private financing of capital projects, in a changing policy climate. As we saw in discussing the growth of PFI in Chapter 4, the restrictive 'Ryrie rules' requiring onerous comparisons with public financing alternatives were scrapped in 1989 and replaced with less rigorous obligations until the political climate once again started to change over PFI schemes in the later 2000s.

A second was the increasing attention paid to environmental and climate-change factors. A supplement devoted to 'natural capital' accounting appeared in 2013, reflecting work by the Department of Environment, Food and Rural Affairs (DEFRA) and criticism from green groups about the way natural capital was valued in investment and policy-making. This criticism led the coalition government to set up an advisory Natural Capital Committee, comprising seven professors, the previous year.[26]

Heavier emphasis also came to be laid on allowing for 'optimism bias'—a recurring feature of project proposals. Earlier Green Books noted the issue in general terms, but after the 2003 edition, a supplement required specific optimism-bias adjustments, reflecting detailed research commissioned by the Treasury from the Mott MacDonald consultancy (2002) on time and cost overruns in fifty major procurement projects over the previous two decades. The study revealed average optimism bias for traditional—that is, non-PFI—procurement of some 17 per cent for time taken, 47 per cent for capital costs and 41 per cent for operating costs.[27]

[26] The issue of the 'greenness' of the Green Book was still in contention at the time of writing. For instance, a 2021 report by Pragmatix (2021: 37) claimed 'the Green Book reinforces incrementalism and inertia' on natural capital matters.
[27] No general update to the Mott MacDonald study had been conducted up to the time of writing, but some departments and agencies produced updates and estimates in particular policy areas, such as nuclear power and transport.

Table 6.3 Four Green Books compared, 1991–2018

Edition	1991	1997	2003	2018
Pages	92	120	118	132
Annexes	8	8	6	6 plus 16 Supplements
Author of preface or foreword	Nick Monck 2nd Permanent Secretary, Public Spending	Norman Glass Director and Chief Micro-Economist	Joe Grice Chief Economist and Director, Public Services	Sir Tom Scholar Permanent Secretary
Notable changes and Selected Highlights	Went beyond basic account of discounted cash flow & net present value analysis to more general principles Main focus on capital projects and physical assets but also applied to uses such as R & D, regulation More on *ex post* evaluation than earlier GBs	Included new annex (D) & appendix on risk analysis of PFI capital projects. First Green Book to mention (briefly) business case and distributional analysis, and said more than earlier GBs about environment issues and other hard-to-value costs and benefits Included a new 30-item checklist	Included a new multi-case framework and approach to option analysis Set out explicit discount for optimism bias (briefly referred to in earlier GBs and bundled into the general discount rate) OGC 'Gateway' procurement approvals linked to GB compliance	A new Chapter (3) set out the 5-case model for analysing business cases and robustness of delivery plans Referred to the Magenta Book (updated in 2007 and 2011) for more guidance on evaluation Drew attention to low-cost 'nudge' methods and the risk of gaming numbers
Discount rate	6 % (real)	6 % (real) 'in most circumstances', said to reflect the cost of capital and time preferences	3.5 % (real), to reflect time preference, and 'unbundling' of optimism bias & other discounts	
Context	Followed 1989 retirement of the 'Ryrie rules' on private finance	Written before 1997 general election but published shortly afterwards	Involved formal consultation for the first time; coincided with a new 'Magenta Book' on policy evaluation	First new GB for 15 years, but supplements had appeared online since the 2003 version

Source: Green Books 1991 to 2018a

Further, from the 2003 Green Book more attention was paid to management and implementation issues, including an options framework and 'five-case model' for appraisal. According to one interviewee that 'five-case model' approach originated in a Treasury satellite body, the former Central Computer and Telecommunications Agency, reflecting CCTA's experience in assessing business cases for IT projects in the 1990s. The model first appeared as a footnote in the 2003 edition of the Green Book, was developed more fully in a Green Book supplement and became a central feature of the 2018 edition. It attracted attention from appraisal bodies across the world. One of our interviewees suggested that pre-2003 Green Books, containing a bewildering multitude of principles, had resembled a fiendishly complicated item of flat-pack furniture without any assembly instructions showing how the pieces fitted together. The importance of the five-case model, according to that interviewee, was that it had finally provided those vital 'assembly' instructions.

Along with reissuing the Green Book went developments in project review processes, notably in a 'gateway' approach, involving multi-stage rather than single-shot reviews of business cases, and later a peer-review element as well. Such changes came in the aftermath of a review of civil procurement by a senior business executive, Sir Peter Gershon, in 1999. That review led to the formation of a centralized unit for 'commercial' activities under Gershon's direction within the Treasury in 2000, the Office of Government Commerce, a body which swallowed up the CCTA and two other arm's-length agencies and brigaded them together with the Treasury's procurement policy and private finance policy teams. It was later absorbed into the Cabinet Office Efficiency and Reform Group (Chapter 5). Along with that organizational restructuring went a new emphasis by the Treasury's guardians of the Green Book—a modest team of one and a half long-serving officials at the time of our study—to socialize their colleagues both in the Treasury and across government into the Book's principles for business case analysis. One interviewee described the work of that team as 'to advocate, educate, advise and police' such analysis, but acknowledged that its work often went against the political and bureaucratic grain and indeed compared it to 'trying to hunt an elephant with a pea-shooter'. The team made extensive efforts to exert leverage and supplement the written guidelines by socialization and training of other officials, and indeed at one point in the mid-2000s the idea of producing a 'little Green Book' was even mooted (presumably to do for rational project evaluation what the Little Red Book had done for Maoist revolutionaries). Predictably enough, no 'Little Green Brook' appeared under that title, but there were efforts to socialize officials into Green Book thinking in two ways. One consisted of training courses (aimed at civil servants in the Treasury or spending departments and other public officials such as parliamentary clerks) through short examinable one- and two-day courses conducted by accredited trainers. The other consisted of workshops aimed at 'winning hearts and minds' and of efforts to draw economists from across government into peer-reviewing major business cases and developing the Green Book.

What does the evidence suggest about how much difference such 'Green-bookery' made to spending control in practice?

What the Green Books said

All four Green Books summarized in Table 6.3 complained (at varying length) about the lack of attention paid to after-the-fact 'lessons-learned' evaluation. For instance, the foreword to the 1997 Green Book said 'There is a natural tendency, once a decision is taken, to move on to the next and let bygones be bygones. To do this, however, is to sacrifice an invaluable source of learning'. Indeed, the Mott MacDonald 'optimism bias' study commissioned in 2002, as mentioned earlier, clearly constituted a key lessons-learned evaluation. But still, the repetition of complaints about weak or absent evaluation after the event in successive editions of the Green Book suggests that the issue did not go away.

What interviewees said

Several interviewees also commented on what they saw as a lack of serious *ex post* evaluation of capital and project spending within government. Several thought institutional memory had declined as a result of poor record keeping in the digital age, together with high turnover and increasing incentives for ambitious high-flying officials to focus exclusively on issues of close interest to ministers at any given moment. On the discipline exerted by the Green Book, only one ex-Treasury interviewee dismissed it outright as a formality to be laid aside whenever the political chips were down, exclaiming: 'No-one pays any attention to the Green Book!' But the tone of many comments, and the examples given, pointed more to a pattern of 'small wins' and gradual change towards more professional financial management than of transformational change in the way politically favoured mega-projects were appraised.

One notable example of that 'small wins' pattern coming from interviews is a contrast between the way the English National Health Service Programme for IT developed in the 2000s, as against what happened under devolved government in Wales. The need for ways of sharing patient records between A & E (emergency room) hospitals and GP surgeries was exacerbated by a new GP contract in 2004, already mentioned, that doubled GPs' pay, leading to a decline in out-of-hours GP services such that many more patients had to use A & E. (emergency rooms) in hospitals instead, The need for effective record-sharing in such circumstances led the English Department for Health to decide that what was needed was a comprehensive, centralized, and uniform country-wide 'single patient record' system. The cost of this ambitious enterprise, strongly backed by spending ministers, spiralled to some £10bn by the time it was scrapped in 2011, later to be described by NAO (2020: 19) as 'largely unsuccessful'. By contrast, in Wales, an initial plan by the Welsh Assembly government to follow a variant of the English patient record model was altered during the appraisal process to produce a different outcome. The plan was scaled down from the English-style centralized single patient record plan in favour of a 'do the minimum at minimum expense' option that enabled effective information sharing between GP surgeries and their local A & E hospitals, using proven 'middleware' rather than untried bespoke state-of-the-art technology. One interviewee said that minimal approach had delivered a functioning system for Wales at a fraction of the £0.5bn funding originally contemplated[28].

What NAO evaluations said

As for evidence from other evaluations, NAO's 2016 report on requests for Ministerial Directions between 1990 and 2015 does not suggest that optimism bias ceased to be an issue for big capital projects in the 2000s. The same picture emerges from NAO's (2014b) report on 'Lessons from Major Rail Infrastructure Programmes', which reviewed five large rail infrastructure programmes in the UK between 1998 and 2014.[29] Those ventures included High Speed 1 (originally known as the Channel Tunnel Rail link) and High Speed 2 phase one (London to Birmingham). Both were classic prestige projects that linked to cherished political narratives (high-tech links with the European continent in the one case, part of a 'growth story' for northern English cities in the other). The key funding decisions for HS1 were made towards the beginning of our period, while HS2 was still at the initial approval stage at the time of writing (House of Commons Transport Committee 2011). Were there clear differences in the way these major projects were handled? Table 6.4, compiled from that NAO report (which itself drew on various earlier NAO reports on HS1 and HS2, such as NAO's (2001b) report on the Channel Tunnel Rail Link over a decade earlier), suggests not. NAO found that in both projects the economic analysis of the case for support was seriously flawed, that the governance arrangements were 'confused' and 'ineffective' in both cases and that choices over how both projects were to be financed were based simply on what funding was available rather than on value-for-money considerations.

---

[28] The final budget available to the Welsh Individual Health Record (IHR) system was £4.7m (Cross 2009).

[29] Similar general conclusions emerged from earlier NAO investigations of evaluation in government spending in 2013 (NAO 2013) and after our period NAO 2021).

Table 6.4 Two mega-rail projects compared: HS1 and HS2

Feature	HS1 (originally Channel Tunnel Rail Link)	HS2 (Phase 1)
Overall timescale	20 years (1987–2007)	15 years planned (2009–2026)
Construction timetable	9 years (1998–2007)	9 years planned (2017–2026)
Scale	109km with 3 new or substantially modified stations	226km with 4 new or substantially modified stations
Cost	£6.2bn (as of 2005)	£21.4bn (as of 2011)
Funding	Initially private (PFI) then public after private financing failed	Initially public, but with declared intention to include some private financing
Shortcomings identified by NAO in economic analysis	Yes (2001 and 2005 reports)	Yes (2013 report)
Confused governance roles and ineffective governance arrangements delaying decision-making identified by NAO	Yes (2001 report)	Yes (2013 report)
Financing choices primarily driven by available funding rather than value for money, according to NAO	Yes (2001 report)	Yes (2013 report)

Source: NAO (2014a and 2014b)

Conclusion

Successive governments over our period made much of the importance of well-managed capital, infrastructure, and investment spending in fostering social and economic development. Issues of how to choose, manage, and finance capital or investment projects figured large, as we have seen, in successive Treasury Green Books, and new administrative machinery developed as well. Putting together such changes with what we learned from interviews, internal Treasury papers and other publications (particularly NAO) reports, there does seem to have been some movement in the direction of rational economic evaluation of capital spending projects over the period covered by this book, in at least three ways.

First, after the 1994 Pergau Dam episode and the parliamentary attention that Direction requests attracted in the same year, spending Ministers and their top civil servants in their role as AOs, could not simply wave away value-for-money issues. The 'subjective' view of Ministers could no longer be considered automatically to trump the Green Book criteria for assessing value for money, even if that is what seems to have happened in practice for some 'pet projects'.

Second, during the most drastic spending squeeze of our period, when plans for capital expenditure were heavily cut by the New Labour government at the end of its term and most (though not all) of those planned cuts were put into effect by the subsequent Conservative-Liberal Democrat coalition after 2010, Green Book principles do seem to have been important to the economists who produced that first cross-government ranking of capital spending projects across departments that we described in the previous chapter.

Third, repeated calls for careful *ex post* evaluation of project spending plans inside Treasury and spending departments seem to have some limited effect. Within the Treasury, the 2002 Mott MacDonald review of fifty projects over two decades to assess optimism bias in capital spending, is a striking example. Further, NAO provided some serious and challenging evaluations, according to several interviewees who thought NAO assessments of project and capital spending had become more hard-hitting over time. Indeed, NAO seems to have played a key part in contesting 'gaming' by the Treasury as well as by the spending departments—including using off-balance sheet PFI funding as a higher-cost means to get round borrowing limits, as we discussed in Chapter 4.

But at the same time, the triumph of cost-benefit analysis and related rational-evaluation techniques seem to have been anything but complete. Even in the unusual political circumstances surrounding the 2010 Spending Review (including a new coalition faced with implementing plans made by its predecessor for big cuts in capital spending and a group of ministers not yet deeply entrenched in their departments), some big spending departments seem to have refused to play by the Treasury's rules, chose not to rank their capital spending proposals on the basis of economic return to investment and simply bid for an aggregate amount of funding. And nothing quite like that intendedly zero-based review appears to have happened again up to the time of writing, while the image of the Treasury's efforts to spread 'Green Book' investment principles still appeared to some of those involved to resemble 'hunting an elephant with a pea-shooter'. More generally, the analysis of Ministerial Directions suggests there were different rules in practice for more everyday proposals put forward by 'small people' and more politically favoured projects pushed hard by powerful ministers and the top civil servants whose careers depended on helping those ministers get what they wanted.

Timeline: Selected Developments over Capital and Related Spending

Pre-1993

- First Treasury 'Green Book' (1973) on appraisal guidance: a terse, internal affair, not published or subject to consultation, applying the 'test discount rate' (first developed for nationalized industry investment proposals in the 1960s) to public services. Followed in 1980 by second Green Book.
- Redefinition of 'public expenditure' (1977) to exclude spending funded from user charges by state-owned enterprises.
- Introduction of the 'Ryrie rules' (1981) for comparing publicly with privately financed funding in project proposals (responding to sale-and-leaseback-type ways of easing short-term budget constraints, particularly by local authorities), later set out in a 1983 Supplementary Note to the Third Green Book).
- End year flexibility (EYF) introduced for 'capital' spending (1982), following complaints about rigid application of annualized cash limits.
- Withdrawal of the Ryrie rules (1989).
- Private Finance Initiative announced and capital charging introduced in the NHS (1992).

1993: Capital spending reported as a separate item in budget documents.

1994: Pergau Dam English High Court case led to changes in practice and reporting of AO requests for Directions (Vignette).

1995: Aggregate Depreciation in capital spending published in Budget Report and Financial Statement.

1997: Sixth Green Book, *Appraisal and Evaluation in Central Government: Treasury Guidance*, written shortly before the 1997 election but published after it.

1997: Adoption of ESA95 national accounts definitions; announcement of 'golden' fiscal rule requiring monitoring of capital spending; first National Asset Register published.

1998: Extension of capital charges from NHS to central government; introduction of capital budgets in central government (splitting DEL into CDEL and RDEL).

1999: Creation of new devolved governments with responsibility for controlling devolved spending, including the capital/current split (and thus potentially affecting the UK's observance of the 'golden rule').

2000: Following the 1999 Gershon review of Civil Procurement in Central Government, the Office of Government Commerce (OGC) was established in the Treasury (bringing together three former executive agencies (Central Computer and Telecommunications Agency (CCTA), Property Advisers to the Civil Estate (PACE) and the Buying Agency (TBA)) together with the Treasury's Procurement Policy Unit and Private Finance Policy Team) and developed a multi-stage 'gateway' process (with peer review added a year later) for assessing large, complicated civil projects at five decision points during their life cycle (OGC's responsibilities excluded MOD and the devolved administrations).

2001: Resource-based Estimates replaced cash Estimates; National Asset Register updated.

2002: Research on fifty major public procurement projects over twenty years (commissioned by Treasury from the Mott MacDonald consulting group) estimated typical optimism bias.

2003: Seventh Green Book, the first to be formally subjected to public consultation, with a supplement requiring optimism bias adjustments based on the Mott MacDonald study.

2004–2005: Internal Treasury Review of the use of the Green Book found improvement in investment appraisal over time, but highlighted evaluation as a continuing problem; imposition of separate control totals for near-cash and non-cash (2005).

2008: Abolition of capital charges following review of resource accounting.

2009: £6bn of capital spending brought forward as stimulus in global financial crisis but plans for fiscal consolidation developed for later cuts in capital spending; establishment of HS2 Ltd as a government-owned company to plan a new high speed rail link.

2009–2010: Following criticisms of insufficient 'greenness' of the Green Book to the Environmental Audit Committee, OGC undertook to develop 'practical guidance' on how to factor in long-term environmental costs and benefits into the VFM assessments required by the Green Book.

2010: Spending Review announced 40 per cent reduction in government capital spending plans (largely from plans inherited from the previous government) and included a ranking of capital project proposals across departments without reference to baselines; OGC moved from Treasury to Cabinet Office Efficiency and Reform Group (ERG); Infrastructure UK established to support major non-PFI infrastructure projects (later merged with Major Projects Authority in 2016 to create the Infrastructure and Projects authority).

2011: Disappearance of OGC and creation of Major Projects Authority (incorporating part of the former OGC) following 2010 Major Projects Review by the ERG. Treasury Select Committee concluded that PFI projects were significantly more expensive to fund over a project's lifetime, with no clear evidence of offsetting savings or benefits.

2012: 'Private Finance 2' announced; publication of 'Accounting for the Value of Nature in the UK' by ONS, with a plan to incorporate natural capital accounting by 2020.

2013: ESA 2010 replaced the earlier European accounting standard ESA 95; supplement to Green Book introduced 'natural capital accounting' for assessing climate and environmental projects; major reversal of the 2010 capital spending cuts in the 2013 budget, bringing forward almost £20bn of extra infrastructure spending in the following Parliament. Review of cross-Whitehall capability to deliver major infrastructure projects announced.

2015: National Infrastructure Commission established to provide government with independent advice and analysis on infrastructure developments.

7

Devolved Administrations and Local Government

Little Moral Hazard but Little True Autonomy

1.8 Responsibility for UK fiscal policy, macroeconomic policy and funding allocation across the United Kingdom remains with the Treasury. As a result, funding from the UK government, as well as that self-financed by the devolved administrations, continues to be determined within this framework. Devolved administration spending falls within a UK-wide system of public expenditure control and budgeting guidance.

(HMT, Statement of Funding Policy, 7th ed. 2015).

[W]ell before devolution in Scotland and Wales brought extra scrutiny into the budgeting process—the team had the acronym 'SWNI' and was known as 'swannee'.

(ex-Treasury interviewee).

Vignette: 'Cash for Ash' in Northern Ireland

The Non-Domestic Renewable Heat Incentive (RHI) was a scheme to encourage businesses to convert their space heating to a system fired by renewable fuel. In 2012, when a scheme was already in place in Great Britain (GB), the devolved administration in Northern Ireland (NI) decided to draw up one of their own. The GB scheme involved 'tiering', in which after a certain number of kilowatt-hours (kWh) of heat generation, the subsidy paid to each generator dropped sharply. The NI scheme largely copied and pasted the GB regulations, but fatally omitted the tiering regulation (CEPA, quoted in McBride 2019: 40).

The scheme was to be run by the UK energy regulator Ofgem, which warned the NI administration that the GB scheme had several flaws that ministers intended to correct. These included perverse incentives to:

- install multiple small boilers rather than one big one;

The Way the Money Goes. Christopher Hood, Maia King, Iain McLean, and Barbara Piotrowska,
Oxford University Press. © Christopher Hood, Maia King, Iain McLean, and Barbara Piotrowska (2023).
DOI: 10.1093/oso/9780198865087.003.0007

- use a boiler to heat and dry wood pellets which were then fed back into it to dry more wood pellets—a perpetual-motion machine at taxpayers' expense;
- supply a house linked to a non-domestic boiler.

The NI administration pressed on regardless of Ofgem's request to wait until these issues had been sorted out (McBride 2019: 54–55).

The killer issue, however, was unique to NI. The NI government's consultants were wrong in their assumption that the subsidy would always be less than the fuel cost. A forthright witness explained:

Well, the equipment we were installing, we used a guy that had been an installer in the UK [sic] and he had worked on the RHI, and even from the first system we put in, you know, the question was, 'What's tier 1?' and 'What's tier 2?'. And we're going, 'What's a tier?'. You know? We weren't aware and, you know, he said, 'When do you fall off?'. And we said, 'No, there is none in Northern Ireland. It's open'. And he was going, 'What? What do you mean it's open? There's no cap?' We're going, 'No. It's just as much as you—'. And suddenly, everyone then suddenly realised, you know, 'I'm paying 4p a kilowatt-hour for fuel here, and I'm getting possibly six at that stage or whatever, so I'm making a third here. And that's it. And I can just use it as much as I want'. So, energy efficiency just went out the window and it was just essentially, 'Use it as much as you can. You can't lose'

(Coghlin 2019. Transcript for 08/2/18, evidence of Neil Elliott).

Installers mentioned the free cash in their advertising:

20 years of free heat. Find out how we can help you get up to 20 years [sic] free heat and payments from the government's RHI 6 scheme... BIOFUEL HEATING SERVICES' (BFH) aim is to provide customers with a replacement heating solution which is both carbon neutral and cost free, to run for up to twenty years after installation. This is possible as the government has introduced an incentive scheme which is greater than the fuel cost–government incentive of 5.9p pkWh, set against Biomass fuel cost of 3.9p pkwh

(Coghlin 2019. Transcript for 08/2/18, advertising flyer read into record during evidence of Brian Hood).

Whistle-blowers started raising concerns as early as 2013, but the scheme was not closed until 2016, after the largest poultry processor in NI had been tipped off that it was about to close (McBride 2019: 363). That processor, Moy Park, was ultimately owned by a Brazilian agrifoods conglomerate (McBride 2019: 288–289). Its suppliers' boilers reduced the cost and improved the quality of the chickens that they supplied to Moy Park, who then changed their contracts to reflect their suppliers' lower input costs. In McBride's (2019) opinion, most of the economic rent generated by the free cash for ash accrued to the international shareholders of Moy Park. Thanks to the tip-off, a last-minute spike of applications from Moy Park suppliers hit the already bust budget ('In absolute confidence. Final push needed on our own farms and contract growers in NI'—Moy Park internal email, 18/01/16. quoted by McBride 2019: 211).

The RHI scandal led to the collapse of devolved government in NI from 2017 until January 2020. The inquiry report (Coghlin 2020) appeared on 13 March 2020—a Friday afternoon when its findings were immediately overshadowed by the growing coronavirus crisis. It contained sharp criticism of numerous politicians, special advisers, and civil servants, but found no corruption. It concluded that RHI was 'a project too far' for the capacity of the NI administration (Coghlin 2020, 56.3.1), which had failed in '[b]asic administration and record-keeping' (56.3.15).

Financially, the disaster was triggered by two factors:

- HM Treasury's offer of time-limited funding up to £25m over four years for a NI scheme. The £25m was the NI population share of the money assigned to the GB scheme. It covered Domestic and Non Domestic Schemes (McBride 2019: 23); and
- NI civil servants' belief that subsidy expenditure would come under uncapped AME (Annually Managed Expenditure) without being aware of the funding cap.

That ministers and civil servants chased £25 million and exposed the NI taxpayer to potential losses of £1.18 billion, according to a BBC estimate (BBC 2016), is an object lesson in being careful how you nudge people.

Readers are already familiar with the DEL/AME distinction. Some special advisers and civil servants treated AME as free money for Northern Ireland. The more flowed to NI under AME, the better. 'I thought this was AME, and we could fill our boots', as a special adviser allegedly told the head of the relevant NI Civil Service division.[1]

HM Treasury had already warned the NI department that support for RHI was not open-ended AME:

[In GB] RHI spending is not being treated as standard AME, where the Exchequer takes on all the risks of overspend. Instead, there is a risk-sharing arrangement whereby should RHI spending in one year exceed the S[pending] R[eview] profile, then DECC would need to repay this in future years.

(J Parker to A. Clydesdale, 15/04/2011. Coghlin 2019 Document WIT-00843)

---

[1] Coghlin 2019, Evidence of Dr Andrew McCormick, Day 111, transcript p. 37. Andrew Crawford, the SPad, has denied using the phrase.

Remarkably, NI civil servants were still assuring their ministers that RHI subsidies were in standard AME in 2015 (McBride 2019: 163). Does the existence of devolved government, therefore, threaten fiscal control?

Fiscal Federalism in the UK

The vignette shows that, although NI has no serious devolved tax powers, it could have posed a threat to the overall control of UK public expenditure. That the threat was not greater is due to three factors. First, NI is so small in relation to the UK (about 3 per cent by population, less by share of GDP or of tax receipts), that even a huge NI overspend would have little impact on the overall UK figure. The RHI overspend estimated at £1.2 billion may be contrasted with UK total managed expenditure of £644 bn in 2018–2019 (HM Treasury 2019, table 6.4). Secondly, AME in Northern Ireland is subject to a 'parity principle' whereby if NI breaks parity with GB the additional cost falls to NI DEL. (For more on parity see FCNI 2021.) Finally, most of the devolved administrations' expenditure is in DEL, with their totals controlled under the Barnett Formula set out periodically in HMT's Statement of Funding Policy (latest HMT 2021). A former devolved finance official has stated that 'the Barnett Formula has only one friend: the Chief Secretary of the day' (personal communication). Hence during the period covered by this book the Treasury mostly kept devolved expenditure on a very tight rein.

The UK's Victorian fiscal constitution was designed for a unitary state. It therefore did not face up to reconciling fiscal autonomy with fiscal responsibility. In 1992, Scotland, Wales, and Northern Ireland had neither fiscal autonomy nor serious fiscal responsibility, though this was just starting to change in Scotland at the end of our period. The Scottish Government set a Scottish Rate of Income Tax for the first time in 2016–2017. Local authorities had no fiscal autonomy. Although there were sanctions against fiscal irresponsibility, no council went bankrupt in our period. There was no threat to the UK government's management of public debt.

Chapter 2 touched on the concept of fiscal federalism in noting the UK's persistently high vertical fiscal gap over our period. Inter-governmental fiscal relations exist in unitary as well as in federal states. The UK is not quite a federal state for two reasons: first, 85 per cent of its people live in England, where there are no autonomous subnational governments; second, politicians in Scotland and NI have had little incentive to act autonomously. In Scotland, the unearmarked transfers from the UK government are enough to pay for locally delivered services. If in fiscal trouble, NI politicians play the security card.

This chapter discusses how much local autonomy there is, or realistically could be, in the UK; and how both VFG and HFE are managed, largely through the Barnett Formula for DEL expenditure and by automatic adjustment for AME expenditure.

Most social protection is in AME, and most health and education is in DEL. The big-ticket items of social protection are state pensions and benefits. They are in AME because they are entitlements. If you have the condition which triggers a payment, and (where relevant) have made the required contributions, then you get the benefit. Government policy establishes the rules of entitlement, but not the amount of spending that flows from those rules. As we noted in Chapter 4, the New Labour governments introduced tax credits extensively as a way of delivering some social protection expenditure to individuals. We also noted how such tax expenditure was recorded in government accounting: until 2014, accounting for tax credits in the National Accounts was split between negative tax for those individuals with a tax liability and spending for those without. This was changed when the requirements of ESA (European System of Accounts) changed in 2014 (Moskalenko and Vassilev 2015). Such issues mattered for the observance of overall fiscal rules, as we saw in Chapter 4 (and see Pope and Waters 2016), but were less important for students of subnational public expenditure, as there is no reason to suppose that distortions introduced by the anomalous treatment of some tax credits fell unevenly across the country.

Tax credits, unemployment and sickness benefits, are automatic stabilizers (Tax Policy Center 2020). If a region suffers a local economic shock, unemployment, and probably sickness, will rise in that region. Therefore it will receive more per head. This is another form of HFE, even though it does not result from deliberate spatial redistribution.

In Northern Ireland, social protection is nominally devolved, but as Northern Ireland has no tax capacity to pay for it and as politicians want to hold rates uniform with the rest of the UK, in practice the UK government has always paid the bill. This practice may have aggravated the behaviour revealed in the vignette.

Health expenditure in England is in DEL. Since the creation of the NHS in 1948 it has never involved locally elected authorities. Rather, the Department of Health does its HFE within a black box that is typically inscrutable even to the Treasury. Health expenditure per head is higher in poorer parts of England, thanks to a resource allocation process started in the 1970s by a medically qualified health minister (David Owen: see further DHSS 1976; Gorsky and Preston 2014). Few details of how it operates its equalization formulae appear to be available. When one of us (IM) was commissioned to review the English regional statistics in the annual HMT publication *Public Expenditure—Statistical Analyses*, we found that the Department of Health reported only twenty numbers: an aggregate total for health expenditure, and a number for expenditure per head, for the benefit of each of the nine standard regions of England, broken down into just two lines (McLean 2003; HM Treasury 2019, Table 9.11).

Health expenditure in Scotland, Wales, and Northern Ireland is the responsibility of the devolved governments there. How much extra they have to spend is essentially a function of how much extra is spent in England. The block grant is delivered by the Barnett mechanism to be described shortly. The devolved authorities have the chance to spend more or less than their 'Barnett equivalent' of health expenditure in England, but they have not varied much. In the annual statistics for the last year of our period, health expenditure per head in each devolved area was higher than in England, but roughly in the same proportion that all public expenditure was higher (HMT 2016, Table A.11). However, health spending per head in Scotland grew more slowly to 2016 than in England (Gallagher 2017).

School education in England was still a local government responsibility at the start of our period but for all practical purposes had ceased to be by the end of it. Like health, it is a devolved responsibility, and the amount available to spend in Scotland, Wales, and Northern Ireland is again determined by Barnett.

Local authorities spend considerably more than they receive in taxes, but the difference is made up by what for most of our period was called Revenue Support Grant, administered by each of the four territorial governments for its local authorities. In this as in many other respects, the UK government doubles as the government of England. Revenue Support Grant and its successors contained an element of HFE, for the same reason as the pooling of Business Rates, namely that poor authorities have a weak Council Tax base but high spending needs. As central governments do not like transfers without strings, HFE is the enemy of local autonomy.

The creation of the NHS in 1948 took health out of local authority hands. Another wave of centralization arose during the Conservative governments headed by Margaret Thatcher (1979–1990). By the natural swing of the political pendulum, the years of Conservative national government were often very good years for Labour in local government elections. A number of Labour-controlled local authorities were captured by members of Militant, a Trotskyist faction who believed that they could help bring about the collapse of capitalism by making impossible promises to spend more than they raised and waiting for the working class to revolt when it saw the results (Crick 2016). The best-known Militant council leaders were Ted Knight in Lambeth (Feldman and McDonnell 2020) and Derek Hatton in Liverpool. The working class did not rise; the district auditor fined Knight and his colleagues for financial impropriety, and Neil Kinnock expelled the Militants from the Labour Party in 1985. Mrs Thatcher liked nothing more than a good enemy, and all remaining financial autonomy for English local authorities effectively ended with the Rates Act 1984. It was not restored in the era of the Poll Tax (Community Charge), which was ending as our period starts (Butler, Adonis and Travers 1994). When Poll Tax was replaced by Council Tax and Business Rates, the pooling and redistribution of the latter drew almost no attention. It increased HFE and diminished local autonomy. (Some modest reforms at the end of our period allowed authorities to retain some of the extra business rates they won by promoting development.) Northern Ireland never endured the Poll Tax, and it retains both domestic and business rates.

As to local authority borrowing, the current regime for England was introduced by the *Local Government Act 2003* c.20. Authorities' borrowing must conform to their financial trade body's *Prudential Code for Capital Finance in Local Authorities* (CIPFA 2017). As part of central government's crackdown on local authority finance in the 1970s and 1980s, authorities were discouraged from issuing bonds, in favour of borrowing at favourable interest rates from the Public Works Loans Board, which is now part of the UK Debt Management Office. Consequently, only a handful of authorities have debt ratings from the commercial rating agencies (Sandford 2020).

Potentially this increases fiscal risk (see OBR 2019, Box 5.2). PWLB borrowings are waved through under the Prudential Code with no Treasury review. Undoubtedly it lowers the cost of borrowing as even a highly credit-worthy LA would suffer a liquidity penalty in the market. However, in aggregate, English local authority capital spending was £24.7 billion at the time of writing (MHLG 2019). This is only about a fifth of UK general government capital expenditure. As most local government debt is held by the PWLB, until it is spent it represents an inter-governmental transfer which nets to zero in the National Accounts.

The Road to Barnett

Scotland, Wales, and Ireland are different. Until 1921, the whole of Ireland was in the UK. It was the poorest and most discontented part of the country. The Liberal government of W. E. Gladstone fell in 1886, when his attempt to give Home Rule (devolution) to Ireland was defeated. The ensuing Unionist government embarked on 'killing Home Rule by kindness' (Redmond 1895). Chancellor George Goschen offered a kindness in his 1888 Budget: to assign some tax revenues in the ratio 80:11:9 to England (with Wales), Scotland, and Ireland. This became known as the Goschen Formula, or Proportion. It was kind to Ireland because Ireland's tax capacity was less than 9 per cent of the UK's.

The Goschen Proportion was very long-lived. Although its direct relevance to Ireland ended with Irish independence in 1921, its relevance to Scotland remained. Scotland's population had fallen below 11/80ths of that of England and Wales by 1921, and continued to fall. But every Secretary of State for Scotland could treat 11/80 as a floor, not a ceiling, for expenditure demands, and could then add special claims for (e.g.) remoteness and bad housing. At times, he would add the sometimes-credible threat that if his demands were refused, the SNP would surge. The Secretary of State during World War II, Tom Johnston, was reputedly a master of this threat (Morrison 1960: 199).

Another long-lived feature of Goschen is that although it purported to be an assignment of tax receipts, it actually functioned as an assignment of expenditure shares. This was probably inevitable. Ireland always was, and Scotland became, a relatively poor part of the UK. Therefore, it had proportionately more need of kindness and proportionately less of a tax base to pay for it. Killing Home Rule by kindness was thus an element of HFE that has existed since 1888.

Although the Government of Ireland Act 1920 described a revenue-based system, the reality (persisting in Northern Ireland to this day) has always been of an expenditure-based system. The 1886 bill and 1920 Act envisaged an Irish Parliament raising its own revenue by levying taxes and spending them on local services, while making an 'Imperial Contribution' to the UK to pay for defence, foreign policy, and debt interest. This was always unrealistic. (Northern) Ireland never had the tax base to pay for even local services. The Imperial Contribution was negative. A revenue-based system requires some fiscal responsibility if there is a credible no-bailout rule. An expenditure-based system encourages fiscal irresponsibility in which the subnational government spends what it thinks it needs (or wants) to and then asks for a transfer payment.

The Goschen Proportion has long been succeeded by the Barnett Formula, which we discuss next. But these structural features, including credible threats of the consequences of violence, may have helped create the RHI fiasco.

Credible threats from Ireland continued into our period. One of our interviewees recalled being 'screamed at' by [the Secretary of State for Northern Ireland] in a meeting about funding for Northern Ireland ... with [the S of S] shouting at [our interviewee] that unless the money was granted there would be a return to the bloodshed of the 1970s and 1980s'.

The Barnett Formula and Public Expenditure Control

Since 1921, UK central governments have worried less about public expenditure in Northern Ireland than in Scotland. The Northern Ireland Joint Exchequer Board was a dignified rather than an efficient part of the fiscal constitution. A Treasury official minuted in 1952:

> If there were a dispute, it would go before the 'Joint Exchequer Board'—a body consisting of an official from Treasury, an official from N. Ireland Ministry of Finance, and an aged Scottish Judge (Lord Alness who lives in Bournemouth). But it is unthinkable that there should be a dispute of this sort
>
> (TNA T 233/1475, as quoted in Mitchell 2009: 78).

Scotland's population is three times larger than Northern Ireland's. Also, Scottish MPs sit on the Government or Opposition front bench, or both; Northern Irish MPs never have. Both Scottish and English MPs knew that public expenditure per head in Scotland was higher than in England. To the former, this showed

Table 7.1 Hypothetical Relative Needs and Relative Expenditure Per Head for the Four Countries of the UK 1977–1978: Services Which Would Have Been Devolved under the Scotland and Wales Acts 1978

	England	Scotland	Wales	N. Ireland
Relative expenditure/head	100	128	100	141
Relative needs/head	100	116	109	131

Source: HM Treasury 1979, paras 2.13 and 6.5

that Scotland's needs were great. To the latter, it showed how much the English subsidized Scotland. Wales gained a separate Welsh Office only in 1964.

The Treasury's *Needs Assessment* of 1979 was run jointly with the Scottish, Welsh, and Northern Ireland Offices, although the Scottish Office refused to sign off on the final numbers. The 'need' calculated in Table 7.1 is the need for services that would have been devolved under the Scotland and Wales Acts 1978 had they proceeded. They are therefore all in DEL (in modern terminology) and exclude benefit expenditure now classed as AME.

Replacing Goschen became urgent when the Scottish National Party won eleven seats and 30 per cent of the Scottish vote in the October 1974 General Election. The Labour governments of 1974–1979 proposed devolved governments in Scotland and Wales. Their first attempt succumbed to a backbench revolt led by MPs from the north-east of England, who complained that their region was poorer than Scotland yet received less public expenditure per head (McLean 2017). The second attempt ended when the proposed assemblies were voted down in referenda (in Scotland there was a narrow majority for devolution, but backbench rebels had imposed a turnout threshold that the result did not meet). Ministers faced an unappealing dilemma: to introduce a needs-based formula for HFE among the four countries of the UK, or to replace Goschen by something still based on population rather than needs, but not frozen into an out-of-date population ratio. The Treasury started out on the former course, but the meagre results were not published until after the change of government in 1979 (HMT 1979).

Meanwhile, what we know as the Barnett Formula was devised in the Treasury (by then-Assistant Secretary David Andren, according to several of our interviewees) as an indirect way of cutting Scotland's 'overspend'. It was first named after Joel (later Lord) Barnett, who was Chief Secretary from 1974 to 1979, by an academic (Heald 1980).

The Barnett Formula is much misunderstood. Here is the Treasury's latest (2021) definition at the time of writing. The bolding is ours:

> 3.6 Under the Barnett formula the Scottish Government, Welsh Government and Northern Ireland Executive receive a **population-based** proportion

of changes in planned UK Government spending on services in England, England and Wales, or Great Britain.

3.7 The Barnett formula therefore determines changes to each devolved administration's funding with reference to changes in **DEL funding** for UK Government departments; it does not determine the total allocation for each devolved administration afresh each time it is applied.

3.8 There are three factors that are multiplied together to determine changes to each devolved administration's block grant under the Barnett formula:
- (A) the change in planned spending by UK Government departments
- (B) the extent to which services delivered by UK Government departments correspond to services delivered by the devolved administrations
- (C) each nation's population as a proportion of England, England and Wales or Great Britain as appropriate....

3.9 Comparability is essentially the extent to which services delivered by UK Government departments correspond to services delivered by the devolved administrations.

3.10 Comparability therefore ranges from 0 per cent (where services are delivered by the UK Government) up to 100 per cent (where services are delivered by the devolved administration) (HMT 2021; our emphases).

The most common misunderstandings of Barnett may be read off the bolded phrases above.

Based on population, not needs per head. There have been many calls for a needs-based formula, which would be a version of HFE. The Treasury made one calculation of it (HMT 1979) but did not proceed. Among many other commentators, a Lords Select Committee on the Barnett Formula, convened at the request of Lord Barnett himself, concluded

> Although the annual increment in funds is made on the basis of recent population figures, the baseline—accumulated over the last thirty years—does not reflect today's population in the devolved administrations. The Barnett Formula also takes no account of the relative needs of any of the devolved administrations.
>
> A new system which allocates resources to the devolved administrations based on an explicit assessment of their relative needs should be introduced. Those devolved administrations which have greater needs should receive more funding, per head of population, than those with lesser needs (House of Lords 2009).

As the Select Committee observed, the population basis is distorted in two ways that take Barnett allocations further away from relative needs, and hence from HFE. These are (1) that population relativities are lagged; and (2) that the resulting bias is then baked into the baseline. The bias is baked in because an over-generous population ratio increases grant in year 1, and this then becomes the baseline for increase in grant in year 2. For the two territories with relatively declining populations—Scotland and Wales—these distortions cumulate to a double advantage.

Driven by changes in spending in England, not on absolute spending in England. The idea behind this is that Scotland began with what Treasury officials perceived as unfairly high public expenditure per head. The formula was therefore designed to converge towards equal public spending per caput (EPC) in all four territories until it could be succeeded by the needs formula. However:

1) there has been very little convergence in practice;
2) convergence to EPC was the wrong target because needs in the three territories are known to be higher than in England.

The Treasury intended for the formula to run for a short time until the 'overspend' had been corrected, and then to move to a needs-based formula. Lord Barnett said in 2009: 'I thought it might last a year or two before a government would decide to change it. It never occurred to me for one moment that it would last this long'.(House of Lords 2009, evidence of Lord Barnett, 28 January).

Based on DEL not AME. Recall that DEL covers expenditure on programmes; AME, essentially, expenditure on entitlements. Therefore aggregate numbers on spending per head in the four countries represent not only the working out of Barnett but also the spatial distribution of AME expenditure. As social protection expenditure is financed out of general taxation and mostly goes to the relatively poor, this element of AME is also an element of HFE.

Amid all these things which Barnett is not, it certainly is one thing: a highly efficient means of exercising central control of public expenditure. Indeed, Lord Barnett often stated that that was one of its attractions. Nothing in Barnett restricts the amount that the devolved administrations spend from their block grants on any one DEL service. They are free to spend more or less per head than the UK government does in England, and some differences have arisen (Table 7.2)

Table 7.2 gives data for 2014–2015, the last financial year fully within our period. It shows that all three devolved authorities spent more per head than in England on 'general public services', agriculture, and 'enterprise and economic development'. The first is probably a scale effect: smaller governments are more expensive per head. The others plausibly reflect differences in their local economies. They spent below average on education, science, and technology.

So the devolved administrations diverged from England on individual spending priorities. But they could not change the overall envelope. And they had (by international standards) very limited borrowing powers. Barnett also curbed the bilateral negotiations between Treasury ministers and the devolved administrations, which had carried a risk of pushing overall public spending up beyond Treasury ministers' plans.

Table 7.2 UK identifiable expenditure on services by function, country, and region, per head indexed, 2014–2015 (UK = 100 in all columns)

	England	Scotland	Wales	NI
General public services	83	192	154	229
Public order and safety	96	115	100	163
Enterprise and economic development	77	224	215	230
Science and technology	101	115	93	48
Employment policies	94	113	117	224
Agriculture, fisheries and forestry	74	219	180	392
Transport	95	156	98	85
Environment protection	94	149	126	83
Housing and community amenities	83	201	123	271
Health	99	105	101	103
Recreation, culture and religion	86	183	137	206
Education	99	107	97	112
Social protection	98	106	115	119
Total Expenditure on Services	97	115	110	123

Source: HM Treasury (2019): Country and Regional Analysis

Barnett was devised in time for the Scotland and Wales Acts 1978, which would have created devolved assemblies in Scotland and Wales if the public had voted for them. After the failure of the ratification referenda, the threat of Scottish and Welsh nationalism seemed in abeyance, and the priorities of the UK government lay elsewhere. So the proposed needs assessment was laid aside. In retrospect, a time when nationalism was in abeyance would have been a good time for a UK government to press ahead. Rather, it focused on making the Barnett process as automatic as possible. In the 1980s, territorial ministers still tried to make special-interest claims for Barnett-busting goodies, and one Conservative Secretary of State for Scotland stressed how good Barnett was for Scotland (Lang 2002; see also Lord Lang's witness examination of Iain McLean in House of Lords 2009). As with Ireland a century earlier, a party with limited support in Scotland resorted to killing Home Rule with kindness.

This changed in 1997. The new Labour government created the Scottish and Welsh parliaments, which held their first elections in 1999. A separate process culminating in the Belfast ('Good Friday') Agreement of 1998 restored devolved government in Northern Ireland. Since then, the Scottish and Welsh parliaments have become entrenched. The history of the Northern Ireland Assembly has been patchier, with long periods of suspension. But the Barnett arrangements were completely unchanged. Our witnesses suggest that killing Home Rule with kindness became redundant in Scotland, which now had Home Rule, but continued in Northern Ireland because of the threat of paramilitary violence there even after the Good Friday Agreement.

Most of the functions of the former Scottish and Welsh Offices were now run by the respective administrations, which by the end of our period were called the Scottish Government, Welsh Government, and NI Executive. One consequence was that the block grant must now cover, for each country, the costs of two administrations. The cost of running the UK civil service did not change. Civil servants working in Scotland and Wales (but not NI) remained members of a unified UK service. But in Scotland, the block grant now had to finance the running costs of the Scottish Parliament, and the new Scotland Office of the UK government, which took over the non-devolved responsibilities of the old Scottish Office. As well as the continuing post of Secretary of State for Scotland, the grant had to fund the new post of Advocate-General for Scotland, who is the UK government's law officer in Scotland. The Lord Advocate is the Scottish government's law officer. Likewise, there are Wales and Northern Ireland Offices of the UK government. There are no separate law officers for Wales as England & Wales is a single legal jurisdiction. Since 2010, the Northern Ireland Executive has had its own Attorney-General, but there is no separate post of UK Advocate-General for NI.

In Wales, which does badly out of Barnett, politicians were rather slow to act. But in 2008, the Welsh Government created a commission (Holtham 2010) to examine the funding of the Welsh parliament and to consider the devolution of further fiscal powers. Its report and working papers demonstrated that if Wales had been a region of England and English departments had applied their HFE formulae to it, public spending per head in Wales in the study period would have been higher. Since then the Welsh government and political parties have pressed for a needs assessment. The areas that would benefit from such a switch from current formulae are Wales, and the eight standard regions of England outside London. But without allies in London, Scotland, or Northern Ireland—the three 'gaining' regions—they are unlikely to prevail. The anomaly that public expenditure per head in Wales has always been lower than in richer Scotland continues. However, in a Westminster Hall Commons debate in 2015, just at the end of our study period, the UK Government agreed to introducing a minimum funding settlement, regardless of Barnett numbers, for Wales (HC Deb 10 Nov 2015, c.61-2). The Welsh floor has been in place since the fiscal year after the end of our study period.

Calman: the First Attempt to Match Marginal Taxing with Marginal Spending

Although the creation of the three devolved assemblies left the Barnett operation unchanged, change began with the SNP (Scottish National Party) victory in the Scottish Parliament election of 2007. From then until the time of writing, the SNP has controlled the Scottish Government, alone or with the Green Party. As in the era of the dominance of the Irish Party (1885 to 1918), one might have expected some more killing of Home Rule with kindness.

However, the situation was different. The kindness had been flowing to Scotland ever since its population ratio dipped below 11/80, which had happened by 1921. In that year's Census, Scotland had 10.3 eightieths of the population of England and Wales. The ratio continued to decline with slower relative population growth in Scotland. In the 1971 Census, the last to be held in the shadow of the Goschen Proportion, the figure was 8.6 eightieths (Authors' calculation from Census 1921 and 1971, E&W, and Scotland). Although massive Barnett block grants accrued to the three territories when the New Labour government turned on the taps after 2000 (see Chapters 1 and 4), the Treasury, headed by a Scotsman, Gordon Brown, refused to go above Barnett. And, as the policy of the SNP was Scottish independence, it could not reasonably complain. In an independent Scotland, there would be no fiscal transfers to or from the rest of the current UK.

Brown's modus operandi was often through independent reviews, with carefully chosen chairs. His vehicle for changing fiscal federalism in Scotland was the Calman Commission, which sat from 2008–2009. It was created by the UK government and the Scottish Parliament. In the latter, the three unionist parties (Labour, Conservative, and Liberal Democrat) voted to establish the commission against the wishes of the minority SNP government. One of us (IM) was a member of the Commission's Independent Expert Group of academic advisers. The source for this section is personal recollections and contemporaneous notes.

The Commission's terms of reference were:

> To review the provisions of the Scotland Act 1998 in the light of experience and to recommend any changes to the present constitutional arrangements that would enable the Scottish Parliament to serve the people of Scotland better, **improve the financial accountability of the Scottish Parliament** and continue to secure the position of Scotland within the United Kingdom
>
> (House of Commons Library 2010; our emphasis).

UK ministers and the Treasury knew that, while Barnett flowed, there was little pressure on the Scottish government to spend funds efficiently, and no accountability to the Scottish taxpayer for them. Although 'cash for ash' in Northern Ireland was still in the future, Treasury ministers knew that overspending without facing the voters' wrath was always possible.

In an ideal model of fiscal federalism, marginal spending should match marginal taxing. In other words, when contemplating any change in policy, the subnational government should be responsible for raising a pound in tax to cover every extra pound spent, or conversely for cutting a pound of spending to match every pound reduction in tax take. Marginal responsibility of this sort is compatible with a VFG (vertical fiscal gap) if the arrangements are carefully designed, as a number of federal regimes including Canada and Australia do.

The Independent Expert Group, which was the engine room of Calman, consulted both the leading Canadian experts on fiscal federalism (François Vaillancourt and Robin Boadway), and the chair of the Commonwealth Grants Commission of Australia. The model it recommended was more Canadian than Australian. An Australian model would have featured robust equalization conducted by a UK equivalent of the Commonwealth Grants Commission. The Canadian model offered focused rather on what Canadians call 'transferring tax points'. A proportion of income tax in Scotland was to be transferred from the UK to the Scottish government, and the Scottish government would be required to set a rate. (It already had the power to vary income tax rates slightly but had never used it). Income tax would still be levied and collected by HM Revenue and Customs, acting as agent for the Scottish government in respect of the Scottish rate. Calman also proposed the transfer of some appropriate small taxes on things that can't move, such as landfill dumps and airports.

After the change of government in 2010, most of Calman's recommendations were enacted in the Scotland Act 2012. The first tax year in which Scotland had the power to set a Scottish rate of income tax was 2014–2015, at the very end of our study period, and the first rate was set for tax year 2016–2017. It is therefore too early to say whether Scotland's fiscal freedom put UK public expenditure management at risk, but every reason to predict that it would not. The SNP government of Scotland, paradoxically but realistically, wanted to have its cake (what it called 'full fiscal autonomy') while continuing to eat Barnett transfers. Both the outgoing and incoming UK governments promised that these would continue. Scottish independence was once again a threat, so killing it with kindness, or at least Barnett, had returned to the UK agenda.

Another Dog That Didn't Bark

We expected a number of our interviewees to mention subnational finance as one of the issues in control of UK public expenditure. In fact, hardly any did. We checked by searching the entire corpus of interview notes for the word 'Barnett', which was used by only six of our interviewees.

The main moral hazard of fiscal federalism is that of a subnational government blowing out its expenditure without facing the consequences (McLean 2015). That was the matter addressed by Alexander Hamilton's Report on Public Credit (Hamilton 1790) at the time when the USA was created as a new state. The issue has never arisen in the UK since the Union of Scotland and England in 1707 (McLean and McMillan 2005).

A different sort of moral hazard arises when central government decides for policy reasons to bail out a subnational government that would otherwise be unsustainable. Typically, the policy reason is a threat to the Union of the United Kingdom. This has been the case for (now Northern) Ireland since 1800. One consequence is shown in the vignette at the outset of this chapter. It has been at a risk for Scotland at times when Scotland posed a credible threat to the unity of the UK. That was the case from 1707 until the final defeat of Bonnie Prince Charlie in 1746, and on and off since the SNP's first major electoral success in 1967. In 1707 one of the sweeteners was to reinstate the wealth that Scotland had lost through the failure of its colony in Darien (Panama) (McLean and McMillan 2005: 13–60). Would it be too cynical to see the continuation of the Barnett Formula since the Scotland Act 2012 as a modern Darien compensation?

However, the scale of any resulting overspending, in any of the three territories outside England, is small from a central perspective. As noted, they comprise only 15 per cent of the UK population between them. They control their own local authority spending within the Barnett envelope. As for English local government, during our period it became more and more a delivery agent for central government, with very limited autonomy in either taxing or spending (as discussed in Chapter 2).

One of our Treasury interviewees recalled that in late 2008, when a potential crisis arose from local authority deposits held in failed Icelandic banks,

> We had decided to put LG spending responsibility together with responsibility for devolved government spending (Scotland, Wales, N.I.). At that time DCLG had been collapsing a number of individual specific grants into one non-ring-fenced pool, which had involved a cross-central-government operation led by [a senior civil servant] to try to establish central priorities for LG spending)
>
> (HMT official).

It made sense for English local government expenditure to be overseen by the Treasury SWaNI ('Swannee') team. But like SWaNI, English local expenditure posed no threat to public expenditure control. As most local government loans are issued by the Public Works Loan Board, the relevant assets and liabilities sum to zero in the UK's national accounts, at least initially. Subnational finance was indeed a dog that didn't bark in our period (OBR 2017, para 6.133).

Innovation through Experiment?

A final question to ask is whether the devolved administrations have functioned as 'laboratories of democracy' in finding ways to do public finance differently, in ways

Table 7.3 Financial innovations in the UK's Devolved Administrations

Year	Territory	Innovation	What it did	Copied in rest of GB/UK?
2011	Wales	Single-Use Carrier Bags Charge Regulations	Clue is in the name. Proceeds to environmental charities	Yes
2012	NI	Devolution of long-haul Air Passenger Duty	Allowed NI to set zero rate for direct long-haul flights. Currently, there are none, but Barnett grant to NI is adjusted downwards	No
2015	Scotland	Land & Buildings Transaction Tax	Replaced Stamp Duty Land Tax (SDLT) in Scotland. Progressive, rather than 'slab'	Yes. SDLT made progressive
2015	NI	Devolution of power over Corporation Tax rate	Enacted but not commenced; now seems unlikely to happen	No
2017	Scotland	Air Departure Tax Act	Enacted but not implemented. Reduction of rates now unlikely to happen	No
2018	Scotland	Minimum unit pricing for alcohol	50p/unit. Not collected as a tax, except indirectly through corporation tax on any increased profits	No

which might be copied by their peers. On the spending side, we found no evidence of this, but on the tax side, there have been some innovations (Table 7.3).

Two of these innovations—plastic bags in Wales and minimum unit alcohol pricing in Scotland—are 'sin taxes' designed to reduce undesired activity rather than to raise revenue. The plastic bag levy raises trivial money, but helped to drive down single-use plastic bags throughout the UK. Minimum unit pricing is claimed to have led to a 'modest' reduction in alcohol consumption in Scotland (Iacobucci 2023). The most successful innovation has been Land & Buildings Transaction Tax in Scotland, which has been 'retrofitted' in the rest of the UK.

The narrow focus of our analysis excludes some other successful innovations that are not tax-related, such as the ban on smoking in public places, introduced in Scotland in 2006 and copied in all three other jurisdictions within a year. In the longer term, the biggest fiscal success of devolution may turn out to be the creation of a separate Crown Estate in Scotland under the Scotland Act 2016, following a recommendation of the Smith Commission in 2014. Revenue from the Crown

Estate Scotland goes to the Scottish Government rather than the UK. This bore fruit with a successful auction of offshore wind generation sites in 2022, raising a reported £700 million.

Conclusion

The creation of elected parliaments in Scotland, Wales, and Northern Ireland was the biggest constitutional change of our study period. Each of them was responsible for the bulk of programme spending, but to begin with had almost no taxing powers. This made the UK more of an outlier than it already was, and it risked conferring power without responsibility on the devolved administrations.

Fiscally, however, almost nothing changed. The devolved administrations continued to receive their DEL block grant through the Barnett Formula. AME expenditure was governed by the level of entitlements in each of the four territories of the UK. There were two main subnational threats to fiscal stability in our period—the loss of local authority deposits in the Icelandic bank collapse and RHI in Northern Ireland—but neither came close to toppling HM Treasury's regime of public spending control.

The academic and professional literature on fiscal federalism insists that ideally responsibility for marginal spending should lie in the same place as responsibility for marginal taxing, to avoid the obvious hazards of politicians spending money they do not have to raise. This principle is very gradually making its way into UK subnational government finance, but it had had almost no practical consequences by the end of our period.

Timeline of Fiscal Events Relevant to the Regions and Nations of the UK

Dates relating to local government in England (rather than Scotland, Wales, or Northern Ireland) starred.

1707: Acts and Treaty of Union united England, Scotland, and Wales as Great Britain.

1800: Act of Union united Great Britain and Ireland into United Kingdom.

1886: Government of Ireland Bill proposed that devolved Irish Parliament raise enough tax to fund its own expenditure and make an Imperial Contribution to the Exchequer to fund services provided by UK. This formula was repeated in the Government of Ireland Acts 1914 and 1920, and was the formal legal position in Northern Ireland until repealed in 1999.

1888: Chancellor George (Viscount) Goschen introduced his 'formula' or proportion'. Some tax receipts to be divided in the proportion 80:11:9 to England (with Wales), Scotland, and Ireland. Although enacted as an assignment of tax, it came to govern expenditure, and continued to apply (as convention, not statute) to Scotland after 1921.

1921: Anglo-Irish treaty. Irish Free State (now Republic of Ireland) left UK; Northern Ireland remained.

*1972. Local Government Act c.70 created metropolitan councils in England and expanded all councils' financial powers, including the power to spend the product of a penny rate on purposes not otherwise authorized by statute.

1977. HM Treasury introduced a formula for funding Scotland in succession to the Goschen proportion. The formula was designed to end bilateral negotiations between HMT and territorial departments, and to cut what HMT saw as relative overspending in Scotland. By 1980, the formula had been extended to cover Wales and Northern Ireland.

1979. HM Treasury Needs Assessment Report showed that on services that would have been devolved to Scotland and Wales under abortive 1978 Acts, Scotland received more than its assessed needs per head and Wales received less.

1980. HM Treasury territorial funding policy first named (in an academic paper) 'Barnett Formula' in honour of Joel Barnett, Chief Secretary 1974–1979.

*1984–1988. Various Acts restricted the financial autonomy of local authorities in England and Wales, including the Rates Act 1984 c.33; Local Government Acts 1985 c.51; 1986 c.10; 1988 c.9.

*1988. Local Government Finance Act c.41: introduced Poll Tax ('Community Charge').

*1992. Local Government Finance Act c.14. Introduced Council Tax to replace Poll Tax. Business Rates continued to be collected locally but at a uniform national rate, with the proceeds pooled and redistributed. Northern Ireland continued to levy domestic rates.

1997. Incoming government announced plans to introduce a Scottish Parliament and a Welsh Assembly.

1998. UK-Irish ('Good Friday') Agreement provided for restored Northern Irish Assembly.

1999. The three devolved assemblies held their first elections. Their expenditure was mostly classed as DEL (Departmental Expenditure Limits) and governed by the Barnett Formula. AME (Annually Managed Expenditure) in Scotland and Wales was mostly delivered by the UK Government. In Northern Ireland rates and entitlements were kept in lockstep with those in GB, and money transferred to pay for them.

2006. Government of Wales Act c.32 separated executive and legislature in Wales.

2007. Scottish National Party (SNP) took control of the Scottish Parliament and campaigned for independence but in the meantime was content with the Barnett Formula.

2008. Calman Commission (Scotland) appointed by UK Government and Scottish Parliament. Reported 2009, recommending an increase in Scotland's fiscal capacity by transferring 10p in the pound of income tax, plus some small taxes, to Scottish Government control. Most of its recommendations were accepted by the incoming government in 2010.

2008. Holtham Commission appointed by Welsh Government. It reported in 2010. It recommended switching Wales' block grant from the Barnett Formula to a needs-based replacement, and showed that if Wales had been a region of England governed by the within-England formulae used by English departments, it would have received a larger block grant per head. Report adopted unanimously by Welsh Assembly. Incoming UK Government announced a further review (the Silk Commission).

2012 Scotland Act c.11. Implemented many Calman recommendations. Gave the Scottish Parliament the power to set a Scottish rate of income tax to be administered by HM Revenue & Customs (HMRC) for Scottish taxpayers. Also fully devolved the tax power on land transactions and on landfill. Scottish rate of income tax first set in tax year 2016–2017; first varied from RUK (rest of the UK) in 2017–2018.

2012. Silk Commission proposed enhanced financial powers for Welsh Assembly.

2012. Renewable Heat Incentive (RHI) for non-domestic boilers introduced in Northern Ireland.

2013. First warnings from NI business people that the RHI payment per unit exceeded the price of fuel.

2014. Wales Act c.29. Gave the Welsh Assembly (now Senedd) the same tax powers as the Scottish Parliament. No change to Barnett arrangements.

2014. Referendum in Scotland: 'Should Scotland be an independent country?' *Yes* 44.7 per cent; *No* 55.3 per cent.

2014. Smith Commission recommended giving near-complete control of Income Tax in Scotland to the Scottish Parliament; assigning a proportion of VAT receipts in Scotland to it; increasing the Scottish Government's previously trivial borrowing powers; and handing control of the Crown Estate in Scotland to the Scottish Parliament. The residual Barnett grant to be calculated by a complicated and contested 'no detriment' principle, designed to ensure that neither the Scottish nor UK governments lost financially from the act of transferring a power.

2016. Scotland Act c.11. Enacted Smith recommendations on transferring tax powers. The 'fiscal framework', designed to implement 'no detriment', remained non-statutory. VAT assignment still not transferred at the time of writing.

2016. RHI closed.

2020. Coghlin Report on RHI published.

8

Letting Sleeping Dogs Lie

Administration Costs and the Tenacity of Input Controls

Vignette: Abolition, Earned Autonomy, Radical Makeover, or Creative Reclassification? Reviewing Administration Cost Controls in the Early 2000s

Administration cost (AC) controls—limits on a sub-category of controlled departmental spending (DEL) that was designated as 'administrative' expenditure and which could only be exceeded with the agreement of the Treasury—were repeatedly reviewed after 1997. In their 2001 general election campaign, the opposition Conservatives pledged to cut central government ACs by nearly £2bn by 2003–2004 and incumbent Labour ministers and their SpAds were uneasy about the political optics of a sharp rise in reported ACs at that time (shown in Figure 8.1). Against that background, the Treasury ran an internal review of AC controls alongside Labour's third spending review in 2002, which ended in a classificatory fudge in the summer of that year.

Treasury ministers rejected options such as scrapping AC controls altogether (an option that had been floated several times before, for instance in the 1998 and 2000 spending reviews) and came out against an 'earned autonomy' approach that would retain central AC approvals only for those departments whose management the Treasury saw as problematic. At the same time the Treasury in effect admitted that it had mis-classified ACs in numerous instances in the past. It had therefore committed itself after the 2002 Spending Review to embark on a process of difficult case-by-case bargaining with departments over how much of their spending was to be classified as 'administration' as against 'front-line service delivery'. Those terms were politically loaded but not clearly defined—and not mutually exclusive either, in that 'administration' can (and arguably should) be a necessary condition for effective front-line service delivery rather than some sort of displacement activity getting in the way of such delivery. Nor did the possibility that AC spending might conceivably be too low in some cases rather than too high ever seem to figure seriously in political debate.[1] Rather, the political presumption throughout seems

---

[1] The 2002 GEP review did aim to explore 'whether over time we could move to a control regime for Departmental expenditure on administration based ... more on what is achieved for the money (outputs), rather than inputs' but nothing much seems to have emerged on that issue at that time.

The Way the Money Goes. Christopher Hood, Maia King, Iain McLean, and Barbara Piotrowska, Oxford University Press. © Christopher Hood, Maia King, Iain McLean, and Barbara Piotrowska (2023). DOI: 10.1093/oso/9780198865087.003.0008

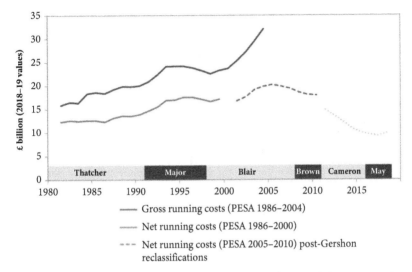

Figure 8.1 Reported running/administration costs of UK civil departments in constant prices 1981–2018

Source: Updated from Hood and Dixon (2015)

to have been that ACs were too high, in absolute terms and particularly relative to front-line delivery, and that governments needed to exhibit conspicuous drive and determination in bearing down on them.

In the aftermath of the 2002 AC review, a GEP paper on 'Administration Costs: Where Do We Go From Here?' began: 'It has been acknowledged for some time that the administration costs regime is flawed. Repeated reviews have not been able to find a clear solution, and so the approach has been to let sleeping dogs lie'.

The paper argued that AC controls were motivated by two different worldviews. One was described as a 'political' or 'populist' worldview, 'which divides public sector workers into "pointless pen-pushers" and a much smaller group of jobs ... admitted to be worthwhile'. To count as 'worthwhile' from this viewpoint, public sector employees needed to have fairly self-explanatory job titles (such as 'prison officer') making it clear what they did, and what they did needed to seem 'reasonably obviously of value to the person in the street'. The aim of AC controls from this viewpoint, was to restrain spending on public sector jobs that did not meet those criteria.

But there was another worldview in play in AC controls, the paper argued: a so-called 'Treasury' view that activities conducted closer to the centre of departments tended to have privileged access to staffing and other resources because units of that kind often had budgets that were very small compared to those of the big service delivery organizations attached to departments, and because 'Departmental management naturally tends to give disproportionate weight to the funding needs of those in the same building/organisation as them'.[2] The aim of AC controls, from what was dubbed the 'Treasury' worldview, was to restrain that tendency by squeezing the central units in departments and thereby limiting what might otherwise be a tendency to top-slice departmental budgets for those high-level central activities at the expense of less glamorous units further down the bureaucratic food chain.

The paper argued that the then existing AC control regime could at best only partly serve either worldview, since it only (or mostly) applied to central government departments at that time and not to other prominent parts of the public sector such as local government or the NHS. Many of the public sector jobs that might be seen as 'useless' from the 'political' or 'populist' viewpoint were outside central government, while the 'Treasury' concern to check possibly self-indulgent spending by privileged HQs and their satellites could equally well be applied 'outside central government to Chief Constables, RHAs [Regional Health Authorities] and so on'.

But there was a deeper and more subtle flaw in the AC control regime, the paper claimed. There was enough overlap between the two worldviews to create a plausible illusion of a workable control system (for example 'both would say that teachers are good, DFES [Department for Education and Skills] officials are not so good and by any reasonable definition, teachers are a "front-line service"'). But several politically important Whitehall departments such as the Foreign and Commonwealth Office (FCO) or the then Department of Trade and Industry (DTI) did not readily fit either of the two worldviews, because those departments were fairly small and did not fund large, separate delivery organizations (such that most of their staff costs counted as 'administration' at that time). The paper argued that it was hardly plausible to see the whole of the FCO as a privileged centre spending its money on worthless 'administration' ('enjoyable though this is...'). But the 'Treasury' justification for AC controls did not really fit such cases either, because departments of that type did not have a privileged centre skimming off funds from service providers down the line. Indeed, in such cases it was often not easy to see what exactly the 'centre' was, as distinct from the 'delivery' operations.

If the Treasury could not credibly count most of the work of such departments as 'administration', the paper argued, nor could it go to the other extreme of treating most of their work as 'front-line service delivery', because to do so would mean that 'the *political* objectives of the [AC] regime are not met' (our emphasis). The fundamental reason for the difficulty, the paper concluded, was that 'there is a third category of activity in government which could not reasonably be described as

---

[2] A view similar to that expounded in several theories of bureaucratic behaviour such as Downs (1967); Niskanen (1971); Dunleavy (1991) and also to Donald Black's (1976) 'relational distance' theory of law enforcement in which stringency is assumed to vary inversely with social distance between enforcer and enforce.

either "administration" or "front-line service delivery" —something like "policy" for example. Most of the Treasury probably falls into that category..."[3]

Faced with such difficulties and the fact that Treasury ministers had already rejected both selective application of AC controls and scrapping such controls altogether, the paper in classic civil service style identified three main options. One was simply to abandon efforts to distinguish 'administration' from 'service delivery' or other activities claimed to be non-administrative in some sense, and return to an older, simpler, Thatcher-era conception of ACs as being all the costs of running central government for whatever it did. A second was a radical redesign of the system to focus on a much narrower pared-down conception of ACs as a few key generic back-office support functions such as IT, HR, and finance, in a scheme that might come closer to a clear distinction between 'overheads' and 'service' delivery and ideally should be applied across the whole public sector rather than just to central government departments. A third was to work with the system as it was and try to tweak it by a creative change in classification, to change the boundary between what counted as 'administration' as against 'front-line service delivery'.

The paper argued that neither the first nor the second option was politically workable at that time. The first option, of going back to a mid-1980s definition of ACs as all the costs of running central government, would fit neither the 'populist' nor the 'Treasury' objectives and it seemed highly unlikely that Treasury ministers (let alone spending departments) would agree to such a change. The second option would be reasonably clear, defensible, and enforceable, but it was said to be politically infeasible except perhaps in the distant future: '...even if Ministers would be willing to agree to it in the long term, it is hard to see them agreeing to it now' (because of the political capital the Labour government had only just invested in securing a 'flat real' settlement for ACs in the 2002 Spending Review to signal how resolutely it was bearing down on bureaucratic waste). 'The accusation of fiddling the figures would be too easy [*for the government's political opponents*] to make, even if the result of this switch was a net increase in the size of ACs'.

That left the third option, of coming up with a new or revised definition of where the boundary lay between 'administration' and 'front-line service delivery' to give the Treasury a new basis for bargaining with politically powerful departments such as FCO over AC controls. The paper argued, 'Whether we like it or not, our arguments with FCO and the Home Office will become arguments about the definition of "front-line". We are therefore better off trying to come up with our own definition first'. Given that background, the paper argued, 'The [AC] system will only be acceptable if we think of ... [it] as essentially covering all the costs of central government, with a few exceptions for politically sellable groups

---

[3] Uncertainty about what should be in and out of ACs also led to repeated requests from NAO for a firmer definition of such costs to help their auditors check outturns against AC limits.

[*sic*], rather than as actually a control on "administration". And as a definition of 'front-line service delivery' that would meet both the 'political' objective and the 'Treasury' one for AC controls, it proposed *'interacting directly with and providing benefit to individual members of the public as one's daily work'*. Conveniently, it argued, the Home Office's border and immigration staff, and FCO consular staff, would meet that test, but FCO's diplomats would not, because their daily work was not spent interacting with individual members of the public. Nor would DTI's various agencies, the paper suggested, because they dealt with firms rather than with individuals. Prison officers might perhaps be marginal but could be argued to meet the test, on the grounds that prisoners counted as members of the public.

That exercise in creative reclassification provided the basis for a politically viable fix at that particular juncture of a long-running story. More broadly, the story shows not only why input controls over ACs are problematic but also why such controls can be surprisingly hard to reform or remove in favour of more output- or outcome-based controls (in which the emphasis goes on the 'public value' results to be achieved in service delivery from whatever resources are available rather than focusing on the particular mix of bureaucratic inputs used to produce those results).

Accordingly, this chapter highlights the contrast between the survival (with numerous classificatory modifications of course) of the AC input control regime over the whole period covered by this book, as against a more variable or volatile picture for output-focused controls. Input controls attracted far less attention than output controls in the public administration and public finance literature over our period. But input-based controls, of which ACs are only one type, not only survived but in some cases grew over that time. The additions took the form both of new ceilings for spending on particular types of inputs but also floors for inputs going into politically favoured 'protected' spending domains.

Unglamorous but Tenacious: Input Controls over Administration Costs

AC (or 'running cost') controls—in the sense of various centrally set limits, reporting and approval systems covering input costs of government activity—have a long history in the UK, although along with other Treasury spending controls they were abandoned in both twentieth-century world wars. In their modern form AC controls date from 1986, and Colin Thain (2010: 47) describes them as the 'most significant by-product' of the Thatcher government's Financial Management Initiative of the early 1980s. Those controls prevented managers in spending departments from switching expenditure between running costs and programme costs, but at the same time allowed those managers to switch between separate items of running costs, some of which had previously been channelled through a set of different common service providers in government (including costs such as property services, IT services, and stationery).

Some of those older common service arrangements reflected a view, going back to the 'economical reforms' of the late eighteenth century, that such arrangements could lead to greater effectiveness and lower costs by concentrating expertise and using government's combined buying power.[4] In 1786 the Treasury created a central stationery office (HMSO) as a state-owned enterprise to cut stationery and printing costs—the equivalent of IT at that time—and two hundred years later the costs of several kinds of common service provision were still charged to departments by expert central providers such as the Central Telecommunications and Computing Agency and the Property Services Agency (Hood and Dixon 2015: 71 fn 21). What the AC control regime therefore added into the mix in the mid-1980s was a bundling of departmental wage costs together with other inputs into a single merged 'running costs' category for reporting and financial control. 'Running costs' in that sense were treated as a block for the purposes of Treasury control, were controlled gross of receipts (with a few minor exceptions) and were ring-fenced from all other departmental expenditure.

That move fitted the political climate of the time, making it possible at least for an approximate answer to be given to questions posed by Thatcherite ministers and their business advisers about how much it cost to 'run' any given government department, or government as a whole. And the change fitted the managerial mood of the 1980s in that it was intended both to enable and oblige departments to manage such costs as a whole and to grapple with trade-offs between different types of input costs, for example between staffing costs and the development of office automation through IT spending (see Hood and Dixon 2015: 53 and Appendix 2: 201).

At first the classification of 'running costs' (as they were termed at that time) made no strong distinction, of the 'populist/political' or 'Treasury' kind referred to in the vignette, between 'tail' and 'teeth' or between 'front-line' and 'back-office' activities. The numbers simply denoted the major costs of operating any central department.[5] In its early days, that cost control system arguably produced some political embarrassment for the government that created it. As can be seen from

[4] See Baity-King (1986); Kleir (1934). Similar ideas resurfaced in the 2000s and 2010s with a new wave of enthusiasm for shared back-office services across public sector organizations to cut costs and for the 'corporate centre' approach to procurement and project management espoused by developments such as the Office of Government Commerce and the Efficiency and Reform Group discussed in Chapters 4 to 6.

[5] The main components of running costs in their original 1980s formulation were (a) civil service pay, travel and subsistence, (b) current expenditure on accommodation—rent, local property taxes, utilities, and maintenance (capital spending, for instance on new offices, was excluded), and (c) office services, stationery, postage, and IT maintenance. The biggest component of cost was civil service wages (about 60 per cent of the total) and likewise roughly 60 per cent of those costs were incurred by four departments, namely Social Security, Home Office and prisons, the tax departments, and the Department of Employment with its employment exchanges (later 'job centres').

Figure 8.1, those costs rose steadily at that time despite the Thatcher government's much-commented-on aspiration to cut costs and 'deprivilege' the civil service (Hood and Dixon 2015: 75). Those increases arose largely because of civil service pay increases, some reflecting obligations inherited from the previous government, but also partly because of reclassifications as new cost items or organizations were included into the AC regime.

The political picture changed for running costs under the succeeding Major government in the 1990s. As noted in Chapter 3 (and shown by Figure 8.1 earlier), reported running costs fell markedly at that time both in constant prices and relative to total managed expenditure. Those numbers presented political credit-claiming opportunities that Chancellor Ken Clarke seized upon in three successive Budget speeches (in fact Clarke mentioned running costs no less than ten times in his 1994 speech). And, following the 1994 'Front Line First' defence costs initiative described in Chapter 3, running costs began to be framed politically in a different way, as representing (unpopular/dispensable) back-office functions, in contrast to more public-facing service activity, as noted in the vignette.

But running cost controls were problematic for Treasury spending control even then, for at least three reasons, some of which were mentioned in the vignette, and some of which are reflected in our interviewees' comments on AC controls during our period (summarized in Table 8.1 below). First, the coverage was not public-sector wide: it applied to most central government departments[6] but not to all non-departmental public bodies or the NHS. The patchy application meant that many key public service providers were outside the scheme, and that there were strong incentives for departments to offload such costs onto satellite bodies, or even to create such bodies to avoid AC limits.[7] Second, whether the running cost numbers for any given department were high or low had much less to do with the efficiency or otherwise with which that organization was managed than with whether it had a large directly employed service delivery workforce, such as prison officers or job centre staff, or whether it funded its service delivery organizations at arm's-length, such as schools or hospitals.

Third, the system was especially problematic in its application to the Ministry of Defence, and indeed after the 1994 Front Line First defence review described in Chapter 3, MOD dropped out of the general AC control regime for a whole decade. That move took some £5bn of what had previously been counted as MOD running costs out of the system and meant that not even approximate numbers could thereafter be given concerning what it cost to run UK central government departments as a whole. For its own planning on 'operating costs', MOD distinguished

---

[6] As well as MOD, the Export Credits Guarantee Department and the Forestry Commission were outside the AC control regime at that time.

[7] One interviewee thought it was commonly believed in the Treasury by 2010 that 'arm's-length bodies got created in part to get around admin [AC] limits' but was not aware of systematic evidence of such practice.

between uniformed combat units and civilian support, a variant of the military dichotomy between 'teeth' and 'tail' that we mentioned in Chapter 3, but which did not readily map onto the Treasury AC regime. As a result, the wages of MOD uniformed service people were counted as programme costs even if the individuals concerned were engaged on non-combatant activities such as accounting, whereas civilian staff doing the same jobs counted towards ACs. So that classification—together with stronger political resistance by ministers to agree cuts in uniformed staff numbers in the armed forces than to authorize reductions in civilian staff—produced perverse incentives for MOD to use (more highly paid) uniformed staff to carry out routine office tasks rather than lower-paid civilian employees.

Running cost controls also came to pose difficulties for New Labour in government. Those difficulties arose as overall public spending began to rise in the early 2000s after the Labour government's initial two years of spending restraint resulting from its pledge to follow the Conservatives' 1996 Survey plans. As already noted, gross running costs were on a sharp upward trajectory at that time, although running costs net of charges for administrative services (to arm's-length bodies, for instance) did not increase so dramatically. The political challenge for New Labour was that of how to deliver on its declared intention to reverse 'underfunding' of public services without being castigated by opposition parties for being soft on bureaucracy. At the same time, public service trade unions and others pressed for the rules to be changed or re-interpreted to prevent in-house bids for service provision from being disadvantaged relative to bids from private sector outsourcing companies in market-testing exercises, where some contracted-out services came to be counted as 'programme' rather than administration costs. Treasury ministers were evidently concerned about this issue: a GEP official reported in 2001 that, 'For some time the Chief Secretary has been vexed by the problem of definition of running costs whereby consultancy counts as programme but civil servants count as admin costs. This has the effect of setting up perverse incentives in that the same piece of work if contracted out to consultants is "good" programme expenditure but if kept in house is "bad" admin costs'.

There was also a certain tension, at least in terms of relative importance, between the input focus of AC controls and a results-oriented focus on 'outputs'. Both the Major government and the Blair/Brown government aspired to put more emphasis on monitoring results and their various exercises in performance management or budgeting attracted an enormous literature, gained much attention on the conference circuit and from international bodies like IMF and OECD, and meant that the civil servants working on them were directly linked to those governments' high-level political and electoral goals. Many of the former Treasury civil servants we interviewed from that era found high-profile work on policy targets to be exhilarating and stretching, while in contrast many saw AC budgets and controls as tedious, less meaningful, and something to be settled perfunctorily at the last minute in spending reviews. As Table 8.1 indicates, a few saw some value in such

Table 8.1 Examples of interviewees' views of AC controls

Negatives	Examples
Perceived susceptibility to gaming and resource distortion	The 'front-line/back office' distinction was 'incredibly permeable'; 'You got into ridiculous arguments' about what counted as ACs; the regime led to 'inappropriate behaviour' by departments in the form of the creation of a 'new class of civil servants' employed on short-term contracts via outsourcing firms to count as programme costs as AC limits tightened in the mid-2000s; 'clever people play the game'.
Perceived irrelevance to key control challenges	Treasury spending teams 'didn't spend much time on ACs and there was 'huge asymmetry of information' over ACs; the Treasury was 'not massively concerned with policing the administration cost/programme costs boundary' because there were bigger things to worry about; AC controls were seen by the Treasury as 'a bit of a waste of time', such that their abolition was discussed by officials at every spending review but 'tenaciously difficult to get rid of because Parliament ... liked it'; 'always settled very briefly right at the end of Spending Reviews after the biggest spending numbers had been fixed'.
Positives	
Perceived utility as a meaningful check on 'bureaucracy'	AC controls were marginally useful in helping the Treasury 'get a grip on the bureaucracy'; perhaps 'politically useful for a reforming spending minister trying to get control of management' in a department; valuable because 'all Permanent Secretaries care about is ACs' and AC controls helped to keep departments' liking for 'big HQs' in check.
Perceived utility for political credit-claiming	AC cost controls were seen by Treasury as a 'relic' that survived only because they allowed easy political credit-claiming over cutting the costs of bureaucracy: 'No-one ever objects to reducing the cost of bureaucracy'; 'Politicians were keen to claim credit for being tough on bureaucracy'.

controls in checking 'bureaucracy' but many were unenthusiastic, seeing AC controls as of little value beyond party-political point-scoring. At the same time, we found no evidence from spending-review post-mortems and interviews of strong and widespread pressure for scrapping AC controls from those who were on the receiving end, though there were evidently some tensions (notably in the MOD's alternative conception of operating costs).

As already noted, what-to-do issues about the running cost regime led to repeated reviews in the late 1990s and early 2000s, of which the 2002 GEP document featured in the vignette was only one. In 1998 Treasury ministers decided to keep AC controls at least for the period of New Labour's first Comprehensive Spending Review. The following year an indication by the Office of Deputy Prime Minister that it would challenge the control system for the 2000 Spending Review led to a review which renamed running costs as 'administration costs' but rejected the idea of modifying those controls by making them more selective. The selectivity or 'earned autonomy' approach would have meant releasing more departments from the control regime (as had happened to MOD in 1994) for departments which could satisfy the Treasury that their management systems were otherwise robust.

Instead, Treasury ministers opted in yet another review in 2002 to handle the problem by the alternative route of creative case-by-case reclassification, as described in the vignette. Departments were encouraged to apply for reclassification of staff from AC into programme costs, wherever there were plausible grounds for arguing, from the 'political-populist' viewpoint, that the people involved could be presented as front-line service providers rather than back-office administrators. At the same time the system of gross cost control and reporting was changed, such that departments could net off against their AC limits the fees they chose to charge for whatever administrative 'services' they provided to their various satellite bodies. So the (embarrassingly growing) gross AC numbers were no longer reported after 2004, as Figure 8.1 shows, making it harder for critical analysts or political opponents to track changes over time on a consistent basis. That step represented a decisive shift away from the original 1980s notion of ACs as representing all the various costs of running any given department.

At first reclassifications from ACs to programme costs through this route were modest. Between 2002 and 2004, only about £0.2bn of AC spending was reclassified. But the overall settlement for ACs in New Labour's 2004 Spending Review was much more restrictive than that of 2002, and the budget of that year capped ACs for all departments at or below 2005–2006 nominal levels. Such a fiscal environment meant that departments by the mid-2000s had very strong incentives to reclassify as much spending as they could from ACs to programme costs. The Chancellor, like his Conservative predecessor, made a point of claiming political credit for reductions in reported ACs in his 2004 budget speech, declaring that the effect of cuts in departmental administration budgets of at least 5 per cent in real terms would lead to planned administration costs falling to 3.7 per cent of total spending by 2008, '…the lowest level since the running costs regime was first introduced' (Brown 2004).

In that Budget speech, the Chancellor also made much of a review he had commissioned from Sir Peter Gershon, the head of the Office of Government Commerce (discussed in Chapter 6). Gershon's review concluded that £15bn a year of 'efficiency savings' across government could be found, thereby reducing government borrowing without affecting front-line services (Gershon 2004). But reclassification was also at work: following the 2004 Spending Review large numbers of staff in the Home Office, Constitutional Affairs, and Law Officers' Departments were reclassified as 'front-line' ('in line with the Efficiency Review's recommendation', as the Spending Review document carefully put it[8]). Further, in the 2004 PESA document that followed the dramatic announcements in the budget, the tables on ACs and staffing numbers were reported in a notably different way from their predecessors. Up to that point those numbers had been reported on a run of eight years, but in 2004, data was omitted for years in which final outturns had previously been published. An apparently minor and technical modification in the numbers presented, the change in reporting turned out to make a substantial and politically convenient difference to the picture the table painted.[9]

After 2004 even more spending items were reclassified away from ACs into programme costs on the grounds that they amounted to 'front-line services' rather than back-office activity. In the 2007 spending review, the definition of 'front-line' arguably began to shift again, this time to include staff who, though not obviously providing front-line services themselves, could be argued to support those who did—a distinction hitherto obscured by the (over) simple dichotomy between 'administration' and 'front-line service'. Key AC-to-front-line reclassifications at this point were applied to the FCO, the Home Office, the Law Officers and the Single Intelligence Account for the security agencies. In the latter case, most staff were moved out of the AC count, and at a time when SIA staff costs were growing rapidly following bomb attacks on central London in July 2005, it would have been harder for government to tell a story of falling ACs without that convenient reclassification. But there was an obvious political risk that going too far or fast with such reclassifications would expose the government to the political charge that it had massaged the figures. That risk perhaps accounts for the ad hoc style of decisions over successive spending reviews, aimed at keeping changes within more or less credible limits.

After the change of government in 2010, the AC control regime altered again, in at least two ways. One striking change, taking place in the 2010 Spending Review, was a big jump in the population of bodies exposed to AC controls, following a reclassification exercise even bolder than those undertaken under the previous government. Most 'arm's-length' bodies (broadly, non-ministerial departments and executive agencies), which had previously been excluded from the reported Treasury numbers,[10] were brought into the scope of the central AC control regime.

[8] HM Treasury 2004b, Table 2.3, p. 21 fn 1.

[9] Data presented for the same run of years as previously reported (that is, the years 1998–1999 to 2005–2006) would have shown ACs rising from £14.1bn in 1998–1999 to £21.3bn in 2005–2006—a rise of £7.2bn.—and civil service numbers up by 66,400 (14 per cent). But the nominal increase in the different selection of numbers published in 2004 (2002–2003 to 2005–2006) was only £2.4bn, reflecting an increase in civil service numbers of only 15,000 (HM Treasury 2004b, Chapter 5, Tables 5.1 and 5.2: 62–63).

[10] Excluded were self-financing public corporations and trading funds plus independent bodies such as the National Audit Office and the Local Government Boundary Commission.

That move reflected a belief, mentioned earlier, that the creation of arm's-length bodies was being used as a way to avoid AC controls, and it also created an opportunity for the Treasury to announce cuts of a dramatic £400m in those bodies' estimated AC budgets in FY 2010–2011. But at the same time the mass-employment 'direct service delivery' parts of the tax department (HMRC) and the Department of Work and Pensions (DWP) were reclassified out of ACs in the 2010 Spending Review. Together with the effects of a two-year public sector pay freeze, that reclassification of the population of organizations in the AC control regime to 'central Whitehall and its arm's-length bodies' produced a huge drop in reported ACs, dwarfing many of the shifts under New Labour. One striking example of that disappearing act is the AC budget of the Department of Work and Pensions, which plunged in a single year from £5.6bn (in 2010/2011) to £1.3bn (in 2011/2012) as a result of the reclassification of its service delivery arm (DWP 2012:219).

The other big change in the AC control regime in the early days of the coalition was the creation of the Efficiency and Reform Group (ERG) in the Cabinet Office, as discussed in Chapter 5. As we saw there, ERG's declared mission was to help deliver on the Coalition's commitment (underlined by Chancellor Osborne's 2010 Mansion House speech) to making big efficiency savings in government in stan-dard corporate style by renegotiating contracts, reducing discretionary spending and keeping a tight grip on 'overheads' (Osborne 2010). As that chapter noted, ERG exercised approval powers on a range of AC items (for example costs of IT, consultancy and meetings) on behalf of the Treasury,[11] within drastically lowered delegation limits, and claimed to have achieved dramatic cost reductions of some £20bn across government in its first three years (Maude 2014). But as we also noted in Chapter 5, tensions over the way ERG exercized its spending approval powers led to a key report in 2013 by a leading Treasury official and a senior departmen-tal Finance Director arguing for a version of the risk-based 'earned autonomy' approach to handling AC controls that had been floated a decade or so earlier. As we have seen, ERG itself disappeared in 2014—but AC controls did not.

The Contrasting Fate of Performance Budgeting and Output-Oriented Controls

In contrast to the traditional emphasis on input cost controls over public spending, of which AC controls are a prime example, one of the central themes of reformers seeking to challenge traditional public administration in the 1980s and 1990s was

---

[11] But in principle the Treasury had a veto, since written approval from its spending teams was needed to avoid NAO qualifying departmental accounts under the Exchequer and Audit Departments Act discussed in Chapter 2. Indeed, those ERG controls that did not use Treasury spending control powers and hence lacked the threat of the NAO qualifying accounts could be flouted by departments without consequence, according to a 2014 'teach-in' on the subject.

the idea of switching emphasis from input or process controls to output controls. The aim of such proposals was to focus the creative efforts of public managers onto better ways of using their resources to provide public services. The title of the high-profile 1993 Gore-Clinton National Performance Review of the US Federal Government, *From Red Tape to Results*, epitomizes that sort of aspiration. David Osborne and Ted Gaebler (1992), whose best-seller *Reinventing Government* was the key text for the National Performance Review, were invited to high-level meetings in the UK to discuss their proposals. That idea of 'managing for results' was reflected in the development of performance measures that captured the key outputs or outcomes for which public managers (and ministers) could be held to account.

As we saw in Chapter 3, several developments under the Major government reflected such aspirations to move to a more output or results-based approach to control. Indeed, John Major (1999: 261) himself interpreted his 1991 'Citizen's Charter' as reflecting the idea that 'we had to end the excessive focus on financial inputs rather than service outputs' and saw the Charter as a forerunner of subsequent developments under New Labour.[12] Another notable effort to put more emphasis on 'service outputs' under that government was the system of centrally reported key performance targets achieved by the 150 or so executive agencies spun out of central departments under the Major government's 'Next Steps' scheme—targets that were originally envisaged as a link between budgetary allocation and agency performance.[13] A third development in output-focused controls under the Major government was the plan for (Schedule E) reporting of results relative to each item of spending in the 1995 White Paper that announced the adoption of a new Resource Accounting and Budgeting system by the early 2000s (to be discussed in Chapter 10).[14]

Under New Labour, some of these specific moves in the direction of output-focused controls were abandoned. The new government scrapped the Citizen's Charter, wound back the central reporting of executive agencies' performance relative to targets, and abolished the scheme for Schedule E reporting of results against each item of spending under the new resource accounting regime. But the new government went ahead with its own version of output-focused controls in the form of performance contracts with central departments in its high-profile system of Public Service Agreements and elaborate accompanying performance

---

[12] Major (1999: 261) also acknowledged with disappointment that the Charter did not play well politically (in a credit claiming sense) for his government at a time when spending on public services was being heavily restrained in consequence of the huge deficits of the mid-1990s. See also Hollingshead (2005) and Mullen (2006).

[13] But according to Pollitt and Talbot (2004: 111–112), the output indicators (KPIs) for the agencies were never truly synched with budget allocation. Those KPIs at first focused more on inputs and processes than on outputs and were decidedly variable in quantity, quality and focus.

[14] The 1994 Fundamental Expenditure Review of the Treasury (Chapter 3) also belonged to the same generation and was arguably compatible with the output approach to control.

indicators, negotiated with the Treasury alongside budgetary allocations in its five spending reviews.

Such developments, much discussed and refined over the period, could all be considered as variants of 'performance budgeting', defined by OECD (2008) as 'the integration of performance information into the budget decision-making process'.[15] OECD distinguishes three different types of performance budgeting, namely 'presentational', 'performance-informed', and 'direct'. The 'presentational' variety involves information about targets, results or both in budget or other government documents as 'background information for accountability and dialogue with legislators and citizens'. In the 'performance-informed' variety, performance information is important in budget decision-making but does not have any automatic or predefined weight in resource allocation. In the 'direct' form, resource allocation links directly to performance information.

In that OECD typology, 'direct' performance budgeting was not generally adopted in the UK at any point in the period, though it was applied in one or two specific areas[16] and figured in the 'Schedule E' RAB accounting-reform plans already mentioned. Rather, over the period covered by this study, the UK moved from a degree of 'presentational' performance budgeting in the 1990s to a more clearly 'performance-informed' approach to budgeting in the 2000s in the form of Public Service Agreements and other performance indicators. In 2010 the Conservative-Liberal Democrat coalition scrapped the PSA system immediately on taking office, to be replaced by departmental business plans with impact indicators that were not centrally reported.

Table 8.2 gives examples of views expressed by our interviewees about the PSA system. In contrast to the mostly dismissive or at best lukewarm views expressed about AC controls, interviewees were more divided over the value of PSAs, with some expressing high praise for the system and regret over its demise. For example, no-one came close to describing AC controls as 'utterly transformative of everything government did', while several interviewees spoke about PSAs in that vein. Moreover, many of our official interviewees thought PSAs improved markedly in a technical sense over the five Labour spending reviews, even though their original form as a hasty concoction at the very end of the 1998 spending review was widely criticized (and indeed the Treasury spending teams seem to have been curiously

---

[15] The idea of performance budgeting goes back at least to the 1930s (and arguably long before that, for instance to Jeremy Bentham's (1962) ideas about public management). A key post-World War II landmark was the 'program planning budgeting system' (PPBS) introduced into the United States Department of Defense (DoD) in the 1960s (Schick 1966). PPBS was later applied across the federal government before being abandoned for the civilian bureaucracy five years later (though retained for defence) and partially brought back in different guises in the 1990s (see West 2011, chapters 2 and 3).

[16] An example is the allocation of public funding for university research on the basis of periodic research quality assessments that ranked and rated every department in every UK university (a system that began in 1986 and became much more consequential for university research funding in the following decades).

Table 8.2 Examples of interviewees' views of PSAs as output controls

Negatives	Examples
Poorly designed and all done in a hurry and 'bolted on afterwards' in 1998, not really linked to budget allocations, ineffective or worse	'…it was all nonsense … largely a waste of time … made no difference at all when [PSAs] were done away with'; 'a mish-mash of input and output targets';'not aligned with [budget allocations] at any point … only [politically] useful for about two years'; 'a PR exercise … very poor [at first]'; 'invented on the hoof … pretty ham-fisted'; improved later but were 'a slightly theological area' because targets cannot capture all government objectives; the lower-level indicators below PSAs [SDAs etc] were 'a complete nightmare … they should have gone'; the 'what gets measured gets done' syndrome led to 'disasters' from excessive focus on PSA targets.
Constitutionally or institutionally dubious or problematic	It was 'staggering' and 'absolutely bonkers' that it had been accepted that the rest of government should have agreements with the Treasury over their policy objectives rather than with Cabinet or Prime Minister; 'the high water mark of the centre trying to dictate to other departments what to do;' at first 'entirely Treasury-driven and had no ownership from departments;' 'became a ridiculous bureaucracy' by 2007; an inferior substitute for the Schedule E accounting for resources against objectives in the 1995 White Paper plans for resource accounting which PSAs replaced.

Positives	
Improved after 1998 up to the time they were abolished, contributed to more 'strategic' conversations about resources between Treasury and departments	'A good idea in principle' though Whitehall was not equipped or motivated to apply it properly, given the huge degree of thought' needed; meant Treasury was 'not just beating people up about money'; a useful shift of Treasury control from just holding down spending by any available means to focusing on what the money was intended to buy; claimed to have produced 'serious negotiations' between Treasury and departments over objectives for the first time; 'a necessary discipline'; valuable because while traditional controls broadly limited corruption, there had been a failure to link spending control to policy outcomes; led to 'more granular conversations' between Treasury and departments over the link between inputs and outputs; after the demise of PSAs, Treasury only cared about whether departments kept to their budgets; 'PSAs were abolished just as they had been sorted out'.
Improved or reshaped incentives for departments to join up, prioritize and/or collect more 'granular' cost data	'a great idea' for Permanent Secretaries of departments … gave them a *raison d'etre* that went beyond just keeping the Minister happy, handling the scandals, getting bills through Parliament etc.'; 'utterly transformative of everything government did … a great achievement'; public spending control without targets left spending debates 'unanchored' and 'meant spending decisions just went back to "how loud people shout"'; made senior officials in departments work together by defining and measuring indicators of joint effort, and had never been replaced as an instrument for engaging joint working; incentivized departments to collect more detailed cost data.

ill-prepared for the task of setting PSA targets in 1998, given how long such ideas had been in the air). Several interviewees thought PSAs had been abolished just as they had been 'sorted out' and regretted their demise. In contrast, some of our politician interviewees said or implied the very opposite, namely that PSAs had been most useful in their early days (in signalling to voters what was being delivered in exchange for extra spending on public services) and thought they were more politically problematic in the final stages of the Labour government as the fiscal climate became more restrictive—an issue to which we return in the next section.

Why Did AC Input Controls Survive while Control over Outputs Did Not?

The politics of credit-claiming and blame-avoidance over 'waste' and 'front-line' protection that we described earlier suggested that AC controls counted throughout our period as a 'valence' issue (that is, an issue on which there is a relatively high degree of consensus among voters over the objective to be sought, such that political parties compete for votes over their competence to deliver such items).[17] Party competition over limiting ACs accordingly took place both at times when overall public spending was increasing and when it was being squeezed. In both conditions, incumbents needed to rebut charges from their political opponents for presiding over avoidable waste, and to seek credit for driving down overhead costs and being tough on bureaucracy without damaging front-line services. All three governments during our period made dramatic claims about cuts in ACs as a sign of success in increasing efficiency. The question of what the 'correct' volume of spending on back-office administration might be for improving (or avoiding collapse in) front-line services was left to backroom debates.

By contrast, it can be argued that for output controls, there is a different logic about political credit claiming and blaming as between times when overall public spending is rising, and times when spending is being restrained or cut back (Hood and Piotrowska 2021).[18] In the former case, there is an obvious political motive for incumbents to show taxpayer-voters that better service performance or policy outcomes are being delivered in exchange for higher levels of spending (and taxes). Many of our interviewees saw New Labour's PSA regime as highly focused on demonstrating such 'more for more' achievements. But when public spending is being restrained or cut back, there is less likely to be good news to

---

[17] See for instance Stokes (1963); Green and Jennings (2017).
[18] Looking at such asymmetry through the prism of bureaucratic rather than electoral politics, Curristine and Flynn (2013) suggest that government departments are more likely to supply meaningful output and outcome data to central agencies in times of fiscal expansionism than in times of austerity, given that in the first case such data will typically be used to justify new spending, whereas in times of austerity it is more likely to be used to look afresh at existing spending to find ways of cutting costs.

deliver to voters from output targets or numbers. Indeed, all else equal, such numbers are more likely to reveal blame-attracting results such as longer wait times or poorer-quality services when spending is cut. Such an observation is consistent with John Major's disappointment at how little political credit he thought his party derived from the 1991 Citizen's Charter, as mentioned earlier. It is also consistent with New Labour's apparently waning political enthusiasm for PSA targets in the government's third term as money became ever tighter. Further, it chimes with the subsequent Coalition's decision to downgrade its predecessor's PSAs with vestigial impact targets in unpublished departmental reports, and instead to put the main political emphasis on the selective protection of inputs in a few favoured spending areas.

It seems possible that some variant of the PSA scheme might have survived as part of the budgeting process had Labour been re-elected in 2010. Some of our Labour interviewees certainly saw that framework as a major achievement, and the same went for numerous official interviewees, as we have seen. Further, although performance budgeting and output targeting were claimed by some observers such as Allen Schick (2013) to have declined in several countries following the 2008 financial crash, Teresa Curristine and Suzanne Flynn (2013) argue that was not the universal pattern in the OECD countries. But not all of our Labour interviewees thought PSAs would have survived in a fourth term in government: several thought they would or should have been scrapped at that point. And in the fiscal-consolidation background to the post-election 2010 spending review, described in Chapter 5, it seems at best doubtful if a continued PSA system would have matched the vigour and political energy put into the targets and indicators in the heyday of spending growth in the early 2000s. In those conditions it seems more plausible that the PSA system might have shared the fate of the 2007 Scottish 'National Performance Framework', namely of moving into a twilight world, still officially in play, but politically sidelined in practice.[19]

Conclusion

Despite or possibly because of repeated aspirations to plan and control public spending by putting more emphasis on the results and outputs such spending produces, such output controls were politically unstable over our period and never amounted to 'direct' performance budgeting in the OECD's terminology. Some disappeared after changes in government (notably the Conservatives' 1995 plans for 'Schedule E' accounting for results relative to inputs in the RAB scheme and

[19] Scotland's 'National Performance Framework', a set of output measures introduced by the Scottish government in 2007, remained formally in place at the time of writing but was said to be largely ignored (see Lapsley and Midwinter 2021; contrast Budget Process Review Group 2017).

New Labour's PSAs, both scrapped by their successors). By contrast, AC input controls survived all the changes in government over the period, even though documents and interviews show that many of those operating those controls saw them as unsatisfactory.

Moreover, the AC control story highlighted by the vignette seems to be part of a wider pattern of survival and even growth of input-focused controls in public spending during a time when virtually saturation coverage was given to performance management and budgeting in the world of think-tanks and academia. One example of such additional input controls, discussed in Chapter 6, was the introduction of separate budgets for 'capital' and 'current' expenditure from the 1990s. And the 2005 health overspend with which we began this book was one of several such episodes that resulted in a different kind of input ring-fence put up by the Treasury, this time between 'near-cash' and 'non-cash'.

Similarly, in Chapters 4 and 5, we noted the extension of 'floor targets' for spending in some protected domains such as international development, health and education, specifying input floors of one kind or another (some in real terms, some as a share of national income, or relative EU average spending, in the case of health care in the early 2000s). That development echoes the much-commented-on decline in the proportion of 'discretionary' spending in the United States federal budget since the early 1970s (see for example Weaver 1988; Posner 2016: 5). Indeed, the remarkably long-lived Barnett funding formula for allocating territorial spending, as discussed in the previous chapter, constitutes another exclusively input-based distributional mechanism.

That ubiquity, growth, and continuing focus on input-based controls and allocation systems in public expenditure seems to contrast with visions of a form of management by objectives as the way of the future and the key to more effective public services and policy delivery. As already noted, several of our interviewees clearly shared that vision and it is true that after the introduction of simplified parliamentary estimates under the Major government in 1996, the spending control system never went back to the previous narrow line-item approach. But input controls on administration did not die away either, and over our period moves in the direction of explicit results-based controls were partial and limited.

Timeline: Selected Milestones in Administration and Running Cost Controls

Pre-1993

1986: A new running cost input control regime was introduced for central government departments, bringing together a set of previously separate spending items.

Late 1980s onwards: The 'next steps' initiative created c.150 civil service executive agencies under arm's-length management with specified goals and performance indicators, but never closely linked or synchronized with budget allocation.

1991 onwards: The 'Citizen's Charter' programme specified performance standards across government as part of a shift to more emphasis on outputs. A 1991 report by Sir Angus Fraser (Cabinet Office Efficiency Adviser) called for more emphasis on outputs and a more strategic approach to Treasury control.

1992: The Labour party's general election manifesto proposed output targets for public service performance (the Conservatives had done so in 1987).

1993–1997

1993: Zero-based reviews of running and programme costs were launched by a new CST (Michael Portillo).

1994: Civil service headcount reduction targets were scrapped; The Treasury Fundamental Expenditure Review (Chapter 3) advocated a 'strategic' approach to spending control with more emphasis on outputs; the 'Front Line First' review of MoD (Chapter 3) claimed to find £1bn of savings in 'non-front-line' activities; MoD taken out of general running costs regime, with an MoD-specific alternative agreed; a Green paper was published on resource accounting and budgeting.

1994–1996: Budget speeches all claimed credit for reductions in running costs while protecting 'front-line' services.

1995: A White Paper confirmed plans for adopting resource accounting and budgeting in central government from 1999–2000, including obligations for departments to report on their main objectives (Schedule D) and provide Output and Performance Analyses (Schedule E) comparing costs of delivering objectives against outputs achieved.

1997–2010

1997: Both Labour and Conservative general election manifestos promised performance targets for public services.

1998: A new Public Service Agreement (PSA) regime (drawing on official experience with target setting for executive agencies and overseas aid) set out 600 output/outcome objectives, agreed between spending departments and Treasury in the 1998 Comprehensive Spending Review (replacing the 1995 plan for 'Schedule E' Output and Performance analyses of outputs relative to spending under Resource Accounting and Budgeting); Treasury ministers decided to retain running cost controls for the 1998 Spending Review period.

1999: An internal GEP review of running cost controls took place, following an indication by one department (ODPM) that it would challenge the case for retaining such controls in the 2000 SR; Treasury ministers decided to keep them; running cost controls were devolved for spending by devolved governments (but at first little changed by those governments in practice); central publication of executive agency performance against KPIs was scrapped.

2000: 'Running costs', renamed 'administration costs' (ACs), remained as a specific control item; Citizen's Charter withdrawn (though 'Chartermarks' survived until 2008, when they were replaced by 'Customer Service Excellence standards').

2000–2007: successive modifications were made to PSAs in 2000, 2002, 2004, and 2007 spending reviews: PSAs cut from 600 to 30 over that period but supplemented by new Service Delivery Agreements from 2000, rebadged as Service Delivery Plans in 2004.

2001: PM's Delivery Unit formed to monitor target performance (separate from Treasury control) and intervene selectively to improve such performance; Conservative general election manifesto promised to cut ACs by £2bn a year by 2003–2004; political alarm by Treasury ministers and SpAds over rising ACs led to further internal Treasury review of AC controls.

2002: AC controls were retained but the Treasury invited departments to apply for reclassification of staff formerly counted under ACs to 'front-line' status (thus counting as programme costs), and allowed departments to net off charges (e.g. to satellite bodies) against ACs.

2004: Budget speech claimed credit for AC reductions and promised that by 2008 ACs would fall to 3.7 per cent of total spending;' the Gershon Efficiency review claimed £15bn a year could be cut from public spending without affecting front-line services, and led to more reclassification of staff to 'front-line' status; three-year freeze of AC budgets announced; MoD returned to the AC control regime; civil service headcount reduction targets reintroduced (a decade after the Conservatives scrapped them in 1994); a new Conservative leader (Michael Howard) used his first party conference speech to attack PSAs and the PMDU, and his first PM's Questions encounter in Parliament to focus on ACs.

2005: The Conservative general election manifesto promised to scrap PSAs, while Labour defended them in its manifesto.

2006: Stricter control of consultancy fees was announced in the Pre-Budget Report.

2007: The 2004 civil service headcount cuts were replaced by real-terms annual cuts in AC budgets; Departmental Delivery Plans were replaced by 'Strategic Objectives', to complement and underpin thirty top-line PSAs.

2010–2015

2010: The Conservatives' general election manifesto promised to scrap 'Labour's failed target regime', the Liberal Democrats attacked 'centralised targets and bureaucracy' in health, while (in contrast to 2005) Labour's manifesto was muted on the subject, merely promising to cut back on central targets; the PMDU was closed down and PSAs scrapped a month after the election; replaced by departmental 'business plans' setting out objectives and performance indicators in departmental reports (but departmental reports later ceased publication as an economy measure and were only issued online); 2010 Spending Review went beyond the 2007 cuts to reduce AC budgets by 34 per cent across government plus a two-year pay freeze; AC controls extended to all arm's-length bodies other than trading funds, public corporations and independent bodies; Cabinet Office Efficiency and Reform group formed (Chapter 5), absorbing the former Treasury Office of Government Commerce and applying a set of AC category controls on behalf of the Treasury with low delegation limits.

2013: White/Douglas Financial Management Review argued for a risk-based 'earned autonomy' approach to spending controls; one-year Spending 'Round' announced a rolling programme of efficiency reviews, beginning with BIS, HMRC, and DWP, with savings targets tailored to individual departments but a 5 per cent cut in RDEL spending as the default.

2014: Francis Maude claimed ERG had achieved efficiency savings of almost £20bn over three years; ERG closed down; AC control responsibilities reverted to the Treasury.

9

Yesterday's Tomorrows

Forecasts and Outturns in Public Spending 1993–2015

Vignette: How a Projected £3.5bn Budget Surplus Turned into a £46bn Deficit

In 1990 the Treasury's Medium-Term Financial Strategy projected a budget surplus for 1993–1994 of some £3½bn at current prices (½ per cent of GDP). In the following year's budget (1991), those official projections changed a little, to forecast a modest deficit in 1993–1994 (under 1 per cent of GDP). But there was still assumed to be an underlying structural surplus—that is, a surplus of revenue over spending corrected for the cyclical effects of a recession that began in that year. That surplus was estimated at about 1 per cent of GDP.

After that, the Treasury's fiscal forecast for 1993–1994 quickly became far more sombre. Between the 1991 and 1992 budgets, its published projections of the 1993–1994 deficit ('Public Sector Borrowing Requirement' (PSBR)) quintupled, shooting up from £6bn to £31½bn. Internally, as late as July 1991, the official Treasury was still predicting a balanced budget in the medium term. But the following June, after a general election in April which unexpectedly returned the incumbent Conservatives to power with a working majority, the unpublished internal forecasts were for a deficit of some 5 per cent of GDP throughout the medium term and a 'best view' of the following year's deficit of £39bn. In the event, the 1993–1994 outturn turned out to be even worse, in the form of a budget deficit of £46bn, 7¼ per cent of GDP, of which the 'structural deficit'—the part of the deficit not attributable to changes in the economic cycle—was estimated at 3¾ per cent of GDP.

That deficit, appearing when only a few years earlier continuing surplus had been predicted, was then the biggest in the UK's post-World War II history (though it was later dwarfed by deficits after the 2008 financial crash and the 2020–2002 Covid pandemic). Indeed, it was larger in real terms and relative to GDP than the legendary 1976 deficit that led to a major IMF bailout with strings attached. And the episode, which was bound up with the surprise ejection of the pound sterling in September 1992 from the then European Exchange Rate Mechanism (ERM, aligning European currencies), had major and long-lasting political repercussions. One of the Conservative party's key electoral advantages over Labour since the 1970s had been a higher rating among voters for management of the economy, and its

The Way the Money Goes. Christopher Hood, Maia King, Iain McLean, and Barbara Piotrowska,
Oxford University Press. © Christopher Hood, Maia King, Iain McLean, and Barbara Piotrowska (2023).
DOI: 10.1093/oso/9780198865087.003.0009

ability to cite the 1976 deficit and subsequent IMF bailout as evidence of fiscal mismanagement by Labour in government. As Figure 9.1 shows, only five months after their surprise general election victory (on a manifesto saying ERM membership was central to the party's economic policy), the Conservatives' poll lead on economic competence abruptly disappeared and was not recovered for a decade and a half (Ipsos 2015).

How did the Treasury get its fiscal forecasting for 1993–1994 so wrong? How did it so greatly underestimate the extent of a deficit that by the summer of 1994 was thought to have dated back as far as the late 1980s (Smith 1994)? As with much else to do with public spending, the answer seems to lie in a mixture of politics and technicalities.

On the technical side, the Treasury was far from alone in failing to forecast that 1993–1994 £46bn deficit. It is true that one respected independent forecaster (Bill Martin of UBS Phillips and Drew) had predicted a 1993–1994 deficit of exactly that size a month before the 1992 general election (Neill 1992). But Martin reduced his forecast of the deficit to £37bn after the election, and most independent forecasters' predictions were closer to those of the Treasury.

In mid-1994 an internal Treasury 'post-mortem' tried to quantify the main sources of error in the Treasury's forecast under eight headings, shown in Table 9.1.

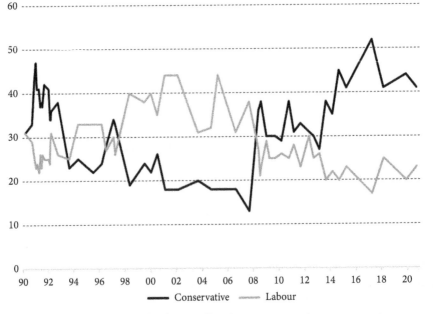

Figure 9.1 Conservative and Labour poll ratings on economic management 1990–2020

Source: Ipsos (2015)

Table 9.1 Treasury analysis of errors in successive forecasts of the 1993–1994 deficit

Per cent of GDP	1990	1991	1992	March 1993
Total error	7.75	6.25	2.5	−0.75
Of which				
'Presentational adjustments' (i.e., adjustments to the forecasters' 'best view'): not the main culprit	0.5	0.5	0.5	0
'Errors in output forecasts'—failure to anticipate the length and depth of the recession; the most important factor	4.5	2.25	1.25	−0.5
Adjustments to output forecast	0.5	0	1	0
Cyclical factors	0.75	0.25	−0.5	0
Tax policy changes	0.25	0	−0.25	0
Spending policy changes (increases in discretionary, non-cyclically related, spending on health, social security, education, transport, and local authorities)	1.5	1.25	0	0
Estimating errors in tax revenue forecasts	0.75	1.25	0.75	0
Residual	−1	0.75	−0.25	−0.25

Source: HM Treasury post-mortem July 1994

It said the biggest source of error was quasi-technical, namely a failure to forecast the length and depth of a recession beginning in 1991 as a result of the high interest rates needed to prop up the pound's exchange rate against the Deutschmark in the ERM.

But, as Table 9.1 shows, pre-election blowouts in public spending also undermined those earlier forecasting assumptions. There were in effect two pre-election spending splurges in 1991 and 1992, since the government originally planned to hold a general election in 1991 and then postponed it to 1992. The result was a combined rise of some £45bn in spending over 1991–1992 and 1992–1993 (including a big rise in health care funding, the lifting of a three-year freeze on child benefit payments and a doubling of spending on roads), but at the same time the Conservatives went into the 1992 General Election committed to low taxation. And the common practice of 'presentational adjustments'—the anodyne term for finessing of forecasts by modified judgements about some of the key numbers, partly to avoid self-fulfilling prophecy—came into the picture too. In the pre-election 1992 budget such adjustments are said to have been larger than usual, in that a so-called 'best view' internal Treasury forecast that put the expected 1993–1994 PSBR at £39bn had been reduced to a published forecast of £32bn. As Table 9.1 shows, the Treasury's post-mortem attributed under 7 per cent of the total forecasting error to over-optimistic presentational adjustments, but of course that was what the political blame game focused on. And what is striking from the table is that all eight types of forecasting error went in the same direction, reinforcing each other rather than cancelling one another out.

A group of senior Treasury officials met in January 1995 to discuss the analysis summarized in Table 9.1. They mulled inconclusively over the difficulty of giving firm and credible official advice to Ministers when the forecast numbers changed so frequently and dramatically; the risk that if advice to Ministers seemed too pessimistic, the officials proffering it were more likely to be ignored; and the risk that while individuals might draw lessons from episodes such as the £46bn deficit, institutional memory was likely to be far more fragile. Several interviewees told us this 'legendary' report was considered secret and sensitive at the time and had very limited circulation. But it evidently did not disappear from the Treasury's institutional memory and re-emerged a decade and a half later when very similar issues were raised by the forecast of GDP growth accompanying the 2008 Budget, described to us as 'the greatest fantasy budget' by a former senior Treasury official. Later in that year, according to another interviewee that 1994 post-mortem helped to inform a move away from the Treasury's most benign planning scenarios to ones that were more pessimistic (though still not pessimistic enough, as things turned out).

Forecasting, the Fiscal Constitution, and Public Spending Control

This story of a rapid lurch from expected surplus to the reality of sudden deficit shows how closely economic forecasting is linked both to the politics and technicalities of the planning and control of public spending. It links to the politics because gaps between official forecasts and outturn can be—and in the 1990s and 2000s often were—construed by opposition parties as avoidable errors resulting from bureaucratic ineptitude or crafty behind-the-scenes fiddling of the numbers, or both. A (possibly) more enlightened view of forecasting error takes gaps between forecasts and outturns mainly as an indicator of the degree of economic uncertainty. In this perspective, the value of obligations to forecast is more a way to force systematic analysis and learning from the inevitable surprises than to avoid such surprises altogether (Josephs 2014).

Still, as this chapter shows, changing institutional arrangements for fiscal forecasting over our period were shaped by political blame-and-credibility factors. As background, Figure 9.2, taken from analysis of reports in *The Times* newspaper over our period, provides some indication of how levels of critical questioning of fiscal forecasting varied over that time.

Forecasting also links to the technicalities of public spending control, because the size of any available spending 'envelope' is limited by expected tax revenue and debt service costs, which themselves depend on predictions of other factors, including inflation and economic cycles. And as we will see, different assumptions

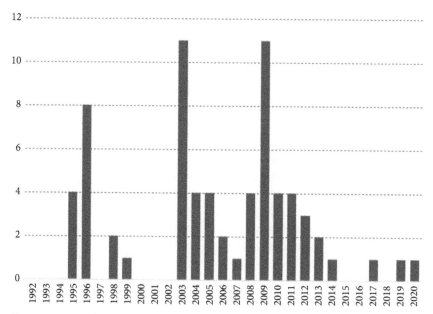

Figure 9.2 Incidence of reports in *The Times* indicating questioning of fiscal forecasting 1992–2021

Source: analysis of Nexis UK articles in The Times where the word "optimist*" appeared within fifteen words of the word "forecast"

over such matters can provide—or remove—convenient 'back pockets' for extra public spending.

This chapter explores three main questions about fiscal forecasting over our period. First, how and why did institutional arrangements for forecasting and reporting vary over that time? Second, how did forecasters fit into the village life of the Treasury and Whitehall, and how did their position change? Third, how did outturns compare with predictions for short-term and longer-term forecasts?

Three Institutional Arrangements for Fiscal Forecasting, 1993–2015

Economic modelling and forecasting was already a well-established part of the public spending planning process at the start of our period. The forecasts described in the vignette were initially produced by a dozen or so middle- or higher-ranking Treasury economists (supported by various other staff). They used a 500-variable, 1,000-equation economic model of the UK to produce two (originally three) official forecasts per year linked to fiscal events (HM Treasury 1994a: 75, Table 7.2).

Those forecasts were not produced robotically through rigid algorithms (nor are their equivalents today). They necessarily included judgements about the likely effect of recent or new developments, like the prospects of the economy nose-diving or real estate prices collapsing, both of which were big worries in the early 1990s. Indeed, one interviewee who worked in the forecasting unit at that time said, 'You could make it [the forecast emerging from the Treasury's economic model] do whatever you wanted' according to which out of several more or less plausible parameters was chosen, within the consistency constraints imposed by the model. After a few months in the job, that interviewee had simply taken to asking 'the policy people', 'What answer do you want?'

Figure 9.2 suggests that levels of sceptical newspaper comment on Treasury forecasts ran high under the Major government, and indeed in the period covered by the vignette forecasting was a blame magnet. Nor was it just opposition parties and sceptical journalists who suspected the forecast numbers accompanying the 1992 giveaway pre-election budget had been politically 'doctored'. One interviewee with senior official experience of Treasury forecasting said the forecast accompanying that budget was 'dishonest' and forecasting 'a dark art'. One or two said forecasts were finessed within the Treasury at that time because of a 'lack of appetite by senior levels [of officials] to tell Ministers bad news'. As such news went up the official hierarchy from the middle-grade economists who produced the forecasts, the numbers were said to have been tweaked by adjustments made at higher levels—meaning that when the bad news reached the Chancellor it had been toned down at least once.[1]

Over-optimistic Treasury forecasts came under political fire when they could be unfavourably compared with other forecasts. In the early 1990s economic forecasting comprised consultancy firms, universities, and think-tanks, as well as the Treasury, whose predictions were compared by the media, political parties, and the Treasury itself. In 1992 the Treasury ranked twenty-ninth out of forty-one in an annual (so-called 'Golden Guru') league table rating economic forecasters for their estimates of economic growth, inflation, and unemployment (Chote 1992; Huhne 1992). Robert Chote (1993) commented, 'Since the mid-Eighties [Treasury forecasters] have failed to predict both the strongest boom in 15 years and the longest recession since the Second World War. The Treasury spent a year forecasting an imminent recovery which still has not arrived...' Even though the Treasury claimed to outperform its most plausible competitors on six key macroeconomic items taken together,[2] an internal Treasury briefing document at the beginning of

---

[1] One interviewee said that no-one knew what the sum of those presentational adjustments was. If so, not all of those official tweaks may have been counted in the 'presentational adjustments' row in Table 9.1.

[2] GDP growth, consumption, investment, current account balance, PSBR and inflation (HM Treasury 1994a: 74)

our period said, 'it became widely asserted that the Treasury forecasts were the worst in the country...'

The reign of the 'Wise Men' 1993–1997

Against that background, the idea of outsourcing the Treasury's modelling and forecasting system altogether was floated more than once in the early 1990s.[3] But the idea was rejected on various grounds (such as: too close to 'policy' for contracting out; potential bidders unenthusiastic about shouldering the blame for erroneous forecasts; risks of even worse performance).

Instead, when in perilous political straits a month after the 1992 ERM debacle, Chancellor Norman Lamont created an official panel of independent economists to provide periodic forecasts to the Treasury, to supplement but not replace the Treasury's regular economic forecasting. The Panel (originally seven, later six, all men) was appointed[4] to produce three (later two) forecasts a year both by working individually and by meeting as a group chaired by a senior Treasury official. They were also invited to comment on policy.

This Panel—dubbed 'The Wise Men' by the media—was not a wholly new departure. Expert advisory groups have long been a feature of UK government and outside economists have been appointed to advisory roles since World War I, if not before. There was even a short-lived 'Economic General Staff' in the 1920s (Heclo and Wildavsky 1974: 268) and the Treasury had an 'Academic Panel' of independent economists in the 1970s and 1980s (Britton 1991: 87). More specifically, from 1986 it published a regular digest of other economic forecasts. This digest could be seen as a 'blame shield' to show it was not alone in making forecasting errors.

The Panel represented a step beyond publishing such digests, and the chance to comment on policy was apparently seen as a necessary inducement to its members for sharing the likely blame about forecast errors. An internal Treasury briefing at the time said,

The original purpose of the Panel was to shift attention away from Treasury forecasts and to demonstrate the range of uncertainty (and degree of error) in outside

[3] A 1993 report from KPMG on possible providers of outsourced forecasting found potential academic bidders fearful of loss of independence and reliance on Treasury funding, and commercial ones of cost-cutting pressures and contractual difficulties. The 1994 Fundamental Expenditure Review of the Treasury, discussed in Chapter 3, also came down against outsourcing forecasting on quality grounds, but called for staffing cutbacks in the modelling and forecasting unit (HM Treasury 1994a: 73).
[4] Probably with tongue in cheek, one Treasury official floated the idea of using a quality threshold followed by an auction (a variant of the method then used for allocating TV franchises) for choosing Panel members. In fact, they were appointed on renewable two-year terms and paid on a modest and uniform fee-per-meeting basis.

forecasts. However, some of the likely candidates...showed that they realised what the game was and insisted that they would only join if they could discuss policy. Since we wished to attract some of our more vociferous critics, the terms of reference included policy discussion.

Commenting from the outside, Robert Chote (1992) highlighted the different economic perspectives represented on the Panel,[5] ranging 'from old-style Keynesian to rabid Thatcherite' and from 'maverick' to 'mainstream'. Chote saw those differences as so wide that official Treasury forecasts would be bound to fit 'snugly' somewhere within the range of views coming from the Panel (as they duly did).[6] Sir Alan Budd (1999), who as the Treasury's Chief Economic Adviser chaired the Panel's meetings, later published an account of how it worked. Budd wrote that in only one of its eleven reports (October 1993) did the Panel come close to agreement on policy advice and there was one strong dissenter even in that case.[7]

There were obvious risks to the Treasury from inviting the Panel to comment on policy, because their views were liable to attract close attention in media and financial markets. Indeed, in February 1993 the Panel's first report did cause a sharp (but short-lived) drop in the value of the pound in the currency markets because it could be interpreted as advocating an interest rate cut. To limit such risks, the Treasury invested substantial energy and skill into chairing this intellectually (though not otherwise) diverse group and shaping its reports to present some semblance of a collective view.

Unlike its predecessor and successor regimes, the four-year 'Wise Men' system did not last long enough to encounter a major economic shock. Figure 9.2 suggests that the incidence of newspaper reports questioning Treasury forecasts did not fall over the four years of the Panel's existence, apart from one notable drop in 1994. None of our interviewees thought the Panel had transformed the landscape, though one believed it might have helped to keep the official Treasury honest by countering the tendency for self-censorship by senior officials over bad news emerging from forecasts, as mentioned earlier. But the Panel did not survive the 1997 change of government.

---

[5] The members were: Andrew Britton (NIESR), Tim Congdon (Lombard Street Research), David Currie (London Business School), Gavyn Davies (Goldman Sachs), Wynne Godley (Kings College Cambridge), Patrick Minford (Liverpool University and Cardiff Business School), and Andrew Sentance (CBI). Four were former Treasury officials.

[6] Several interviewees from that era said the same.

[7] Reflecting on the experience, Budd (1999: 47) remarked wryly: 'I have never completely given up the hope that, if one economist says A and another economist says Not A, it should be possible to determine...who is right and who is wrong. But I am still waiting...for the first example of such a demonstration'.

The New Labour approach: official validation of Treasury forecasting assumptions 1997–2010

New Labour took a different approach to 'honesty-signalling' over forecasts and projections. Its 1997 manifesto included a pledge to create an independent national statistical service but said nothing about any similar move over economic and fiscal forecasting. The Liberal Democrat party and some other individuals at that time advocated the creation of a small independent office of experts to advise Parliament on Treasury forecasting and adherence to fiscal rules (Parker 1996; Tyrie 1996). But such proposals stopped well short of handing over fiscal forecasting to an outside body, and a senior New Labour interviewee said the new government did not even consider such a step.[8] The 'Wise Men' panel, that interviewee said, was dismissed by New Labour as just 'a piece of obfuscation', since the Treasury's own forecasting had been kept separate from the Panel's deliberations. An ex-Treasury official thought moving to an independent Bank of England in 1997 had been such a big step towards granting autonomy to expert technocrats within the Treasury's domain that it precluded other types of independent 'expertization' at that time.

Still, in a partial embrace of the idea of providing independent advice to Parliament on fiscal forecasting and reporting, the new government 'invited' the National Audit Office (NAO), the parliamentary public audit body headed by an autonomous official (the Comptroller and Auditor General) with judicial tenure, to report to Parliament on the broad reasonableness of the conventions and assumptions made in the Treasury's official forecasts. The Chancellor declared, 'We will not leave ourselves open to accusations of accounting tricks, dubious figures or rigging of the rules...' (quoted in Chote 1997). NAO's new task was duly enshrined in the government's statutory Code for Fiscal Stability.[9]

Figure 9.2 shows a markedly lower incidence of critical reports about forecasts in the two newspapers surveyed in New Labour's early years. Conditions for fiscal forecasting were benign, with low inflation, rising revenues, and falling cyclical spending. Such conditions provided fiscal headroom for extra spending to respond to political emergencies (such as a winter hospital-beds crisis in 1997–1998 that tested the credibility of New Labour's election pledge to 'save the NHS') without accusations about fiddled forecasts of the kind that were levelled at the forecast in the vignette.

---

[8] That interviewee said no-one outside the Treasury was capable of providing forecasts at that time, but later said NAO had had no difficulty in recruiting people with the necessary skills to certify forecasts.

[9] Written into the 1998 Finance Act, Section 155 and covering Financial Statements and Budget Reports, Economic and Fiscal Strategy Reports and Debt Management Reports.

But (as Figure 9.2 also shows), over-optimistic fiscal forecasting became a blame magnet again in the middle and later New Labour years.[10] Critics noted five successive years of Treasury over-forecasts of tax revenue, especially of revenue from the financial sector following a stock market drop in the early 2000s. They challenged what they saw as implausible assumptions about likely GDP growth and the size of the 'output gap' in the economy (which determined how much government borrowing was counted as 'structural' rather than 'cyclical') (OBR 2022). They accused the Treasury of 'moving the goalposts' over its fiscal rules when in July 2005—shortly after New Labour's third successive general election victory—it redated the economic cycle by pushing the start date back by two years to 1997–1998. That apparently technical decision to add two 'good years' to the cycle conveniently allowed the Treasury to claim the 'golden rule' of only borrowing to invest had been met over the cycle—a rule that would otherwise have been broken (IFS 2009: 82).

What challenge did NAO present over such issues? As with the earlier forecasting regimes (and no doubt for similar self-protective reasons) NAO consulted with other experts and institutions,[11] comparing their estimates of items such as the trend rate of growth with those made in the Treasury forecasts. But the 'invitation' it had accepted was quite circumscribed. The task was not to audit the numbers themselves but the reasonableness of any conventions and assumptions the Treasury chose to submit for review (plus, after 2000, a review of any changes and a review of every convention or assumption once every three years).

One ex-Treasury interviewee recalled exchanges with NAO over underestimated Treasury forecasts of tax credit spending and said the Treasury sometimes 'had to work quite hard to prevent NAO drawing blood'. One of the major political figures said there had been 'some quite intensive difficult discussions...you couldn't come up with things that were off the wall'. Another played down the difference between NAO validation and the subsequent OBR system, asserting that NAO 'grew into that job' and over time had come to present a credible challenge. And a senior ex-Treasury official said that although NAO's validation of forecasts was largely 'symbolic' and limited in credibility, it enabled Treasury mandarins to 'play the NAO card'—that is, invoke risk of political embarrassment from non-validation by NAO in their discussions with ministers, 'to ensure we stayed honest'.

But apart from the tax credit example (which itself can be argued to be a case of the NAO doing its normal day job and consequently more likely to be able to 'draw blood') none of our interviewees came up with a specific instance of NAO obliging

---

[10] See House of Commons Treasury Select Committee 2005 §14; IFS 2006: 7; IFS 2009: 82 and 85, Table 5.1.

[11] Among those NAO consulted were Professor Peter Spencer (University of York); Ernst and Young ITEM Club; the Bank of England; the CBI; the European Central Bank; the European Commission (Economic and Financial DG); IMF; Morgan Stanley; NIESR; OECD; and Oxford Economics Ltd.

the Treasury to change course overtly. And whereas the Treasury's re-dating of the 'economic cycle' after the 2005 general election was challenged by outside critics and was cynically described by one of our ex-official interviewees as 'finding money down the back of the sofa', NAO chose to approve the revision with only minor caveats that were apparently largely resolved at middle-grade official level.

Indeed, there were obvious question marks about the technical capacity of an audit body primarily concerned with assessing regularity and value for money issues in public spending to evaluate assumptions about issues like the size of the 'output gap' and trend rates of economic growth. Professional macro-economists were divided over such issues and there were no universally recognized conventions, while on interest rates, the Treasury never revealed its forecasting assumptions because of the obvious market sensitivity (Chote 1997). A leading academic commentator, David Heald, complained:

> ...NAO does not have, nor could it have, the technical macroeconomic expertise to match that of the Treasury. Second, this arrangement ('look only at what we ask you to look at') breaches the fundamental postulate of auditing that there must be independence to investigate as well as independence to report...the NAO has allowed itself to be misused.
>
> (Heald 2009: §6; see also Heald and MacLeod 2002: §505).

Indeed, as far back as 2001, the Treasury's budget briefings to the Chancellor included defensive points to make against possible accusations that 'NAO audit process is a sham/NAO merely a puppet of HMT'.

Several interviewees from that era said there was debate inside government about possible transfer of responsibility for fiscal forecasting and reporting to an independent public body, at roughly the same time as the government announced a decision to give independence to the Office for National Statistics in November 2005 (a late delivery of Labour's 1997 manifesto pledge). We were also told that in New Labour's final years, in the immediate aftermath of the 2008 financial crisis, some senior officials 'pushed quite hard' for such a move. As in the 1990s, various schemes for enhanced independent assessments were also floated outside government. The Institute for Fiscal Studies said in its pre-election 2005 'Green Budget' that 'credibility might be improved' by delegating more fiscal policymaking to independent bodies and set out several possible models (IFS 2005: 6 and 39). As in 1997, the Liberal Democrats' 2005 election manifesto promised more independent assessment of whether the Treasury was meeting fiscal rules, by beefed-up NAO validation. And in 2008 the Conservatives went further by announcing plans for a separate Office for Budget Responsibility (OBR) to provide neutral fiscal forecasts and set out an independent view of the state of the public finances.

Former Labour ministers we interviewed said the time was not ripe for such a move, when the Treasury was grappling with a global financial crisis, though all said it might have been adopted later, had Labour been re-elected in 2010. One pointed out that no other forecasters had avoided the forecasting errors made by the Treasury in 2007/2008. And there was certainly an issue of political timing that could have made any shift to a different forecasting regime awkward at that point. Several interviewees thought that after a decade of New Labour in government and Gordon Brown's ascent from Chancellor to Prime Minister, any such a move would have risked being taken as an admission that the government's earlier forecasting regime had failed. So in its final months the Labour government instead countered the opposition parties' proposals by passing a Fiscal Responsibility Act, binding itself—and, perhaps more to the point, its successor—to reductions in debt and deficit but with no change in forecasting machinery.

Stop me before I kill again: the OBR Era, 2010–

The IFS's 2005 options for greater independence in fiscal machinery comprised eight schemes listed in order of radicalism. Those options ranged from independent forecasting through autonomous policy advice to completely independent setting of fiscal objectives and associated policy choices. One option, close to the centre of this spectrum, involved independent fiscal forecasting and reporting (judging adherence to fiscal rules) but government retention of fiscal policy making—essentially describing what became OBR. One of the key players said the idea, taken up by the Conservatives in 2008, had been influenced more by the Monetary Policy Committee (MPC) of the Bank of England than by the 'Wise Men' under the Major government. But MPC had appeared in a snap announcement immediately after Labour came to power in 1997 (its election manifesto had contained only a single line vaguely alluding to 'reform' of the Bank of England). By contrast, the pledge to set up OBR figured prominently in the Conservatives' 2010 manifesto and the party had established OBR in 'shadow' form before the election, headed by Sir Alan Budd.

So just as it was primed for a major spending squeeze in 2010 (described in Chapter 5), the official Treasury had plenty of time to prepare for a change in the fiscal forecasting and reporting regime after the 2010 election. Predictably enough, the 2010 Conservative/Liberal Democrat coalition agreement included the OBR promised in the Conservative manifesto (and repeal of the previous government's Fiscal Responsibility Act) but not the all-party Council for Fiscal Stability in that of the Liberal Democrats.

It took a year to establish OBR in legislation and in its own premises, such that the interim OBR was still part of the Treasury in terms of location, pay, and rations at the time of the crucial post-election 2010 emergency budget and the spending review which followed it. The Treasury also continued to operate the IT technology and infrastructure for handling the budget numbers. But, in contrast to the NAO validation regime, OBR from the outset made the judgements behind the fiscal forecasts accompanying the new government's spending plans, and Treasury officials were precluded from making the sort of presentational adjustments that were described in the vignette. Indeed, in contrast to the position in (say) 1992 or 2008, a bad forecast was if anything likely to be politically helpful for the government's post-election fiscal squeeze in 2010, as described in Chapter 5.

In its early life, the political path of the new body was rocky. The political impartiality of its interim head, Sir Alan Budd, was challenged.[12] The interim OBR's forecast of economic growth accompanying the post-election emergency budget in June 2010 was attacked as over-optimistic by some other forecasters, such as Schroders and Capital Economics.[13] The extent to which the fledgling OBR was genuinely independent from the Treasury was questioned too, for example over the fact that the Treasury handled OBR media inquiries and that Treasury officials were seconded to staff the new organisation, using Treasury selection procedures (Inman 2010).

There were some other tricky blame issues for OBR later in the life of the Coalition government. One was OBR's acceptance of the revenue department's (HMRC) estimates of the yield of the top rate of income tax, in a review that was used by the government to justify the cutting of top tax rates from 50 to 45 per cent in the 2012 Budget (Seely 2018: 22 and 27–28). Another was a challenge by the SNP over what it claimed were unduly pessimistic OBR forecasts of North Sea oil revenues at the time of the Scottish independence referendum in 2014 (BBC 2014). In the event OBR proved too optimistic: oil revenues subsequently crashed.

Still, Figure 9.2 suggests that after 2011 OBR mostly attracted a lower incidence of reports indicating blame or criticism than its predecessor forecasting regimes. Indeed, it was 'blessed' in advance in the 'Green Budget' issued before the 2010 election by the Institute for Fiscal Studies which said an OBR-type body was more likely to be effective than NAO validation because:

[It] might have discouraged Gordon Brown and his advisers from 'sniffing round the forecasters' pockets' from 2002 onwards... Mr Brown might have felt constrained to ...restrain government borrowing more quickly than he did as revenues fell short of his forecasts...when the financial crisis hit, we would have

[12] The subsequent appointment of Robert Chote, former Director of the Institute of Fiscal Studies, as head of OBR a few months after the election brought to the position a prominent critic of the Treasury's earlier forecasting regimes.

[13] In defensive mode reminiscent of its predecessors, OBR said its forecast lay within the range of predictions by other forecasters and was 'bang in line with the consensus' (House of Commons Treasury Committee 2010: 7–8).

had a...smaller structural budget deficit and...public debt. Perhaps more impor-
tantly, voters and investors may have seen the government's fiscal promises as
more believable.

(IFS 2010: 262).

Nor did enthusiasm for OBR from outside experts stop there. An external review
(mandated by the 2011 Act that set up OBR) conducted in 2014 by the former First
Parliamentary Budget Officer in Canada (Kevin Page) gave the organization a rave
review (Page 2014). Similar praise was bestowed on OBR shortly after the end of
our period by IMF's 2016 'fiscal transparency review' of the UK (IMF 2016), to
which we return in Chapter 11.

Describing how OBR impacted on the planning of public spending, one senior
figure in the Coalition government said last-minute changes in OBR forecasts gave
Treasury ministers and officials little time to adjust their spending plans (but the
same applied in the previous regime, and hasty last-minute changes are arguably
inherent in any planning exercise that has a lot of moving parts). At the same time,
the obligation on Treasury to submit documents to OBR well in advance of fiscal
events ('not the night before') was seen by another interviewee as making more
of a reality of the aspiration to fix the spending envelope in advance of spending
allocations. A third said the officials who transferred to the new organization were
conspicuously cautious about sharing information with their Treasury colleagues,
to emphasize their independence.

Several interviewees also commented on the disappearance of some of the 'back
pockets' available to the Treasury under the previous forecasting regime. One
example was the so-called 'AME margin', a buffer for forecast error in AME spending introduced after AME and DEL spending were split in 1998. The Treasury
tried to reinvent this *de facto* reserve on top of the main Reserve in 2010 but OBR
insisted it be taken out. Similarly, while the Treasury had previously left out of
its forecasts the long-established tendency of departments to under-spend their
budgets,[14] OBR's forecasts incorporated assumptions of underspending, removing
another long-standing 'fudge factor' from the Treasury's repertoire. The existence
of OBR also ruled out the option of changing forecasts rather than spending plans
to make the figures add up. One senior interviewee thought that for the Treasury 'there was nowhere to go in fiddling the numbers'. It certainly seems to have
changed the way the game was played, in that after our period the Treasury simply chose not to set any clear numerical fiscal targets for OBR to assess during the
Brexit and coronavirus crises. We return to the issue of 'fiddling the numbers' in
the next chapter.

---

[14] Already noted by Heclo and Wildavsky (1974: 105). Underspending ran at between 1 and 2 per
cent of estimates throughout our period, even in the austerity years (see OBR 2021b, Table 3.5).

'Golden Gurus?' Forecasts Compared to Outturns

So what if any difference did those various institutional forms make to forecasting performance, in terms of accuracy and bias? Figure 9.3, based on OBR's historical database going back to 1990, compares the gap between outturn and forecast for receipts, spending, deficit and GDP growth over the different forecasting eras covered in this study. It also includes Treasury forecasts in the two years preceding the 'Wise Men' era, and comprises a separate calculation to exclude major crisis years from the analysis for the NAO validation and OBR era, to allow a non-crisis comparison with the 'Wise Men' system. The numbers are 'two-year ahead' errors, with the errors for receipts and spending errors are expressed as changes in ratios to GDP rather than as absolute errors.[15]

Figure 9.3 shows that the forecast errors for receipts, deficit and GDP growth in the two pre-Wise Men years were strikingly higher than any of the other regimes, though the same does not apply to forecasts of spending growth. For the two longer-lived regimes (NAO validation and OBR), OBR showed rather lower forecast errors for spending growth while the NAO validation regime shows markedly

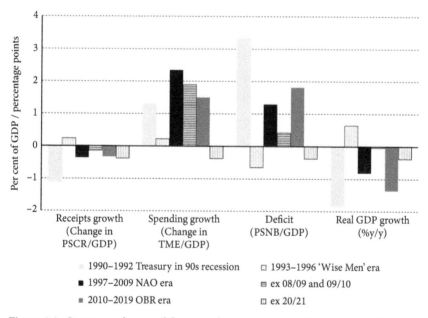

Figure 9.3 Outturns, plans, and forecasts for receipts, spending growth, deficit, and GDP growth in different forecasting eras

Source: Update of Chart 2.2 from OBR (2014)

---

[15] Especially upward revisions to nominal GDP through methodological changes that make outturn levels hard to compare with forecasts.

lower errors for GDP growth (in both cases, for both crisis and non-crisis conditions). The figure indicates optimism in forecasts of receipts for most of the
time (except for the Wise Men era, in which there was no major financial crisis),
while public spending growth exceeded forecast in most of the different forecasting
regimes, with consequent errors in forecasts of deficits.

That pattern chimes with a remark by a veteran forecaster, who said, 'Tax
revenue always turns out to be more cyclically responsive than expected, and
always takes the Treasury by surprise.'[16] In the early 2000s, such over-forecasting
of tax receipts took place even during periods of reasonably accurate GDP
forecasts.[17] But turning from forecast accuracy to the issue of bias, the IMF found
less bias in the OBR's forecasting record up to that date than under the previous
Treasury regime, notably in forecasts of revenue and fiscal balance (IMF 2016:
47 §75 and Figure 2.13). Their analysis would suggest that over our period at
least, OBR's forecasting errors were more evenly divided between optimism and
pessimism than its predecessor regimes—precisely the issue to which the creation
of OBR was directed.

Figure 9.4 shows what happened to GDP deflator forecasts and outturns over the
same time span. It demonstrates that, as noted in Chapter 1, inflation was mostly
low and stable over the period compared to the 1970s and 1980s (Davies 2006),

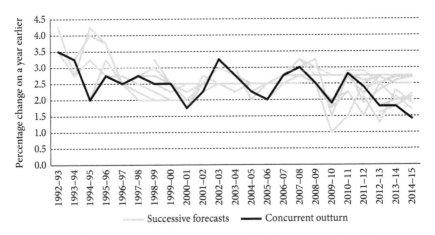

Figure 9.4 GDP deflator forecasts and outturns 1992–1993 to 2014–2015

Source: Official Treasury and OBR forecast documents and authors' calculations. Concurrent
outturn calculated based on methodology in Crawford et al 2018.

---

[16] How surprising it really was in the pre-OBR era is perhaps debatable: one interviewee observed
'HMT knew the forecasts were too optimistic and it would all end in tears'.
[17] For 2010/2011 there were also marked divergences between forecast and outturn for income and
corporation taxes (Riley and Chote 2014: 66, Table 4.1), which also resembled the pattern of our
opening vignette. In both cases the result was a huge tax shortfall that precipitated a major spending
squeeze.

such that forecasts mostly aligned fairly closely to outturns. Along with lower inflation went lower and less volatile interest rates than in earlier times, in turn leading
to reduced and more predictable debt service costs. The two main exceptions,
shown in Figure 9.4, were lower than forecast inflation in the early 1990s and
after the 2008 international financial crisis, when oil prices collapsed. That over-
forecasting of inflation in the early 1990s had the convenient 'back pocket' effect of
making it easier for departments to meet apparently tough cash spending targets.
Similarly, a big un-forecasted drop in inflation in 2009, when oil prices collapsed,
gave the Chancellor the option of banking approximately £15bn of savings in
lower borrowing with no reduction in real-terms spending) or of increasing public spending both in real terms and as a proportion of GDP, by choosing not to
reduce cash limits.[18]

Looking Wider and Looking Further Ahead: Long-Term Fiscal Sustainability Projections

What was forecast and reported also changed. The National Assets Register in
1998, the introduction of accrual accounts in central government in 2000 and
the advent of 'whole of government accounts' first published in 2010 represented
efforts to take a wider look at public assets and liabilities. But the period also wit-
nessed a development of forecasts or projections extending over decades rather
than just the next year or two.

In defence, there was a long-established tradition of ten-year policy reviews
(cutting across annuality in spending allocations), and 'forward looks' projecting
possible spending patterns beyond a single electoral term had been undertaken
for other policy domains in earlier times too.[19] During our period there were
some 'longer look' fiscal forecasts associated with proposals for major constitutional change, notably over the Scottish independence referendum in 2014 (and
just after the end of our period, over the prospects for the UK in or out of the EU
in the context of the 2016 Brexit referendum). But longer-term analysis of 'fiscal
sustainability', extending over decades, became a regular and systematic feature of
budget reporting from the late 1990s.

New Labour's 1998 Code for Fiscal Stability required 'projections of the outlook
for the key fiscal aggregates' for at least ten years ahead, to be published in Budget documents 'to shed light on the intergenerational impact and sustainability

---

[18] Arguably an echo of 1920s spending cutback politics (Hood and Himaz 2017: 26 (Table 2.1 and
50) but in this case it was the second option that was chosen.

[19] For example, the Treasury had run a 'forward look' exercise in 1949, aiming to project at least some
types of spending up to 1960. Some officials were evidently sceptical of this venture: a senior mandarin,
Sir Bernard Gilbert, commented, 'I doubt whether more can be done than to make...a shot at 1950 and
possibly 1951. Looking ahead as far as 1955 cannot...be much more than crystal-gazing'. (T230/151
Forward Planning of Government Expenditure 1949, EAS 50/02, note dated 10 March 1949.)

of fiscal policy'. Further, from 2003 the Treasury and the Government Actuary's Department began to publish long-term projections of public sector retirement pension costs, while previously government accounts simply reported the costs of pensions paid out, not the expected longer-term costs. Those long-term projections provided much of the evidence for a major review of public sector pensions after the 2010 election (Independent Public Service Pensions Commission 2011).

An ex-Treasury interviewee said 'generational accounting' (focusing on transfers between generations in public spending) had been in 'high fashion' in international policy circles at that time. The EU Commission was also concerned about fiscal sustainability, given that ageing populations raised questions about the future ability of member states to meet the conditions of the 1997 EU Stability and Growth Pact preceding the adoption of the Euro. But that interviewee thought the adoption of long-term fiscal forecasting in the UK at that time had more to do with seizing credit-claiming opportunities in a fiscally benign period than with the serious worry about fiscal sustainability that existed in the early 1990s or the early 2010s.

Like much else in the public spending world, the convoluted terminology ('illustrative projection') in the 1998 Code for Fiscal Stability was there for a reason. It denoted 'what if' exercises based on the beguiling assumption that the then prevailing fiscal rules would be met over the decades. The projections were thus not strictly 'forecasts' in the sense of attempts to predict what was most likely to happen in the future, for example by projecting historical patterns of revenue and spending separately to discover whether the rules were in fact likely to be met.

Arguably the most noticeable feature of the 1999 fiscal sustainability forecast viewed in the light of hindsight two decades or so later is its expectation of long-term GDP growth to underpin the sustainability of increased public spending. Figure 9.5 shows how optimistic those expectations look against the outturns up to 2015 (a gap widened still further by later developments), though they were notably pessimistic for the first half of the 2000s. Real GDP was approximately 7 per cent lower in 2016 than that 1999 projection.

Figure 9.6 compares outturns at the time of writing with the forecasts of public spending growth and public sector net debt in those 1999 'illustrative projections'. As can be seen, the 1999 expectation was that current 'consumption' spending would increase particularly through the effects of more spending on health care (which did indeed occur). But it conveniently assumed that 'transfers'—including big-ticket welfare payments such as the state retirement pension and means-tested benefits—would fall correspondingly as a share of GDP as GDP grew, since indexation policy at that time was to link those benefits to prices rather than earnings, creating fiscally sustainable space for an increase in current consumption spending.

But Figure 9.6 shows that in the outturn there was no long-term fall in transfer spending relative to GDP. Rather, such spending stayed flat or rose slightly (reflecting political choices for above-inflation uprating of retirement pensions,

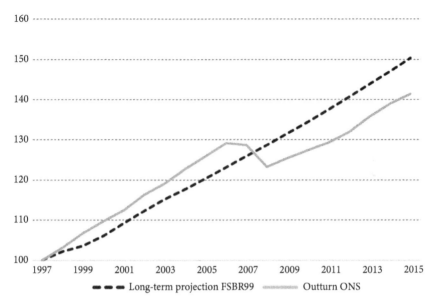

Figure 9.5 1999 forecast of long-term GDP growth compared to outturn, 1997–2015

Source: Long-term forecast: FSBR 1999; outturn ONS

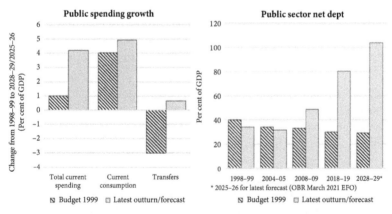

Figure 9.6 Latest outturn or forecast and 1999 long-term projections of public spending growth and public sector net debt

Source: OBR databank

higher disability benefits spending and the effect of two big recessions on working-age spending). But that spending surprise pales into insignificance compared to the effect on public sector net debt of a deep financial crisis followed by a global pandemic. At the time of writing some fifty percentage points of the rise in public debt over the past two decades had been incurred in just four years (2008/2009, 2009/2010, 2020–2021, and 2021–2022). The reassuring 'projection' in the 1999 Budget document that 'unlike in many countries, Britain does not have long-term fiscal problems in store' and that 'given the assumptions for transfer payments, public current consumption can grow at an average real rate of around 2½ per cent for the next thirty years and still remain consistent with the fiscal rules' (HM Treasury 1999, 31 and 89) looks remarkably optimistic in retrospect. Assessment of long-term fiscal prospects passed to OBR after 2010 and it remains to be seen whether OBR's rather less optimistic conclusions on that subject[20] will prove to be more accurate than those produced by earlier forecasting regimes.

Conclusion

This chapter shows that the 1993–1994 deficit forecast episode described in the vignette, while dramatic even three decades later, was not a once-in-a-century occurrence but rather one instance of major economic shocks frequently taking fiscal forecasters by surprise. The gap between the March 2008 budget forecast of the deficit in 2010–2011 and the outturn was of much the same order (7 per cent of GDP) as that between the 1990 Medium Term Financial Strategy forecast and the 1993–1994 outturn in our vignette (Riley and Chote 2014: 2, Table 1.1).

Returning to the three questions we raised at the outset about how forecasting fitted into the UK's fiscal constitution over our period, the first related to how and why politicians chose institutional arrangements for forecasting and reporting. Here the creation of OBR is a particularly striking instance of ministers choosing to adopt constitutional arrangements relating to public spending that on the face of it seemed guaranteed to embarrass and constrain them. This development is a notable example of elected politicians preferring blame-avoidance to credit-claiming opportunities (Weaver 1986 and 1988), following several earlier efforts to shift or share the blame for forecast errors. But there was certainly some political credit to be claimed for creating a new independent watchdog as well.

Indeed, the move took place in a particular political window, namely the inauguration of the 2010 Coalition. Had the incumbents won re-election in 1997 or 2010, major change in the forecasting arrangements might have run more political risk of being counted as an admission of earlier failure: as it was, creating OBR provided a way for the Conservatives and Liberal Democrats to keep reminding voters and the media about the over-optimism of their predecessors' forecasts. And the advent of a coalition government in 2010 could arguably have increased

---

[20] At the time of writing OBR's long-term fiscal projections assumed transfer payments would be uprated in line with earnings rather than prices, even though the indexation policy for most such transfers (other than the state pension) was to uprate with prices.

the risk of deadlock over key fiscal judgements among the two coalition part-
ners in the absence of OBR.[21] Similar conditions did not apply at other times in
our period.

The second question concerned how fiscal forecasting fitted into Heclo and Wildavsky's (1974) 'village life' of the Treasury, and how that relationship changed.
Broadly, there were moves to bring in new institutional players (Wise Men, NAO,
OBR), making the rules of the game more explicit and by the end of the period
making the official relationships more arms-length as between the technocrats
who produced the forecasts on the one hand, and Treasury ministers and their
SpAds on the other.[22]

At the same time, it was clear from our interviews that almost all the players in
the OBR system had been part of the same department in their previous lives, knew
each other well and continued to work within the Whitehall square mile even if
not in the same building. Whitehall did not become 'a government of strangers'
(Heclo 1977) overnight and how OBR-type arrangements would operate in different circumstances has yet to be demonstrated.[23] Indeed the OBR regime might
possibly be interpreted as a reactive movement, compensating for what one interviewee saw as a weakening of an older egalitarian Treasury culture of 'challenge
and be challenged' (irrespective of rank or grade or political status), being replaced
by a more hierarchist culture in which Treasury ministers and especially their
SpAds were harder to challenge when they moved into the detail of Treasury
operations.

When it comes to our third question, of what happened to the size of forecast errors (the gap between outturns and predictions), our analysis in section
7 showed that while those different institutional arrangements arguably made a
difference to how political credit was to be claimed and blame resisted, the technology of forecasting did not alter greatly. Similarly, while the IMF's (2016) 'fiscal
transparency' analysis quoted in section 6 found the OBR did better than NAO,
our analysis in Figure 9.3 shows that gaps between forecast and outturn by no
means disappeared, even in non-crisis times. It remained true that no-one found
a reliable way to foretell dramatic shifts and shocks in the economy for the purpose
of planning public spending.

---

[21] An issue that threatened to break up the Liberal-Conservative coalition in the early 1920s, before
it eventually collapsed over foreign policy.

[22] The system arguably went 'up-grid' and possibly 'down-group' in cultural theory terminology
(Thompson Ellis and Wildavsky 1990) as forecasts and key fiscal judgements moved out of the Treasury
'nuclear family' into a separate group and from implicit understandings about how forecasting was
produced to formally enacted rules.

[23] As happened for example with regulation of formerly privatised utilities after a first generation in
which both the new regulators and the industry players had previously worked in the same departments
and enterprises (Hall et al. 2000).

Timeline: Institutional Arrangements for Official Economic and Fiscal Forecasting 1993–2015

1975: Industry Act required the Treasury to maintain a publicly accessible economic model to demonstrate likely effects on the economy of different assumptions about policies and events, and to use that model to publish forecasts twice a year. Treasury officials produced forecasts for Ministers in the shadow of competition from outside forecasters.

1986: The Treasury began to publish summaries of a range of other forecasts.

1993: In addition to, but separate from, Treasury forecasting, a Panel of seven (later six) Independent Forecasters was created with a Treasury chair and secretariat, reporting three times (later twice) a year.

1996: Liberal Democrats and others proposed an independent committee to advise Parliament on fiscal forecasting.

1997/1998: Panel of Independent Forecasters scrapped; the Code for Fiscal Stability in the 1998 Finance Act provided for certification of the reasonableness and transparency of the underlying economic assumptions of Treasury forecasts by NAO and for the Treasury to produce long-term 'illustrative projections' of spending prospects over future decades.

1999: The first long-term fiscal projections appeared in the Budget 'Red Book', concluding 'Britain does not have long-term fiscal problems in store'.

2000: NAO initiated a rolling three-year review of forecasting assumptions and conventions in addition to its review of changes and of assumptions/conventions proposed by the Treasury.

2002: The first Long-Term Public Finance report appeared as a separate analytic publication.

Mid-2000s: Over-optimistic revenue forecasts in SR2002 and 2004 attracted criticism.

2005: Liberal Democrat election manifesto pledged to empower NAO to check budget numbers for observance of fiscal rules; the IFS pre-election Green Budget set out options for a greater role for independent actors in fiscal policy, including revenue forecasting and reporting; the Treasury chose to retrospectively re-date the onset of the then current economic cycle, thereby enabling the government to claim it had met the 'golden rule'.

2006 onwards: successive IFS Green Budgets returned to the idea of handing over some reporting and forecasting functions to a body independent of the Treasury.

2008: The Conservatives in opposition announced plans for an independent Office of Budget Responsibility for fiscal reporting and forecasts, constituted as a non-ministerial department run by autonomous experts and reporting to Parliament.

2009: The Conservatives set up OBR on a shadow basis, headed by Sir Alan Budd, former Chief Economic Adviser to the Treasury.

2010: Shortly before losing the 2010 general election, Labour in government enacted a Fiscal Responsibility Act requiring reductions in debt and deficit, as an alternative to OBR. After the election, OBR set up on an interim basis in the Treasury and staffed by Treasury officials on secondment under the direction of an independent chair and two other directors; its first forecast was attacked by opposition critics as over-optimistic, together with accusations of political interference on the grounds that media inquiries to OBR were handled by the Treasury and allegations that Prime Minister David Cameron had gained early access to some OBR figures that enabled him to wrongfoot the opposition in Parliament. Robert Chote, formerly Director of IFS, replaced interim head Sir Alan Budd as head of OBR.

2011: The Budget Responsibility and National Audit Act formally established OBR to report on fiscal performance against rules or targets and to produce short and longer-term forecasts and projections of revenue and other fiscal aggregates for the UK government. OBR obtained in its own premises, separate but only a short walk away from Treasury.

2012: OBR was given responsibility for forecasting tax revenues for Scotland.

2014: OBR was given responsibility for forecasting tax revenues for Wales.

2014: OBR's projections of future North Sea oil revenues were attacked by the SNP in the Scottish independence referendum campaign.

2015: Treasury review of OBR (HM Treasury 2015b) recommended OBR and the devolved governments should provide more information and analysis to each other, that OBR should have a rolling three-year budget to underpin its independence, that no change should be made to OBR's policy remit, and that OBR should produce a regular report on fiscal risks in line with IMF's fiscal transparency code (see Chapter 11).

10

The People, the Rules, and the Numbers

The introduction of more sophisticated financial information on costs…has provided the means to achieve better management in government which is not available to countries which do not have the information.

(Senior ex-Treasury interviewee).

RAB…didn't work. We tried.

(Senior ex-Treasury interviewee).

Vignette: Cash in the Attic? Responses to a New Accounting Regime 2002/2003

In February 2003, the Ministry of Defence (MOD) surprised its Treasury spending team—but apparently not the Treasury's accounting group—by announcing a switch of about £1bn per year from 'non-cash' into cash (or 'near-cash') spending between 2003 and 2006. By revaluing its assets downwards (and hence its non-cash depreciation charges), MOD could reduce its non-cash spending and then switch a phantom gain into spendable cash—something often done to flatter corporate balance sheets.

Described as a 'bolt from the blue' by one Treasury spending official, this announcement caused alarm among the Treasury's ministers and its Defence spending team, because, just as with the 2005 Department of Health overspend described in the vignette to Chapter 1, a switch of that size from non-cash to near-cash threatened New Labour's 'golden' fiscal rule. What counted for that golden rule was the National Accounts estimate of depreciation or capital consumption (which was not linked to departmental accounts), plus other current spending (which did reflect near-cash spending by departments). And those technicalities meant that MOD's abrupt switch would serve to increase current spending in the National Accounts at a time when the government had little fiscal headroom over meeting its much-vaunted rule.[1]

---

[1] MOD's announcement was not a claim on the Reserve, but it came at a time when the total Reserve (for 2003–2004) amounted to only £1.4bn. And in the event, that Reserve turned out to have been spent

The Way the Money Goes. Christopher Hood, Maia King, Iain McLean, and Barbara Piotrowska,
Oxford University Press. © Christopher Hood, Maia King, Iain McLean, and Barbara Piotrowska (2023).
DOI: 10.1093/oso/9780198865087.003.0010

At that time, 'non-cash' and 'near-cash' spending were a relative novelty in the UK central government public spending world. Those new adjectival terms had appeared respectively in the first and second stages of a two-part move to a new resource or accruals-based accounting and budgeting (RAB) system between 2000 and 2002. 'Near-cash' was the spendable cash element of the new accounting framework. It represented actual cash payments, with accruals adjustments applied to allocate it to the year in which the activity took place rather than in the year in which it was paid for (typically after the event). By contrast, 'non-cash' represented items such as depreciation and the costs of holding land and other assets that had not previously been recorded under the traditional cash-in, cash-out system of government accounting, and the RAB framework required departments to manage non-cash within their controlled spending totals.[2]

As we noted in Chapter 4, the new RAB system had been initiated by Kenneth Clarke, Chancellor in the previous government, with a Green Paper in 1994 (HM Treasury 1994b) followed by a White Paper the following year (HM Treasury 1995). The assumption behind the move was that when government departments were given the opportunity to switch between cash and non-cash costs in managing their budgets, their managers would be less inclined than before to ignore important but previously 'off-balance-sheet' costs like depreciation and the cost of capital and other assets. Bringing those non-cash costs into the budgetary framework and allowing departments to switch between near-cash and non-cash, the argument went, could be expected to result in more efficient use of overall public resources. For example, it was expected to remove what one of our senior interviewees claimed to be an 'implicit bias' in cash accounting against capital spending, and to incentivize departments to dispose of surplus assets such as land and buildings that would otherwise be hoarded.[3] The idea of greater efficiency through business-type accounting 'resonated with Ministers, Parliament, and departments alike', according to one interviewee.

To allow such potential gains to be realized, the Treasury under the new regime controlled only the combined total of (near) cash and non-cash spending and did not impose separate control totals on near-cash as against non-cash. But as matters turned out, central government was still in transition to the new accounting framework at the time of New Labour's third spending review in the summer of 2002, so MOD's budgetary settlement was originally worked out in cash alone. The new non-cash category was added on hastily at the very end of the review process,

twice over by October 2003, well before the end of the financial year, as a result of an extra £1.2bn of expenditure on the Iraq war, plus a further £1.6bn of extra spending on other items, including asylum costs and the London underground.

[2] Near-cash was calculated as Resource and Capital Departmental Expenditure (DEL) less depreciation, cost of capital charges, impairments, stock write-offs, and other adjustments.

[3] Before RAB, central government accounting rules simply said departments should review their fixed assets regularly and sell surplus assets 'as quickly as possible', and capital charging was introduced in 1998 to incentivize them to do so.

when the Treasury asked MOD to estimate its expected breakdown of spending as between near-cash and non-cash. Those MOD estimates appeared in the Treasury 'Settlement Letter' to MOD after the spending review, summarized in Table 10.1.

The 2016 Chilcot report into the UK government's 2003 decision to go to war in Iraq showed that in early 2003 MOD had both motive and opportunity to find ways of increasing its spendable cash (Chilcot 2016: 505–520). The motive was a belief in the higher echelons of the department that MOD was underfunded to the tune of about £0.5bn a year relative to its agreed mission and responsibilities, particularly on the logistics side (though for its part the Treasury maintained that the 2002 Review was the best Defence settlement for twenty years). And the opportunity came in the form of the ability to switch between non-cash and near-cash in the then-new Resource Accounting and Budgeting ('RAB2') framework.

Hence MOD's abrupt move in February 2003, sharply reducing the 2002 forecasts for its non-cash spending shown in Table 10.1 and thereby giving itself the opportunity to switch about £1bn per year from unspendable non-cash into spendable near-cash. Under the newly introduced RAB2 rules, which it had studied closely and on which it carefully sought advice from the Treasury's accountants, MOD claimed it was entitled to make that switch, because it had reduced its asset base in three ways. First, at the very last minute before the new rules took effect, it opted to write down some £3.6bn of its assets under the previous transition-period RAB1 rules in which the cost of such write-offs did not count against the departmental control total (DEL). Second, it announced delays in some big procurement projects, thereby reducing the associated non-cash costs that would have applied had the projects run to their originally forecast timetables. Third, it extended the predicted lives of some of its major assets such as airframes, meaning that its

Table 10.1 Estimates of near-cash and non-cash in Ministry of Defence settlement letter for Spending Review 2002

		£bn			
		2002–2003 (Baseline)	2003–2004 (Plan)	2004–2005 (Plan)	2005–2006 (Plan)
	Resource DEL	31.4	33.0	33.8	34.7
	Capital DEL	5.5	6.0	6.3	6.9
Non-cash	Depreciation	7.6	8.1	8.3	8.8
	Cost of capital	5.1	5.2	5.3	5.4
	Other charges	–	0.1	–	–
Near-cash	Estimated cash spending	24.2	25.6	26.5	27.4
	Total DEL	29.3	30.9	31.8	32.8

Source: Calculated from Spending Review 2002 (HM Treasury 2002) and Report of the Iraq Inquiry (2016 Vol X, 13.1 Resources p. 508)

expected depreciation costs fell sharply as well. At the same time, MOD promptly allocated the proposed cash windfalls to its own key budget holders (Army, Navy, RAF, Defence Logistics Organisation) in January 2003—which ensured that the military top brass would see any subsequent reductions as spending cuts and cry foul to the media, as they duly did (Evans 2003).

MOD's Accounting Officer insisted that the department had followed all the official rules for financial management, but the relevant Treasury spending team ('DDI') evidently saw MOD's move as an effort to 'bounce' the Treasury by eleventh-hour creative accounting.[4] An internal Treasury document declared, 'MOD have acted in bad faith... there are no hard and fast rules in some areas...we need to be able to trust departments to work within the spirit of RAB and check with us where clarification is obviously required....this cash windfall has nothing to do with the RAB principles of efficiency or improved asset utilisation...MOD have constantly reassured us, until the very last minute, that non-cash forecasts in SR2002 were understated...It would appear that they have misled us'. Indeed, the episode was still vividly recalled by interviewees from both departments fifteen years or so later.

For the Treasury, the timing for a battle with MOD could hardly have been worse, since the Blair government's fateful decision to go to war in Iraq the following month (March 2003) meant that any moves that could be portrayed as cutting defence funding at such a time would inevitably create serious political embarrassment. So a stopgap deal was struck between Treasury and MOD officials, in which MOD agreed to switch no more than £200m a year from non-cash to near-cash for the time being. After months of wrangling, ministers settled the issue with a deal that included an external review of MOD's finances by a private-sector accountancy expert (as a sop to the Treasury), while MOD was allowed £400m per year of extra near-cash to spend instead of the £1bn a year it had originally aimed for.

Part of the reason for the Treasury's alarm over MOD's scheme for turning non-cash into near-cash was that it could open the floodgates for other departments to follow. Such fear was not unfounded. Similar though smaller switches did indeed occur in other departments in 2003–2004, notably the then Department of Constitutional Affairs (£345m) and the Department of Health (£90m), followed by the much larger Department of Health near-cash overspend of about £2.6bn which suddenly emerged in mid-2005, taking the Treasury's Health spending team by surprise, as we saw in Chapter 1. At that time the Treasury apparently had not read across from this MOD episode to grasp the equivalent risk to the 'Golden Rule' posed by another major spending department whose 2002 settlement had left it awash with capital and non-cash allocations it could not spend.

---

[4] Indicating that Heclo and Wildavsky's (1974: 93) observation that 'bounces' were 'anathema to the Treasury' still applied.

The Treasury's eventual response to these non-cash to near-cash switches was to impose separate control totals on near-cash and non-cash spending such that switching could not take place without Treasury consent (a change officially enacted after the subsequent spending review in 2005 but applied through informal pressure before that). That response reduced the risk to the Treasury of unexpected large switches into near-cash, but arguably at the cost of seriously weakening the incentives RAB was originally intended to provide for departments to manage their assets and use their resources more efficiently by switching freely between near-cash and non-cash.

This MOD story might look like a tale of arcane small-print accounting rules, but it brings out some critical tensions between the formal and informal aspects of the fiscal constitution as discussed in Chapter 1—enacted rules on the one hand, unwritten expectations on the other (notably about trust, consultation and information-sharing). The story generally supports the analysis of several academic studies of Treasury spending control (including Heclo and Wildavsky 1974; Thain and Wright 1995; Deakin and Parry 2000) which stress the limitations of Treasury power, the efforts put into consultation to avoid 'bounces', and the practical necessity of proceeding by often messy bargaining with other key players (No 10, heavyweight Cabinet ministers, powerful departments).

More specifically this story also reflects two kinds of social tensions or disconnects in the UK public spending world at that time. One was the rocky relationship between the Treasury and MOD, the fourth largest spending department (often seen as a 'problem child' by the Treasury for reasons we set out in discussing the 1994 'Front Line First' episode in Chapter 3). The other was a disconnect between the Treasury's 'porthole' spending teams (mostly populated by economists or 'policy' officials) and its accountants during a time when ambitious changes in public sector accounting rules were in train. Those two epistemic groups within the bureaucracy worked in different places, under separate commands, with distinct frames of reference and (judging by what our interviewees said) fairly limited social interaction.

In this chapter, we begin by briefly describing the official rules and categories concerning public spending control numbers and some of the ways in which those rules and numbers changed over our period. Then we look at how the rules were applied, exploring who saw what as problematic gaming of those numbers and what measures or mechanisms were adopted to keep such gaming in check. We argue that 'relational distance' (or 'group')—a term denoting social closeness or distancing between players in a system—was a central focus of efforts to deal with gaming and ambiguities in the rules. But whereas the Treasury's efforts to limit 'gaming' by departments in the 2000s included an emphasis on informal 'togetherness' to cut relational distance, some major efforts to curb gaming by the Treasury itself took exactly the opposite form, by changes in the formal organization designed to increase the distance between the Treasury and other players in the system.

Budget Guidance, Classification Frameworks, and 'The Spirit of the Rules'

A manual entitled *Consolidated Budgeting Guidance* (CBG) first appeared in the later 2000s as an attempt to put all the accounting rules for budgeting into a single document that could be easily updated. As one of three documents replacing a hefty paper-age book (*The Government Accounting Manual*), CBG from 2008–2009[5] was a forbidding 50,000 word, 152-page document that combined stern exposition of formalities ('Treasury Ministers have the right to modify the budgeting guidance at any time') with repeated pleas to departments to keep their Treasury teams abreast of troubles as they developed, rather than springing unpleasant surprises on the Treasury at the last minute. It also contained numerous exhortations not to 'play the system': 'Departments are asked to go with the *spirit* of the spending control framework...departments should follow the *spirit* of the rules' [our emphasis: the all-important 'spirit of the rules' was of course not defined.]

In a section entitled 'Keeping Track of the Numbers', this document said:

1.50. Departments are expected to keep track of their authorized control totals as these change with Machinery of Government changes, other classification and transfer changes, issues from central funds, authorized transfers to near-cash, and...issues from the Reserve. Departments and spending teams should at all times have a common understanding of the authorized levels of:
* Resource Budget DEL and within it
    1. Near-cash...
    2. Administration Budget
* Capital Budget DEL

1.51. Departments and spending teams should also have a common understanding of the planned levels—and risks of variances to plans—of:
* Resource Budget AME
* Capital Budget AME

1.52. Departments are expected to monitor spending against plan and to share information with their Treasury spending team (via bilaterally agreed information supply) and the Treasury collectively (via COINS).[6]

---

[5] The Government Accounting Manual contained all the guidance later to be found in *Managing Public Money* (HM Treasury 2007a, reissued annually), *The Estimates Manual*, and *Consolidated Budgeting Guidance*.

[6] COINS (Combined Online Information System) was the digital database and monitoring system for public spending operating in the Treasury from 2007 to 2013. It was a bespoke system bought from a niche software provider based in New Zealand. In the face of persistent difficulties in operating the system—graphically described to us by several interviewees—the Treasury eventually chose to replace COINS with a completely new and more standard 'off the shelf' system, OSCAR (Online System for Central Accounting and Reporting) from 2013.

Even this daunting list was not complete. For example, as well as the four over-all 'control totals' mentioned, delegation limits (designating the maximum sums that could be spent on defined items without specific Treasury approval) had to be remembered—sometimes with difficulty, it appears.[7] The sums available within departmentally specific reserves (so-called 'Departmental Unallocated Provisions', which dated back to the 1960s in development aid but which were extended across government in 1998) also had to be tracked and reported. The same went for contingent liabilities (extra costs that might need to be paid out dependent on some factor outside government's control, such as court decisions over medical negligence cases or payments arising from government guarantees), which had to be reported to Parliament. There were also other 'policy ring-fences' set out in Spending Reviews, representing earmarked levels of spending for particular policies or services that could not be switched within any given control total. 'Baselines' (meaning the agreed cost of delivering existing policies, without reference to one-off increases from claims on the Reserve and the like) were another all-important and often disputed number that needed to be tracked both by Treasury and departments, because they almost invariably served as the starting-point for negotiations of future allocations in spending reviews.[8]

Those expenditure numbers kept changing, partly because of Prime Ministerial re-orderings of the Cabinet and central departments, policy changes from spending departments and new spending initiatives announced by the Chancellor at every fiscal event. The control and classification categories altered for other reasons as well, such as changes in the international and national accounting conventions: indeed, as we showed in Chapter 6, whether some types of spending counted as 'capital' or not depended on which accounting convention was used. Building on a 2002 GEP presentation, Figure 10.1 gives an indication of some of the major changes in the classification and control framework in the eventful decade between 1996 and 2006.

How the Rules and Categories Were Applied

The opening vignette to this chapter shows that a major department and its Treasury spending team clearly did not 'at all times have a common understanding' of the near-cash position and evidently had different views of what was meant by 'the spirit of the spending control framework' or 'the spirit of the rules'. The episode shows that departments did not invariably 'contact their Treasury spending team early so that alternative courses of action [could] be fully discussed while there

---

[7] For example, a 2007 survey by GEP revealed that numerous delegation limits had not been reviewed or changed for over a decade. Several spending teams were not certain they had submitted the most recent versions of those limits, and for some departments (notably Health) no written documentation on the subject could be found.

[8] They were a key component of GEP's sensitive, secret, and jealously guarded 'scorecard' for each spending review (a spreadsheet listing baselines, bids, and settlements for each department).

(a) 1996 top-line categorization of spending controls (all items in cash)

'Controlled' spending: ' New control total' (dating from 1992)	Running (Administration) costs	Programme costs
Uncontrolled or forecast spending	Spending outside 'control total' (e.g. cyclical social security, dept interest payments)	

(b) 1998 (still all cash, but 'current' and 'capital' divided, and also a new split between DEL and AME spending)

	Current (cash)	Capital (cash)
'Controlled' spending: DEL (3 year budget)	Most current programme spending Administration costs Current grants to NDPBs	Capital spending net of asset sales Capital grants
Uncontrolled or forecast spending: AME (annual forecast)	Most social security, debt, CAP, LG self-financed current Lottery current NDPBs own expenditure	Lottery capital LG self financed capital Public corporations capex including self-financed PCs

(c) 2000 ('accruals' partially replacing old cash system, with consequential categorization changes and additions)

	Resource (accruals)	Capital (accruals)
'Controlled' spending: DEL (3 year budget)	Main operating spend Administration costs NDPBs current spend	Capital spend net of asset sales Capital grants NDPBs capital spend Public corporations capex
Uncontrolled or forecast spending: AME (annual forecast)	Soc. security, debt, CAP, LG self-financed & lottery current Depreciation Cost of capital Provisions	Lottery capital LG self financed capital self-financed public corporations

(d) 2002 (next stage of 'accruals' with further categorisation changes)

	Resource (accruals)	Capital (accruals)
'Controlled' spending: DEL (3 year budget)	Main operating spend , incl. NDPBs Administration costs Capital grants Depreciation Cost of capital Provisions	Net capital spend including NDPBs
Uncontrolled or forecast spending: AME (annual forecast)	Soc. security, debt, CAP, LG self-financed & lottery current	Public corporations Capital AME e.g., self-financing PCs

(e) 2006 (more categorisation changes including a ring-fence between near-cash and non-cash)

	Resource (accruals)		Capital (accruals)
'Controlled' spending: DEL (3 year budget)	Programme spend: near cash	Programme spend: non cash (Provisions, etc.)	Net capital spend including NDPBs
	Administration spend: near cash	Administration spend: non cash	
Uncontrolled or forecast spending: AME (annual forecast)	Soc. security, debt, CAP, LG self-financed & lottery current		Public corporations Capital AME e.g., self-financing PCs

Figure 10.1 Ten years of changing classification frameworks for Treasury spending controls, 1996–2006

[was] still time to put them into effect...' The story thus raises the issue of who saw what as 'gaming', 'fiddles', 'cheating', or 'manipulation' in handling the public spending numbers. Where did the boundary lie between those creative interpretations of rules and categories that were considered damaging or reprehensible (therefore cheating of some kind), as against interpretations seen as legitimate or even as useful, constructive or creative workarounds?

The term 'gaming'

'Gaming' was a word we frequently heard in interviews and it appeared in numerous internal Treasury documents too. It was mostly used in a particular sense, to denote strategic interpretation of classification categories for departmental or policy advantage—as opposed to propriety issues like embezzlement, fraud, or other forms of misappropriation of public funds for private personal gain. The term thus connoted behaviour that, while not illegal, was seen to breach or stretch 'the spirit of the rules', as interpreted by the Treasury or other players. We heard the term, or its analogues, applied by Treasury people to denote strategic behaviour by departments or other spending bodies, but it was also sometimes used to denote such behaviour by the Treasury itself. For example, one interviewee recalled a so-called 'one fiddle rule' to which the Treasury had limited itself in a major spending review. And another interviewee, as already mentioned, recalled an old Treasury joke that 'there is no fiscal crisis that cannot be dealt with by swingeing classification changes'.

Spending control lends itself to gaming in that sense in at least two ways. One is through the inevitable ambiguity of the words used to describe the classification categories, such as the terms 'administration', 'front line', and 'back office' in the AC control regime that we explored in Chapter 8. All language is inherently ambiguous for reasons that have been discussed at least since the exposition of the 'Sorites paradox' by Eubulides in ancient Greece, namely that the world contains more things—items, objects, relationships—to be described than the words that are available in any language to denote them. As well as providing the source of puzzles, riddles, paradoxes, and jokes, such ambiguity of language creates opportunities for gaming and its analogues whenever words are used administratively.[9] The literature on 'incomplete contracts' in economics also stresses the practical impossibility of specifying what is to be done in every contingency that could conceivably arise (see for instance Grossman and Hart 1986; Hart and Moore 1990; Hart 1995).

Table 10.2 provides an illustrative list of spending categorizations, together with examples of ways of 'gaming' them by stretching or blurring tactics on the part of departments or the Treasury or both, that we came across in the course of this study and some of which we have explored in previous chapters.

[9] See Collins 2018; Hood 1976; Bevan and Hood 2006; Hood and Piotrowska 2021.

Table 10.2 Examples of 'gaming' by blurring or jumping categorical distinctions in public spending control

Boundary lines	Type of spending	Examples of creative (re)categorization
'Public spending'	Non-public spending or public non-spending such as loans	Taking spending off balance sheet by creating notionally 'private' debt liabilities (Chapter 4)
Spending consistent with stated fiscal or spending rules e.g. of budget balance or debt quotients	Spending that exceeds the level specified by fiscal or spending rules	Creating extra fiscal headroom by presentational adjustments in forecasts related to fiscal rules, e.g. expected tax revenue (Chapter 9)
'Controlled public spending' (subject to a full array of approvals or limitations)	Less- or non-controlled spending (subject to exemptions or to lighter oversight)	Using types of spending outside the normal control framework e.g. lottery funding for Olympic games (Chapter 12)
'Committed' or allocated spending	Unallocated or 'reserve' spending	Leaving spending allocations not fully agreed in practice, to be settled later through reserve claims (Chapter 3)
'Baseline' spending Costs of existing policy	Additional spending beyond current policy	Padding the baseline by adding costs of new or changed policies (Chapter 10)
'Protected' or 'ring fenced' domain specific spending	'Unprotected', vireable or 'non-ring fenced' spending	Adding unfunded liabilities to protected spending ('tuck unders') (Chapter 10)
'Capital' spending	Current or resource spending	Switching out of capital to fund extra resource spending (Chapters 4, 6, 10)
Spending within a budget period	Spending outside a budget period	Strategic deferral or rescheduling of spending from one budget period to another (Chapters 3, 4, 5)
'Administration' or 'back office' costs	'Programme' or 'front line' costs	Redescribing activity as 'front line' to turn it into programme costs (Chapter 8)
Cash or near-cash (spendable funds)	Non-cash outlays such as depreciation/capital cost	Turning non-cash into near-cash by reclassification (Chapter 10)

Source: adapted from Hood and Piotrowska (2021)

Miles' Law, and who saw what as helpful creativity, acceptable leeway, or culpable cheating

Social or anthropological studies of fiddling or cheating commonly find that some or all players in a given social setting see a certain amount of licence with formal rules as acceptable as long as it is modest or limited in extent. Such licence may

even be seen as desirable in some ways[10]. On similar lines, some of our interviewees said or implied that some degree of 'gaming' of the numbers was allowable
and to be expected, and a few long-serving Treasury officials with in-depth classification expertise were in much demand as potential problem-solvers. An example
of creative classification whose value was contested was the case of 'tuck unders'
(in 2010s Treasury jargon, though the phenomenon long pre-dated that particular name), as shown in Table 10.2. The term meant moving existing items of
spending as new charges under budgetary categories such as 'health' and 'overseas
aid' whose aggregate spending levels were protected by international agreements
or other policy pledges. A case in point is funding for the BBC World Service,
moved into the protected overseas aid budget in 2014 (BBC 2011). Views differed
as to whether such moves were to be deplored as stealthy back-door spending cuts
by landing new unfunded mandates on input-protected budgets, or whether they
could be seen as helpful remediation of earlier mis-classifications when attention
was concentrated by financial constraints.

Similarly, from the departmental side, one former Finance Director of a major
spending department told us that a certain amount of 'padding' of baselines ahead
of spending review negotiations was taken by Treasury and departments alike
as normal and expected behaviour. Indeed, in Chapter 8, we saw that efforts by
departments and agencies to reclassify staffing expenditure out of 'administration'
into 'programme' costs were encouraged by the Treasury after the 2002 review of
AC controls. By contrast, the vignette to this chapter is a clear case in which there
were starkly different views about the application of the rules over non-cash to
near-cash transfers. Treasury ministers and spending officials saw MOD's moves
as unacceptable 'manipulation' (the word chosen by a former senior minister to
describe what happened). But their counterparts in MOD saw those moves as a
legitimate use of opportunities—taken up after consultation with the Treasury's
own accountants—to switch between spending categories to release much-needed
cash to correct for persistent under-funding of a key department's agreed mission. Who saw what as 'gaming' was evidently shaped in this case by 'Miles' Law',
to which we referred in Chapter 1: the famous observation that in bureaucratic
settings, 'where you stand depends on where you sit'.

Contrasting Recipes for Countering Gaming: More and Less Relational Distance

Recipes for countering gaming in the spending control process varied too. It
was striking that several ideas and initiatives aimed at reducing the Treasury's

---

[10] See for instance Mars 1982; Hood and Lodge 2006: 63. The notion of 'honest graft'—famously
expounded by George Washington Plunkitt, political machine boss of Tammany Hall in New York in
the early twentieth century (Riordon 1905) is a classic example of such a view.

opportunities to game the spending numbers tended to take the form of efforts to increase social distance between Treasury ministers (and those who worked under their direction) and some of the more technocratic players, while the Treasury's efforts to counter or forestall gaming by spending departments went in the other direction, involving efforts to keep spending teams close to departments and to bring finance professionals and policy officials such as economists closer together, within the Treasury and across government.

Social distance or closeness figures large in academic accounts of how rules are enforced and how social interactions work in human organizations, as reflected in concepts such as 'relational distance' in law enforcement (Black (1976; 1984) and 'group' as a measure of social cohesion in accounts of cultural bias and workplace cheating (Douglas 1982: 183–254; Mars 1982). In principle 'relational distance' and 'group' are quantifiable items,[11] but we were not able to measure them in this study. Nor did any of our interviewees or the official papers we read ever use those particular jargon words. But nevertheless, the underlying concepts kept coming up in ideas about institutional design to keep gaming at bay. Here we compare efforts to limit gaming of spending numbers on the part of the Treasury itself by putting those numbers under the control of autonomous experts, with efforts by the Treasury to avoid being 'bounced' itself in the sort of way illustrated in the vignette. In the latter case, the efforts to limit gaming took the form of bringing Treasury spending teams and departmental Finance Directors closer together, and related efforts by the Treasury to reduce the social distance between finance professionals and economists or policy experts in a world of more complex accounting rules. This social response was far from new[12] but it was certainly in evidence during our period.

Efforts to limit Treasury gaming by outsourcing functions to increase RD

Earlier chapters (4 and 9) showed that a series of measures intended to 'keep the Treasury honest' and to provide assurance that the Treasury was not gaming its forecast numbers culminated in a move in 2010–2011 to constitute forecasting and reporting functions under a separate bureaucracy, OBR, not controlled by Treasury ministers. As we noted, that effort to limit the Treasury's power to finesse key numbers or influence judgements by increasing RD and moving key parts of the bureaucracy 'down-group' in some ways resembled the creation of

---

[11] For Black (1976: 40–1), relational distance is in principle measurable in terms of scope, frequency, and length of social interactions among different individuals or groups to denote variations in 'the degree to which [people] participate in one another's lives. This defines their intimacy, or relational distance.'

[12] Heclo and Wildavsky (1974: 93) in their discussion of 'bounces' remark that, 'The Treasury's way around it [the risk of being bounced] is to stay close to the department so as to know what is going on.'

the independent Monetary Policy Committee of the Bank of England in 1997, and perhaps also what happened to the public audit function in the early 1980s when the more independent NAO had replaced the former Exchequer and Audit Department. More broadly that move followed an approach to keeping governments and bureaucracies honest by a mixture of autonomy and challenge that stretches back at least to the famous Censorate of Imperial China (though it was much less drastic in the amount of social 'apartness' required[13]).

The re-constitution of the Office for National Statistics (ONS) in 2007–2008 represents the other notable case over our period of efforts to limit Treasury opportunities for gaming spending numbers by removing key functions from the direct control of Treasury ministers and putting them under the control of autonomous officials directly responsible to Parliament. ONS, the product of a 1996 merger between the former Central Statistical Office and the Office of Population Censuses and Surveys, was re-constituted in 2008 as a non-ministerial department overseen by a Statistics Authority with an independent chair directly accountable to Parliament (a former high-ranking civil servant who had the right to chide Ministers and departments for misleading use of national statistics). That change was a late delivery of a 1997 Labour manifesto commitment, but it was also endorsed by the Conservatives and Liberal Democrats.

It is notable that the new ONS arrangements began at a time when a Eurobarometer survey indicated the UK had the lowest level of public trust in its official statistics of all EU member states (Eurobarometer, 2007) but at the end of our period in 2015 the proportion of UK respondents who said they trusted official statistics over those who did not had risen by some nineteen percentage points, placing the UK rather above the EU average (Eurobarometer, 2015). From the perspective of our interviewees, there were several interlinked ways in which they thought efforts to increase RD between the Treasury and ONS had made a difference to the planning and control of public spending. One consisted of bringing forms of debt previously classified as off-balance sheet into the realm of public sector debt, of which probably the most important episode during our period was ONS's decision in 2014, to count as public debt the £30bn debt of Network Rail, a quango created in 2001 in the guise of a government-owned company after the collapse of the privatized Railtrack (Wynne 2013).[14] Another was ONS's power to determine which statistics sufficiently met its quality standards to count as 'National Statistics' (or not, as in the case of the ever-changing AC numbers we

---

[13] A disciplinary body which only employed fresh graduates who were not closely related to anyone else of high rank in the imperial bureaucracy (Hsieh 1925: 98). Division of the UK public service bureaucracy as between working for ministers in executive government and working for parliament in challenging the executive was also advocated by Sidney and Beatrice Webb in their ideas for constitutional reform after World War I (Webb and Webb 1920).

[14] These balance sheet issues were described to us as 'partly ONS and partly NAO territory', and they were part of a switch to new National Accounting guidelines from Eurostat (from ESA 95 to ESA10).

discussed in Chapter 8). Related to that was ONS's role (together with its international counterparts) as guardian of the conventions for National Accounts, for example in whether to classify 'single-use' military equipment as current or capital in those Accounts, as discussed in Chapter 6. One interviewee commented, 'It was certainly Treasury orthodoxy that ONS was a lot more afraid of Eurostat than of HMT on classification issues!'

By deciding which data and publications could be kitemarked as 'National Statistics', ONS certified that such statistics met international standards of clarity, reliability, validity, and political non-interference, and on occasion such certification had high political significance. For example, as already noted, the Scottish Government publishes annually *Government Expenditure and Revenue Scotland* (*GERS*), which carries the National Statistics kitemark. And as we saw above, *GERS* for 2014–2015 contained tables (E1–E4), showing trends in Scottish revenue and expenditure, including numbers calculated on the assumption (favoured by the Scottish Government but not the UK Government) that revenues from Scotland's geographical share of North Sea oil taxation were assigned to Scotland. At the same time, the Scottish Government published its manifesto for independence (Scottish Government 2013), seeking a 'yes' vote in the 2014 Scottish independence referendum. The manifesto contained many pictures, but almost no statistics. It was not submitted for, nor would it have met, the National Statistics kitemark. Annex C of the manifesto showed a rosy forecast for Scottish public finances by 2016–2017, the year the Scottish Government hoped to achieve independence if the referendum vote was 'Yes', taken from 'scenarios published in the Scottish Government Oil and Gas Analytical Bulletin'—presenting a picture strikingly different to the trends shown in *GERS* (and which was not borne out when 2016–2017 came round).

Treasury efforts to limit gaming by departments through reduced RD

Treasury efforts to limit gaming by spending departments present a contrasting picture over social distance. In the decade following the MOD episode described in the vignette, the Treasury's efforts to limit what its spending controllers saw as gaming by departments took at least two forms. As we have seen, one consisted of rule changes, scrapping capital charges, and building an administrative wall between non-cash and near-cash by imposing separate control totals on those two types of spending. But the other consisted of continuing or renewed emphasis on social 'togetherness' between Treasury and departments.

One or two ex-Treasury interviewees thought the only real way to counter gaming by spending departments was to keep changing the rules and categories—as did indeed happen over much of our period, as the succession of changes charted in Figure 10.1 shows. But that was a minority view, and our vignette shows that a keep-the-plates-spinning approach could work against the Treasury as well as for it. A more common view among spending controllers we interviewed was that the best way to limit gaming and avoid unpleasant surprises was to emphasize social interaction and information-sharing to secure 'common understanding' of the various spending numbers. Such an approach has a long history: Heclo and Wildavsky (1974: 62) commented on it as a marked feature of the Treasury's mode of operation half a century ago.

Documents and interviews revealed variations in RD between the Treasury and spending departments over the period covered by this book, ranging from close and amicable relations to distant and antagonistic ones, at official or ministerial level—or both, as in our vignette.[15] When relationships between departments and the Treasury were frosty at ministerial level, there seem to have been efforts at least sometimes to 'keep the official relationships going whatever the politics', as one former Finance Director of a spending department put it, but several interviewees told us that suspicious spending ministers were apt to tell their officials not to talk freely to the Treasury. One former Treasury spending team leader said that finance officials in spending departments 'don't tell you what's coming until their Ministers tell them to', and if powerful departments opted for a strategy of minimal engagement with the Treasury in spending reviews (as happened with the Home Office in the 2002 spending review, for instance) retaliation by the Treasury could be tricky.

RD between Treasury spending teams and spending departments was reduced in a sense by the movement of people between the Treasury and other parts of government (about half of the fifteen Chief Secretaries to the Treasury over the period moved on to be ministers of spending departments, for instance, and at official level there was likewise traffic in both directions between spending departments and the Treasury, as well as between the Treasury, No. 10 and the Cabinet Office. Echoing, 'Miles' Law', as mentioned earlier, one former Permanent Secretary said he had recruited ex-Treasury people to his department 'to work the system in our small way against the Treasury'. But experienced former departmental Finance Directors were far less likely to be hired to head the relevant Treasury spending teams in a full-blown 'poacher-to-gamekeeper' mode.

Indeed, that asymmetric movement within the bureaucracy was part of a very long-standing institutional pattern in which Treasury spending teams tended to

---

[15] One ex-Treasury interviewee boldly distinguished between parts of government like International Development, Work and Pensions, or Culture, Media and Sport which were staffed by the Treasury's 'natural government bedfellows', as against those departments run by what that interviewee called 'Neanderthals'. 'Natural government bedfellows' here evidently meant departments staffed by economists who had 'a similar worldview' to that of many of their Treasury spending team counterparts (reflected, we were told, in an inclination to long-termism, an aversion to vested interests, and a predisposition in favour of open markets rather than economic nationalism and protectionism). 'Neanderthals' for that interviewee included the FCO, Home Office, Department of Trade, and MOD.

be staffed by a changing cast of people who were markedly younger and less experienced than the departmental finance or policy officials with whom they were interacting. Those conditions arguably had the advantage of bringing fresh eyes, youthful energy, and new perspectives to the Treasury's scrutiny of expenditure plans. But several interviewees thought it led to resentment and social tension as well, as indicated by barbed phrases like 'Teenage Treasury Taliban', 'kids who'd never run anything...', '22-year-olds...with no social skills and no manners'.

There were also recurrent and deliberate attempts to reduce RD between Treasury spending teams and the departments they oversaw. The Treasury's role in the 1994 'Front Line First' defence review was one notable case in point, as described in Chapter 3, and early in the following decade, there was another concerted attempt to bring Treasury spending teams and departments' finance directorates more closely together. Indeed, in the aftermath of the problems over resource accounting described earlier and in an effort to counter long-standing accusations of Treasury arrogance, a set of 'Treasury values' including 'collaboration and openness' was officially promoted in the 2000s. Spending teams were encouraged to get closer to their departmental counterparts by meeting them weekly or fortnightly to gather intelligence. Several interviewees contrasted what they saw as a more distant and confrontational style on the part of Treasury spending control officials vis-à-vis their departments in the fiscally constrained 1990s (using phrases such as 'capricious and hostile' or 'adversarial'), as against efforts to develop greater 'togetherness' and a more listening-style in different fiscal circumstances in the following decade.[16] One ex-Treasury interviewee from that later period declared with great emphasis that 'being a .... good listener' was the most important quality of a spending team leader.

Those interviewees suggested two reasons for the renewed emphasis placed on efforts to reduce RD between Treasury and departments in the 2000s. One or two thought the Treasury's spending teams had moved away from a previous approach to handling departments that relied on simply 'being cleverer' than their official opposite numbers in departments, in the sense of ability to deploy economic analysis and specifically cost-benefit and time-discounting analysis (evaluative weapons the Treasury had developed from the 1960s and incorporated into the 'Green book' discussed in Chapter 6). But none of our Treasury interviewees from the 2000s said or implied that the Treasury could rely on being 'cleverer' at least by that stage (while one senior official in a large department pointedly told us he had far more trained economists than the Treasury). Most of them placed heavy stress on the need to get closer to their opposite numbers.

---

[16] A 2002 review of Treasury external relations found the proposition 'Our relationship with departments is necessarily adversarial' to be 'not universal, but a common view' among Treasury officials.

Efforts to reduce RD between finance professionals and policy officials: 'out of the bean-counting hinterlands'

A final 'group' or RD issue that figures large in our opening vignette concerned relations among different epistemic or specialist players within the Treasury. The 1994 Fundamental Expenditure Review of the Treasury that we discussed in Chapter 3, led to the 'bedding out' of a formerly separate corps of specialist economists into the Treasury's spending teams and was designed to reduce the RD that was said to have previously existed between those two groups (against competing arguments for creative tension). But no similar integration seems to have taken place at that time between spending teams and the Treasury's finance professionals, and the social gap between those two sets of players is part of the story in our vignette.

A 2007 booklet,[17] published to mark twenty-five years of the UK's Government Finance Profession, celebrated the rise of Whitehall's qualified finance professionals since 1982, from what it described as 'bean-counting hinterlands' to senior and central positions in Whitehall departments and from a population of a mere 600 or so to some 7,000 in 2006[18]. The booklet included reminiscences and commentary from all the major players in the central government accounting world over the previous two decades. It traced the ascent of finance professionals in Whitehall from the status of a group said to have been originally regarded with 'scepticism' and 'indifference' to positions of power and influence 'at the very centre of government' in the 2000s.[19] One of the key elements of that change was the increased status of those officials who headed departmental finance units, traditionally known as Principal Finance Officers (PFOs) but renamed Finance Directors in 2003 to signify a status that merited membership of departmental boards. Interviewees told us that traditionally PFO roles had often been filled by policy civil servants who had worked in the Treasury earlier in their careers and consequently had some knowledge both of its people and its ways of working. But in the 2000s these departmental positions came to be filled exclusively by qualified finance professionals, reflecting a policy formally announced in 2004 and completed in 2007 (and a striking instance of the Treasury insisting on a policy for other departments that it did not apply to itself, meaning it risked being outgunned by departments over accounting technicalities). That new breed of departmental Finance Directors did not necessarily have Treasury experience, and indeed some of them were said to have sent their deputies along to regular meetings with

---

[17] Government Finance Profession (2007).

[18] One of those we interviewed in 2019 put the number by then at 10,000.

[19] The booklet (and many of our interviewees) attributed much of what it called a 'seismic shift in central government culture' to the ability and charisma of Professor Sir Andrew Likierman, who served as Head of the Government Accountancy Service (then known as HOTGAS) in the Treasury from 1993 to 2004.

Treasury spending teams because of the typical disparity in grade levels between Treasury spending teams and the senior departmental officials they dealt with.

Within the Treasury too, during the period that saw arguably the biggest change in UK public sector accounting since the introduction of double-entry book-keeping in the mid-nineteenth century, there seems to have been a measure of social 'apartness' between the Treasury's accounting specialists and its spending team officials. That RD seems to have arisen out of a mixture of formal and informal elements.

As for the formal elements, accountants (or finance professionals) were in a Treasury command separate from the public spending teams. That organizational division survived the 1994 Treasury Fundamental Expenditure Review discussed in Chapter 3, on the grounds that the development of the RAB project required concentrated and specialist direction. The division meant that the Treasury finance professionals did not routinely participate in the weekly spending team meetings that took stock of developments in their departments, and they worked in a separate physical location ('silo-ed off in the TOA [Treasury Officer of Accounts] room', according to the recollection of one interviewee).

Any such physical distance between the finance professionals and the spending teams might not have mattered had it not apparently been reinforced in informal ways. Many of our interviewees from the era covered by the vignette commented on differences in outlook between the two groups. For instance, one said the Treasury had been 'entirely split' on the RAB issue; another said RAB had been developed within the Treasury 'in a silo', 'didn't touch the sides' of other parts of the Treasury and 'almost crept up on us;' a third even saw it as 'some sort of accountant conspiracy'. In the same vein, a former spending team director who we interviewed had been 'deeply sceptical' of RAB, was 'not convinced that it made real sense' and railed against changes of the kind that had brought in capital charges in the 1990s as 'ridiculous accounting rules'. A former senior official in a major spending department said there had been 'a complete disconnect between the two halves of the Treasury' and a former GEP official stressed the depth of 'the social gulf' in the Treasury between what were as described as 'purist accountants brought in from outside' and most of the Treasury's spending teams. One even said 'No one thought of accountants as proper Treasury people'.

Several of those who had been members of spending teams at that time echoed a claim by one of interviewees, who said, 'No one on the spending side understood it [RAB]...' One described it as, like the Unified Budget of 1993, 'a bit of an IFS [Institute for Fiscal Studies] policy'. We were told that spending teams tended to be 'obsessed' by policy issues in the early 2000s—which were catnip for the Treasury's politically minded economists—rather than detailed understanding of management accounting, and that those officials took their cue from what one interviewee described as 'zero political interest' in RAB from ministers and SpAds at that time 'despite a real risk of things going seriously wrong'.[20] At the same time, we were told that, while financially qualified departmental Finance Directors successfully bridged the gap between policy and accounting, Treasury accountants seldom if ever met ministers and were mostly detached from policy issues.

Attempts to reduce this apparent social divide between finance professionals in the Treasury and those who worked in the spending control teams seem to have been a third area of efforts at reduction in RD, aiming to limit the risk of unpleasant surprises of the type represented by the MOD and later Department of Health near-cash overspends in the early to mid-2000s. Those measures included serious efforts to inject more knowledge and understanding of accountancy and finance into the spending teams, by including accountancy apprentices who were interested in policy into the spending teams, encouraging spending control officials to gain finance qualifications and (for a while at least) appointing a financially qualified head of public spending in the Treasury.

Conclusion

This chapter has shown that common understanding of the changing numbers and classificatory frameworks, information-sharing and perceptions of what was 'gaming' rather than action within 'the spirit of the rules', were central and continuing issues in the UK spending control world over the period of this study.

The MOD near-cash overspend story shows the 'spirit of the rules' (and likewise what was to be counted as 'gaming') governing a major new accounting framework could be and was interpreted in different ways by the various players in the public spending system, in line with Miles' Law, as mentioned earlier. That episode also shows that the 2005 Department of Health overspend episode with which we began this book was by no means the only substantial near-cash overspend that followed the introduction of RAB (and over RAB, GEP seems to have been curiously slow to develop the wider view that is often said to be afforded by its central position in government, namely to read across from experience in one spending domain to inform policy or practice in another). Further, this chapter suggests that the cash/non-cash classificatory boundary was only one of many such administrative boundaries that could be blurred by the Treasury or departments, or both, when it was convenient to do so.

As described earlier, part of the Treasury's response to the political bruises that resulted from those near-cash overspends in the mid-2000s took the form

---

[20] Several interviewees told us that ministers after 2002 had still thought wholly in terms of cash. Perhaps contrasting with the 1993–1997 period when Treasury ministers included two former Ministers of Health who had experienced the introduction of accrual accounting in the National Health Service, one former Treasury official said that in the early 2000s 'No ministers understood RAB at all. Blunkett was the only one that got it'.

of formal rule changes forbidding departments from exercising the discretion to switch between non-cash and near-cash without specific Treasury approval. But its other response to those episodes—not showing up in formal organograms or rule books—were the renewed efforts by its spending teams to get closer to the spending departments in new circumstances. Both the DH and MOD episodes described above exposed weaknesses in the Treasury's capability to keep track of a more complex set of spending numbers, despite or perhaps because of its well-established focus on conducting ambitious policy analysis and reading the political runes.[21]

Finally, this chapter brings out a striking contrast between the Treasury's own efforts to get closer to spending departments to gather better intelligence to forestall gaming and efforts by other players to limit gaming on the part of the Treasury itself. The first stressed informal organization and 'togetherness', while the latter put more emphasis on formal organization and 'apartness' in creation of bodies such as OBR and ONS.

Timeline: Some Selected Developments in Spending Control Numbers and Categories

1992: 'New Control Total' replaced previous 'Planning Total; capital charging introduced in NHS; *Government Expenditure and Revenue Scotland* (GERS) first published.

1993: Capital and current spending separately identified in Budget documents (Chapter 6); The November budget statement and 'Red Book' for the first time included tax proposals with spending plans, thus combining the Budget and the Autumn Statement (Chapter 4).

1994: Treasury Green Paper on Resource Accounting and Budgeting (RAB).

1995: Treasury White Paper announced RAB as policy to come into effect in 2001.

1996: Simplified Supply Estimates introduced.

1997: New DEL/AME framework replaced NCT; separate budgets for capital spending, new fiscal rules; National Assets Register published; ESA95 European National Accounts definitions adopted (Chapter 5).

1998: Capital charges extended from NHS to all of central government; first Public Service Agreements (PSAs) published as output/outcome targets alongside Labour's first Comprehensive Spending Review. Statutory Code for Fiscal Stability enshrined fiscal rules and provided for NAO to audit the conventions and assumptions in the Treasury's fiscal forecasts (Chapter 9).

---

[21] One interviewee vividly described it as a place whose denizens spent their time 'reading between the lines and preparing for ministerial meetings that don't happen'.

1999: First long-term fiscal sustainability forecast published (in accordance with the 1998 Code for Fiscal Stability) (Chapter 9).

2000: Government Resources and Accounts Act 2000 amended the 1866 and 1921 Exchequer and Audit Departments Acts and provided for publication of 'Whole of Government accounts' to give a wider picture of assets and liabilities; DEL settlements in the 2000 spending review were agreed between Treasury and departments on an accruals basis in stage 1 of the RAB programme.

2001/2002: Resource-based Estimates replaced previous cash Estimates; National Assets Register updated.

2002: Stage 2 of RAB (non-cash costs incorporated into DELs); First Long-Term Public Finance Report included in the Budget documents (Chapter 9).

2003: MOD near-cash overspend; departmental Principal Financial Officers renamed Finance Directors; the Treasury and Government Actuary began to publish long-term projections of public sector pension costs.

2004: Announcement of policy that all future departmental Finance Directors should be qualified finance professionals (implemented by 2007).

2005: Department of Health overspend (Chapter 1); separate control totals introduced for near-cash and non-cash spending, after an announcement the previous year; COINS (Combined Online Information System) introduced as a new IT system for spending control; the Treasury pushed back the start date for the 'economic cycle' by two years, with the effect that the 'Golden Rule' applying to budget balance was easier to meet (Chapter 5).

2007/2008: A 2007 Eurobarometer poll revealed the UK to have the lowest level of public trust in its official statistics out of all EU member countries; The Statistics and Registration Services Act created an independent Statistics Board to oversee ONS; *Consolidated Budget Guidance* (with *Managing Public Money* and the Estimates Manual) replaced the *Government Accounting Manual*; the Scottish government produced its first National Performance Framework, based on the US state of Virginia.

2010: OBR started work on an interim basis (Chapter 9), including rejection of the previous 'AME margin' on top of the Reserve and incorporation of assumptions of under-spending into fiscal forecasting for the first time. Decision to replace COINS with a new spending control database (Project OSCAR), involving scrutiny from Cabinet Office Efficiency and Reform Group; PSAs were officially scrapped, with performance information to be included in departmental reports; first Whole of Government Accounts published, based on International Financial Reporting Standards.

2011: 'Clear Line of Sight' Project (first announced in a 2007 Green Paper) aligned the numbers used for Treasury planning of expenditure and departmental budgets with those in the parliamentary Supply estimates; spending

PEOPLE, RULES AND NUMBERS

by 'arms length' bodies, previously all classified as programme expenditure, now split between administration and programme costs.

2012/2013: OSCAR (Online System for Central Accounting and Recording) replaced COINS as the Treasury spending control IT system.

2014: Switch from ESA95 to ESA10 National Accounting Guidelines, including counting Network Rail's £30bn debt as public debt for the first time, counting all tax credits as additional public spending and counting 'single-use' military assets under capital spending (Chapter 6).

PART IV

UK PUBLIC SPENDING CONTROL
IN PERSPECTIVE

11

As Others Saw It

Rating and Comparing UK Public Spending Control

...to achieve world-class standards of financial management in government

> (one of eight strategic objectives: HM Treasury 2007b: 9).

How do we measure up against the kind of performance measurement systems we are beginning to require of others?

> (1992 Treasury document for a top management awayday during a period of election 'purdah' in April 1992).

Nowhere is the budgetary decline of parliaments more noticeable than in Britain...[the] House of Commons, the cradle of budgetary democracy [has] lost all formal influence over revenues and expenditures

> (Schick 2002: 27).

It didn't cross any of our minds to find out [if there was a useful international literature on budgeting]

> (Ex-Treasury interviewee reflecting on work on budgeting changes in the early 1990s).

Vignette: The Highs and Lows of Roller-Coasting in Public Spending

Several of our interviewees talked of 'feast and famine' or 'roller-coaster ride' as something they saw as a marked, negative, and distinctive feature of UK public spending control over our period. For instance, one leading commentator thought violent shifts between sudden acceleration and sharp braking typically led to poor value for money and wasteful underspends during spending spikes and to service collapse requiring reopening of budget settlements in extended periods of restraint. That interviewee thought such volatility was particularly damaging for capital expenditure, on the grounds that changes in direction for that crucial type of spending needed to be kept 'modest'. The same was said at an event we organized

The Way the Money Goes. Christopher Hood, Maia King, Iain McLean, and Barbara Piotrowska,
Oxford University Press. © Christopher Hood, Maia King, Iain McLean, and Barbara Piotrowska (2023).
DOI: 10.1093/oso/9780198865087.003.0011

in 2019 to compare how different countries approached public spending control, when an experienced and respected public finance expert declared the UK to have a 'bad record' of high volatility in its approach to public spending over time. Another senior Treasury interviewee cited rail electrification as a classic case where the UK's feast-and-famine approach (as he saw it) was 'exactly the wrong way to control costs', in contrast to a more measured and incremental pattern reported for Germany over many decades.[1]

There were several ways in which interviewees critical of volatility thought a stop-start approach damaged the quality of public spending. One was the extra risks it presented for cost blowouts in the upswings, particularly for items (like railway electrification) for which the stock of real resources was relatively fixed in the short term. Several cited the steep upward spike in healthcare spending in the 2000s (discussed in Chapters 1 and 4) as a case in point. Given the limited stock of trained medical staff available, those interviewees thought that legendary spending surge did not secure the amount of extra medical care that it might have done if the additional billions had been fed in more gradually. As it was, they said, the rapid rise in spending led to plunging hospital productivity and a big jump in medical pay that left the UK with some of the highest-paid doctors in the developed world (OECD 2009: 71 Tables 3.5.1 and 3.5.2) and unintendedly led GPs (family doctors) to opt out of providing out-of-hours care, putting extra pressure on hospital accident and emergency services. One interviewee thought its handling of that spending spike was the Treasury's greatest failure in expenditure control over the whole period of our study; another said the Treasury 'shouldn't be proud' of how it had handled the episode, while a third said of the controversial 2004 GP contract that was a central feature of the spending uplift, 'We should have stopped it; we couldn't say we didn't know...it was a political deal...imposed on us by No. 10'.

But unnecessarily high cost was not the only issue that interviewees associated with a roller-coaster approach to spending. A former senior Treasury official said, 'The trouble always starts when the brakes come off', meaning that policy fiascos were inevitable when money was poured too rapidly into new initiatives that were not piloted, were politically protected from vigorous Treasury challenge and rested largely on 'policy-based evidence'. And in the bad times, steep downward swings of the roller coaster risked heavily cut services 'falling over' in Treasury parlance, meaning serious collapse forcing a reopening of spending allocations. One striking example we were given of the latter problem towards the end of our period was a tale of prisoners making overnight journeys in vans because there was nowhere for them to sleep overnight as a result of lack of funding for prison places. Palpable service failures of that type meant not only avoidable human suffering and political damage but also the likelihood of costly remedial spending down the line and

---

[1] For the steadiness of German rail electrification, a claim by David Shirres (2018) has been widely cited.

irresistible pressure to reopen budgets for on-the-hoof emergency bailouts, for instance in the frequent top-ups and capital-to-current switches in NHS spending towards and after the end of our period after some years of squeeze.[2]

A third negative effect associated by interviewees with a roller-coaster pattern of spending was the powerful incentives it provided for departments, local authorities, schools, and public authorities generally to squirrel away financial reserves whenever they could (in the pessimistic or perhaps realistic belief that 'tomorrow will be worse'). Several interviewees recalled such under-spending as a central feature of the 2000s spending boom, when departments and agencies, both at central and subnational level, built up huge unspent balances (eventually amounting to some £20bn, particularly in capital spending) under the end-year flexibility regime then in force (HM Treasury 2011). Others commented on similar efforts by local authorities to accumulate reserves to protect themselves from subsequent cutbacks, with one saying that from a whole-of-government perspective it seemed 'crazy' for different public organizations to build up reserves to guard against future changes in policy.

The preference expressed by such interviewees for avoiding what they saw as excessive swings between feast and famine in public spending echoed—and from one especially erudite ex-Treasury interviewee even involved an explicit reference to—Nobel Prize-winning economist Milton Friedman's (1960: 90–93) preference for 'straight line' monetary policies by government.[3] But as with Friedman's doctrine, the negative view of expenditure volatility did not go wholly unchallenged. Against the value of stability in spending over time, some interviewees implicitly or explicitly pointed to potential advantages of ups and downs in public spending.[4]

Some thought innovative cross-departmental initiatives like the 'Sure Start' programme (a flagship New Labour scheme in the late 1990s providing support to parents and children under the age of four in deprived areas, with heavy emphasis on experimentation) were more likely to flourish during sharp upward spending spikes because then the spending was additional to, and not at the expense of, the baselines of the various departments whose collaboration and engagement was needed to make such initiatives work.[5] But others commented that

---

[2] Culminating in a £30bn multi-year settlement announced in 2018 as a '70th birthday present' to the institution after six years of spending restraint between 2010 and 2016.

[3] Friedman (1960) argued that to control inflation in the long run, the money supply should be increased at a constant percentage rate every year, irrespective of business cycles. Interviewees' frustration with spending volatility over our period was reminiscent of criticisms of 'stop-go' management of the UK economy in the 1950s and 1960s (Scott and Walker 2019) and of those comparative studies which link public spending volatility to weak fiscal institutions and lower economic growth (Albuquerque, 2011; Brzozowski and Siwińska-Gorzelak, 2010; Furceri and Poplawski Ribiero 2008; Afonso and Jalles 2012; Fatas and Mihov 2013).

[4] Reminiscent of the case for periodic changes in the spending control rules to limit gaming, as discussed in the previous chapter.

[5] Consistent with this view, it is striking that Sure Start spending in England fell steeply after 2010 (from £1.2bn in 2010–2011 to £691m in 2015–2016) when the Coalition removed the ring-fence for Sure Start funding (Bate and Foster 2017).

expenditure restraint could help to foster effective spending control in other ways, because departments were then forced to make tough choices over spending that would otherwise be avoided, and departmental incentives were more likely to align with the Treasury's search for value for money. One interviewee thought swings of the pendulum could be salutary in the short term (since fat was accumulated in booms, while unmet needs built up in periods of restraint) but had negative effects if either feast or famine was pursued for too long. One senior official floated the possibility that if public spending allocations had invariably followed the incremental, inflation-plus pattern implicitly favoured by critics of volatility, no department would ever need to give up on anything, zero-based reviews would never bite, and pet projects, failing policies, or flawed practices would live for ever. As it was, changes in party incumbency accompanied by a spending squeeze could provide political windows for scrapping troubled but hitherto politically favoured spending items, as in the case of the 'Building Schools for the Future' programme, axed in the early days of the Coalition government.

Viewing UK Performance in International Perspective: Two Issues

Up until now, we have mainly looked at developments in the UK's fiscal constitution in their own right, with a few glancing references to practice in other countries. That approach follows the focus of most earlier studies of UK spending control. A generation or two ago, such studies were mainly country-specific, and the quotation from the ex-Treasury interviewee in the final epigraph to this chapter suggests that the same applied to Whitehall's own deliberations about the budgeting system at the start of our period. But as is shown by those interviewees' complaints about excessive spending volatility in the vignette, those debates also included some more or less explicit comparisons of the UK's performance in public spending control with that of other countries.

This chapter does not aim for any comprehensive comparison. It focuses instead on two ways of looking at the UK's performance in international perspective. One is the issue highlighted by the vignette, concerning how far the UK displayed a roller-coaster, feast-and-famine approach to public spending compared to other countries—something that several interviewees claimed or implied, but which seems to be easier to assert than to prove. The other issue we look at concerns how the UK was assessed over our period in international rankings and ratings for 'public financial management'. Exploring how its public spending control system was assessed in three sets of such ratings, we suggest that the way the UK system was evaluated depended on the relative weight given to the more 'political' as against the more 'technocratic' features of its fiscal constitution.

Chronic roller-coaster or malade imaginaire?

Our opening vignette shows that several of our interviewees saw volatility as a central—and undesirable—issue in expenditure planning and control, although a few thought alternating surges and squeezes could present some advantages and opportunities.

But leaving aside those pros and cons of spending volatility in the abstract, it is not exactly self-evident from the official statistics available that the UK was far out of line with other countries on such volatility over our period. Figure 1.3 in Chapter 1 (drawing on IMF data on government expenditure from 1900 to 2011), showed that at least since the late 1940s the UK did not greatly stand out from seven other comparable countries in the way its overall public spending changed over time. None of the other seven had anything approximating to a 'straight line' profile and their spending was evidently subject to broadly similar cyclical shocks of economic boom and bust.

So did the picture change if we focus more on the kinds of spending that critics of 'feast-and-famine' were most concerned with? Figure 11.1 draws on OECD data to compare the UK's annual percentage change in general government spending on gross fixed capital formation over our period against selected OECD countries, tracking year-on-year changes over time. For a dramatic 'feast-and-famine' pattern, we would expect to find some years of changes close to zero, punctuated with big swings above and below the zero line. On those OECD numbers the UK appeared at first sight to be way out of line with all the others in the mid-2000s as it swung from a deep plunge to an equally dramatic spike. But that apparent roller-coaster pattern reflects a classificatory shift rather than true changes in spending—a £15.6bn transfer of the UK's nuclear reactors from one quango to another (that is, from a government-owned company to a non-departmental public body) that happened to score for OECD purposes as a huge negative investment for the 'private sector' and subsequently as positive investment by 'government'. Once those reclassification effects are stripped out (Figure 11.1 (b)) the UK ceased to score as the most volatile spender on fixed capital formation. But it is true that the UK's volatility on that item was markedly above that of Germany, whose volatility hovered around 0 per cent over most of the period.

This discussion suggests that comparative evaluation of the UK's record on 'roller coasting' in public spending is complicated not just by slipperiness of the available numbers, but also and more fundamentally by the fact that contradictory values turn out to be in play (is roller-coasting good or bad, how much is too much, how conducive is steady incrementalism to novel initiatives or searching reviews?). Nor do such conclusions apply to spending volatility alone. Exactly the same issues arise for cross-national attempts to rank and rate the UK's spending control performance more broadly over our period, the issue to which we now turn.

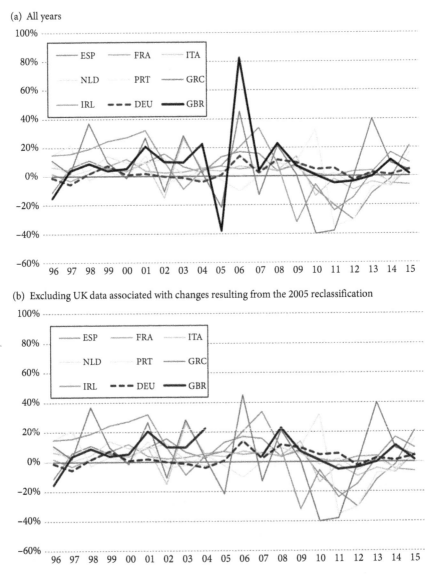

Figure 11.1 Year-on-year change in general government investment 1996–2015, selected OECD countries

Source: OECD (2022b)

Public spending control and international ratings

Over our period more explicit ratings and rankings were developed by public international bodies assessing and comparing countries' performance in public financial management. A new generation of such ratings aimed to be systematic, actionable, and expressible in terms of numerical ratings based largely on documentary evidence, measuring key aspects of the system of fiscal governance in any given country as against explicitly stated standards of good or best practice. That approach partially echoed the established practice of international commercial credit-rating agencies assessing the riskiness of sovereign debt (by awarding 'triple A' ratings and the like). Commercial credit rating of that type applied to the UK's debt since it returned to the New York bond market in the 1970s, four decades after defaulting on its American World War I debt (Gill 2015). Such ratings are part of the background to the planning and control of spending, but they evaluate creditworthiness in the round and revenue capacity rather than spending control specifically. Other rankings and ratings developed over our period, both of 'public financial management' and of 'good governance' more broadly, for instance in Transparency International's corruption perception index starting in in 1993 and of the World Bank's World Governance Indicators three years later (Besançon 2003; Hood, Dixon and Beeston 2008).

For public financial management, new ranking and rating exercises construed 'best practice' in several ways, including: how much scrutiny was applied to spending and taxes by legislatures and other actors; the level of propriety and rule-of-law (as opposed to fraud and corruption) in the handling of public money; and the extent to which explicit objectives were set in fiscal rules or targets (specifying ceilings for debt and deficit) and longer-term trends monitored, going beyond the traditional annual budgeting cycle. Other items included the extent to which government balance sheets contained a comprehensive account of assets and liabilities, and how far budgeting processes focused on outputs or outcomes rather than inputs alone.

How did the UK's fiscal constitution rate in that changing world of rankings and ratings? As for credit ratings of its sovereign debt, the UK maintained a 'triple A' rating for most of our period, although its ratings slipped a little in 2009 and 2013 (and fell again after our period in the turbulent aftermath of the 2016 Brexit referendum). As for the non-commercial evaluations of public financial management, three different sets of rating exercises seem to have rated some parts of the UK's fiscal constitution less positively than others.

How the UK was rated in three sets of non-commercial reviews

Of those three sets of non-commercial international reviews,[6] one is the periodic evaluation of 'fiscal transparency' in its member states, applied to the UK in 1999

---

[6] We could add other more general governance rankings, notably the Transparency International Corruption Perception Index (on which the UK was rated in the top decile throughout our period) and the six 'Worldwide Governance Indicators' from the WGI programme part-funded and sponsored by the World Bank (though not representing the Bank's official views). The UK ranked consistently in or around the top decile on five out of those six WGI indicators over our period, but it rated noticeably lower on 'political stability and the absence of violence or terrorism', with its ranking on that item dropping by over ten places over our period.

234 THE WAY THE MONEY GOES

and 2016 by the International Monetary Fund (IMF, founded in 1944). A second consists of reviews and summaries of budgeting practices in its member states by the Organisation for Economic Cooperation and Development (OECD, founded in 1961) and in particular a review carried out a few years after our period in 2019. A third comprised several rounds of comparative evaluations of fiscal performance carried out by the International Budget Partnership over the second decade or so of our period. Both IMF and OECD reports traditionally consisted of descriptive summaries and qualitative comments on institutional processes (and in the case of OECD covered topics that changed over time and between countries). But in both cases the style of reporting became more explicitly comparative over our period.

IMF Fiscal Transparency Reports: changing performance or moving goalposts?

The IMF conducted two reviews of the UK's 'fiscal transparency' that are relevant to our theme. One was presented as an experimental review (IMF 1999), and the other was a regular review carried out in 2016, just after the end of our period (IMF 2016). Those two reviews were very different in style and format, reflecting the changing styles of analysis mentioned earlier. The 1999 experimental report was a slim affair of sixteen pages, only three of which were devoted to fiscal transparency (the rest of the report dealt with banking and the management and regulation of insurance and financial services) and it consisted only of text, with no tables or figures at all. Its successor in 2016 devoted eighty-six pages to fiscal transparency alone, including some sixty-two figures and tables (many of them in league-table format ranking the UK against other countries). Further, there was an attention-grabbing summary table using traffic-light colour codes to express the UK's overall performance on 46 of the forty-eight elements that made up the IMF's Fiscal Transparency Code. The scoring system ranged from red to denote areas in which the standards of that Code were not met at all, to dark green to signify performance considered to be an advanced application of those standards.

The mood music of the IMF commentary was different as well. The 1999 report in its section on fiscal transparency gave a glowing account of the UK's then newly enacted Code for Fiscal Stability (a central part of the 1998 suite of New Labour reforms described in Chapter 4). The report declared that the UK had 'achieved a very high level of fiscal transparency. The requirements of the Code [The IMF Code of Good Practices on Fiscal Transparency] are met in almost all respects and exceeded in many. The various provisions of the CFS [Code for Fiscal Stability] …have made a major contribution in this regard'. The IMF made only two qualifications to that laudatory assessment, by asking for already-published statements of contingent liabilities (as already mentioned, 'known unknown' financial risks arising from government guarantees or similar liabilities such as likely payouts for claims of medical negligence in public health care) to be integrated into the budget documents and for a more detailed breakdown of government expenditure to be published in the main budget documents rather than coming out later in a series of departmental reports.

The 2016 IMF report appeared at a time when the UK had suspended explicit fiscal rules, but the then Chancellor, Philip Hammond, had declared his intention to return to such rules (and also to move back to a single once-a-year budget in the autumn well before the start of the financial year, going back to the budgeting system described in Chapter 3). That second report painted a rather more mixed picture of UK practice. As already noted, the IMF's assessment by then covered a larger and more systematic set of categories, two of which were not assessed for the UK). The striking traffic-light summary of the results of its indicated ratings of the UK's fiscal management practice at both ends of the scale.

Table 11.1 compares the IMF's overall rating of the UK's fiscal transparency in 2016 with its ratings for six other EU countries that were reviewed on the same criteria between 2013 and 2018. On the negative side, the table shows that with four 'not met' red ratings (indicating practices considered to have failed to meet the standards of the IMF's Fiscal Transparency Code), the UK was in the bottom half of the seven countries reviewed. But on the positive side, with twenty-three 'advanced' dark-green ratings at the other end of the scale it topped the whole league by a large margin. The UK was thus rated as an uneven performer, leading the field in several respects, but lagging on some other criteria.

Of the four features of the UK system that the IMF rated 'red' in 2016, one concerned delay in publication of end of year financial statements, a form of delay in documentation somewhat different to the timing of publication of detailed breakdowns of expenditure by department that featured in the 1999 review. Another (on the absence of a summary statement of fiscal risks) more sharply reiterated IMF's

Table 11.1 IMF Fiscal Transparency Reviews: Summary assessments of seven EU member states on the IMF Fiscal Transparency Code, 2013–2018

Country	Review Date	Rating of Elements of Performance against the IMF Code				
		'Not Met' Red	'Basic' Yellow	'Good' Light Green	'Advanced' Dark Green	Not evaluated
UK	2016	4	9	10	23	2
Finland	2014	1	6	12	17	0
Malta	2018	2	12	10	11	1
Ireland	2013	3	14	11	10	0
Austria	2017	7	5	12	9	0
Romania	2015	5	15	8	7	1
Portugal	2014	2	13	15	6	1

Source: IMF Fiscal Transparency Evaluations (IMF 2013, 2014, 2015a, 2015b, 2016, 2018a, 2018b)

mildly expressed concerns in 1999 about reporting of fiscal risks in the form of contingent liabilities, but it was calling for something that was already on the way. A Treasury review of OBR the year before (HM Treasury 2015b: 90 §6.36) had asked for OBR to produce regular reports on fiscal risks, a change which was duly written into the Charter for Budget Responsibility the month before the IMF's Fiscal Transparency Evaluation came out.) So it was the comfortable kind of 'red' in the rating game that was politically convenient for both IMF and Treasury since the issue was about to be resolved in a way that allowed IMF to say its advice was followed and the Treasury to say it was following international best practice.[7]

Of the two other 'reds', one related to the fact that specific fiscal targets had been abandoned at that time, in contrast to the Code for Fiscal Stability over which the IMF had enthused in 1999. Its 2016 report said simply, 'Adopt new fiscal objectives as a matter of priority...' (IMF 2016: 9). But the fourth red-rated negative represented a more critical evaluation of features of the UK system that could equally have been singled out for criticism in 1999, notably its limitedly codified and convention-heavy budgeting system that we counted as a relatively enduring feature of the fiscal constitution in Chapter 2. That negative judgement might therefore be seen as a certain shifting of the evaluative goalposts over a long-standing 'political' feature of the spending-control system.

OECD assessments: median notability

OECD, with thirty-four member states at the time of this study, also ran two surveys of its member states' budgetary practices and procedures during our period. Those surveys drew largely on self-reporting by the states concerned, were essentially drafted by consensus such that the governments being reported on had rather more say over the wording than applied to IMF reports[8] and which were published without any overall rating or critical commentary.

When it came to evaluation of member states' practices, OECD traditionally published reports on its member states in a qualitative textual style, meaning they could only be interpreted by reading between the lines and carefully parsing the obscurantist language of the economic mandarinate in which they were written. But that style began to change in 2009, when OECD started publishing *Government at a Glance* reports every two years. Those reports comprised a set of quantitative indicators ranking OECD member states on matters of governance as well as fiscal and economic aggregates, and each issue included a chapter on 'Budgeting Practices and Procedures'. That budgeting chapter focused on different issues in each edition of *Government at a Glance*, meaning there was no

---

[7] OBR (2017) duly published its first Fiscal Risks Report the following year, which in turn received a glowing write-up from the IMF Fiscal Affairs Department (IMF 2017).

[8] Though Peretz's (2010: 20 §43) account of the IMF's Article IV assessment of financial risks in the UK prior to the 2008 financial crash records detailed discussions with the Treasury over the wording of the report's conclusions.

continuous series on which the UK's ranking on budgeting procedures could be tracked.

But in 2019, a few years after the end of our period, OECD edged closer towards an IMF-style ratings approach to budgetary practices and procedures (OECD 2019a), and its rating of the UK system, summarized in Table 11.2, in several respects resembled the IMF ratings discussed earlier. Unlike the IMF, the OECD did not sum up its evaluations in traffic-light terms, and while it rated some applications of its principles as 'notable' in a positive sense, there was no explicit equivalent to the red 'not met' IMF category at the negative end of the evaluation. As Table 11.2 shows, the UK was clearly well above the median 'notable' score, since it was rated ahead of twenty-four OECD countries on that item, equal on six and behind on only four.

For the negatives in the OECD's rating, clues have to be sought in the tone of the text, which includes critical comments on three relatively enduring features of the UK fiscal constitution that we have commented on in earlier chapters, namely: the UK Parliament's 'very limited power to amend executive budget proposals' (the Crown initiative rule discussed in Chapter 2); the 'limited public participation in the process of budget preparation' (discussed in Chapter 5); and the limited information provided to Parliament in budgetary documents (such as the much simplified and highly aggregated Estimates first presented for 1996–1997) that were reported to be 'highly aggregated...lacks detail' (OECD 2019a: 252–253).

That profile, and those specific criticisms, echo the portrayal of the UK as an uneven fiscal management performer in the 2016 IMF review described earlier. OECD's assessment of the UK's PFM system mentioned several features that its international assessors saw as commendable or advanced in comparison with other developed countries (notably the formal arrangements for handling capital and infrastructure spending, the accruals and whole-of-government approach to accounting and financial reporting and the arrangements for quality assurance and audit). But those plaudits from OECD mainly applied to more 'technocratic' features of the fiscal constitution and were mixed with negative comments, several of which concerned the features that had been red-rated in the IMF's 2016 assessment.

Open Budget Survey Evaluations 2006–2015: dropping down the league?

How does the picture change when we turn from ratings conducted or associated with international organizations answerable to and at least in part influenced by, member state governments (IMF and OECD), and look at ratings conducted by more independent bodies? One indication is provided by Table 11.3, which shows how the UK scored in a series of 'Open Budget Surveys'—OBS—conducted by the International Budget Partnership, an independent international body set up to promote budgetary transparency by periodic rankings and ratings of countries conducted by expert academic or independent evaluators. The first OBS scores

Table 11.2 Number of applications of ten OECD 'Budget Principles' rated as
'Notable' in thirty-four OECD member states in 2019

Number of items rated 'Notable'	1	2	3	4	5	6
Number of countries	7	17	7	2	0	1
Country names	Belgium Greece Iceland Israel Norway Poland Turkey	Chile Czech Rep Denmark Finland France Germany Hungary Ireland Italy Japan Korea Portugal Slovak Rep Slovenia Spain Sweden Switzerland	Australia Austria Estonia Latvia Mexico Netherlands **United Kingdom**	Luxembourg New Zealand	(Nil)	Canada

Source: Assembled from OECD (2019a)

and rankings came out in 2006, around the middle of our period, with subsequent
iterations every two or three years. As Table 11.3 shows, the UK ranked second out
of some fifty-nine states in that first OBS survey in 2006 and it topped the whole
league two years later. It ranked third in 2010 and 2012 but dropped to eighth in
2015 (and slid further to nineteenth place in 2019).

That change does not seem to be explicable by new high-performing countries
being included in the ranking. So did that change in the UK's rank order reflect
some clear decline in the quality of its fiscal management, or a change in the way
its fiscal institutions or practices were evaluated?

There seems to have been some element of the latter, because the 2015 slide in
the UK ranking coincides with a change in the composition of OBS's 'Open Budget Index' (its measures of good practice) in that year. The revised index included
twenty-two new questions (out of a total of 109), increasing the weight given to
budget documents other than the Executive's budget proposals, which had the
effect of lowering the UK's ranking (International Budget Partnership 2015: 63–
66). As for the dramatic drop in the UK's ranking in 2019, a few years after our
period, it was an unusual time in that no budget statement at all was issued in that

Table 11.3 UK rating in 'Open Budget' Surveys, 2006–2019

Year	2006	2008	2010	2012	2015	(2017)	(2019)
UK score out of 100	88	88	87	88	75	74	70
Tier (out of 5 or 6), where 1 = 'extensive' 2 = 'substantial'	1	1	1	1	2	2	2
UK ranking	2	1	3	3	8	10	19
Number of countries	59	85	94	100	102	115	117

Source: OBS Survey Reports 2006–2019 (International Budget Partnership 2006 and thereafter)

eventful calendar year. As already noted, the background was the deep political crisis over post-Brexit negotiations between the UK and the EU, which dramatically split the ruling Conservative party, caused the downfall of the Prime Minister and led to a snap general election. In those conditions a budget planned for the autumn under a new fiscal regime that would allow much more time for parliamentary scrutiny before the start of the financial year was abruptly postponed and did not take place until the following March. So while the first drop in the UK's ranking in 2015 might plausibly be argued to have reflected the new questions included in the 2015 OBS evaluation, the second drop in 2019 seems more likely to have been caused by abandonment of normal procedure in a major political crisis.

How the players saw it: UK interviewees' views

Despite the Treasury's aspirations in the 2000s 'to achieve world-class standards of financial management', as noted in the first epigraph to this chapter, none of the various domestic reviews of the Treasury that we came across over the period (including the root-and-branch 1994 Fundamental Expenditure Review discussed in Chapter 3) involved any in-depth cross-national comparisons with other finance ministries, meaning that international benchmarking conducted by the Treasury itself was at most fragmentary and informal. A few of the Treasury high-fliers we interviewed had spent time at the IMF in Washington, several had worked in other finance ministries (in France, Germany, New Zealand, South Africa), and some of the classification experts displayed impressive in-depth knowledge of the quirks of the international accounting conventions with which they had to operate, as mentioned in the previous chapter. Others gleaned knowledge about how spending control worked in other national systems from ad hoc encounters, snippets picked up from contacts overseas, and from the constant stream of international visitors passing through the Treasury.

Several interviewees were sceptical about the value of international rankings and ratings of expenditure planning and control. One senior office-holder with extensive experience of both government and business practice declared that no attention at all should be paid to such surveys, arguing that the assessments tended to reflect presentation or gaming rather than true performance.[9] From a slightly different angle, one experienced evaluator thought international ratings, like domestic NAO reports on spending reviews, often tended to be based more on box-ticking assessments of formal documents rather than more substantive results (such as the incidence of fiscal emergencies, the sums involved in underspends on capital projects, or the amount of spending that had to be funded from reserves outside regular budgetary provision).

When our interviewees themselves reflected on positive and negative aspects of UK systems and practices, several recalled episodes or developments that they saw as having been in the front rank of international practice for some parts of our period. Particularly but not only reflecting on the early New Labour period in the 1990s, some recalled a sense of having been on the crest of an international wave, noting for example that the UK was one of only a handful of countries that adopted multi-year budgeting with any seriousness and was one of only two or three producing what one technocrat called 'state of the art' long-term fiscal sustainability forecasts at a time when 'generational accounting' was in high fashion (as discussed in Chapter 9). Other developments mentioned as leading-edge internationally included some of the accounting reforms discussed in the previous chapter [10] and the establishment of autonomous expert bodies for the handling of national statistics and fiscal forecasting and reporting. Further, as we saw in Chapter 6, some pointed out that the UK's approach to 'business case' analysis for evaluation of spending projects or policies had also been recognized as in the forefront of international practice.

But interviewees brought up negatives as well, in the sense of UK developments they thought other countries should avoid rather than follow. As mentioned earlier, some thought that (contrary to the long-lived Haldane principle described in Chapter 2 and aspirations for a 'Unified Budget') UK public expenditure might be better planned and controlled if it followed a path taken by countries such as Ireland or Australia and separated the taxing and spending-oversight parts of the

---

[9] The withdrawal of the World Bank's influential 'Ease of Doing Business' index in 2021 following criticisms of political manipulation interacting with lack of transparency and frequent changes in the underlying methodology (Shmulyan 2021) is a notable recent instance of the susceptibility of international governance rankings to gaming.

[10] Including the adoption of resource accounting and budgeting, the compilation of a National Assets register and the move towards 'whole of government' accounts that put more items on the government balance sheet.

Treasury.[11] As we saw in the previous chapter, many thought the 'budgeting' side of the UK's introduction of resource accounting and budgeting had been a step too far. Several expressed doubts about the much-discussed DEL-AME framework for spending control that was part of New Labour's revamp of the previous New Control Total in 1998. Indeed, one dismissed that distinction as 'bonkers...no decent justification for it'. Others suggested that what came to be classified as DEL or AME sometimes reflected raw politics rather than consistent and analytically defensible distinctions (for example with asylum budgets classified as DEL despite the uncontrollability of asylum spending in practice). One interviewee even recalled an occasion in which a visiting group from another country had been informally but firmly advised by Treasury officials not to copy the UK's DEL-AME framework, given the undesirability of putting close to half of public spending into a category that was in practice outside the spending review process at the time.

Further, the UK style of synchronized multi-year spending reviews was seen as a negative by several interviewees who saw the approach as dysfunctional political 'theatre' or 'circuses'. One senior official wryly imagined a world in which departments' spending review settlements would be made by a robot or algorithm, thereby 'freeing analytic resources for more intelligent decisions over detailed spending'. Indeed, several interviewees expressed admiration for the Dutch tradition of transparent costing of rival parties' policy proposals, and spending reviews of different areas of policy that were conducted sequentially rather than simultaneously and de-linked from the budget allocation cycle, in a country with a strong tradition of civil service autonomy and a PR electoral system normally producing coalition governments.

Only one high-level ex-Treasury interviewee expressed strong criticism of the ex post bias in the UK parliament's engagement with public spending, deplored an attitude that saw the planning of public spending in the UK as 'almost entirely a matter of politics within the executive', and declared that approach to be out of line with practice in other 'serious democratic systems'.[12] That interviewee also dismissed the idea that decision-making over tax should be exclusively the province of the Treasury, witheringly describing that doctrine as 'absurd theology'.

Conclusion: Miles' Law Again?

In an age of international rankings aiming to distinguish 'poster children' from 'problem children' in fiscal management (and public administration more

[11] One ex-Chief Secretary said he had toyed with the idea of splitting the 'OMB' (US Office of Management and Budget) functions of the Treasury from its tax-raising responsibilities.
[12] By contrast another interviewee defended the 'Crown initiative' rule as a valuable antidote to 'pork barrel' (as mentioned in Chapter 1), while a third thought pork-barrel was by no means eliminated by the Crown initiative rule, merely confined to an inner core of ministers while denied to backbench MPs.

generally), the UK was by and large closer to the first category than the second in the three sets of ratings discussed in this chapter. As we noted in the first epigraph to this chapter, the Treasury aspired to be among the best in the world, and indeed the UK never emerged as anything less than 'good second rate' in those three sets of evaluations (with the possible exception of the OBS 2019 survey). In fact, it rated as 'leader of the pack' in the 2008 OBS survey and, arguably, in the 2016 IMF survey as well. But it did not invariably do so, and it rated unevenly on different criteria. As shown earlier, it tended to score well on some of the more technocratic features of spending control, but the long-standing idiosyncrasies and limitations of parliamentary procedure around the planning and approval of spending attracted more negative ratings, especially in some more recent reviews.

But the features we noted about discussions of 'roller coasting' in our opening vignette are also to be found in the comparative ratings of fiscal management systems described in this chapter. As we saw earlier, the composition of those international ratings changed from one iteration to another in all cases, especially in the change in the OBS ratings between 2012 and 2015, so comparing country scores over time can be difficult. Despite efforts to standardize accounting conventions, different institutional traditions or public service delivery systems can affect what gets counted as what in published numbers, and the same goes for the kind of game-playing over categorization that we discussed in the previous chapter.

Further, for all the rhetorical stress laid on identifying and following best practice in institutional design, different and conflicting values are in play in comparative assessments such as those discussed earlier. For instance, one senior former Treasury official said, 'Critics like IMF, IfG, IFS, and NAO make good points about the desirability of rules-based, evidence-based documentary review processes. But the essential feature of a Spending Review is that it's about **bargaining**'.

That observation—not the only one we heard on that theme—about the adversarial and political part of the expenditure planning and control process, raises tricky issues for evaluators. If the central feature of public spending control is indeed to be understood as bargaining, assessments of how effectively the participants played the cards available to them inevitably takes us into tricky counterfactuals (what would have happened if...) and means that serious evaluation of the bargaining process has to go beyond merely noting the existence and quality of the documents produced.[13]

The lower-rated aspects of the UK's spending control system tended to concern the more 'political' rather than the more 'technocratic' features of its fiscal constitution, and in particular the weakness of *ex ante* parliamentary scrutiny of

---

[13] Because, as Fisher (1971: 44–45) notes, 'a law against X can be interpreted as evidence for the existence of X or for its non-existence' and only other kinds of information can resolve such 'reversible reference' issues. Still, gaps in documentation can be revealing about political behaviour, if they reflect choices by spending ministers to withhold information from the Treasury or choices by Chancellors to do political deals ad hoc, short-circuiting the official review machinery.

spending plans. But what counts as a weakness from one perspective or worldview can be seen as a strength from another, just as would be expected from Miles' Law ('where you stand depends on where you sit') that was mentioned in the previous chapter.

Specifically, the UK's limited *ex ante* legislative scrutiny of spending plans— identified as a weakness by academic critics (Wehner 2006), by the OBS and even to some extent by the IMF and OECD ratings discussed earlier—might be portrayed in a different light to other players such as commercial credit-rating agencies which could be expected to be more impressed by the institutional ability to make public spending turn on a dime than by the sort of extensive parliamentary engagement that carried the accompanying risk of delay, deadlock and government shutdowns. It may have been that sort of credit-rating readership that the Treasury was aiming to reach when in a report on Fiscal Risks a few years after our period—and at a time when several credit-rating agencies had moved to class UK sovereign debt as AA negative—it declared: 'The UK's record of controlling spending is underpinned by a world-leading system of expenditure management...UK has the best record of any EU country in meeting its medium-term spending forecasts over the last 15 years' (HM Treasury 2018: 12).

So it may be that 'Miles Law' applies here as well. Such a conclusion would be consistent with the Treasury's behaviour in embracing and encouraging recommendations to develop technocratic practice over our period, while largely ignoring or pushing back on recommendations to enhance the role of the legislature or the public at large (as in the Budget committee issue described in Chapter 5). The former developments at least in some cases could help to strengthen the Treasury's hand in its dealings with departments and ministers,[14] while the latter would risk weakening its grip on *ex ante* control of public spending. Perhaps the asymmetry between the UK's rating on the 'technocratic' and 'political' aspects of its fiscal constitution is not merely a matter of happenstance or coincidence. It might just be down to the fact that different values are inevitably in play over such ratings and the sort of things that would matter to some players might be counted differently by others.

However that may be, it leaves open the question as to whether the international profile of the UK system that emerges from such comparisons might be expected to continue, and what might be the future of the features that made the UK fiscal constitution distinctive in the past. We discuss that issue in the next, concluding chapter.

---

[14] For example, one former senior official who had spent time in the IMF thought international reports such as those from the IMF were one way of exposing Chancellors to criticism by accredited experts (NAO reports and reports from the Institute for Fiscal Studies were other ways). That interviewee said that, as with those other sources of potential criticism, the prospect of negative IMF reactions could sometimes be usefully played as a 'card' to help restrain Treasury ministers from becoming too cavalier about public spending decisions.

12

Conclusion and Epilogue

The Fiscal Constitution, Then, Now, and to Come

Why don't we [just] tell everyone what their budgets are?
(Question said to have been asked
in a Treasury meeting by an impatient SpAd).

What 'unlocks the code' [of a spending review] is *politics*
(Former spending minister).

There is an awful lot of acknowledged and unacknowledged politics
going on around the accounting
(Interviewee commenting on the tension between
following the rules and helping governments
to achieve their political programmes).

Their description of what they call the 'village life' of Whitehall...seems to me misguided because their analysis is solely in terms
of...the technocratic dimension and misses...the political dimension,
which is ultimately decisive
(Sir Leo Pliatzky (1982: 35) criticizing
Heclo and Wildavsky (1974)).

Introduction

This final chapter is divided into three unequal parts, roughly corresponding to
past, present, and future.

First, we return to some of the issues raised in the opening chapter and discuss
three main findings about how the UK's fiscal constitution operated during the
period covered by this study. Those findings are:

- There were several important underlying continuities in the system; some of
the fundamentals did not alter.

The Way the Money Goes. Christopher Hood, Maia King, Iain McLean, and Barbara Piotrowska,
Oxford University Press. © Christopher Hood, Maia King, Iain McLean, and Barbara Piotrowska (2023).
DOI: 10.1093/oso/9780198865087.003.0012

- The rules of the game were often indeterminate and/or selectively applied; and
- Classification and categorization were central to the way the public spending game was played.

It is not a coincidence that those three findings all span the distinctions we drew in Chapter 1 between formal and informal behaviour and between the more 'political' and the more 'bureaucratic' aspects of spending control.

The second part of the chapter is an epilogue, briefly commenting on three dramatic developments that took place like a set of volcanic eruptions in the aftermath of the period covered by this study, and which are likely to affect the UK's public spending for years to come. They were: the UK's exit from the European Union in 2020 following the 2016 Brexit referendum; the coronavirus pandemic that began to hit the UK in 2020 and upended almost all social and economic life as well as the public finances on a scale not seen since World War II; and the big question mark over the future political geography of the British islands, and their component countries. All those developments were still playing out as we finished writing this book in 2022. Each raises fundamental questions about the future of public expenditure control. Their combined effect takes us into further imponderables, and on past form other eruptions can be expected, for example in the form of new defence and security issues, in the same way that the 2001 9/11 attacks on the United States during our period changed the security landscape.[1]

Third, we follow up on our discussion of 'yesterday's tomorrows' in Chapter 9, when we looked back at past visions of the future in the form of forecasts, scenarios, and 'illustrative projections' to compare them with what happened later. In this final section we briefly look ahead at possible future prospects for the fiscal constitution, in the light both of what happened over our period and from a longer-term perspective. We look at those prospects with more of a focus on politics and bureaucracy than on possible future economic performance, exploring four different possible ways in which the UK's fiscal constitution might develop in coming decades. We do not claim ability to predict the future. But we can at least tentatively identify some possible futures.

How the Fiscal Constitution Worked over the Period:
Three Conclusions

Returning to the questions raised in Chapter 1, three broad interlocking conclusions stand out from this study. First, not everything changed. Amid all the

---

[1] Russia's invasion of Ukraine was taking place as we finished writing this book.

detailed developments in public spending control, there were several underlying continuities that often received less attention than the new departures.

Second, the formal rules or procedures often seem to have been selectively applied in practice. The 'negotiated discretion' that Colin Thain and Maurice Wright (1995) highlighted as the key characteristic of Treasury spending control from the 1970s to the early 1990s by no means disappeared. Both documents and interviews suggested that the application of the rules often differed as between the 'big beasts' and the rest, for instance over the point at which spending departments chose to convey bad news to the Treasury; how (sometimes whether) those departments chose to engage with Treasury during spending reviews; and how much attention they paid to the Treasury's post-spending review 'settlement letters' that aimed to lay out what had been agreed over how the funds allocated were to be spent.

Third, 'creative classification' was pervasive in the way the system worked and it was at the heart of some of the major developments in public spending over the period. By 'creative classification' we mean innovations at the edge of what counted as 'public spending' or on the boundaries between different forms of spending. Over our period a lot of ingenuity and energy went into developments at the margin of official definitions of 'public expenditure' and of its various sub-types.

Not everything changed: Some underlying continuities

Too much focus on change can risk obscuring those often less commented-on parts of the system that were not rearranged or replaced—the dog-that-didn't-bark issue. That is why Chapter 2 began by identifying seven elements of the UK's fiscal constitution that either persisted or recurred over our period. Those elements included features of the parliamentary process of controlling public spending and the Barnett territorial funding formula (described in Chapter 7 and characterized by one of our interviewees as a scheme carefully designed to 'allow politicians in Scotland, Wales, Northern Ireland, and England not to speak to one another') as well as the organization of the Treasury itself as a mixture of the porthole principle and the military-type 'staff and line' principle. Most of those seven long-lived features of the fiscal constitution were cut across or violated over the period to a greater or lesser extent. But none disappeared entirely or permanently.

There were also numerous changes in the arrangements for public spending control over our period, as discussed in our earlier chapters and noted in the accompanying timelines. Some of those changes were loudly trumpeted when they were introduced, others more low-key. They also followed different pathways, varying in how long they lasted and how linear or circular the direction of change

Table 12.1 Selected examples of shorter-lived and more durable changes in the handling of public spending 1993–2015

Shorter-Lived, Cyclical or Recurring	More Durable or Once-For-All
Capital charges (intended to promote more efficient use of government's assets) introduced 1998, abolished 2009	The 1998 distinction of DEL and AME, itself a refinement of the earlier 1992 'New Control Total', which survived after 2010
End-Year-Flexibility (right to carry over unspent funds from one year to another), intended to limit wasteful end-year spending surges—stopped in 1994, brought back 1998, heavily restricted from the mid-2000s, replaced by 'Budget Exchange' 2010	The separate reporting and budgeting of 'capital' spending in 1992 and 1998 (Chapter 6), even after resource accounting and budgeting in the early 2000s arguably made separate capital and current budgets unnecessary
One-fiscal-event-a-year budgeting in parliament (introduced as part of the move to unified budgeting in 1993, scrapped for a two-fiscal-event-a year approach in 1997, reintroduced after our period in 2017)	Devolved parliaments and governments with spending-control functions in the UK's non-English territories (Chapter 7), though the Northern Ireland. Assembly was suspended four times during our period
The five different balanced-budget or deficit-reduction fiscal rules in operation over our period, the longest lasting of which were the 'golden' and 'sustainable investment' rules formally operating from 1998 to 2009	The move of key functions to autonomous actors, notably statistical classification and quality control to ONS and the Statistics Authority in 2008 and economic/fiscal forecasting and reporting to OBR in 2010 (Chapter 9)
Resource budgeting (right to switch between non-cash and near-cash spending to reflect changing asset levels or depreciation costs), introduced in 2002, withdrawn and replaced by a Treasury approval regime from 2005	Resource Accounting (production of accounts to reflect cost and depreciation of assets rather than simply cash in and out), introduced for Parliamentary accounts after six years of preparation from 2001 and retained thereafter

proved to be. Table 12.1 gives a few selected examples of more and less durable changes in the control and management system over our period.

Interviewees and archive documents suggest that the key 'veto players' in the system—those with the power to stop policies or institutional changes—were the political actors (Prime Ministers, Chancellors, CSTs, spending ministers, and SpAds). That observation aligns with the fourth epigraph to this chapter, which is a comment from a former senior Treasury mandarin criticizing Heclo and Wildavsky's 1970s study for downplaying the role of those actors relative to the civil service mandarinate. It was largely those political actors' judgements of the advantages of the status quo compared to alternatives that served to block, continue, reverse, or foster major change in processes and institutions.

But there were also areas (such as the Resource Accounting and Budgeting developments described in Chapter 10) where those 'big beast' actors were less engaged or were divided or competing with one another, providing conditions in which other actors or institutions could come into play. And, in line with our observations in the previous chapter about the mixed picture of the UK's position in international rankings on public financial management, it is striking that the enduring changes noted in Table 12.1 tended to be ones that strengthened the institutional Treasury's hand, whereas changes that faltered were in several cases initiatives that were pushed through without wholehearted buy-in from the Treasury and later dismantled once the relevant champion (Minister, SpAd or official) departed or once the Treasury reached the conclusion that it had given up more control than it was comfortable with. The circular path of End Year Flexibility and the U-turn over non-cash to near-cash switches are clear cases of change in that second category, and the same goes for the recurring idea of having a single fiscal event per year to allow the Treasury to make all the tradeoffs between tax and spending on its own terms. Sometimes the institutional Treasury seems to have been its own worst enemy—for instance falling into the classic IT procurement trap of depending on non-standard bespoke software for the vital task of keeping track of the spending numbers, failing to apply to its own spending teams the changes it insisted on for other departments (in bringing in qualified financial professionals) and being relatively slow to up-skill its spending teams for the PSA and RAB eras. But nevertheless, over our period the Treasury managed to maintain or regain its central position in public expenditure control.

'Apparent' rules, selective application: How to unlock a spending review

Alexis de Tocqueville (1866: 99) famously declared that the government of pre-revolutionary France featured 'rigid rules and lax enforcement'.[2] In similar vein, a senior ex-Treasury official told us gnomically that *Managing Public Money* (the Treasury's official guide to procedures and standards in the handling of public expenditure, described in Chapter 6) was 'an apparent rule book', with the emphasis laid on 'apparent'.

That statement might be interpreted in several ways. It could mean that some of the precepts and guidelines in that official tome were not really 'rules', possibly because (*à la* Tocqueville) they were not uniformly enforced, perhaps not even

---

[2] '*L'ancien régime, c'est là tout entier: une règle rigide, une pratique molle: tel est son caractère.*' (Ch VI '*Des Moeurs Administratives Sous l'Ancien Régime*')

intended to be binding in all cases, or possibly were just too ambiguous to count as rules. It might alternatively mean that the rules were crafted to allow more discretion to the Treasury than to spending departments: *MPM*'s repeated emphasis on the need for departments to keep the Treasury in the loop, observe the 'spirit of the rules' and avoid 'bounces' was certainly not matched by equal clarity about what the Treasury was expected to do with the information volunteered by spending departments. Or again, the statement might imply that the 'real rules' in practice differed from what was set out in the book, in the same sense that politics is sometimes said to follow no hard-and-fast rules but those of expediency.

Our observations were consistent with all those possible interpretations. What seemed to be strict reporting requirements or bidding procedures for some departments, projects, or ministers appear to have been applied variably or not at all to others. Often the rules seem to have been different in practice for political heavyweights as against players who were further down the pecking order.

The most obvious case in point, highlighted in the second epigraph to this chapter, is the ability of spending ministers with sufficient political clout to 'unlock' spending reviews by securing Prime Ministerial backing for special ad hoc political deals struck outside the apparently rigid timetable and information-provision requirements set by the Treasury for submissions. In earlier chapters we noted two dramatic cases of such unlocking in the New Labour period. One was the pre-emption of New Labour's second (2000) spending review by the Department of Health (under a newly appointed Health minister, Alan Milburn, who had been CST only three months earlier). That move took the form of a policy announcement pledge made on a Sunday morning TV show by Prime Minister Tony Blair in January 2000. Significantly, 2000 was a pre-election year and in the winter of 1999–2000 the Labour government was under political fire for cancelled hospital operations and severe bed shortages during a winter 'flu crisis, when the party had made 'saving the NHS' its central campaign pledge in the 1997 election (Watt 2000). In that TV show, Tony Blair pre-empted Labour's second Spending Review, due to start later in the year, by committing his government to raise health care spending to at least the EU average as a proportion of GDP by 2006. The £12bn pledge implied a real rate of growth in health care spending of over 5 per cent a year for five years, such that spending would go from 6.7 per cent of GDP to 8 per cent. 'And that was the Spending Review...' commented one of the players to us, '...it worked a treat'.

Another dramatic 'unlocking' example recounted earlier (Chapter 10), is the way the Ministry of Defence in effect reopened the 2002 Spending Review (which the Department believed had left it inadequately funded for its agreed mission) a month before the UK embarked on the controversial invasion of Iraq in 2003. As we saw, MOD managed to reopen that settlement by making the most of opportunities offered by the new Resource Accounting and Budgeting system. By announcing the intention to release cash amounting to extra £1bn a year from switches out of non-cash funding, it forced the Treasury into a special deal which eventually yielded an extra £0.4bn a year of spendable cash to MOD. In both of those cases the political 'key' (in the words of our second epigraph) was the ability to play the Prime Minister against the Chancellor.

Of course, there were also times where the Treasury itself did the unlocking. One dramatic example came in the aftermath of the 2007 Spending Review, the results of which were published only a fortnight or so before the first UK bank failure (Northern Rock) that heralded the global financial crash of 2008, one of the two big volcanic eruptions of our period. In the new, suddenly much more adverse, fiscal climate the Treasury in effect reopened the Spending Review by developing a blandly titled 'Operational Efficiency Programme' aimed at finding recoverable savings from the allocations already agreed and announced. A key element of that unlocking operation was a plan announced in the 2009 Pre-Budget Report to secure £8bn of reductions in planned spending by 2012/2013, involving a concerted effort to claw back agreed administration budgets.

Formal expectations and practice also often seemed to diverge over the provision of advance notice, prompt reporting, and submission of supporting evidence or analytic assessments. An example is the major fiscal consolidation exercise in the 2010 Coalition government spending review (Chapter 5), when the Treasury asked departments to rank their proposed capital spending projects in order of priority with elaborate supporting evidence about the expected benefits, so that the priorities could be adjudicated on a cross-government basis on common Green Book-type criteria by a panel of economic experts. In principle, this development represented a major change from the longstanding tradition of haggling from a starting-point of 'baseline' spending in that it implied a zero-based, evidence-driven, cross-government competition. But, following a long line of selective or non-responses by departments requested by the Treasury to identify spending priorities in times of fiscal consolidation (Hood and Himaz 2017: 103–107), several big departments appear to have simply declined to play the game by those rules, offered no ranking and relied on their Ministers' 'big beast' political clout to shape the final outcome.

Some of our interviewees described other instances in which ministers refused to allow their officials to talk to Treasury officials to follow up on political-level meetings. One interviewee from a local government background had been 'shocked' to find there was no-one in central government 'whose job it was to challenge warring ministers who had instructed their officials to reinterpret in private discussions with the Treasury what the Cabinet had agreed to the previous week and send [those ministers] back round the formal decision loop' (which was 'what you do all the time in local government').

The phrase 'apparent rules, selectively applied' also seems to apply to the responses of departmental Permanent Secretaries in their role as Accounting Officers empowered to call for written 'directions' from their Ministers over spending proposals deemed to be out of line with Treasury rules. As we saw in Chapter 6, despite the value-for-money requirements for spending proposals laid out in the Treasury's Green Book and in *Managing Public Money*, most of the major government 'blunders' (wasteful and ill-thought-out ventures) identified by Anthony King and Ivor Crewe (2013), did not result in requests for such directions. There were few such requests over our period (though their incidence sharply increased after 2015), mostly applying to smaller or middle-ranking items and conspicuously absent for many political 'pet projects'.

The Treasury as a 'classification machine': Public spending by other means

For decades the term 'quango' has been loosely used in the UK to denote any public organization outside ministries and local councils (such as advisory committees, state-owned enterprises, or statutory boards). But the term—originally standing for 'quasi-non-government organization'—was first coined by Alan Pifer (1967), then President of the Carnegie Corporation of New York, to denote a narrower and arguably more problematic institutional phenomenon. It denoted organizations that *look* as if they are private or independent but are in fact creatures of government, as with 'front' organizations in espionage, covert operations, or economic warfare.

In precisely the same vein, there are ways of funding services or policies that do not count as public spending on formal or official definitions but do a similar job. Indeed, in the European Union, the main way for governments to game the 'Maastricht' (Stability and Growth Pact) rules was to pass spending and borrowing out to state-owned enterprises or similar bodies, because the Maastricht fiscal rules were set at the 'general government' rather than 'public sector' level, in contrast to the UK's traditional practice. And as we have seen repeatedly in earlier chapters, it was often convenient for UK governments to find and develop funding methods that did not quite—or fully—count as 'public spending' on ordinary classifications, or at least not as the 'wrong kind' of public spending. Sometimes those political moves backfired, as we saw in Chapter 5, in the case of the Millennium Dome under New Labour, but a great deal of official and political energy and ingenuity went into 'public spending by other means'.

We highlighted that process in Chapter 10, when we discussed some of the intricacies of classification in public spending and the central feature of the Treasury as a 'classification machine'—summed up in the old Treasury joke that 'there is no fiscal crisis that cannot be tackled by swingeing classification changes'. That ironic overstatement draws attention to the never-ending search by departments and the Treasury for creative ways of categorizing spending or spending substitutes to fit within fiscal rules or budgetary constraints.

That thread runs through most of our chapters and several of our vignettes. The issue of what counts as what in public spending might at first sight be dismissed as 'nerdy', in the same vein as the comment we quoted in Chapter 1, by an interviewee from a non-civil service background who was bemused by all the time and effort spent on wrangling about classification issues in the Treasury, when it was 'all cash to government'. But such a conclusion would miss much of the action in public spending control. As we have seen, those categorizations affect the size of deficits and therefore governments' ability to claim to be meeting fiscal rules. They affect which funds held by departments are just notional accounting items and which are cash that can actually be spent. They can play into party-political arguments over the size and growth of 'the state', and over governments' track records of spending both in more politically favoured areas (healthcare, education, 'front line' services) and less favoured ones ('back office bureaucracy'). Just as private companies can flatter their financial performance by being creative with numbers over matters such as depreciation, government bodies can do something similar, as we showed in the vignette to Chapter 10. Such finessing of the numbers is reflected in the third epigraph to this chapter about the 'politics going on around the accounting'.

Each of the three governments in office over our period presided over the development of new categories of 'spending' which did not—quite or fully—count as such in existing classifications. At the start of our period, the reintroduction of a National Lottery for the first time in over a century produced what was in effect a new category of public spending from 1994 in the form of the 12 per cent of the ticket sales that went into 'good causes'. That spending was counted as 'uncontrollable' (it was classified as a special category of AME at the time of writing) and allocated to fund sport, arts, and culture activity outside the normal processes of budgeting and spending review. But the 'additionality' principle and the separate status of Lottery funding wore decidedly thin in places, not only for the Millennium Dome as already mentioned but also over the funding of the 2012 London Olympic games, when some £0.5bn was taken from the Big Lottery Fund to build the Olympic Village, with promises to repay it after the Games when the Olympic facilities were eventually sold (Doward 2016).

In similar category-blurring vein, we saw in Chapters 3 and 4 that, having battled in the early 1980s to stop local authorities doing 'sale and leaseback' deals to fund their spending, the Treasury withdrew the restrictive Ryrie Rules in 1989 and three years later launched its own private finance initiative enabling a new generation of schemes for leased facilities in central government, some of which conveniently did not count as 'debt' in National Accounts. Some New Labour figures in opposition castigated the PFI scheme as a disreputable way to move public debt off balance sheet while increasing government's underlying borrowing costs, but Labour in government produced its own supercharged version.

In higher education financing, a much bigger move to 'public spending by other means' took place over our period (Chapter 4). Here, too New Labour in government markedly extended the modest steps its predecessor had taken towards funding higher education teaching in most of the UK out of loans and tuition fees for undergraduate courses. By a variant of the 'swingeing reclassification' approach, it created another whole domain of spending and debt that did not officially count as 'public expenditure'.[3] And the succeeding Coalition government took the approach still further by switching from grants to fees and loans for most adult further education courses below university level (for learners over twenty-five studying courses at level 3 or above). The switch meant that spending on loans was classed as a financial transaction instead of public sector current spending (even if most of the money would never be repaid).[4] Significantly, too, the welfare payments made through the giant tax credits empire built by the Treasury under New Labour (amounting to an average of £24bn per year in 2012/2013 prices between 2003/2004 and 2009/2010 (DWP 2013)) did not all count as 'public expenditure', as explained in Chapter 4, because some of them counted as 'negative tax'.

Creative classification was not confined to developments in 'public spending by other means'. As we also saw in earlier chapters, such finessing of the categories could be observed in other contexts wherever there was a boundary line to be drawn between types of spending that were deemed 'good' or 'bad', or were governed by different rules. Examples of fuzzy boundary lines inviting creative categorization that we have encountered in earlier chapters include the distinction between capital and current spending (Chapter 6) and between 'protected' and unprotected items of spending, which led to reclassifications in the form of so-called tuck-unders (Chapters 5 and 10).

Similarly, Chapter 8 brought out the creative reclassification that took place over our period across the boundary between (good) 'front line programme' spending and (bad) 'back office administration'. The boundary lines between those categories kept being moved, for example when the salary costs of Foreign and Commonwealth Office staff working 'overseas directly on strategic priorities' were reclassified out of administration costs into programme spending in the 2007 Spending Review, producing what might appear at a casual glance to be a steep reduction of some 12 per cent in FCO's AC spending. Finally, as we showed in Chapter 10, describing the 2003 MOD near-cash overspend, the advent of resource budgeting on top of resource accounting from 2002 to 2005 offered new

[3] As we saw in Chapter 4, even for student loans expected to be written off, the outlays were only scored against the public finances at the end of the loan period, thirty years in the future—a classic 'fiscal illusion' that took a long time to be corrected by reclassification (Ebdon and Waite 2018)
[4] It had to stop short of extending the switch from grants to loans and fees to younger learners and lower-level FE courses because such a move would have cut across statutory human rights to a 'basic level of education', defined as a full Level 2 qualification.

opportunities for creative reclassification exercises by several departments, turning items such as provisions and depreciation from abstruse accounting entries into sizeable amounts of spendable cash.

As we saw there, despite the Treasury's central role as a 'classification machine', some of the potential creative-classification issues opened up by resource accounting and budgeting evidently posed challenges to the Treasury's 'porthole' spending teams. In contrast to the move to professionally qualified finance directors that the Treasury insisted on for spending departments in the mid-2000s, it kept its own accountants separate from the spending teams, which at the time of our study tended to be dominated more by economists, steeped in distributional analysis and policy design issues, than by accountants skilled in reading balance sheets.

We began this book by distinguishing between political and bureaucratic elements of the UK's fiscal constitution, and also between formal and informal elements. All of the three conclusions set out earlier—the persistence of many long-standing features of that fiscal constitution, the 'apparent' rules, selectively applied, and innovation through creative classification—reflect combinations of those four elements, all of which come into play in determining whether or when change is to be substantial or lasting. It may be easier to keep the formal rules in place where there is scope for creative classification to accommodate the pressures of politics, for example with the Coalition's tuck-unders or New Labour's debt and deficit rules. Equally, change in the formal rules often seems to have taken effect in windows where both political imperatives and technocratic or bureaucratic opinion pointed in the same direction, for example with the move to top-down budgeting after the ERM fiasco in 1992 and the adoption of multi-year spending settlements under New Labour.[5] Volcanic-type eruptions could play a part in such shifts as well, and it is to those that we now turn.

Epilogue: Three Volcanoes that Erupted between 2015 and 2021 and Their Implications for Public Spending Control

As we noted at the outset, some readers might think a history of UK spending control up to 2015 is a bit like telling the story of Pompeii and Herculaneum up to 78 CE, of the island of Sumbawa up to 1814 before Mount Tambora produced the largest volcanic eruption in recorded human history, or of the Island of Krakatoa up to 1882, before it too was suddenly buried under millions of tons of volcanic ash. Is our story of public spending control up to 2015 just a record of a forgotten world, utterly dwarfed by largely unforeseen and political life-changing

---

[5] This observation aligns with John Kingdon's (1984) well-known 'windows' analysis of policy change.

developments that came shortly afterwards, including Brexit, coronavirus, and the move towards the disintegration of the UK marked by the SNP's successive election victories in Scotland since 2007, plus a set of other stresses on the Union with no precedent since its partial dismantling in 1921?

Vesuvius: The 2016 Brexit referendum and public spending control

On 23 July 2016, a few weeks after the Nuffield Foundations' research call that resulted in this study, the UK's political landscape was dramatically and unexpectedly changed by the Brexit referendum on UK membership of the European Union, which split the country down the middle, with two of the UK's component countries returning majorities for 'remain' and the other two for 'leave', and a tiny 'leave' majority overall. In contrast to countries that require super-majorities for constitutional change, no qualified majority-rule had been set. The political turmoil that followed led to three general elections in five years (something not seen in the UK since the 1970s), several major constitutional crises over the powers of the executive relative to the legislature under a government with no majority in Parliament, and cliff-hanging negotiations with the EU, particularly over border arrangements in Ireland provided for in a disputed Withdrawal Agreement and Trade and Cooperation Agreement, both signed (but not really concluded) in 2020.

Public spending certainly played into the politics of Brexit. The 'leave' campaign included a bitterly contested claim that leaving the EU would release substantial funds for extra domestic spending on public services. It was commonly asserted that years of austerity in the sense of restraint on public spending growth after 2010 had contributed to the appeal of 'populism' among voters that the Brexit vote was often said to represent. Many economists thought Brexit would slow economic growth, with negative consequences for tax revenue and thus for the affordability of extra public spending. Further, the fiscal constitution was clearly affected by a move away from subjection to EU rules on matters such as VAT and state aid, and the repatriation of spending responsibilities, notably in agriculture, led to conflicts between the Westminster government and the devolved countries, particularly in SNP-ruled Scotland. But given that the UK had been a net contributor to the EU budget, that by 2020 EU 'Structural Fund' spending was no longer a major source of funding to poorer areas in the UK, and that EU spending within the UK (notably over agricultural subsidies) was channelled through the UK spending bureaucracy, Brexit arguably did not fundamentally alter the fiscal system described in previous chapters. Its impact on that system seems more likely to be indirect, in its effect on the politics of separation within the UK (see 'Krakatoa' below) and its effect on economic growth.

Tambora: Public debt suddenly leapt up in a global pandemic

If the Brexit referendum transformed the political landscape just before we began this study, a second volcano in the form of the global coronavirus pandemic after 2019 transformed social and economic life across the world as we worked on the project. As in many other countries, the UK's Covid response involved a compulsory shutdown of much of the economy in successive lockdowns as well as a public-health and medical response of unprecedented scale (involving extra funding for healthcare, for businesses forced to close and for workers 'furloughed' by their employers). Public debt jumped from 78 per cent to 95 per cent of GDP (at the time of writing) and the immediate effect of the Covid response was a bigger change in the fiscal landscape than the global financial crisis of the previous decade, though its longer-term effects are not currently expected to be anything like as large (OBR 2021a). It was likened to the twentieth-century world wars by the then Chancellor (Rishi Sunak) in his 2021 Budget speech: 'The amount we've borrowed is comparable only with the amount we borrowed during the two world wars. It is going to be the work of many governments, over many decades, to pay it back' (Sunak 2021).

If we follow the war finance analogy, the question is, which of the two twentieth-century World Wars is that UK coronavirus response most likely to resemble? Treasury control of spending was not formally abandoned for 'votes of credit', as happened in both world wars, though it seems to have greatly diminished in practice for massive, hastily developed initiatives, such as the allocation of some £37bn to a 'Test and Trace' scheme (described by one former Treasury Permanent Secretary, Lord Macpherson, as 'the most wasteful and inept public spending programme of all time' (Cecil 2021).[6] The response to the crisis also consisted of monetary as well as fiscal measures, since it included 'quantitative easing'—printing about £450bn to buy government bonds over the course of 2020—which seems to have come more from the playbook of the response to the 2008 financial crisis than that of the twentieth-century world wars.

The impact of the pandemic on public debt was considerably smaller than that of the world wars (and also of the 2008 financial crisis) but if Sunak and others are correct in comparing the fiscal response to Covid 19 with that of the twentieth-century World Wars, which of those wars is it most likely to resemble? As Table 12.2 notes, World War II was financed not only by borrowing but by also by a big increase in mass taxation imposed during the war (in the form of taxing the incomes of middle earners by the introduction of the deduction-at-source 'pay as you earn' system in 1942 and also of a general sales tax, Purchase Tax, imposed at the start of the war). By contrast, World War I (like the United States' post-9/11

---

[6] It might be argued that the procurement of PPE (personal protective equipment) better merited such a description (House of Commons Public Accounts Committee 2021).

Table 12.2 Fiscal response to coronavirus and three other episodes compared

	World War I response	World War II response	Response to 2008 Financial crisis	Covid 19 response 2020–2021
Was there a substantial increase in mass taxation?	No	Yes	No	Not at first
Was there quantitative easing on top of Borrowing?	No	No	Yes	Yes
Was there substantial restraint on domestic public spending?	Yes	Yes	Yes	No
Were policies developed for future extension of the welfare state?	Yes	Yes	No	Not yet clear

wars in Iraq and Afghanistan) was largely financed by borrowing and no general taxes on middle or lower earners were introduced (because of government fears that extra taxation of industrial workers could lead to a Russian-style revolution, according to Martin Daunton (2002: 42–43)). With large tax increases announced but not yet fully implemented and still hotly debated within the Conservative party at the time of writing, the fiscal response to Covid seems to have differed from that adopted in response to the 2008 financial crisis, and to have come somewhere between that of World War I and World War II.

It remains to be seen whether the aftermath of the Covid pandemic will more closely resemble the handling of the quantum increase in debt after World War I (which involved high interest rates, debt defaults, currency crises, inflation followed by falling prices, extended recessions—and some highly unstable politics) or that of the post-World War II decades, with variable inflation and stop-go economic performance. It also remains to be seen how post-Covid governments will handle a challenging combination of debt at levels not seen for decades together with importunate calls for extra spending to deliver on promises for reconstruction and to deal with new crises at a time when debt is already high and expectations have been raised by the Covid response.

...And Krakatoa? The political geography of the UK in question

As we were drafting this book, the 2021 Scottish Parliament election resulted in the fourth successive SNP government in Scotland since devolution and the second majority in the Scottish parliament for parties committed to taking Scotland out of the UK to form an independent state belonging to the EU. Some saw the result as producing a sufficient mandate for independence talks with Westminster to start immediately (as happened in Ireland after Sinn Féin swept to victory in almost every constituency in what is now the Republic of Ireland in the 1918 'khaki' election after World War I). Others saw the election as a mandate to demand a second referendum on Scottish independence (with successive opinion polls indicating support for independence among voters running at roughly the 50 per cent level necessary to secure such a change). Either way, that election result dramatically called the future political geography of the UK into question.

The case for—and against—Scottish separation from the rest of the UK of course was not confined to matters of taxing and spending, any more than were the debates over Irish independence a century before or the Brexit debates over membership of the EU. Visceral issues of identity politics are at stake as well. But from a tax and spend perspective, Scotland continued to receive relatively favourable treatment over public spending allocations within the Union under the long-lived Barnett Formula, producing remarkable stability in the spending numbers shown in Table 12.3. Over our period Scotland continued to be favoured by comparison to its relative GDP. Wales did much better than in 1979, and Northern Ireland slipped. But, in 2021 as in 1979, these public spending allocations did not map from or to relative GDP per head.

So what sort of volcano would Scottish independence be for the fiscal constitution? From a rest-of-UK perspective, the quantitative effect of Scottish independence would be likely to be fairly small. Even taken together, the expenditure of the three devolved countries within the UK amounted to only the size of one small spending department, and in that sense was not of overwhelming fiscal significance. But from a Scottish perspective, the numbers look very different. Given the big gap between Scottish spending and tax receipts (discussed in Chapter 7), independence would require measures to cover that gap by higher taxes, lower spending,

Table 12.3 Services suitable for devolution and relative public spending per head, 1979 and 2021

England = 100		
	1979	2021
Scotland	128	126
Wales	100	120
Northern Ireland	141	121

Sources: 1979, HM Treasury 1979, 2.13. 2021: HM Treasury 2021, Table 4C. 1979 figures relate to FY 1976-77. 2021 figures are projections for FYs 2022-3 to 2024-5

extra borrowing, or some combination of all three. Indeed, from a fiscal viewpoint, Scottish independence would be likely to involve a far harder landing in terms of a tax or spending squeeze than would apply to Irish unification if a 'border poll' on that issue were to be triggered and gain a majority—another issue regularly being raised at the time of writing.[7]

But while small in terms of the amount of spending at stake, Scottish independence would be likely to mean a greater qualitative change in the UK's fiscal constitution than either the Vesuvius of Brexit or the Tambora of coronavirus. By creating two fully autonomous spending and taxing jurisdictions in the island of Great Britain for the first time in over three centuries, it would mean finally dissolving the cosy interior world of the Barnett Formula-funding arrangements whose remarkable survival we explored in Chapter 7. Nicholas Deakin and Richard Parry (2000: 159) correctly predicted that after devolution in 1999 relations between the Treasury and the Scottish government would increasingly resemble international diplomacy rather than internal dealings within a single government system. Scottish independence would complete that process.

Further, it would be surprising if negotiations over Scotland's inherited share of UK debt (greatly inflated by coronavirus) could be quickly settled on the basis of the Barnett Formula. In the Irish case, the inherited debt, originally amounting to some 80 per cent of Irish GDP, was eventually waived as part of a deal to leave the land border with Northern Ireland unchanged (Fitzgerald and Kenny 2020). In the Scottish case, it is not difficult to imagine such negotiations cross-cutting with EU-UK post-Brexit negotiations, since SNP aspirations for an independent Scotland to rejoin the EU would create a new EU land border within Great Britain.

There are at least two other complications that Scottish independence would be likely to bring to the fiscal constitution in the British islands. First it would introduce new possibilities for fiscal competition on the British mainland, to which we turn in the next section. Second, after centuries of union extending into an era of complex modern information systems such as air traffic control and driver and vehicle licensing (unlike the simpler systems applying to state break-ups in earlier eras, such as the dissolution of the union of Norway and Sweden in 1905 or what is now the Republic of Ireland from the UK a century ago), decades of 'sharing' or 'splitting' issues can be expected.

Other volcanic eruptions affecting the UK's fiscal constitution are of course possible. But without speculating on what else might follow, the three developments we have mentioned, occurring in a mere half-decade following the period covered by this book, present some obvious potential challenges to the fiscal constitution.

[7] Because the border down the Irish Sea that formed part of the 2021 Brexit deal was destabilizing Northern Ireland, with Sinn Féin topping the popular vote in elections in both Northern Ireland and the Republic, and Irish unification becoming a topic of serious non-partisan discussion for the first time since 1921.

Looking Ahead: Some Possible Political Futures for the Fiscal Constitution

As for the future, normal academic caution makes us leery of star-gazing and dramatic prophecies, and our exploration of forecasting in Chapter 9, pointed to some of the pitfalls. After all, Heclo and Wildavsky (1974: xvii) conspicuously failed to predict the swift demise of the UK's PAR and PESC arrangements for expenditure review and planning which they had praised as 'the most important innovation in its field in any western nation'. Colin Thain and Maurice Wright (1995) in their study of UK public spending control from 1976 to 1993 carefully limited their horizon to less than a decade and judiciously set out several possible scenarios for the future development of the system rather than a single one.

Here we follow Thain and Wright's approach by sketching out several possible directions of change. But unlike Thain and Wright, we focus less on prospects for future economic growth (important though they are) than on possible developments in politics and bureaucracy. We return to the distinctions we drew in Chapter 1 (Table 1.1), when we distinguished formal from informal aspects of fiscal constitutions, and the more political aspects from the more bureaucratic or technocratic ones. Within that framework, Table 12.4 sketches out four possible future directions of travel for the UK's fiscal constitution.

Table 12.4 Some possible future directions of travel for the UK fiscal constitution

	More Formal	More Informal
More 'Political'	(1) Greater *ex* ante parliamentary involvement in spending allocation **Exemplar:** US Congressional Budgeting and Impoundment Control Act 1974	(2) Greater element of 'Tiebout competition' shaping spending relative to tax in rival jurisdictions **Exemplar:** Tax and spending dynamics across US states
More bureaucratic or technocratic	(3) Greater legal entrenchment of fiscal operating rules and institutions **Exemplar:** German Basic Law entrenching fiscal rules and the position of the Ministry of Finance	(4) Greater application of economic rationalism by 'superbureaucrats' in spending reviews etc **Exemplar:** The Dutch spending review system

More parliamentary involvement in *ex ante* spending allocation?

As we have seen, one of the distinctive political features of UK's fiscal constitution has been the lack of close engagement by the Westminster parliament in shaping spending proposals. There is no powerful budget committee that matches the *ex post* scrutiny carried out by the Public Accounts Committee, Estimates debates rarely go deep into spending proposals and Parliamentary voting on estimates is often believed to be a 'confidence' issue (though this belief has been contested by Paul Einzig (1959) and others). No budget estimate has been defeated on the floor of the House for a century or so. There is a stark contrast with the greater role in shaping budgets played by the US Congress (with the accompanying government shutdowns that ensue when President and Congress deadlock over the Budget) and by other legislatures that score higher than the UK in the 'Open Budget' reviews discussed in Chapter 10.

So what would it take for the UK's fiscal constitution to move in the direction of a more 'American' future involving serious parliamentary engagement in weighing up spending proposals? It took the bitter political divisions following a decade or so of unsuccessful warfare in Vietnam for the United States to move in the 1970s from the older more executive-dominated system dominated by the Bureau of the Budget to new formal institutional arrangements giving greater scope to Congress in shaping the budget. In the case of the UK, we saw in Chapter 5, that a one-parliament Coalition government did not suffice to move the system in that direction, though it did put the issue on the agenda briefly in 2013 as a result of pressure by Liberal Democrat ministers in the Cabinet. It might therefore take a sustained period of minority or coalition government, and a change in the voting system, to change this feature of the fiscal constitution; and even then such a move would require agreement by the powerful Public Accounts Committee to shed some of its powers and compete with a Budget committee for support resources.

More polycentricity and competition in public spending systems?

Moving to cell (2) of Table 12.4, rivalry or competition—for votes, inward investors, international prestige, for instance—can play into the way fiscal constitutions work in practice, instead of or as well as justiciable rules or parliamentary pressure. Politicians and bureaucrats can glean 'bragging rights' from high credit ratings or favourable international rankings of their countries and corresponding embarrassment from less favourable ones. As we saw in Chapter 11, the development of international rankings and ratings of public spending systems was a feature of our period, and several of our Treasury interviewees were evidently animated by the sense of being in the forefront of international developments and leading the field.

The international PFM ranking and rating business that we described in Chapter 11, seems unlikely to disappear, though its impact is harder to predict. But competition within and among fiscal systems can also take the form of so-called 'Tiebout competition' (Tiebout 1956). That term denotes competition among contiguous (or otherwise similar) jurisdictions over tax and expenditure policies in conditions where resident individuals or firms can readily move among those jurisdictions. Both at national and local level, governments plainly do compete against each other to attract business development, and such competition can play into public spending decisions. But at local government level in the UK, evidence of effective competition for residents (as opposed to corporations) through tax and service packages has proved elusive in studies of metropolitan areas (see for example Dowding et al 1994; John et al. 1995; Kay and Marsh 2007; Norris 2016). Indeed, the scope for local authorities to compete on property tax rates to attract businesses has been deliberately restricted by uniform business rate regimes in the interests of HFE, as explained in Chapter 7.

Still, devolution from the 1990s in principle created opportunities for a limited degree of Tiebout competition over tax and spending among the component countries of the UK as well as on the island of Ireland. And two of the volcanic developments discussed earlier, namely Brexit and the possible break-up of the UK, could in principle set the stage for a fiscal world involving greater tax-and-benefit competition among rival government units.

More judicial and legal entrenchment of fiscal rules and operating systems?

As already said, many have noted that the UK's fiscal constitution is not highly juridified in the sense of extensive codification of the rules in some form of higher-level law or in regular judicial involvement in the process. But Chapter 6, showed how in some conditions judicial intervention can tighten up indefinite rules—in that case, arguably contributing to the tightening up of the previously non-transparent and vaguely specified rules applying to the role of Accounting Officers than the occasional pressures from backbench MPs acting alone.

The Pergau Dam case indicates what can be achieved in efforts to shape the fiscal constitution through the courts by public interest pressure groups. That episode points to another conceivable direction of formal change in the constitution—towards a more 'German' approach (quadrant (3) of Table 12.4), involving more codification, legal entrenchment and judicially interpreted rules of the game.

Arguably the UK's fiscal constitution did move to some extent in the direction of greater legal enactment over our period, for instance in the devolution legislation, the first statutory enactment of fiscal rules in the 1997 Code for Fiscal Stability, and the statutory powers given to bodies such as the Office of National Statistics and the Office for Budget Responsibility. But such movement was limited. The Pergau case did not prove to be the start of a flood of judicial interventions in public spending. And statutes establishing independent bodies in the public spending field can be changed, as happened our period to the Audit Commission, created by the Thatcher government in 1983 but scrapped under the Coalition.

New roles for 'superbureaucrats': Populism in reverse?

Turning to the final quadrant (4) of Table 12.4, our earlier chapters have touched on the role played by various official experts in the public spending world, acting as authorities in some way or another. For instance, in the Netherlands, the distinctive system of spending reviews conducted separately from budgetary allocations (discussed in Chapter 11 and much admired by several of our interviewees) largely rests on unwritten rules, the traditionally high prestige of the Dutch civil service, and conventions of civil service autonomy, working with a PR electoral system that usually produces coalition governments.

Within the UK, too, there is an epistemic community of experts in economics, public finance, and public management, operating in parts of the civil service, the audit establishment and third-sector bodies as well as the academic world. As we have seen, the knowledge and skills of that community came to be more institutionally entrenched over our period, for instance in enhanced value-for-money auditing and in the creation of more autonomous bodies to exercise key functions previously handled under ministerial direction, notably economic forecasting and statistical validation. And as well as empowering experts in such ways, a recurring item in the handling of public spending over our period took the form of using authority figures from business, government, or the third sector to review public spending issues. Notable examples over our period were Sir Ron Dearing's review of higher education funding in 1997 (part of an unofficial pact between the two main political parties to keep the issue out of party contention during the 1997 general election campaign) and the successor review of higher education funding in England by Lord Browne (a review of higher education fees, launched late in 2009 and reporting in October 2010, five months after the general election and immediately after the 2010 party conferences).

It would be surprising if either the autonomous economic professionals or the other outside authority figures disappeared from the public spending control playbook, but is it possible to imagine a 'Dutch' or even 'Italian' future in the fiscal constitutions of the UK or its successor states, where autonomous superbureaucrats of one sort or another played a still greater role in the planning and control of public spending?

Unlike Italy, which had two 'technocratic' governments over our period during times of fiscal crisis, the closest the UK came over our period to a general review by professional economists of spending across government was the panel which ranked departmental capital projects in the 2010 spending review (Chapter 5), and the closest it came to using outside authority figures to review current spending across the board was the 2004 Gershon efficiency review.[8] In principle, there would seem to be powerful blame-avoidance incentives to put fiscal decision-making into the hands of experts, especially in conditions of deep crisis. But despite claims by some that economic policy-making was increasingly conducted by economic experts (dubbed disapprovingly by their critics as an 'economic establishment' or 'econocrats'[9]), nothing like the Italian 'technocratic' governments occurred in the UK over our period, the two major fiscal consolidations during that time were not outsourced to experts and the Liberal Democrats' 2010 manifesto proposal for an all-party 'Council for Fiscal Stability' to set the spending envelope for the 2010 post-election spending review did not make it into the Coalition agreement. So over our period, expertization had its limits as a part of the fiscal constitution. It remains to be seen whether that feature might change in the future.

A Final Word

The old joke that 'the future is always the same: it's the past that keeps changing' (Flynn 1999) is a reminder that characterizing the past is hard enough, without venturing into prophecies about the future. And the possible directions of change in the future sketched out above and summarized in Table 12.4, are neither mutually exclusive nor jointly exhaustive. But whatever else results from the smoking volcanoes mentioned in the previous section (and whatever other eruptions are destined to follow) serious spending control seems unlikely to disappear from the fiscal constitution. 'Wild West' periods favouring free-wheeling entrepreneurial players in executive government (people 'of push and go', in the phrase associated with David Lloyd George's use of figures from business to cut corners and break bottlenecks in government in World War I) tend to be followed by more emphasis on tighter central control, as happened after both twentieth-century World Wars. If so, the issues explored in the preceding chapters over how to manage and control public spending will be back.

[8] The 2010 'Spending Challenge' group described in Chapter 5, might possibly be added, but as we saw those 'Challengers' were senior civil servants in the main.
[9] See for instance Earle, Moran and Ward-Perkins 2016.

References and Sources

Our sources include interviews and some unpublished documents not yet in the public domain. HM Treasury also gave us access to some records not yet transferred to the National Archives. We anticipate that they will be available when the relevant documents have been passed to the National Archives.

Some other sources are not, or not fully, in the alphabetical list that follows:

- We have not produced separate Tables of Cases and Statutes. All cases and statutes cited are in the general index.
- Parliamentary records in Hansard are cited in the text in the form HC Deb. [date]. Hansard is fully searchable by date and speaker at https://hansard.parliament.uk/. This wonderful source incorporates the database of Hansard from 1803–2005, created by a then-Commons clerks' team under the banner of 'Millbank Systems'.
- House of Commons and House of Lords papers are numbered HC [sequential number] [parliamentary session] and HL [sequential number] [parliamentary session]. Unlike Hansard, there is unfortunately no single online archive of them.
- Similarly, each Select Committee of both houses maintains its own website, reachable from www.parliament.uk. There is no standard reporting format although most of those cited, from the period covered by our book, remain available.
- The citation format for other government, agency, and international organisation publications is non-standardised and changed over our period. Many are now published online only. When a UK government publication has a Command Paper number (in our period Cmnd xxxx, or Cm xxxx), we give it as a finding aid.

All hyperlinks were live at the time of writing.

References

Afonso, A. and J. T. Jalles. 2012. 'Fiscal Volatility, Financial Crises and Growth'. *Applied Economics Letters* 19:18, pp. 1821–1826, DOI: 10.1080/13504851.2012.667531

Aitken, J. 2000. *Pride and Perjury*. London: Continuum.

Albuquerque, B. 2011. 'Fiscal Institutions and Public Spending Volatility in Europe'. *Economic Modelling*, 286, pp. 2544–2559.

Allen, R. 2014. 'Evaluating the Capability of the UK Treasury 1990-2013'. *OECD Journal on Budgeting* 13(3): pp. 1–29. https://read.oecd-ilibrary.org/governance/evaluating-the-capability-of-the-uk-treasury-1990-2013_budget-13-5jxx2xcvjpth# page 18

Allen, R. and D. Tommasi, 2001. *Managing Public Expenditure: A Reference Book for Transition Countries*. Paris: OECD.

Apps, P. 2010. 'UK Govt Pulls Interactive Spending Website'. *Reuters Technology News* 21 July 2010. https://www.reuters.com/article/us-britain-cuts-website/uk-govt-pulls-interactive-spending-cuts-website-idUSTRE66K31L20100721?feedType=RSSand feedName=internetNews

Armstrong, W. 1980. *Budgetary Reform in the UK: Report of a Committee*. London: Institute for Fiscal Studies, and Oxford University Press.

Asteris, M. 1994. 'UK Defence Spending: Trends and Implications'. *RUSI Journal* 139(5): pp. 38–71.

Audit Scotland. 2022. 'Multiple failings have led to delays and cost overruns which continue to obstruct delivery of island ferries'. Edinburgh: Audit Scotland, March. https://www.audit-scotland.gov.uk/news/multiple-failings-have-led-to-delays-and-cost-overruns-which-continue-to-obstruct-delivery-of

Baity-King, H. 1986. *Her Majesty's Stationery Office: The Story of the First 200 Years*. Norwich: HMSO.

Balls, Ed. 2016. *Speaking Out: Lessons in Life and Politics*. London: Hutchinson.

Barker, A. 1982. *Quangos in Britain*. London: Macmillan.

Bate, A. and D. Foster. 2017. *Sure Start (England)*. Briefing Paper 7257. London: House of Commons Library.

BBC. 1999. 'Lid Lifted off Dome Designs'. 14 June 1999. http://news.bbc.co.uk/1/hi/uk/368525.stm

BBC. 2006. 'NHS Deficits My Problem – Hewitt'. 21 November 2006. http://news.bbc.co.uk/1/hi/health/6168926.stm

BBC. 2011. 'Government grant for BBC World Service Trust'. 13 November 2011. https://www.bbc.co.uk/news/entertainment-arts-15711864

BBC. 2014. 'Scottish independence: Report Claims UK Oil Forecasts "too Pessimistic"'. 18 August 2014. https://www.bbc.co.uk/news/uk-scotland-scotland-politics-28827295

BBC. 2016. 'RHI Scandal: Pressure Mounts for RHI Public Inquiry'. 16 December 2016. https://www.bbc.co.uk/news/uk-northern-ireland-38339530

Bentham, J. 1962. *The Works of Jeremy Bentham*. New York: Russell and Russell.

Besançon, M. 2003. Good Governance Rankings: The Art of Measurement, WPF Reports No 36. Cambridge, MA: World Peace Foundation.

Bevan, G. and C. Hood. 2006. 'What's Measured is What Matters: Targets and Gaming in the English Public Health Care System'. *Public Administration* 84(3): pp. 517–538.

Black, D. J. 1976. *The Behavior of Law*. New York: Academic Press.

Black, D. J. 1984. *Toward a General Theory of Social Control*. Orlando, FL: Academic Press.

Blair, Tony. 2010. *A Journey*. London: Hutchinson.

Bolton, P. 2022. Student Loan Statistics, Commons Library Research Briefing, 19 July 2022 Number CBP01079.

Bosanquet, N. 1988. *The Ghost of PAR? Public Expenditure Beyond Plowden. Centre for Economic Policy Research Discussion Paper 259*. London: Centre for Economic Policy.

Brennan, G. and J. Buchanan. 1980. *The Power to Tax: Analytical Foundations of a Fiscal Constitution*. Cambridge University Press.

Brennan, G. and J. Buchanan. 1985. *The Reason of Rules: Constitutional Political Economy*. Cambridge: Cambridge University Press.

Brewer, M. 2003. 'The New Tax Credits'. Briefing Note no 35. London: Institute for Fiscal Studies. https://www.ifs.org.uk/bns/bn35.pdf

Bridges, E. 1957. 'Haldane and the Machinery of Government'. *Public Administration* 35(3): pp. 254–265.

Britton, A. 1991. *Macroeconomic Policy in Britain 1974-87*. Cambridge: Cambridge University Press.

Brown, G. 1998. The Chancellor's 1998 Budget Speech. 17 March 1998. https://webarchive.nationalarchives.gov.uk/ukgwa/20100407170757/http:/www.hm-treasury.gov.uk/bud_budget98_speech.htm

Brown, G. 2004. 'The Budget 2004: Full Text: Gordon Brown's Budget Statement'. *Guardian*, 17 March, 2004. https://www.theguardian.com/money/2004/mar/17/budget. budget20044

Brown, G., R. Cook, and J. Prescott, 1994. 'Financing Infrastructure Investment: Promoting a Partnership between Public and Private Finance'. Joint Consultative paper prepared for the Labour Finance and Industry Group Symposium on Public/Private Finance. London: Labour Party.

Brzozowski, M., and J. Siwińska-Gorzelak 2010. "The Impact of Fiscal Rules on Fiscal Policy Volatility". *Journal of Applied Economics*, 132: pp. 205–231.

Budd, A. 1999. 'Learning from the Wise People'. *Manchester School Supplement* 1463–6786: pp. 36–48.

Budget Process Review Group. 2017. Final Report. Edinburgh: Scottish Parliament. https://archive2021.parliament.scot/S5_Finance/Reports/BPRG_-_Final_Report_30. 06.17.pdf

Butler, D., A. Adonis, and T. Travers. 1994. *Failure in British Government: The Politics of the Poll Tax*. Oxford: Oxford University Press.

Cameron, G., I. McLean, and C. Wlezien. 2004. 'Public Expenditure in the English Regions: Measurement Problems and (Partial) Solutions'. *Political Quarterly* 75(2): 121–131.

Cecil, N. 2021. 'Test and Trace Most Wasteful and Inept Public Spending Programme of All Time, Says Former Treasury Chief'. Evening Standard 10 March. https://www.standard. co.uk/news/politics/test-and-trace-wasteful-public-spending-former-treasury-chief-report-b923249.html

Chapman, R. A. 1997. *The Treasury in Public Policy-Making*. London: Routledge.

Chapman, R. A. and A. Dunsire. 1971. *Style in Administration: Readings in British Public Administration*. London: Allen and Unwin.

Chilcot, S. 2016. Iraq Inquiry - The Report Vol X, 13.1 Resources: pp. 505-520. [online] Iraqinquiry.org.uk. Available at: http://www.iraqinquiry.org.uk/the-report/

Chote, R. 1992. 'The Not Quite So Magnificent Seven: The Treasury Plans to Set up a Panel of Outside Advisers'. *Independent on Sunday*, 23 October.

Chote, R. 1993. 'Demise of the Golden Guru'. Independent, 10 April.

Chote, R. 1997. 'Audit Office to Take on an Awkward Task: The Scrutinising of Treasury Forecasts does not Necessarily Mean They will be more Accurate'. *Financial Times*, 21 May.

Chote, R., C. Emmerson, and G. Tetlow. 2009. *The IFS Green Budget 2009*. Ch. 5. The Fiscal Rules and Policy Framework. London: Institute for Fiscal Studies. https://ifs.org.uk/ budgets/gb2009/09chap5.pdf

Chubb, B. 1952. *The Control of Public Expenditure*. Oxford: Oxford University Press.

CIPFA (Chartered Institute of Public Finance and Accountancy). 2017. The Prudential Code for Capital Finance in Local Authorities 3rd edn. London: CIPFA. Available from landing page https://www.cipfa.org/policy-and-guidance/publications/t/the-prudential-code-for-capital-finance-in-local-authorities-2017-edition-book

Coghlin, Sir P. (chair). 2019. Renewable Heat Incentive Inquiry. Belfast: The Inquiry. Transcripts and documents available from landing site at https://wayback.archive-it.org/ 11112/20200911103439/https://www.rhiinquiry.org/

Coghlin, Sir P. (chair). 2020. Report of the Independent Inquiry into the Non-Domestic Renewable Heat Incentive RHI Scheme. Belfast: The Inquiry. At https://www.rhiinquiry. org/report-independent-public-inquiry-non-domestic-renewable-heat-incentive-rhi-scheme

Collins, R. 2018. 'On the Borders of Vagueness and the Vagueness of Borders'. *Vassar College Journal of Philosophy Issue* 5: 3. pp. 30–44.

Conservative Party. 2010. *The 2010 Conservative Manifesto*. London: Conservative Party. https://issuu.com/conservatives/docs/cpmanifesto2010_hires

Crawford, R., P. Johnson, and B. Zaranko. 2018. *The Planning and Control of UK Public Expenditure, 1993–2015*. London: IFS. https://ifs.org.uk/publications/13155

Crick, M. 2016. *Militant*, 3rd ed. London: Biteback. Originally published in 1984.

Cross, M. 2009. A Welsh cure for a nation's ills. *Guardian*. 29 January. https://www.theguardian.com/technology/2009/jan/29/computing-nhs

Curristine, T. and S. Flynn. 2013. 'In Search of Results: Strengthening Public Sector Performance'. In M. Cangiano, T. Curristine, and M. Lazare, *Public Financial Management and Its Emerging Architecture*, pp. 225–258. Washington, DC: IMF. https://www.elibrary.imf.org/doc/IMF071/20033-9781475531091/20033-9781475531091/Other_formats/Source_PDF/20033-9781475512212.pdf

Daunton, M. 2001. *Trusting Leviathan: The Politics of Taxation in Britain, 1799-1914*. Cambridge: Cambridge University Press.

Daunton, M. 2002. *Just Taxes: The Politics of Taxation in Britain 1914-1979*. Cambridge: Cambridge University Press.

Davey, E. 2000. 'Making MPs Work for Our Money: Reforming Parliament's Role in Budget Scrutiny'. Centre for Reform Paper No. 19. London: Centre for Reform.

Davies, H. (ed.). 2006. *The Chancellors' Tales: Managing the British Economy*. London: Wiley.

De Tocqueville, A. 1866. *L'Ancien Régime et la Revolution*, Septième Edition. Paris: Michel Levy Frères.

Deakin, N. and R. Parry. 2000. *The Treasury and Social Policy: The Contest for Control of Welfare Strategy*. London: Palgrave Macmillan.

Department for Work and Pensions (DWP). 2012. *Annual Report and Accounts 2011–12*. https://assets.publishing.service.gov.uk/government/uploads/system/uploads/attachment_data/file/214340/dwp-annual-report-and-accounts-2011-2012.pdf

Department of Health and Social Security. 1976. *Sharing Resources for Health in England: Report of the Resource Allocation Working Party*. London: HMSO. Archived at https://webarchive.nationalarchives.gov.uk/20130124071316/http://www.dh.gov.uk/prod_consum_dh/groups/dh_digitalassets/@dh/@en/documents/digitalasset/dh_4122318.pdf

Dilnot, A. and J. McCrae. 1999. 'Family Credit and the Working Families' Tax Credit, *Briefing Note no 3*. London: Institute for Fiscal Studies https://www.ifs.org.uk/bns/bn3.pdf

Dodd, T. 1994. *Frontline First: The Defence Costs Study*, Research Paper 94/101. London: House of Commons.

Douglas, M. 1982. 'Cultural Bias'. In M. Douglas, *In the Active Voice*, pp. 183–254. London: Routledge.

Doward, J. 2016. 'Charities Seek Return of £425m Lotto Cash Used for London Olympics'. *Guardian* 6 August. https://www.theguardian.com/uk-news/2016/aug/06/charities-demand-return-olympics-london-2012-lottery-cash.

Dowding, K., P. John, and S. Briggs. 1994. 'Tiebout: A Survey of the Empirical Evidence'. *Urban Studies* 31(4/5): pp. 247–273.

Downs, A. 1967. *Inside Bureaucracy*. Boston: Little, Brown.

Duffet, H. 2010. 'Nick Clegg Launches "Your Freedom."' Liberal Democrat Voice, 1 July. https://www.libdemvoice.org/nick-clegg-launches-your-freedom-20123.html

Dunleavy, P. 1991. *Democracy, Bureaucracy and Public Choice: Economic Explanations in Political Science*. London: Harvester-Wheatsheaf.

DWP. 2013. *Tax Credit Expenditure in Great Britain*, https://assets.publishing.service.gov.uk/government/uploads/system/uploads/attachment_data/file/223090/gb_tax_credit_estimates.pdf

Earle, J., C. Moran, and Z. Ward-Perkins. 2016. *The Econocracy: The Perils of Leaving Economics to the Experts*. Manchester: Manchester University Press.

Ebdon, J. and R. Waite. 2018. Student Loans and Fiscal Illusions, OBR Working Paper No. 12. https://obr.uk//docs/dlm_uploads/WorkingPaperNo12.pdf

Einzig, P. 1959. *The Control of the Purse: Progress and Decline of Parliament's Financial Control*. London: Secker and Warburg.

Else, P. K. and G. P. Marshall. 1981. 'The Unplanning of Public Expenditure: Recent Problems in Expenditure Planning and the Consequences of Cash Limits'. *Public Administration* 59(3): pp. 253–278.

Eurobarometer. 2007. *Standard Eurobarometer 67*. Brussels: European Commission. https://ec.europa.eu/commission/presscorner/detail/en/IP_07_853

Eurobarometer. 2015. *Standard Eurobarometer 83*. Brussels: European Commission. https://data.europa.eu/data/datasets/s2099_83_3_std83_eng?locale=en

Evans, M. 2003. 'We've Run Out of Cash, Say Defence Chiefs'. *The Times* online. 28 November 2003. https://www.thetimes.co.uk/article/weve-run-out-of-cash-say-defence-chiefs-2k0wb70050k

Fatás, A. and I. Mihov, 2013. 'Policy volatility, institutions, and economic growth'. *Review of Economics and Statistics* 95-2: pp. 362–376.

Feldman, P. and J. McDonnell. 2020. 'A Giant of Our Movement: Ted Knight, Former Leader of Lambeth Council, Dies at 86'. https://www.john-mcdonnell.net/news/2020/03/30/a-giant-of-our-movement/

Fiscal Commission for Northern Ireland (FCNI). 2021. *Interim Report: More Fiscal Devolution for Northern Ireland*. Belfast: FCNI. https://www.fiscalcommissionni.org/files/fiscalcommissionni/documents/2021-12/fcni-more-fiscal-devolution-for-ni-interim-report-accessible_1.pdf

Fisher, D. 1971. *Historians' Fallacies: Toward a Logic of Historical Thought*. London: Routledge and Kegan Paul.

Fitzgerald, J. and S. Kenny. 2020. '"Till Debt Us Do Part": Financial Implications of the Divorce of the Irish Free State from the United Kingdom 1922-1926'. *European Review of Economic History* 24(4): pp. 818–842.

Flynn, P. 1999. *Dragons Led by Poodles: The Inside Story of a New Labour Stitch-Up*. London: Politico's Publishing Ltd.

Foot, P. 2004. 'P.F.Eye: An Idiot's Guide to the Private Finance Initiative'. Special Report attached to Private Eye No. 1102, 19 March–1 April, pp. 1–11.

Fraser, A. 1991. *Making the Most of Next Steps: The Management of Ministers' Departments and their Agencies*. London: HMSO.

Friedman, M. 1960. *A Program for Monetary Stability*. New York: Fordham University Press.

FullFact. 2012. 'Are British Doctors among the Best Paid in the World?' https://fullfact.org/news/are-british-doctors-among-best-paid-world/

Furceri, D. and M. P. Ribeiro. 2008. *Government Spending Volatility and the Size of Nations* August 14. ECB Working Paper No. 924, Available at SSRN : https://ssrn.com/abstract=1188506.

Gallagher, J. D. 2017. 'Public Spending in Scotland: Relativities and Priotrities'. Nuffield College Working Paper in Politics 2017/08. https://www.nuffield.ox.ac.uk/media/1972/2017-10-public-spending-in-scotland-relativities-and-priorities.pdf

Gershon, P. 2004. 'Releasing *Resources to the Front Line*'. London: HMSO. https://www.civilservant.org.uk/library/2004_gershon_releasing_resources_to_the_front_line.pdf

Gill, D. J. 2015. 'Rating the UK: The British Government's Sovereign Credit Ratings 1976-8'. *Economic History Review* 68(3): pp. 1016–1037. DOI.org/10.1111/ehr.12095

Gorsky, M. and V. Preston (eds). 2014. 'The Resource Allocation Working Party: Origins, Implementation and Development, 1974-1990 transcript of witness seminar'. London: Institute of Contemporary British History. https://www.kcl.ac.uk/sspp/assets/icbh-witness/rawp.pdf

GOV.UK. 2013. 'Forecasts for the UK economy'. https://www.gov.uk/government/collections/data-forecasts

Government Finance Profession. 2007. *Government Finance Profession: A Celebration of 25 Years*. London: Government Finance Profession November 2007.

Government Office for Science. 2013. '*Science and Analysis Assurance Review of Her Majesty's Treasury*'. https://assets.publishing.service.gov.uk/government/uploads/system/uploads/attachment_data/file/369440/13-1143-science-review-hm-treasury-update.pdf

Green, J. and W. Jennings. 2017. *The Politics of Competence: Parties, Public Opinion and Voters*. Cambridge: Cambridge University Press.

Groom, B. and C. Hepburn. 2017. 'Looking Back at Social Discounting Policy: The Influence of Papers, Presentations, Political Preconditions, and Personalities'. *Review of Environmental Economics and Policy* 11(2): pp. 336–356. DOI:10.1093/reep/rex015

Grossman, S. J. and O. D. Hart. 1986. 'The Costs and Benefits of Ownership: A Theory of Vertical and Lateral Integration'. *Journal of Political Economy* 94 (4): pp. 691–719. DOI:10.1086/261404. hdl:1721.1/63378

Haldane, R. B. (chair). 1918. *Report of the Machinery of Government committee*. London: HMSO.

Hall, C, C. Scott, and C. Hood. C. 2000. *Telecommunications Regulation: Culture, Chaos and Interdependence Inside the Regulatory Process*. London: Routledge.

Hamilton, Alexander. 1790. 'First Report on Public Credit'. Facsimile available at https://oll.libertyfund.org/page/1790-hamilton-first-report-on-public-credit

Harden, I., F. White, and K. Hollingsworth. 1996. 'Value for Money and Administrative Law'. *Public Law* 1996, pp. 661–681.

Harris, J. 2013. *Following the Pound: The Accounting Officer in Central Government*. London: Institute for Government.

Hart, O. D. 1995. *Firms, Contracts, and Financial Structure*. Oxford: Oxford University Press.

Hart, O. D. and J. Moore. 1990. 'Property Rights and the Nature of the Firm'. *Journal of Political Economy* 98(6): pp. 1119–1158.

Hartley, C. 2010. 'The Axe Factor – Chancellor's Cuts Plea: I Want YOU to suggest Big Savings'. *Sun* 9 July.

Hawkes, A. 2010. 'PFI deal costs Treasury and Taxman £17m to stay in their own building and that's just since the election'. *Guardian* 19 November.

Heald, D. A. 1980. Territorial Equity and Public Finances: Concepts and Confusion, *Studies in Public Policy 75*, Centre for Study of Public Policy. Glasgow: University of Strathclyde.

Heald, D. A. 1983. *Public Expenditure: Its Defence and Reform*. Oxford: Martin Robertson.

Heald, D. A. 1995. 'Steering Public Expenditure with Defective Maps'. *Public Administration* 73(2): pp. 213–240.

Heald, D. A. 1997. 'Privately Financed Capital in Public Services'. The Manchester School 65, December: pp. 568–598.

Heald, D. A. 2009. 'Pre-Budget Report 2009: A Holding Statement'. Written evidence submitted to the Treasury Select Committee, Fourth Report: Pre Budget Report 2009. HC 529 Session 2009/10. https://publications.parliament.uk/pa/cm200910/cmselect/cmtreasy/180/180we02.htm

Heald, D. A. and R. Hodges, 2015. 'Will "Austerity" be a Critical Juncture in European Public Sector Financial Reporting?' *Accounting, Auditing and Accountability Journal* 28(6): pp. 993–1015.

Heald, D. A. and A. MacLeod. 2002 'Public Expenditure'. In *The Laws of Scotland: The Stair Memorial Encyclopaedia*, Constitutional Law volume. Edinburgh: LexisNexis Butterworths, paras 480-551.

Heaven, W. 2010 'Your Freedom: The Coalition Government Proves it is Ready to Listen'. Daily Telegraph 1 July.

Heclo, H. 1977. *A Government of Strangers: Executive Politics in Washington.* Washington, DC: Brookings.

Heclo, H. and A. B. Wildavsky. 1974. *The Private Government of Public Money: Community and Policy in British Political Administration.* London: Macmillan.

Hencke, D. 2008. 'Chinook Blunders Cost MOD £500m'. *Guardian* 4 June. https://www.theguardian.com/uk/2008/jun/04/military.defence

Heywood, S. 2020. *What does Jeremy think? Jeremy Heywood and the making of modern Britain.* London: Collins.

HM Government. 2010. 'The Coalition: Our Programme for Government'. https://assets.publishing.service.gov.uk/government/uploads/system/uploads/attachment_data/file/78977/coalition_programme_for_government.pdf

HM Treasury. (Annual) *Public Expenditure: Statistical Analyses.* https://www.gov.uk/government/collections/public-expenditure-statistical-analyses-pesa

HM Treasury. 1979. *Needs Assessment: Report.* London: HMT. Released to the authors following an FOI request.

HM Treasury. 1992. *Budgetary Reform.* London: HMSO. Cm 1867.

HM Treasury. 1994a. *Fundamental Review of Running Costs.* London: HM Treasury.

HM Treasury. 1994b. *Better Accounting for the Taxpayer's Money: Resource Accounting and Budgeting in Government: a Consultation Paper.* Cm 2626. London: HMSO.

HM Treasury. 1995. *Better Accounting for the Taxpayer's Money. The Government's Proposals: Resource Accounting and Budgeting in Government.* Cm2929.

HM Treasury. 1998. *The Code for Fiscal Stability.* London: HMT.

HM Treasury. 1999. *Budget 1999: Building a Stronger Economic Future for Britain: Economic and Fiscal Strategy Report and Financial Statement and Budget Report* HC298 1999–2000. London: HMSO.

HM Treasury. 2002. *2002 Spending Review, Cm 5570.* London: HMSO.

HM Treasury. 2004a. *2004 Spending Review, Cm 6237,* London: HMSO.

HM Treasury. 2004b. *Public Expenditure Statistical Analyses 2004,* Cm 6201. London: HMSO.

HM Treasury. 2007a, reissued annually. *Managing Public Money.* Norwich: HMSO.

HM Treasury. 2007b. 'Capability Review of HM Treasury'. https://assets.publishing.service.gov.uk/government/uploads/system/uploads/attachment_data/file/191692/HM_Treasury_capability_review.pdf

HM Treasury. 2010. *Spending Review 2010.* Cm 7942. London: HMT.

HM Treasury. 2011. 'Alexander Announces New Budget Flexibility for Devolved Administrations'. https://www.gov.uk/government/news/alexander-announces-new-budget-flexibility-for-devolved-administrations

HM Treasury. 2012a. 'Review of HM Treasury's Management Response to the Financial Crisis'. London: HMT. https://web.archive.org/web/20120405120847/http:/www.hm-treasury.gov.uk/d/review_fincrisis_response_290312.pdf

HM Treasury. 2012b. 'Capability Action Plan'. London: HMT. https://assets.publishing.service.gov.uk/government/uploads/system/uploads/attachment_data/file/191691/HM_Treasury_capability_action_plan.pdf

HM Treasury. 2015a/2021. 'Statement of Funding Policy 7th edn/8th edn'. https://assets.publishing.service.gov.uk/government/uploads/system/uploads/attachment_data/file/479717/statement_of_funding_2015_print.pdf. 9th edn 2021. https://assets.publishing.service.gov.uk/government/uploads/system/uploads/attachment_data/file/1030043/Statement_of_Funding_Policy_2021_-_FINAL.pdf

HM Treasury. 2015b. *Review of the Office for Budget Responsibility* (led by Sir David Ramsden). London: HM Treasury.

HM Treasury. 2016. Country and Regional Analysis November 2016. https://assets.publishing.service.gov.uk/government/uploads/system/uploads/attachment_data/file/569815/Country_and_Regional_Analysis_November_2016.pdf

HM Treasury. 2018. *Managing Fiscal Risks: Government Response to the 2018 Fiscal Risks Report*, Cm 9647 2018. London: HMT and OBR. https://www.gov.uk/government/publications/managing-fiscal-risks-government-response-to-the-2017-fiscal-risks-report

HM Treasury. 2019. Public Expenditure: Statistical Analyses 2019. London: HMT. CP 143. https://assets.publishing.service.gov.uk/government/uploads/system/uploads/attachment_data/file/818217/PESA_2019_print.pdf

HM Treasury. 2021. 'Block Grant Transparency Explanatory Note'. https://www.gov.uk/government/publications/block-grant-transparency-december–2021

Hollingshead, I. 2005. 'Loose Ends. Whatever Happened to the Citizen's Charter?' *Guardian* 17 September. https://www.theguardian.com/politics/2005/sep/17/past.comment

Holtham, G. (chair). 2010. *Final Report: Fairness and Accountability: A New Funding Settlement for Wales.* Cardiff: Independent Commission on Funding and Finance for Wales.

Hood, C. 1976. *The Limits of Administration.* London and Toronto: Wiley.

Hood, C. and R. Dixon. 2015. *A Government that Worked Better and Cost Less: Evaluating Three Decades of Reform and Change in UK Central Government.* Oxford: Oxford University Press.

Hood, C., R. Dixon, and C. Beeston. 2008. 'Rating the Rankings: Assessing International Rankings of Public Service Performance'. *International Public Management Journal* 11(3): pp. 298–328.

Hood, C. and R. Himaz. 2017. *A Century of Fiscal Squeeze Politics: 100 Years of Austerity, Politics, and Bureaucracy in Britain.* Oxford: Oxford University Press.

Hood, C. and M. Lodge. 2006. *The Politics of Public Service Bargains: Reward, Competency, Loyalty – and Blame*. Oxford: Oxford University Press.

Hood, C. and B. Piotrowska. 2021. 'Goodhart's Law and the Gaming of UK Public Spending Numbers'. *Public Performance and Management Review* 44(2): pp. 250–271.

House of Commons Defence Select Committee. 1994. *Eighth Report: The Defence Costs Study*. HC 655 1993–94.

House of Commons Defence Select Committee. 1998. *Eighth Report 1997-98: The Defence Costs Study*. HC 138 1997–98.

House of Commons Expenditure Committee. 1975. *The Financing of Public Expenditure, First Report*. Volume II Minutes of Evidence and Appendix.

House of Commons Library. 2010. 'The Commission on Scottish Devolution – the Calman Commission'. Standard Note SN/PC/04744. https://commonslibrary.parliament. uk/research-briefings/sn04744/

House of Commons Library. 2021. *Student Loan Statistics*. Research Briefing https:// commonslibrary.parliament.uk/research-briefings/sn01079/

House of Commons Procedure Committee. 2019. '*Should there be a Commons Budget Committee?*' 10th Report HC1482, session 2017–2019. https://publications.parliament.uk/ pa/cm201719/cmselect/cmproced/1482/1482.pdf

House of Commons Public Accounts Committee. 2003. '*Minutes of Evidence: 3 December Inland Revenue and Electronic Data Systems Corporation*'. https://publications. parliament.uk/pa/cm200304/cmselect/cmpubacc/89/3120306.htm

House of Commons Public Accounts Committee. 2010. *Department for Transport: The Failure of Metronet*, 14th Report of Session 2009-10. https://publications.parliament.uk/pa/ cm200910/cmselect/cmpubacc/390/39002.htm

House of Commons Public Accounts Committee. 2021. *Covid-19: Government Procurement and the Supply of Personal Protective Equipment*. https://publications.parliament. uk/pa/cm5801/cmselect/cmpubacc/928/92802.htm

House of Commons Reform Committee. 2009. *Rebuilding the House First Report of Session 2008–09*. HC 1117. https://publications.parliament.uk/pa/cm200809/cmselect/ cmrefhoc/1117/1117.pdf

House of Commons Transport Committee. 2011. *High Speed Rail*. https://publications. parliament.uk/pa/cm201012/cmselect/cmtran/1185/118504.htm

House of Commons Treasury Committee. 2003. *Letter and Memorandum Submitted by HM Treasury: Revised Spring Supplementary Estimate 30 April 2003*. https://publications. parliament.uk/pa/cm200203/cmselect/cmtreasy/1079/3091010.htm

House of Commons Treasury Committee. 2005. *First Report 2004–5*, HC 138 2004–5.

House of Commons Treasury Committee. 2007. *The 2007 Budget: Fifth Report of Session 2006–07*.

House of Commons Treasury Committee. 2010. June 2010 Budget, HC350 Session 2010/11.

House of Commons Treasury Committee. 2010. *Spending Review 2010*, Sixth Report, Cm 201011, 3 Process.

House of Lords. 2009. *Select Committee on the Barnett Formula: First Report*. https:// publications.parliament.uk/pa/ld200809/ldselect/ldbarnett/139/13902.htm

House of Lords Constitution Committee. 2013. *Thirteenth Report: The Pre-Emption of Parliament*. https://publications.parliament.uk/pa/ld201213/ldselect/ldconst/165/ 16502.htm

Hsieh, P. C. 1925. *The Government of China 1644-1911*. Baltimore: Johns Hopkins University Press.

Hughes R., J. Leslie, C. Pacitti, and J. Smith. 2019. *Totally (Net) Worth It: The Next Generation of UK Fiscal Rules*. London: Resolution Foundation.

Huhne, C. 1992. 'Economics: A Prophet of Gloom Takes Golden Guru'. *Independent on Sunday*. 23 October.

Hull, R. and G. Gausden. 2021. 'Revealed: The Council that Raked in £10.6m from Parking Fines in just a YEAR as the Average Authority Issues more than £850,000 in Tickets'. ThisIsMoney.co.uk, 18 January 2021. https://www.thisismoney.co.uk/money/cars/article-9159111/The-council-thats-raking-10-6MILLION-parking-fine-revenues-year.html

Hurd, D. 2003. *Truth Game*. London: Time Warner.

Iacobucci, G. 2023. 'Minimum Unit Pricing in Scotland is Associated with 13% Fall in Alcohol Deaths, Study Finds', *BMJ* 380: p672

IMF (International Monetary Fund). 1999. *Experimental Report on Transparency Practices: United Kingdom*. http://www.imf.org/external/np/rosc/gbr.

IMF. 2014. *Portugal: Fiscal Transparency Evaluation*; IMF Country Report No. 14/306. Washington, DC: IMF.

IMF. 2015a. *Finland: Fiscal Transparency Evaluation*; IMF Country Report No. FO/FIS/15/60. Washington, DC: IMF.

IMF. 2015b. *Romania: Fiscal Transparency Evaluation*, IMF Country Report No. 15/17. Washington, DC: IMF.

IMF. 2016. *United Kingdom: Fiscal Transparency Evaluation*; IMF Country Report No. 16/351. Washington, DC: IMF.

IMF. 2017. 'Stressing the Public Finances: the UK Raises the Bar', posted by Vitor Gaspar and Jason Harris 14 July. PFM blog: Stressing the Public Finances – the UK Raises the Bar.

IMF. 2018a. *Austria: Fiscal Transparency Evaluation*; IMF Country Report No. 18/193. Washington, DC: IMF.

IMF. 2018b. *Malta: Technical Assistance Report – Fiscal Transparency Evaluation*; IMF Country Report No. 18/284. Washington, DC: IMF.

IMF. 2013. *Ireland: Fiscal Transparency Assessment*; IMF Country Report No. 13/209. Washington, DC: IMF.

IMF (2022) Datamapper. https://www.imf.org/external/datamapper/exp@FPP/USA/FRA/JPN/GBR/SWE/ESP/ITA/ZAF/IND

Independent Public Service Pensions Commission. 2011. *Final Report*. London: HMSO.

Inman, P. 2010. 'Sir Alan Budd Defends his Reliance on Treasury Staff'. *Guardian* 20 July.

Institute for Fiscal Studies. 2005. *Green Budget 2005*. London: Institute for Fiscal Studies.

Institute for Fiscal Studies. 2006. *Green Budget 2006*. London: Institute for Fiscal Studies.

Institute for Fiscal Studies. 2009. *Green Budget 2009*. London: Institute for Fiscal Studies.

Institute for Fiscal Studies. 2010. *Green Budget 2010*. London: Institute for Fiscal Studies.

Institute for Government. 2015. 'Ministerial Directions 1990-July 2015'. https://www.google.com/url?sa=t&rct=j&q=&esrc=s&source=web&cd=&ved=2ahUKEwiM1JaUzZHtAhUdQEEAHfAEAY0QFjABegQIAxAC&url=https%3A%2F%2Fwww.institutefor government.org.uk%2Fsites%2Fdefault%2Ffiles%2Fblog%2Fwp-content%2Fuploads%2F2015%2F08%2FWMMinisterialDirectionsAugust2015.xlsx&usg=AOvVaw18iwSPTj7EUgHvzbRBIjL7

Institute for Government. 2018. 'The 2019 Spending Review: How to Run it Well'. London, Institute for Government. https://www.instituteforgovernment.org.uk/publications/2019-spending-review

Institute for Government. 2021. 'Local Government Funding in England'. https://www.instituteforgovernment.org.uk/printpdf/9553

International Budget Partnership. 2006. *Open Budget Survey 2006*. https://www. internationalbudget.org/publications/open-budget-survey–2006/

International Budget Partnership. 2015. *Open Budget Survey 2015*. https:// internationalbudget.org/wp-content/uploads/OBS2015-Report-English.pdf

Ipsos. 2015. https://www.ipsos.com/en-uk/best-party-key-issues-managing-economy

Jeffery, S. 2010. 'Has the Government's Crowdslicing Exercise been Given the Chop?' *Guardian Politics Blog* 19 July. https://www.theguardian.com/politics/blog/2010/jul/ 19/crowdslicing-government-treasury-spending-cuts

Jennings, W. 2004. 'Public Policy, Implementation and Public Opinion: The Case of Public Celebrations (Canada 1967, USA 1976, Australia 1988 and the UK 2000)'. Oxford University: DPhil thesis.

John, P., K. Dowding, and S. Briggs. 1995. 'Residential Mobility in London: A Micro-Level Test of the Behavioral Assumptions of the Tiebout Model'. *British Journal of Political Science* 25(3): pp. 379–397.

Josephs, T. 2014. 'In Defense of Forecasting: Its Importance in the Budget Process'. *IMF Public Financial Management Blog* 23 June 2014.

Kay, A. and A. Marsh. 2007. 'The Methodology of the Public Choice Research Programme: The Case of "Voting with Feet"'. *New Political Economy* 12(2): pp. 167–183.

Kelly, R. 2015. *House Business Committee*, Briefing Paper 06394. 28 October 2015. London: House of Commons Library.

King, A. and I. Crewe. 2013. *The Blunders of Our Governments*. London: Oneworld.

Kingdon, J. 1984. *Agendas, Alternatives and Public Policies*. Boston: Little, Brown.

Kleir, D. L. 1934. 'Economical Reform 1779-1787'. *Law Quarterly Review* 50: pp. 368–385.

Labour Party. 2010. 'Labour Manifesto 2010: A Future Fair for All'. London, Labour Party. https://manifesto.deryn.co.uk/labour-manifesto-2010-a-future-fair-for-all/

Lamont, N. 1992. 'Mansion House speech'. https://assets.publishing.service.gov.uk/ government/uploads/system/uploads/attachment_data/file/220822/Chancellors_ Mansion_House_Speech_1992.pdf

Lamont, N. 1999. *In Office*. London: Little, Brown.

Lang, I. 2002. *Blue Remembered Years: A Political Memoir*. London: Politico's Publishing Ltd.

Lankester, T. 2013. *The Politics and Economics of Britain's Foreign Aid: The Pergau Dam Affair*. London: Routledge.

Lapsley, I and A. Midwinter. 2021. 'Results, Results, Results: Can Outcome Budgeting Deliver?' In Z. Hoque (ed.). *Public Sector Reform and Performance Management in Developed Economies: Outcomes-Based Approaches in Practice*, pp. 91–124. New York: Routledge.

Lenkowsky, L. 1986. *Politics, Economics and Welfare Reform: The Failure of the Negative Income Tax in Britain and the United States*. New York, NY: University Press of America.

Liberal Democrat Party. 2010. 'Liberal Democrat Manifesto'. London: Liberal Democrats. https://www.markpack.org.uk/files/2015/01/Liberal-Democrat-manifesto-2010.pdf

Lewin, L. 1991. *Self-Interest and Public Interest in Western Politics*. Oxford: Oxford University Press.

Likierman, A. 1988. *Public Expenditure: Who Really Controls it and How*. London: Penguin Books.

Lowe, R. 1997. 'Milestone or Millstone: The 1959-61 Plowden Committee and its Impact on British Welfare Policy'. *The Historical Journal* 40(2): pp. 463–491.

MacDonald, M. 2002. *Review of Large Public Procurement in the UK*. Croydon: Mott MacDonald.

Mackenzie, W. J. M. 1963. 'The Plowden Report: A Translation'. *Australian Journal of Public Administration* 22(2): pp. 155–163.

MacLeod, D. 2000. 'Don't Spurn the Sporran'. *Guardian* 3 March. https://www.theguardian.com/education/2000/mar/03/highereducation.scotland

Major, J. 1999. *The Autobiography*. London: Harper-Collins.

Marre, A. S. 1957. 'Departmental Financial Control'. *Public Administration* 35(2): pp. 169–178.

Mars, G. 1982. *Cheats at Work: An Introduction of Workplace Crime*. London: Counterpoint.

Maude, F. 2014. 'Francis Maude Announces End of Year Savings 2013 to 2014'. https://www.gov.uk/government/speeches/francis-maude-announces-end-of-year-savings-2013-to-2014

McBride, S. 2019. *Burned: The Inside Story of the 'Cash-for-Ash' Scandal and Northern Ireland's Secretive New Elite*. Newbridge, Co. Kildare: Merrion Press.

McCrae, J. 2011. 'Fiscal Consolidation'. In Institute for Government, *One Year On: The First Year of Coalition Government: A Collection of Views*, pp. 35–39. https://www.instituteforgovernment.org.uk/sites/default/files/publications/One%20Year%20On_0.pdf

McCubbins, M. and T. Schwartz. 1984. 'Congressional Oversight Overlooked: Police Patrols versus Fire Alarms'. *American Journal of Political Science* 28(1): pp. 165–179.

McDonald, A. 1989. 'The Geddes Committee and the Formulation of Public Expenditure Policy 1921-1922'. *The Historical Journal* 32(3): pp. 643–674.

McGettigan, A. 2015. The Accounting and Budgeting of Student Loans HEPI Report 75. https://www.hepi.ac.uk/wp-content/uploads/2015/05/Accounting-and-Budgeting-FINAL.pdf

McLean, I. and 15 others. 2003. 'Identifying the Flow of Domestic and European Expenditure' ODPM, July. Copies available in Nuffield College Library, Oxford.

McLean, I. 2005a. *The Fiscal Crisis of the United Kingdom*. Basingstoke: Palgrave.

McLean, I. 2005b. 'Scotland after Barnett: Towards Fiscal Autonomy'. In G. Hassan, E. Gibb, and L. Howland (eds), *Scotland 2020: hopeful stories for a northern nation*, pp. 134–148. London: Demos.

McLean, I. 2009b. "The 1909 Budget and the Destruction of the Unwritten Constitution". *History and Policy* 2009. https://www.historyandpolicy.org/policy-papers/papers/the-1909-budget-and-the-destruction-of-the-unwritten-constitution. https://publications.parliament.uk/pa/ld200809/ldselect/ldbarnett/139/9020406.htm

McLean, I. 2015. 'Spending too Much, Taxing too Little? Parliaments in Fiscal Federalism'. *European Political Science* 14: pp. 15–27.

McLean, I. 2017. 'The No-men of England: Tyne and Wear County Council and the failure of the Scotland and Wales Acts 1978'. *Journal of Borderlands Studies* 33(1): pp. 19–33.

McLean, I. 2018a. 'England in a Changing Fiscal Union'. In M. Kenny, I. McLean and A. Paun (eds), *Governing England: English Identity and Institutions in a Changing United Kingdom. Proceedings of the British Academy* 217: pp. 227–244. Oxford: Oxford University Press.

McLean, I. 2018b. 'Fiscal Federalism and Fiscal Responsibility: The Case of Scotland'. In A. López-Basaguren and L. San-Epifanio (eds), *Claims for Secession and Federalism*, pp. 163–181. Cham, CH: Springer.

McLean, I., G. Lodge, and K. Schmuecker. 2008. *Fair Shares? Barnett and the Politics of Public Expenditure*. London/Newcastle: ippr/ippr north.

McLean, I. and A. McMillan. 2005. *State of the Union: Unionism and the Alternatives in the United Kingdom since 1707*. Oxford: Oxford University Press.

McQuillan, M. 2016. 'Graduate Tax: A Short History of a Long-Lasting Bad Idea'. *Guardian* 7 September 2016, https://www.theguardian.com/higher-education-network/2016/sep/07/graduate-tax-history-bad-idea

Miles, R. 1978. 'The Origin and Meaning of Miles' Law'. *Public Administration Review* 38(5): pp. 399–403.

Ministry of Housing, Communities and Local Government. 2019. 'Local Authority Capital Expenditure and Receipts, England: Provisional Outturn, April 2018 to March 2019 and forecast, April 2019 to March 2020'. MHCLG. https://assets.publishing.service.gov.uk/government/uploads/system/uploads/attachment_data/file/862423/CER_2019-20_CPR4_2018-19_NS_release.pdf

Ministry of Reconstruction. 1918. *Report of the Machinery of Government Committee*. London: HMSO, Cd 9230.

Mitchell, J. 2009. *Devolution in the UK*. Manchester: Manchester University Press.

Morrison, H. 1960. *Herbert Morrison: An Autobiography*. London: Odhams.

Moskalenko, E. and G. Vassilev. 2015. 'Methodological Improvements to National Accounts for Blue Book 2015: Classifications'. Newport, Gwent: Office for National Statistics. Available from landing page at www.ons.gov.uk

Mullen, J. C. 2006. 'John Major's Citizens Charter: Fifteen Years Later'. In Raphaéle Espiet-Kilty and Timothy Whitton (eds), *Les Mutations Rhétoriques et Politiques au Royaume-Uni*, pp. 1–14. Clermont-Ferrand: PU Clermont.

Musgrave, R. 1959. *The Theory of Public Finance: A Study in Political Economy*. New York: McGraw-Hill.

Musson, S. 2009. 'The Geography of the Private Finance Initiative'. Geographical Paper No. 188, University of Reading. https://www.reading.ac.uk/web/files/geographyandenvironmentalscience/GP188.pdf

NAO (National Audit Office). 1997. *The Sale of the Married Quarters Estate, HC 239 1997-98*. London: HMSO.

NAO. 2001a. *Department of the Environment, Transport and the Regions: The Channel Tunnel Rail Link*, Report by the Comptroller and Auditor General. HC 302, 2000–01.

NAO. 2001b. *Innovation in PFI: Financing the Treasury Building Project*. HC 328 2001–02.

NAO. 2008. *Ministry of Defence: Chinook Helicopters*. HC 512 2007–08. https://www.nao.org.uk/wp-content/uploads/2008/06/0708512.pdf

NAO. 2009. *Department of Transport: The Failure of Metronet*. HC 512 2008-9. https://www.nao.org.uk/report/the-department-for-transport-the-failure-of-metronet/

NAO. 2013. *Evaluation in Government*. https://www.nao.org.uk/wp-content/uploads/2013/12/10331-001-Evaluation-in-government_NEW.pdf

NAO. 2014a. *Department for Transport: The Completion and Sale of High Speed 1*. Report by the Comptroller and Auditor-General. HC 1834, 2010–12.

NAO. 2014b. *Department for Transport: Lessons from Major Rail Infrastructure Programmes*. HC 267, 2014–15.

NAO. 2014c. *Cabinet Office: The 2013–14 Savings Reported by the Efficiency and Reform Group*, HC442 2014/15.

NAO. 2016. *Accountability to Parliament for Taxpayers' Money*. HC 849 2015–16. https://www.nao.org.uk/wp-content/uploads/2016/02/Accountability-for-Taxpayers-money.pdf

NAO. 2020. *Department of Health and Social Care, NHS England and NHS Improvement. NHS Digital: Digital Transformation in the NHS*. HC 317 2019–21.

NAO. 2021. *Evaluating Government Spending*. HC 860 20221–22. https://www.nao.org.uk/wp-content/uploads/2021/12/Evaluating-government-spending.pdf

Neill, M. 1992. 'Brokers Fear UK Debt Mountain'. *Evening Standard* 11 March 1992: 29.

Niskanen, W. 1971. *Bureaucracy and Representative Government*. Chicago and New York: Aldine-Atherton.

Norris, D. F. 2016. *Metropolitan Governance in America*. Burlington, VT: Ashgate Publishing Company.

O'Leary, J. 2007. 'Higher Education', Chapter 21 in Anthony Selden (ed) *Blair's Britain 1997-2007*. Cambridge: Cambridge University Press: 468–484.

Oates, W. E. 1999. 'An Essay on Fiscal Federalism'. *Journal of Economic Literature* 37: pp. 1120–1149.

OBR (Office for Budget Responsibility). 2017. 'Fiscal Risks Report'. Cm 9459. London: HMSO.

OBR. 2019. 'Fiscal Risks Report'. CP 131. London: HMSO. https://obr.uk//docs/dlm_uploads/Fiscalrisksreport2019.pd

OBR. 2021a. 'Repairing the Public Finances: The Pandemic Versus the Financial Crisis'. https://obr.uk/box/repairing-the-public-finances-the-pandemic-versus-the-financial-crisis/

OBR. 2021b. 'Fiscal Supplementary Tables Expenditure October 2021'. htttps://obr.uk.docs. Fiscal_Supplementary_Tables

OBR. 2022. 'Potential Output and the Output Gap'. https://obr.uk/forecasts-in-depth/the-economy-forecast/potential-output-and-the-output-gap/

OBR. 2014. 'Welfare Trends Report'. https://obr.uk/wtr/welfare-trends-report-october-2014/

OECD (Organization for Economic Co-operation and Development). 2009. 'Health at a Glance 2009': OECD. Paris: OECD. https://www.oecd.org/health/health-systems/44117530.pdf

OECD. 2019a. 'Budgeting and Public Expenditures in OECD Countries 2019'. Paris: OECD. https://doi.org/10.1787/9789264307957-en

OECD. 2019b. 'Government at a Glance 2019'. Paris: OECD.

OECD. 2022a. 'Global Revenue Statistics Database'. http://stats.oecd.org/Index.aspx?DataSetCode=RS_GBL

OECD. 2022b. 'Investment by sector'. https://data.oecd.org/gdp/investment-by-sector.htm

OECD. 2008. 'Performance Budgeting: A Users' Guide'. https://www.oecd.org/gov/budgeting/Performance-Budgeting-Guide.pdf

Office of National Statistics. 2014. 'Latest Developments in National Accounts: Changes to be Implemented for Blue Book and Pink Book 2014'. https://webarchive.nationalarchives.gov.uk/20160106163150/http://www.ons.gov.uk/ons/rel/naa1-rd/national-accounts-articles/changes-to-national-accounts/sty-national-account-changes.html

Osborne, D. and T. Gaebler. 1992. *Reinventing Government: How the Entrepreneurial Spirit is Transforming the Public Sector*. Reading, MA: Addison Wesley.

Osborne, G. 2010. 'Mais Lecture – A New Economic Model, Rt Hon George Osborne'. https://www.primeeconomics.org/articles/ann-pettifor-on-austerity-osbornomics-and-what-labour-should-be-doing/

Ostrom, V. 1971. *The Political Theory of a Compound Republic: Designing the American Experiment*. Lincoln: University of Nebraska Press.

Page, K. 2014. 'External review of the Office for Budget Responsibility'. HMSO.https://
assets.publishing.service.gov.uk/government/uploads/system/uploads/attachment_
data/file/349961/external_review_of_the_OBR_print.pdf

Parker, D. 2009. 'Editorial: PPP/PFI – Solution or Problem?'. *Economic Affairs 29 (1)*: pp.
2–5. https://iea.org.uk/wp-content/uploads/2016/07/upldeconomicAffairs339pdf.pdf

Parker, G. 1996. 'Lib Dems Seek to Open Tax Debate'. *Financial Times* 21 November.

Parry, R., C. Hood, and O. James. 1997. 'Reinventing the Treasury: Economic Rationalism
or an Econocrat's Fallacy of Control?'. *Public Administration* 75(3): pp. 395–415.

Peacock, A. T. and J. Wiseman. 1961. *The Growth of Public Expenditure in the United
Kingdom*. Princeton, NJ: Princeton University Press.

Peretz, D. 2010. 'IMF Performance in the Run-Up to the Financial and Economic Crisis:
Bilateral Surveillance of the United Kingdom' Background Paper BP/10/05, Independent
Evaluation Office of the IMF. www.01102011crisis-bp5-uk-bilateral-surveillance.pdf

Persson, T. and G. Tabellini. 2005. *The Economic Effects of Constitutions*. Cambridge, MA:
MIT Press.

Peters, B.G. 1998. 'Managing Horizontal Government: The Politics of Co-ordination'. *Public
Administration* 76 (2), pp. 295–311.

Pifer, A. 1967. *The Quasi Nongovernmental Organisation*. New York, NY: Carnegie Corporation of New York.

Pliatzky, L. 1982. *Getting and Spending: Public expenditure, Employment and Inflation*.
Oxford: Blackwell.

Plowden, Lord (chair). 1961. *Control of Public Expenditure, Cmnd 1432*. London: HMSO.

Pollitt, C. and C. Talbot (eds). 2004. *Unbundled Government: A Critical Analysis of the
Global Trend to Agencies, Quangos and Contractualisation*. London: Routledge.

Pollock, A. 1998. 'Public Health and the Private Finance Initiative'. *Journal of Public Health
Medicine* 20(1): pp. 1–2.

Pope, T. and T. Waters. 2016. A Survey of the UK Tax System, updated edition. London:
Institute for fiscal Studies, Briefing Note BN09. https://www.ifs.org.uk/bns/bn09.pdf,
accessed 29.04.2020

Posner, P. 2016. 'Can We Institutionalize More Comprehensive Oversight in Federal Budgeting? Statement of Dr. Paul L. Posner, for "Spending on Unauthorized Programs"'.
Hearing before The Committee on the Budget United States Senate Wednesday, February
3. https://www.budget.senate.gov/imo/media/doc/Posner-Testimony.pdf

Pragmatix. 2021. *Towards a Greener Green Book Process*. Chelmsford: Pragmatix.

Rawnsley, A. 2000. *Servants of the People: The Inside Story of New Labour*. London: Hamish
Hamilton.

Rawnsley, A. 2010. *The End of the Party*. London: Viking.

Redmond, J. 1895. 'The Policy of "Killing Home Rule by Kindness"'. *The Nineteenth Century*
38: pp. 905–914.

Riley, J. and R. Chote. 2014. 'Crisis and Consolidation in the Public Finances, Office of
Budget Responsibility Working Paper No 7'. London: Office of Budget Responsibility.
https://obr.uk/docs/dlm_uploads/WorkingPaper7a.pdf

Riordon, W. (ed.). 1905. *Plunkitt of Tammany Hall; a Series of Very Plain Talks on Very
Practical Politics*. New York, NY: McClure, Phillips.

Robinson, W. 1993a. 'The Hole in Our Pocket: The Chancellor's Dilemma, an Inside View'.
Financial Times, 13 July.

Robinson, W. 1993b. 'Kenneth Clarke 1, Treasury 1: Bill Robinson Former Special Adviser
to Norman Lamont, Assesses the First Battle for the Mind of the New Chancellor'. The
Independent 16 June.

Rodgers, K. 2016. 'Boaty McBoatface: What You Get When You Let the Internet Decide'. New York Times, 21 March 2016. https://www.nytimes.com/2016/03/22/world/europe/boaty-mcboatface-what-you-get-when-you-let-the-internet-decide.html

Sandford, M. 2020. Local Government in England: Capital Finance. House of Commons Library Briefing Paper no. 05797, May.

Savoie, D. J. 1999. Governing from the Centre: The Concentration of Power in Canadian Politics. Toronto: University of Toronto Press.

Savoie, D. J. 2014. 'A Perfect Storm in Reverse: The 1994–1997 Program Review in Canada'. In C. Hood, D. A. Heald, and R. Himaz (eds). 'When the Party's Over: The Politics of Fiscal Squeeze in Perspective'. Proceedings of the British Academy 197. Oxford: Oxford University Press, pp. 207–227.

Schick, A. 2002. 'Can National Legislatures Regain an Effective Voice in Budget Policy?' OECD Journal on Budgeting 1(3): pp. 15–42.

Schick, Allen. 1966. 'The Road to PPB: The Stages of Budget Reform'. Public Administration Review 26: pp. 243–258.

Scott, P. M. and J. T. Walker. 2019. 'Stop-Go Policy and the Restriction of Post-War British House-Building'. Economic History Review 72(2): pp. 716–737. DOI: 10.1111/her.12700

Scottish Government. 2013. 'Scotland's Future'. https://www.gov.scot/publications/scotlands-future/

Scottish Government. 2021. 'Ministerial Written Authority under Section 15 (8) of the Public Accountability (Scotland) Act 2000'. FOI Release 21 December 2021. https://www.gov.scot/publications/foi-202100252510/

Sedley, S. 2011. Ashes and Sparks: Essays on Law and Justice. Cambridge: Cambridge University Press.

Seely, A. 2018. 'Income Tax: The Additional 50p Rate'. London: House of Commons Briefing Paper No 249, 26 September.

Shaoul, J. 2005. 'The Private Finance Initiative or the public funding of private profit?'. In G. A. Hodge and C. Greve (eds), The Challenge of Public–Private Partnerships, chapter 10. Cheltenham: Elgar.

Shapiro, D. 1978. 'The Policy Implications of Treasury Organisation'. Paper presented to the Annual Conference of the Public Administration Committee, University of York, September.

Shapiro, D. 1984. 'Passing Judgment on Public Spending'. Letter to The Times, 30 November.

Schick, A. 2013. "The Metamorphoses of Performance Budgeting". OECD Journal on Budgeting 2013 (2): 1–31.

Shirres, D. 2018. 'Getting Electrification Right'. Rail Engineer 13 4 June 2018. https://www.railengineer.co.uk/getting-electrification-right/

Shmulyan, L. 2021. 'Manipulation of the World Bank's Ease of Doing Business Index, LSE International Development Blog 5 October 2021'. https://blogs.lse.ac.uk/internationaldevelopment/2021/10/05

Sloman, P. 2015. 'Activation or Redistribution? The Mystery of Tax Credits'. LSE British Politics and Policy Blog, 24 November 2015. https://blogs.lse.ac.uk/politicsandpolicy/tax-credit-cuts-mystery/?utm_content=buffer4b43aandutm_medium=socialandutm_source=twitter.comandutm_campaign=buffer

Sloman, P. 2016. 'The Pragmatist's Solution to Poverty: The Heath Government's Tax Credit Scheme and the Politics of the Social Policy in the 1970s'. Twentieth Century Political History 27(2): pp. 220–241.

Smith, D. 1994. 'Broken Promises – Conservative Party Tax Policies'. Sunday Times 10 April.

Spackman, M. 2004. 'Time Discounting and the Cost of Capital in Government'. *Fiscal Studies* 25(4): pp. 467–518.

Spackman, M. 2013. 'Discounting and Required Rates of Return: UK History and Current Issues'. *Economic Affairs* 33(2): pp. 190–206.

Stokes, D. E. 1963. 'Spatial Models of Party Competition'. *American Political Science Review* 57(2): 368–377.

Sumption, Jonathan. 2011. 'Judicial and Political Decision-Making: The Uncertain Boundary'. *Judicial Review* 16(4): pp. 301–315.

Sunak, R. 2021. 'Budget Speech 2021'. https://www.gov.uk/government/speeches/budget-speech-2021

Tax Policy Center 2020. 'What Are Automatic Stabilizers and How Do they Work?'. https://www.taxpolicycenter.org/briefing-book/what-are-automatic-stabilizers-and-how-do-they-work

Thain, C. 2010. 'Budget Reform in the United Kingdom: The Rocky Road to Controlled Discretion'. In J. Wanna, L. Jensen, and J. de Vries (eds), *The Reality of Budgetary Reform in OECD Nations*, pp. 35–64. Cheltenham: Edward Elgar.

Thain, C. and M. Wright. 1995. *The Treasury and Whitehall: The Planning and Control of Public Expenditure, 1976-1993*. Oxford: Clarendon.

Thompson, M., R. Ellis, and A. Wildavsky. 1990. *Cultural Theory*: Boulder: Westview.

Tiebout, C. 1956. 'A Pure Theory of Local Expenditures'. *Journal of Political Economy* 64(5): pp. 416–424.

Tyrie, A. 1996. *The Prospects for Public Spending*. London: Social Market Foundation.

Ussher, K. and I. Walfrod 2011. *National Treasure*. London: Demos.

Waldegrave, W. 2015. *A Different Kind of Weather: A Memoir*. London: Constable.

Watt, N. 2000. 'Blair's £12bn Pledge to NHS'. *Guardian* 17 January.

Weaver, R. K. 1986. 'The Politics of Blame Avoidance'. *Journal of Public Policy* 6(4): pp. 371–398.

Weaver, R. K. 1988. *Automatic government: the politics of indexation*. Washington, DC: Brookings Institution Press.

Webb, S. and B. Webb. 1920. *A Constitution for the Socialist Commonwealth of Great Britain*. London: Longmans Green.

Webb, T. 2009. 'Taxpayer Bails Out Europe's Biggest Waste-to-Energy Scheme in Manchester', *Guardian* 8 April. https://www.theguardian.com/business/2009/apr/08/utilities-pfi

Wehner, J. 2006. 'Assessing the Power of the Purse: An index of Legislative Budget Institutions'. *Political Studies* 54 (4): 767–785.

Weight, D. 2014. 'Budget Reviews and Commissions of Audit in Australia, Research Paper Series 2013–14', 9 April. Canberra: Parliament of Australia Department of Parliamentary Services. https://parlinfo.aph.gov.au/parlInfo/download/library/prspub/3102584/upload_binary/3102584.pdf;fileType=application/pdf

West, W. F. 2011. *Program Budgeting and the Performance Movement: The Elusive Quest for Efficiency in Government*. Washington, DC: Georgetown University Press.

Treasury publication. http://www.hmtreasury.gov.uk/d/review_fincrisis_response_290312.pdf

Wildavsky, A., 1964. *The Politics of the Budgetary Process*. Boston, MA: Little, Brown.

Wildavsky, A. 1976. *How to Limit Government Spending*, Berkeley, CA: University of California Press,

Wildavsky, A. 1988. *The New Politics of the Budgetary Process*. Glenview, IL: Scott, Foresman.

Wildavsky, A. B. and N. Caiden. 1997. *The New Politics of the Budgetary Process*. New York: Longman.

Willis, J. R. and P. J. Hardwick. 1978. *Tax Expenditures in the United Kingdom*. London: Heinemann for the Institute of Fiscal Studies.

Wilson, J.Q. 1989. *Bureaucracy: What Government Agencies Do and Why They Do It*. New York: Basic Books.

Wintour, P. 2002. 'Chancellor at Odds with Blair Over Top-Up Fees'. *Guardian* 20 November. https://www.theguardian.com/politics/2002/nov/20/uk.studentpolitics

Woodward, L. 1962. *The Age of Reform 1815–1870*. Oxford: Clarendon.

Wright, K. 1997. 'The National Health Service (Private Finance) Bill', Research Paper 97/88, 9 July 1997, Social policy Section, July. London: House of Commons Library.

Wright, M. 1977. 'Public expenditure in Britain: the crisis of control'. *Public Administration* 552: pp. 143–169.

Wynne, A. 2013. 'Network Rail Debt to Go on Government Balance Sheet'. *New Civil Engineer* 19 December.

Index

For the benefit of digital users, indexed terms that span two pages (e.g., 52–53) may, on occasion, appear on only one of those pages.

NB, for continuity of reference, we have indexed every term that appears in the index of our predecessor volume, Colin Thain and Maurice Wright, *The Treasury and Whitehall: The Planning and Control of Public Expenditure, 1976-1993*, (Oxford, Clarendon 1995), apart from names of people and entities that do not feature in our account. Two further notes: a) All individuals are cited in the form <surname>, <forename or initials>. Readers who wish to know whether they became Sir or Lord must look elsewhere; b) bodies and concepts with acronyms are cited by the acronym if it is more familiar than the full title. All are cross-referenced unless they would be adjacent in the alphabetical list.